Microsoft

Microsoft XNA Framework Edition: Programming Windows Phone 7

Charles Petzold

PUBLISHED BY
Microsoft Press
A Division of Microsoft Corporation
One Microsoft Way
Redmond, Washington 98052-6399

Library of Congress Control Number: 2010941603
ISBN: 978-0-7356-5669-7

Printed and bound in the United States of America.

Microsoft Press books are available through booksellers and distributors worldwide. For further information about international editions, contact your local Microsoft Corporation office or contact Microsoft Press International directly at fax (425) 936-7329. Tell us what you think of this book at http://www.microsoft.com/learning/booksurvey. Send comments to mspinput@microsoft.com.

Acquisitions Editor: Devon Musgrave
Developmental Editor: Devon Musgrave
Project Editor: Devon Musgrave
Editorial Production: Ashley Schneider, S4Carlisle Publishing Services
Technical Reviewer: Per Blomqvist; Technical Review Services provided by Content Master, a member of CM Group, Ltd.

Body Part No. X17-35782

Contents at a Glance

Part I **The Basics**

1 Hello, Windows Phone 7 3
2 Getting Oriented. 31
3 An Introduction to Touch 49
4 Bitmaps, Also Known as Textures. 65
5 Sensors and Services 83
6 Issues in Application Architecture 107

Part II **XNA**

7 Principles of Movement. 143
8 Textures and Sprites. 169
9 Dynamic Textures 193
10 From Gestures to Transforms 233
11 Touch and Play 293
12 Tilt and Play. 345

Table of Contents

Introduction xi

Part I   The Basics

1   Hello, Windows Phone 7 3
      Targeting Windows Phone 7. 3
      The Hardware Chassis. 5
      Sensors and Services. 7
      File | New | Project 8
      A First Silverlight Phone Program 9
      The Standard Silverlight Files 11
      Color Themes. 18
      Points and Pixels 19
      The XAP is a ZIP. 21
      An XNA Program for the Phone. 21

2   Getting Oriented. 31
      Silverlight and Dynamic Layout 31
      Orientation Events 38
      XNA Orientation 40
      Simple Clocks (*Very* Simple Clocks) 43

3   An Introduction to Touch 49
      Low-Level Touch Handling in XNA 49
      The XNA Gesture Interface 53
      Low-Level Touch Events in Silverlight 54
      The Manipulation Events 58
      Routed Events 61
      Some Odd Behavior? 63

What do you think of this book? We want to hear from you!

Microsoft is interested in hearing your feedback so we can continually improve our
books and learning resources for you. To participate in a brief online survey, please visit:

microsoft.com/learning/booksurvey

4   Bitmaps, Also Known as Textures........................ 65

XNA Texture Drawing...66

The Silverlight *Image* Element 68

Images Via the Web 69

Image and ImageSource 73

Loading Local Bitmaps from Code....................................74

Capturing from the Camera 76

The Phone's Photo Library..79

5   Sensors and Services 83

Accelerometer...83

A Simple Bubble Level 89

Geographic Location 94

Using a Map Service...98

6   Issues in Application Architecture 107

Basic Navigation 107

Passing Data to Pages 114

Sharing Data Among Pages..116

Retaining Data across Instances...................................121

The Multitasking Ideal 124

Task Switching on the Phone 124

Page State..126

Isolated Storage 130

Xna Tombstoning and Settings......................................134

Testing and Experimentation 140

Part II   XNA

7   Principles of Movement. 143

The Naïve Approach..143

A Brief Review of Vectors 146

Moving Sprites with Vectors.......................................151

Working with Parametric Equations 153

Fiddling with the Transfer Function...............................156

Scaling the Text..157

Two Text Rotation Programs..161

8   Textures and Sprites **169**

    The *Draw* Variants 169

    Another Hello Program? 171

    Driving Around the Block 176

    Movement Along a Polyline 180

    The Elliptical Course 185

    A Generalized Curve Solution 188

9   Dynamic Textures **193**

    The Render Target 193

    Preserving Render Target Contents 202

    Drawing Lines 206

    Manipulating the Pixel Bits 213

    The Geometry of Line Drawing 217

    Modifying Existing Images 229

10   From Gestures to Transforms **233**

    Gestures and Properties 233

    Scale and Rotate 237

    Matrix Transforms 245

    The *Pinch* Gesture 249

    Flick and Inertia 257

    The Mandelbrot Set 260

    Pan and Zoom 271

    Game Components 278

    Affine and Non-Affine Transforms 282

11   Touch and Play **293**

    More Game Components 293

    The PhingerPaint Canvas 299

    A Little Tour Through SpinPaint 309

    The SpinPaint Code 311

    The Actual Drawing 316

    PhreeCell and a Deck of Cards 321

    The Playing Field 322

    Play and Replay 331

12 Tilt and Play **345**

3D Vectors 345

A Better Bubble Visualization 347

The Graphical Rendition 356

Follow the Rolling Ball 364

Navigating a Maze 376

Index 389

What do you think of this book? We want to hear from you!

Microsoft is interested in hearing your feedback so we can continually improve our books and learning resources for you. To participate in a brief online survey, please visit:

microsoft.com/learning/booksurvey

Introduction

> **Important** This book and *Microsoft Silverlight Edition: Programming Windows Phone 7* are fully indexed, print-book versions of a single free, electronic edition titled *Programming Windows Phone 7*, which you can find on the Microsoft Press blog: *http://blogs.msdn.com/b/microsoft_press/.* No changes have been made to the original edition's text, including references to the color of the original images, which appear black and white in this book. What follows is the Introduction that originally appeared in *Programming Windows Phone 7*; "Code Samples" is the only section in this Introduction that has been updated.

This book is a gift from the Windows Phone 7 team at Microsoft to the programming community, and I am proud to have been a part of it. Within the pages that follow, I show you the basics of writing applications for Windows Phone 7 using the C# programming language with the Silverlight and XNA 2D frameworks.

Yes, *Programming Windows Phone 7* is truly a free download, but for those readers who still love paper—as I certainly do—this book will also be available (for sale) divided into two fully-indexed print editions: *Microsoft Silverlight Edition: Programming Windows Phone 7* and *Microsoft XNA Framework Edition: Programming Windows Phone 7.*

With the money you've saved downloading this book, please buy other books. Despite the plethora of information available online, books are still the best way to learn about programming within a coherent and cohesive tutorial narrative. Every book sale brings a tear of joy to an author's eye, so please help make them weep overflowing rivers.

In particular, you might want to buy other books to *supplement* the material in this book. For example, I barely mention Web services in this book, and that's a serious deficiency because Web services are likely to become increasingly important in Windows Phone 7 applications. My coverage of XNA is limited to 2D graphics and while I hope to add several 3D chapters in the next edition of this book, I don't really get into the whole Xbox LIVE community aspect of game development. Nor do I discuss any programming tools beyond Visual Studio—not even Expression Blend.

My publisher Microsoft Press has a couple additional Windows Phone 7 books coming soon: *Windows Phone 7 Silverlight Development Step by Step* by Andy Wigley & Peter Foot offers a more tools-oriented approach. Although Michael Stroh's *Windows Phone 7 Plain & Simple* is a guide to *using* the phone rather than developing for it, I suspect it will give developers some insights and ideas.

Moreover, I also hear that my old friend Doug Boling is working hard on a Windows Phone 7 enterprise-programming book that is likely to be considered his masterpiece. Be sure to check out that one.

Organization

This book is divided into three parts. The first part discusses basic concepts of Windows Phone 7 programming using example programs that target both Silverlight and the XNA framework. It is likely that many Windows Phone 7 developers will choose either one platform or the other, but I think it's important for all developers who have at least a *little* knowledge of the alternative to their chosen path.

The second part of this book focuses entirely on Silverlight, and the third part on XNA 2D. For your convenience, the chapters in each part build upon previous knowledge in a progressive tutorial narrative, and hence are intended to be read sequentially.

My Assumptions About You

I assume that you know the basic principles of .NET programming and you have a working familiarity with the C# programming language. If not, you might benefit from reading my free online book *.NET Book Zero: What the C or C++ Programmer Needs to Know about C# and the .NET Framework*, available from my website at *www.charlespetzold.com/dotnet*.

System Requirements

To use this book properly you'll need to download and install the Windows Phone Developer Tools, which includes Visual Studio 2010 Express for Windows Phone, XNA Game Studio 4.0, and an on-screen Windows Phone Emulator to test your programs in the absence of an actual device. Get the latest information and downloads at *http://developer .windowsphone.com*.

You can install these tools on top of Visual Studio 2010, in effect enhancing Visual Studio 2010 for phone development. That's the configuration I used.

Although you can do quite a bit with the phone emulator, at some point you'll want to deploy your programs to an actual Windows Phone 7 device. You can register as a phone developer at *http://developer.windowsphone.com* and then have the ability to unlock your phone so you can deploy your programs from Visual Studio.

Since late July 2010, I've had an LG GW910 phone to test the programs in this book. For the record, the final build I installed was 7.0.7003.0.

Using the Phone Emulator

Windows Phone 7 supports multi-touch, and working with multi-touch is an important part of developing programs for the phone. When using the Windows Phone Emulator, mouse clicks and mouse movement on the PC can mimic touch on the emulator, but for only one finger. You can test out multi-touch for real on the phone emulator if you have a multi-touch monitor running under Windows 7.

In the absence of a multi-touch monitor, you might want to explore simulating multi-touch with multiple mouse devices. The site *http://multitouchvista.codeplex.com* has the download you'll need and includes a link to *http://michaelsync.net/2010/04/06/step-by-step-tutorial-installing-multi-touch-simulator-for-silverlight-phone-7* that provides instructions.

Windows Phone 7 devices also have a built-in accelerometer, which can be *very* difficult to simulate in an emulator. Per Blomqvist, the Technical Reviewer for this book, found an application at *http://accelkit.codeplex.com* that utilizes the webcam and ARToolkit to emulate the accelerometer sensor and feed that data into the Windows Phone 7 emulator through a TCP/HTTP Server, and although neither of us have tried it out, it sounds quite intriguing.

Code Samples

To illustrate Silverlight and XNA programming concepts, this book describes about 190 complete programs. Many of them are small and simple, but others are larger and more interesting.

Some people like to learn new programming environments by re-creating the projects in Visual Studio and typing in the source code themselves from the pages of the book. Others prefer to study the code and run the pre-existing programs to see what the code does. If you fall into the latter category, you can download all the source code in a ZIP file via the Companion Content link at *http://oreilly.com/catalog/0790145316899/*.

If you find something in the code that is useful in your own software project, feel free to use the code without restriction—either straight up or modified in whatever way you want. That's what it's there for.

Last-Minute Items

As I was nearing the completion this book, the first version of the Silverlight for Windows Phone Toolkit was released with some additional elements and controls, and is available for downloading at *http://silverlight.codeplex.com*. Historically, these Silverlight toolkits very often contain previews of elements and controls that are incorporated into later Silverlight releases. I regret that I could not include a discussion of the toolkit contents in the appropriate chapters of this book.

With XNA programs, sometimes Visual Studio complains that it can't build or deploy the program. If you encounter that problem, in the Solution Platforms drop-down list on the standard toolbar, select "Windows Phone" rather than "Any CPU". Or, invoke the Configuration Manager from the Build menu, and in the Active Solution Platform drop-down select "Windows Phone" rather than "Any CPU".

The *www.charlespetzold.com/phone* page on my website will contain information about this book and perhaps even some information about a future edition. I also hope to blog about Windows Phone 7 programming as much as possible.

The Essential People

This book owes its existence to Dave Edson—an old friend from the early 1990s era of *Microsoft Systems Journal*—who had the brilliant idea that I would be the perfect person to write a tutorial on Windows Phone 7. Dave arranged for me to attend a technical deep dive on the phone at Microsoft in December 2009, and I was hooked. Todd Brix gave the thumbs up on the book, and Anand Iyer coordinated the project with Microsoft Press.

At Microsoft Press, Ben Ryan launched the project and Devon Musgrave had the unenviable job of trying to make my code and prose resemble an actual book. (We all go way back: You'll see Ben and Devon's names on the bottom of the copyright page of *Programming Windows*, fifth edition, published in 1998.)

My Technical Reviewer was the diligent Per Blomqvist, who apparently tested all the code in both the sample files and as the listings appear in the book, and who in the process caught several errors on my part that were truly, well, shocking.

Dave Edson also reviewed some chapters and served as conduit to the Windows Phone team to deal with my technical problems and questions. Early on, Aaron Stebner provided essential guidance; Michael Klucher reviewed chapters, and Kirti Deshpande, Charlie Kindel, Casey McGee, and Shawn Oster also had important things to tell me. Thanks to Bonnie Lehenbauer for reviewing a chapter.

I am also indebted to Shawn Hargreaves for his XNA expertise, and Yochay Kiriaty and Richard Bailey for the lowdown on tombstoning.

My wife Deirdre Sinnott has been a marvel of patience and tolerance over the past months as she dealt with an author given to sudden mood swings, insane yelling at the computer screen, and the conviction that the difficulty of writing a book relieves one of the responsibility of performing basic household chores.

Alas, I can't blame any of them for bugs or other problems that remain in this book. Those are all mine.

Charles Petzold
New York City and Roscoe, New York
October 22, 2010

Errata & Book Support

We've made every effort to ensure the accuracy of this book and its companion content. If you do find an error, e-mail Microsoft Press Book Support at *mspinput@microsoft.com*. (Please note that product support for Microsoft software is not offered through this address.)

We Want to Hear from You

At Microsoft Press, your satisfaction is our top priority, and your feedback our most valuable asset. Please tell us what you think of this book at:

http://www.microsoft.com/learning/booksurvey

The survey is short, and we read *every one* of your comments and ideas. Thanks in advance for your input.

Stay in Touch

Let's keep the conversation going! We're on Twitter: *http://twitter.com/MicrosoftPress*

Part I
The Basics

Chapter 1
Hello, Windows Phone 7

Sometimes it becomes apparent that previous approaches to a problem haven't quite worked the way you anticipated. Perhaps you just need to clear away the smoky residue of the past, take a deep breath, and try again with a new attitude and fresh ideas. In golf, it's known as a "mulligan"; in schoolyard sports, it's called a "do-over"; and in the computer industry, we say it's a "reboot."

A reboot is what Microsoft has initiated with its new approach to the mobile phone market. With its clean look, striking fonts, and new organizational paradigms, Microsoft Windows Phone 7 not only represents a break with the Windows Mobile past but also differentiates itself from other smartphones currently in the market. Windows Phone 7 devices will be made by several manufacturers and available with a variety of cell providers.

For programmers, Windows Phone 7 is also exciting, for it supports two popular and modern programming platforms: Silverlight and XNA.

Silverlight—a spinoff of the client-based Windows Presentation Foundation (WPF)—has already given Web programmers unprecedented power to develop sophisticated user interfaces with a mix of traditional controls, high-quality text, vector graphics, media, animation, and data binding that run on multiple platforms and browsers. Windows Phone 7 extends Silverlight to mobile devices.

XNA—the three letters stand for something like "XNA is Not an Acronym"—is Microsoft's game platform supporting both 2D sprite-based and 3D graphics with a traditional game-loop architecture. Although XNA is mostly associated with writing games for the Xbox 360 console, developers can also use XNA to target the PC itself, as well as Microsoft's classy audio player, the Zune HD.

Either Silverlight or XNA would make good sense as the sole application platform for the Windows Phone 7, but programmers have a choice. And this we call "an embarrassment of riches."

Targeting Windows Phone 7

All programs for Windows Phone 7 are written in .NET managed code. Although the sample programs in this book are written in the C# programming language, it is also possible to write Windows Phone 7 applications in Visual Basic .NET. The free downloadable Microsoft Visual Studio 2010 Express for Windows Phone includes XNA Game Studio 4.0 and an on-screen phone emulator, and also integrates with Visual Studio 2010. You can develop visuals and animations for Silverlight applications using Microsoft Expression Blend.

The Silverlight and XNA platforms for Windows Phone 7 share some libraries, and you can use some XNA libraries in a Silverlight program and vice versa. But you can't create a program that mixes visuals from both platforms. Maybe that will be possible in the future, but not now. Before you create a Visual Studio project, you must decide whether your million-dollar idea is a Silverlight program or an XNA program.

Generally you'll choose Silverlight for writing programs you might classify as applications or utilities. These programs are built from a combination of markup and code. The markup is the Extensible Application Markup Language, or XAML and pronounced "zammel." The XAML mostly defines a layout of user-interface controls and panels. Code-behind files can also perform some initialization and logic, but are generally relegated to handling events from the controls. Silverlight is great for bringing to the Windows Phone the style of Rich Internet Applications (RIA), including media and the Web. Silverlight for Windows Phone is a version of Silverlight 3 excluding some features not appropriate for the phone, but compensating with some enhancements.

XNA is primarily for writing high-performance games. For 2D games, you define sprites and backgrounds based around bitmaps; for 3D games you define models in 3D space. The action of the game, which includes moving graphical objects around the screen and polling for user input, is synchronized by the built-in XNA game loop.

The differentiation between Silverlight-based applications and XNA-based games is convenient but not restrictive. You can certainly use Silverlight for writing games and you can even write traditional applications using XNA, although doing so might sometimes be challenging.

In particular, Silverlight might be ideal for games that are less graphically oriented, or use vector graphics rather than bitmap graphics, or are paced by user-time rather than clock-time. A Tetris-type program might work quite well in Silverlight. You'll probably find XNA to be a bit harder to stretch into Silverlight territory, however. Implementing a list box in XNA might be considered "fun" by some programmers but a torture by many others.

The first several chapters in this book describe Silverlight and XNA together, and then the book splits into different parts for the two platforms. I suspect that some developers will stick with either Silverlight or XNA exclusively and won't even bother learning the other environment. I hope that's not a common attitude. The good news is that Silverlight and XNA are so dissimilar that you can probably bounce back and forth between them without confusion!

Microsoft has been positioning Silverlight as the front end or "face" of the cloud, so cloud services and Windows Azure form an important part of Windows Phone 7 development. The Windows Phone is "cloud-ready." Programs are location-aware and have access to maps and other data through Bing and Windows Live. One of the available cloud services is Xbox Live, which allows XNA-based programs to participate in online multiplayer games, and can also be accessed by Silverlight applications.

Programs you write for the Windows Phone 7 will be sold and deployed through the Windows Phone Marketplace, which provides registration services and certifies that programs meet minimum standards of reliability, efficiency, and good behavior.

I've characterized Windows Phone 7 as representing a severe break with the past. If you compare it with past versions of Windows Mobile, that is certainly true. But the support of Silverlight, XNA, and C# are not breaks with the past, but a balance of continuity and innovation. As young as they are, Silverlight and XNA have already proven themselves as powerful and popular platforms. Many skilled programmers are already working with either one framework or the other—probably not so many with both just yet—and they have expressed their enthusiasm with a wealth of online information and communities. C# has become the favorite language of many programmers (myself included), and developers can use C# to share libraries between their Silverlight and XNA programs as well as programs for other .NET environments.

The Hardware Chassis

Developers with experience targeting Windows Mobile devices of the past will find significant changes in Microsoft's strategy for the Windows Phone 7. Microsoft has been extremely proactive in defining the hardware specification, often referred to as a "chassis."

Initial releases of Windows Phone 7 devices will have one consistent screen size. (A second screen size is expected in the future.) Many other hardware features are guaranteed to exist on each device.

The front of the phone consists of a multi-touch display and three hardware buttons generally positioned in a row below the display. From left to right, these buttons are called Back, Start, and Search:

- **Back**   Programs can use this button for their own navigation needs, much like the Back button on a Web browser. From the home page of a program, the button causes the program to terminate.
- **Start**   This button takes the user to the start screen of the phone; it is otherwise inaccessible to programs running on the phone.
- **Search**   The operating system uses this button to initiate a search feature.

The initial releases of Windows Phone 7 devices have a display size of 480 × 800 pixels. In the future, screens of 320 × 480 pixels are also expected. There are no other screen options for Windows Phone 7, so obviously these two screen sizes play a very important role in phone development.

In theory, it's usually considered best to write programs that adapt themselves to any screen size, but that's not always possible, particularly with game development. You will probably find yourself specifically targeting these two screen sizes, even to the extent of having conditional code paths and different XAML files for layout that is size-dependent.

I will generally refer to these two sizes as the "large" screen and the "small" screen. The greatest common denominator of the horizontal and vertical dimensions of both screens is 160, so you can visualize the two screens as multiples of 160-pixel squares:

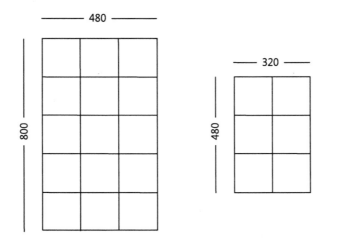

I'm showing these screens in portrait mode because that's usually the way smartphones are designed. The screen of the original Zune is 240 × 320 pixels; the Zune HD is 272 × 480.

Of course, phones can be rotated to put the screen into landscape mode. Some programs might require the phone to be held in a certain orientation; others might be more adaptable.

You have complete control over the extent to which you support orientation. By default, Silverlight applications appear in portrait mode, but you'll probably want to write your Silverlight applications so they adjust themselves to orientation changes. New events are available specifically for the purpose of detecting orientation change, and some orientation shifts are handled automatically. In contrast, game programmers can usually impose a particular orientation on the user. XNA programs use landscape mode by default, but it's easy to override that.

In portrait mode, the small screen is half of an old VGA screen (that is, 640 × 480). In landscape mode, the large screen has a dimension sometimes called WVGA ("wide VGA"). In landscape mode, the small screen has an aspect ratio of 3:2 or 1.5; the large screen has an aspect ratio of 5:3 or 1.66…. Neither of these matches the aspect ratio of television, which for standard definition is 4:3 or 1.33… and for high-definition is 16:9 or 1.77…. The Zune HD screen has an aspect ratio of 16:9.

Like many recent phones and the Zune HD, the Windows Phone 7 displays will likely use OLED ("organic light emitting diode") technology, although this isn't a hardware requirement. OLEDs are different from flat displays of the past in that power consumption is proportional to the light emitted from the display. For example, an OLED display consumes less than half the power of an LCD display of the same size, but only when the screen is mostly black. For an all-white screen, an OLED consumes more than three times the power of an LCD.

Because battery life is extremely important on mobile devices, this characteristic of OLED displays implies an aesthetic of mostly black backgrounds with sparse graphics and light-stroked fonts. Regardless, Windows Phone 7 users can choose between two major color themes: light text on a dark background, or dark text on a light background.

Most user input to a Windows Phone 7 program will come through multi-touch. The screens incorporate capacitance-touch technology, which means that they respond to a human fingertip but not to a stylus or other forms of pressure. Windows Phone 7 screens are required to respond to at least four simultaneous touch-points.

A hardware keyboard is optional. Keep in mind that phones can be designed in different ways, so when the keyboard is in use, the screen might be in either portrait mode or landscape mode. A Silverlight program that uses keyboard input *must* respond to orientation changes so that the user can both view the screen and use the keyboard without wondering what idiot designed the program sideways. An on-screen keyboard is also provided, known in Windows circles as the Soft Input Panel or SIP. XNA programs also have access to the hardware keyboard and SIP.

Sensors and Services

A Windows Phone 7 device is required to contain several other hardware features—sometimes called sensors—and provide some software services, perhaps through the assistance of hardware. These are the ones that affect developers the most:

- **Wi-Fi**   The phone has Wi-Fi for Internet access to complement 3G data access through the cell provider. Software on the phone includes a version of Internet Explorer.

- **Camera**   The phone has at least a 5-megapixel camera with flash. Programs can invoke the camera program for their own input, or register themselves as a Photos Extra Application and appear on a menu to obtain access to photographed images, perhaps for some image processing.

- **Accelerometer**   An accelerometer detects acceleration, which in physics is a change in velocity. When the camera is still, the accelerometer responds to gravity. Programs can obtain a three-dimensional vector that indicates how the camera is oriented with respect to the earth. The accelerometer can also detect sharp movements of the phone.

- **Location**   If the user so desires, the phone can use multiple strategies for determining where it is geographically located. The phone supplements a hardware GPS device with information from the Web or cell phone towers. If the phone is moving, course and speed might also be available.

- **Vibration**   The phone can be vibrated through program control.

- **FM Radio**   An FM Radio is available and accessible through program control.

- **Push Notifications**   Some Web services would normally require the phone to frequently poll the service to obtain updated information. This can drain battery **life. To** help out, a push notification service has been developed that will allow any required polling to occur outside the phone and for the phone to receive notifications only when data has been updated.

File | New | Project

I'll assume that you have Visual Studio 2010 Express for Windows Phone installed, either by itself or supplementing a regular version of Visual Studio 2010. For convenience, I'm going to refer to this development environment simply as "Visual Studio."

The traditional "hello, world" program that displays just a little bit of text might seem silly to nonprogrammers, but programmers have discovered that such a program serves at least two useful purposes: First, the program provides a way to examine how easy (or ridiculously complex) it is to display a simple text string. Second, it gives the programmer an opportunity to experience the process of creating, compiling, and running a program without a lot of distractions. When developing programs that run on a mobile device, this process is a little more complex than customary because you'll be creating and compiling programs on the PC but you'll be deploying and running them on an actual phone or at least an emulator.

This chapter presents programs for both Microsoft Silverlight and Microsoft XNA that display the text "Hello, Windows Phone 7!"

Just to make these programs a little more interesting, I want to display the text in the center of the display. The Silverlight program will use the background and foreground colors selected by the user in the Themes section of the phone's Settings screen. In the XNA program, the text will be white on a dark background to use less power on OLED.

If you're playing along, it's time to bring up Visual Studio and from the File menu select New and then Project.

A First Silverlight Phone Program

In the New Project dialog box, on the left under Installed Templates, choose Visual C# and then Silverlight for Windows Phone. In the middle area, choose Windows Phone Application. Select a location for the project, and enter the project name: SilverlightHelloPhone.

As the project is created you'll see an image of a large-screen phone in portrait mode with a screen area 480 × 800 pixels in size. This is the design view. Although you can interactively pull controls from a toolbox to design the application, I'm going to focus instead on showing you how to write your own code and markup.

Several files have been created for this SilverlightHelloPhone project and are listed under the project name in the Solution Explorer over at the right. In the Properties folder are three files that you can usually ignore when you're just creating little sample Silverlight programs for the phone. Only when you're actually in the process of making a real application do these files become important.

However, you might want to open the WMAppManifest.xml file. In the App tag near the top, you'll see the attribute:

```
Title="SilverlightHelloPhone"
```

That's just the project name you selected. Insert some spaces to make it a little friendlier:

```
Title="Silverlight Hello Phone"
```

This is the name used by the phone and the phone emulator to display the program in the list of installed applications presented to the user. If you're really ambitious, you can also edit the ApplicationIcon.png and Background.png files that the phone uses to visually symbolize the program. The SplashScreenImage.jpg file is what the program displays as it's initializing.

In the standard Visual Studio toolbar under the program's menu, you'll see a drop-down list probably displaying "Windows Phone 7 Emulator." The other choice is "Windows Phone 7 Device." This is how you deploy your program to either the emulator or an actual phone connected to your computer via USB.

Just to see that everything's working OK, select Windows Phone 7 Emulator and press F5 (or select Start Debugging from the Debug menu). Your program will quickly build and in the status bar you'll see the text "Connecting to Windows Phone 7 Emulator…" The first time you use the emulator during a session, it might take a little time to start up. If you leave the emulator running between edit/build/run cycles, Visual Studio doesn't need to establish this connection again.

Soon the phone emulator will appear on the desktop and you'll see the opening screen, followed soon by this little do-nothing Silverlight program as it is deployed and run on the emulator. On the phone you'll see pretty much the same image you saw in the design view.

The phone emulator has a little floating menu at the upper right that comes into view when you move the mouse to that location. You can change orientation through this menu, or change the emulator size. By default, the emulator is displayed at 50% actual size, about the same size as the image on this page. When you display the emulator at 100%, it becomes enormous, and you might wonder "How will I ever fit a phone this big into my pocket?"

The difference involves pixel density. Your computer screen probably has about 100 pixels per inch. (By default, Windows assumes that screens are 96 DPI.) The screen on an actual Windows Phone 7 device is more than 2½ times that. When you display the emulator at 100%, you're seeing all the pixels of the phone's screen, but at about 250% their actual size.

You can terminate execution of this program and return to editing the program either though Visual Studio (using Shift-F5 or by selecting Stop Debugging from the Debug menu) or by clicking the Back button on the emulator.

Don't exit the emulator itself by clicking the X at the top of the floating menu! Keeping the emulator running will make subsequent deployments go much faster.

While the emulator is still running, it retains all programs deployed to it. If you click the arrow at the upper-right of the Start screen, you'll get a list that will include this program identified by the text "Silverlight Hello Phone" and you can run the program again. The program will disappear from this list when you exit the emulator.

If you have a Windows Phone 7 device, you'll need to register for the marketplace at the Windows Phone 7 portal, *http://developer.windowsphone.com*. After you're approved, you'll to connect the phone to your PC and run the Zune desktop software. You can unlock the phone for development by running the Windows Phone Developer Registration program and entering your Windows Live ID. You can then deploy programs to the phone from Visual Studio.

The Standard Silverlight Files

With the project loaded in Visual Studio, take a look at the Solution Explorer for the project. You'll see two pairs of skeleton files: App.xaml and App.xaml.cs, and MainPage.xaml and MainPage.xaml.cs. The App.xaml and MainPage.xaml files are Extensible Application Markup Language (XAML) files, while App.xaml.cs and MainPage.xaml.cs are C# code files. This peculiar naming scheme is meant to imply that the two C# code files are "code-behind" files associated with the two XAML files. They provide code in support of the markup. This is a basic Silverlight concept.

I want to give you a little tour of these four files. If you look at the App.xaml.cs file, you'll see a namespace definition that is the same as the project name and a class named *App* that derives from the Silverlight class *Application*. Here's an excerpt showing the general structure:

Silverlight Project: **SilverlightHelloPhone**   File: **App.xaml.cs** (excerpt)

```
namespace SilverlightHelloPhone
{
    public partial class App : Application
    {
        public App()
        {
            ...
            InitializeComponent();
            ...
        }
        ...
    }
}
```

All Silverlight programs contain an *App* class that derives from *Application*; this class performs application-wide initialization, startup, and shutdown chores. You'll notice this class is defined as a *partial* class, meaning that the project should probably include another C# file that contains additional members of the *App* class. But where is it?

The project also contains an App.xaml file, which has an overall structure like this:

Silverlight Project: **SilverlightHelloPhone**   File: **App.xaml** (excerpt)

```
<Application
    x:Class="SilverlightHelloPhone.App"
    xmlns="http://schemas.microsoft.com/winfx/2006/xaml/presentation"
    xmlns:x="http://schemas.microsoft.com/winfx/2006/xaml"
    xmlns:phone="clr-namespace:Microsoft.Phone.Controls;assembly=Microsoft.Phone"
    xmlns:shell="clr-namespace:Microsoft.Phone.Shell;assembly=Microsoft.Phone">
    ...
</Application>
```

You'll recognize this file as XML, but more precisely it is a XAML file, which is an important part of Silverlight programming. In particular, developers often use the App.xaml file for storing *resources* that are used throughout the application. These resources might include color schemes, gradient brushes, styles, and so forth.

The root element is *Application*, which is the Silverlight class that the *App* class derives from. The root element contains four XML namespace declarations. Two are common in all Silverlight applications; two are unique to the phone.

The first XML namespace declaration ("xmlns") is the standard namespace for Silverlight, and it helps the compiler locate and identify Silverlight classes such as *Application* itself. As with most XML namespace declarations, this URI doesn't actually point to anything; it's just a URI that Microsoft owns and which it has defined for this purpose.

The second XML namespace declaration is associated with XAML itself, and it allows the file to reference some elements and attributes that are part of XAML rather than specifically Silverlight. By convention, this namespace is associated with a prefix of "x" (meaning "XAML").

Among the several attributes supported by XAML and referenced with this "x" prefix is *Class*, which is often pronounced "x class." In this particular XAML file *x:Class* is assigned the name *SilverlightHelloPhone.App*. This means that a class named *App* in the .NET *SilverlightHelloPhone* namespace derives from the Silverlight *Application* class, the root element. It's the same class definition you saw in the App.xaml.cs file but with very different syntax.

The App.xaml.cs and App.xaml files really define two halves of the same *App* class. During compilation, Visual Studio parses App.xaml and generates another code file named App.g.cs. The "g" stands for "generated." If you want to look at this file, you can find it in the \obj\ Debug subdirectory of the project. The App.g.cs file contains another partial definition of the *App* class, and it contains a method named *InitializeComponent* that is called from the constructor in the App.xaml.cs file.

You're free to edit the App.xaml and App.xaml.cs files, but don't mess around with App.g.cs. That file is recreated when you build the project.

When a program is run, the *App* class creates an object of type *PhoneApplicationFrame* and sets that object to its own *RootVisual* property. This frame is 480 pixels wide and 800 pixels tall and occupies the entire display surface of the phone. The *PhoneApplicationFrame* object then behaves somewhat like a web browser by navigating to an object called *MainPage*.

MainPage is the second major class in every Silverlight program and is defined in the second pair of files, MainPage.xaml and MainPage.xaml.cs. In smaller Silverlight programs, it is in these two files that you'll be spending most of your time.

Aside from a long list of *using* directives, the MainPage.xaml.cs file is very simple:

```
Silverlight Project: SilverlightHelloPhone   File: MainPage.xaml.cs (excerpt)

using System;
using System.Collections.Generic;
using System.Linq;
using System.Net;
using System.Windows;
using System.Windows.Controls;
using System.Windows.Documents;
using System.Windows.Input;
using System.Windows.Media;
using System.Windows.Media.Animation;
using System.Windows.Shapes;
using Microsoft.Phone.Controls;

namespace SilverlightHelloPhone
{
    public partial class MainPage : PhoneApplicationPage
    {
        // Constructor
        public MainPage()
        {
            InitializeComponent();
        }
    }
}
```

The *using* directives for namespaces that begin with the words *System.Windows* are for the Silverlight classes; sometimes you'll need to supplement these with some other *using* directives as well. The *Microsoft.Phone.Controls* namespace contains extensions to Silverlight for the phone, including the *PhoneApplicationPage* class.

Again, we see another *partial* class definition. This one defines a class named *MainPage* that derives from the Silverlight class *PhoneApplicationPage*. This is the class that defines the visuals you'll actually see on the screen when you run the SilverlightHelloPhone program.

The other half of this *MainPage* class is defined in the MainPage.xaml file. Here's the nearly complete file, reformatted a bit to fit the printed page, and excluding a section that's commented out at the end, but still a rather frightening chunk of markup:

Silverlight Project: **SilverlightHelloPhone**   File: **MainPage.xaml** (almost complete)

```
<phone:PhoneApplicationPage
    x:Class="SilverlightHelloPhone.MainPage"
    xmlns="http://schemas.microsoft.com/winfx/2006/xaml/presentation"
    xmlns:x="http://schemas.microsoft.com/winfx/2006/xaml"
    xmlns:phone="clr-namespace:Microsoft.Phone.Controls;assembly=Microsoft.Phone"
    xmlns:shell="clr-namespace:Microsoft.Phone.Shell;assembly=Microsoft.Phone"
    xmlns:d="http://schemas.microsoft.com/expression/blend/2008"
    xmlns:mc="http://schemas.openxmlformats.org/markup-compatibility/2006"
    mc:Ignorable="d" d:DesignWidth="480" d:DesignHeight="768"
    FontFamily="{StaticResource PhoneFontFamilyNormal}"
    FontSize="{StaticResource PhoneFontSizeNormal}"
    Foreground="{StaticResource PhoneForegroundBrush}"
    SupportedOrientations="Portrait" Orientation="Portrait"
    shell:SystemTray.IsVisible="True">

    <!--LayoutRoot is the root grid where all page content is placed-->
    <Grid x:Name="LayoutRoot" Background="Transparent">
        <Grid.RowDefinitions>
            <RowDefinition Height="Auto"/>
            <RowDefinition Height="*"/>
        </Grid.RowDefinitions>

        <!--TitlePanel contains the name of the application and page title-->
        <StackPanel x:Name="TitlePanel" Grid.Row="0" Margin="12,17,0,28">
            <TextBlock x:Name="ApplicationTitle" Text="MY APPLICATION"
                       Style="{StaticResource PhoneTextNormalStyle}"/>
            <TextBlock x:Name="PageTitle" Text="page name" Margin="9,-7,0,0"
                       Style="{StaticResource PhoneTextTitle1Style}"/>
        </StackPanel>

        <!--ContentPanel - place additional content here-->
        <Grid x:Name="ContentPanel" Grid.Row="1" Margin="12,0,12,0">
        </Grid>
    </Grid>
</phone:PhoneApplicationPage>
```

The first four XML namespace declarations are the same as in App.xaml. As in the App .xaml file, an *x:Class* attribute also appears in the root element. Here it indicates that the *MainPage* class in the *SilverlightHelloPhone* namespace derives from the Silverlight *PhoneApplicationPage* class. This *PhoneApplicationPage* class requires its own XML namespace declaration because it is not a part of standard Silverlight.

The "d" (for "designer") and "mc" (for "markup compatibility") namespace declarations are for the benefit of XAML design programs, such as Expression Blend and the designer in

Visual Studio itself. The *DesignerWidth* and *DesignerHeight* attributes are ignored during compilation.

The compilation of the program generates a file name MainPage.g.cs that contains another partial class definition for *MainPage* (you can look at it in the \obj\Debug subdirectory) with the *InitializeComponent* method called from the constructor in MainPage.xaml.cs.

In theory, the App.g.cs and MainPage.g.cs files generated during the build process are solely for internal use by the compiler and can be ignored by the programmer. However, sometimes when a buggy program raises an exception, one of these files comes popping up into view. It might help your understanding of the problem to have seen these files before they mysteriously appear in front of your face. However, don't try to edit these files to fix the problem! The real problem is probably somewhere in the corresponding XAML file.

In the root element of MainPage.xaml you'll see settings for *FontFamily*, *FontSize*, and *Foreground* that apply to the whole page. I'll describe *StaticResource* and this syntax in Chapter 7.

The body of the MainPage.xaml file contains several nested elements named *Grid*, *StackPanel*, and *TextBlock* in a parent-child hierarchy.

Notice the word I used: *element*. In Silverlight programming, this word has two related meanings. It's an XML term used to indicate items delimited by start tags and end tags. But it's also a word used in Silverlight to refer to visual objects, and in fact, the word *element* shows up in the names of two actual Silverlight classes.

Many of the classes you use in Silverlight are part of this important class hierarchy:

Object
      DependencyObject (abstract)
          UIElement (abstract)
              FrameworkElement (abstract)

Besides *UIElement*, many other Silverlight classes derive from *DependencyObject*. But *UIElement* has the distinction of being the class that has the power to appear as a visual object on the screen and to receive user input. (In Silverlight, all visual objects can receive user input.) Traditionally, this user input comes from the keyboard and mouse; on the phone, most user input comes from touch.

The only class that derives from *UIElement* is *FrameworkElement*. The distinction between these two classes is a historical artifact of the Windows Presentation Foundation. In WPF, it is possible for developers to create their own unique frameworks by deriving from *UIElement*. In Silverlight this is not possible, so the distinction is fairly meaningless.

One of the classes that derives from *FrameworkElement* is *Control*, a word more common than *element* in traditional graphical user-interface programming. Some objects commonly referred to as *controls* in other programming environments are more correctly referred to as *elements* in Silverlight. Control derivatives include buttons and sliders that I'll discuss in Chapter 10.

Another class that derives from *FrameworkElement* is *Panel*, which is the parent class to the *Grid* and *StackPanel* elements you see in MainPage.xaml. Panels are elements that can host multiple children and arrange them in particular ways on the screen. I'll discuss panels in more depth in Chapter 9.

Another class that derives from *FrameworkElement* is *TextBlock*, the element you'll use most often in displaying blocks of text up to about a paragraph in length. The two *TextBlock* elements in MainPage.xaml display the two chunks of title text in a new Silverlight program.

PhoneApplicationPage, *Grid*, *StackPanel*, and *TextBlock* are all Silverlight classes. In Markup these become XML elements. Properties of these classes become XML attributes.

The nesting of elements in MainPage.xaml is said to define a *visual tree*. In a Silverlight program for Windows Phone 7, the visual tree always begins with an object of type *PhoneApplicationFrame*, which occupies the entire visual surface of the phone. A Silverlight program for Windows Phone 7 always has one and only one instance of *PhoneApplicationFrame*, referred to informally as the *frame*.

In contrast, a program can have multiple instances of *PhoneApplicationPage*, referred to informally as a *page*. At any one time, the frame hosts one page, but lets you navigate to the other pages. By default, the page does not occupy the full display surface of the frame because it makes room for the system tray (also known as the status bar) at the top of the phone.

Our simple application has only one page, appropriately called *MainPage*. This *MainPage* contains a *Grid*, which contains a *StackPanel* with a couple *TextBlock* elements, and another *Grid*, all in a hierarchical tree. The visual tree of a Silverlight program creates by Visual Studio is:

PhoneApplicationFrame
    PhoneApplicationPage
        Grid named "LayoutRoot"
            StackPanel named "TitlePanel"
                TextBlock named "ApplicationTitle"
                TextBlock named "PageTitle"
            Grid named "ContentPanel"

Our original goal was to create a Silverlight program that displays some text in the center of the display, but given the presence of a couple titles, let's amend that goal to displaying the text in the center of the page apart from the titles. The area of the page for program content is the *Grid* towards the bottom of the file preceded by the comment "ContentPanel - place additional content here." This *Grid* has a name of "ContentPanel" and I'm going to refer to it informally as the "content panel" or "content grid". The area of the screen corresponding to this *Grid* apart from the titles I'll often refer to as the "content area".

In the content grid, you can insert a new *TextBlock*:

Silverlight Project: **SilverlightHelloPhone**   File: **MainPage.xaml (excerpt)**

```
<Grid x:Name="ContentPanel" Grid.Row="1" Margin="12,0,12,0">
    <TextBlock Text="Hello, Windows Phone 7!"
               HorizontalAlignment="Center"
               VerticalAlignment="Center" />
</Grid>
```

Text, *HorizontalAlignment*, and *VerticalAlignment* are all properties of the *TextBlock* class. The *Text* property is of type *string*. The *HorizontalAlignment* and *VerticalAlignment* properties are of numeration types HorizontalAlignment and *VerticalAlignment*, respectively. When you reference an enumeration type in XAML, you only need the member name.

While you're editing MainPage.xaml you might also want to fix the other *TextBlock* elements so that they aren't so generic. Change

```
<TextBlock ... Text="MY APPLICATION" ... />
```

to

```
<TextBlock ... Text="SILVERLIGHT HELLO PHONE" ... />
```

and

```
<TextBlock ... Text="page title" ... />
```

to:

```
<TextBlock ... Text="main page" ... />
```

It doesn't make much sense to have a page title in a Silverlight application with only a single page, and you can delete that second *TextBlock* if you'd like. The changes you make to this XAML file will be reflected in the design view. You can now compile and run this program:

This screen shot—and most of the remaining screen shots in this book—are shown on the pages of this book with a size that approximates the size of the actual phone, surrounded by some simple "chrome" that symbolizes either the actual phone or the phone emulator.

As simple as it is, this program demonstrates some essential concepts of Silverlight programming, including dynamic layout. The XAML file defines a layout of elements in a visual tree. These elements are capable of arranging themselves dynamically. The *HorizontalAlignment* and *VerticalAlignment* properties can put an element in the center of another element, or (as you might suppose) along one of the edges or in one of the corners. *TextBlock* is one of a number of possible elements you can use in a Silverlight program; others include bitmap images, movies, and familiar controls like buttons, sliders, and list boxes.

Color Themes

From the Start screen of the phone or phone emulator, click or touch the right arrow at the upper right and navigate to the Settings page and then select Theme. A Windows Phone 7 theme consists of a Background and an Accent color. For the Background you can select either Dark (light text on a dark background, which you've been seeing) or Light (the opposite). Select the Light theme, run SilverlightHelloPhone again, and express some satisfaction that the theme colors are automatically applied:

Although these colors are applied automatically, you're not stuck with them in your application. If you'd like the text to be displayed in a different color, you can try setting the *Foreground* attribute in the *TextBlock* tag, for example:

```
Foreground="Red"
```

You can put it anywhere in the tag as long as you leave spaces on either side. As you type this attribute, you'll see a list of colors pop up. Silverlight supports the 140 color names supported by many browsers, as well as a bonus 141st color, *Transparent*.

In a real-world program, you'll want to test out any custom colors with the available themes so text doesn't mysteriously disappear or becomes hard to read.

Points and Pixels

Another property of the *TextBlock* that you can easily change is *FontSize*:

```
FontSize="36"
```

But what exactly does this mean?

All dimensions in Silverlight are in units of pixels, and the *FontSize* is no exception. When you specify 36, you get a font that from the top of its ascenders to the bottom of its descenders measures approximately 36 pixels.

But fonts are never this simple. The resultant *TextBlock* will actually have a height more like 48 pixels—about 33% higher than the *FontSize* would imply. This additional space (called *leading*) prevents successive lines of text from jamming against each other.

Traditionally, font sizes are expressed in units of *points*. In classical typography, a point is very close to 1/72nd inch but in digital typography the point is often assumed to be exactly 1/72nd inch. A font with a size of 72 points measures approximately an inch from the top of its characters to the bottom. (I say "approximately" because the point size indicates a typographic design height, and it's really the creator of the font who determines exactly how large the characters of a 72-point font should be.)

How do you convert between pixels and points? Obviously you can't except for a particular output device. On a 600 dots-per-inch (DPI) printer, for example, the 72-point font will be 600 pixels tall.

Desktop video displays in common use today usually have a resolution somewhere in the region of 100 DPI. For example, consider a 21" monitor that displays 1600 pixels horizontally and 1200 pixels vertically. That's 2000 pixels diagonally, which divided by 21" is about 95 DPI.

By default, Microsoft Windows assumes that video displays have a resolution of 96 DPI. Under that assumption, font sizes and pixels are related by the following formulas:

points = ¾ × pixels

pixels = 4/3 × points

Although this relationship applies only to common video displays, people so much enjoy having these conversion formulas, they show up in Windows Phone 7 programming as well.

So, when you set a *FontSize* property such as

```
FontSize="36"
```

you can also claim to be setting a 27-point font.

For a particular point size, increase by 33% to get a pixel size. This is what you set to the *FontSize* property of *TextBlock*. The resultant *TextBlock* will then be another 33% taller than the *FontSize* setting.

The issue of font size becomes more complex when dealing with high-resolution screens found on devices such as Windows Phone 7. The 480 × 800 pixel display has a diagonal of 933 pixels. The phone I used for this book has a screen with about 3½" for a pixel density closer to 264 DPI. (Screen resolution is usually expressed as a multiple of 24.) Roughly that's 2½ times the resolution of conventional video displays.

This doesn't necessarily mean that all the font sizes used on a conventional screen need to be increased by 2½ times on the phone. The higher resolution of the phone—and the closer viewing distance common with phones—allows smaller font sizes to be more readable.

When running in a Web browser, the default Silverlight *FontSize* is 11 pixels, corresponding to a font size of 8.25 points, which is fine for a desktop video display but a little too small for the phone. For that reason, Silverlight for Windows Phone defines a collection of common font sizes that you can use. (I'll describe how these work in Chapter 7.) The standard MainPage .xaml file includes the following attribute in the root element:

```
FontSize="{StaticResource PhoneFontSizeNormal}"
```

This *FontSize* is inherited through the visual tree and applies to all *TextBlock* elements that don't set their own *FontSize* properties. It has a value of 20 pixels—almost double the default Silverlight *FontSize* on the desktop. Using the standard formulas, this 20-pixel *FontSize* corresponds to 15 points, but as actually displayed on the phone, it's about 2/5 the size that a 15-point font would appear in printed text.

The actual height of the *TextBlock* displaying text with this font is about 33% more than the *FontSize*, in this case about 27 pixels.

The XAP is a ZIP

If you navigate to the \bin\Debug directory of the Visual Studio project for SilverlightHelloPhone, you'll find a file named SilverlightHelloPhone.xap. This is commonly referred to as a XAP file, pronounced "zap." This is the file that is deployed to the phone or phone emulator.

The XAP file is a package of other files, in the very popular compression format known as ZIP. (Shouting "The XAP is a ZIP" in a crowded room will quickly attract other Silverlight programmers.) If you rename SilverlightHelloPhone.xap to SilverlightHelloPhone.zip, you can look inside. You'll see several bitmap files that are part of the project, an XML file, a XAML file, and a SilverlightHelloPhone.dll file, which is the compiled binary of your program.

Any assets that your program needs can be made part of the Visual Studio project and added to this XAP file. Your program can access these files at runtime. I'll discuss some of the concepts in Chapter 4.

An XNA Program for the Phone

Next up on the agenda is an XNA program that displays a little greeting in the center of the screen. While text is often prevalent in Silverlight applications, it is less common in graphical games. In games, text is usually relegated to describing how the game works or displaying the score, so the very concept of a "hello, world" program doesn't quite fit in with the whole XNA programming paradigm.

In fact, XNA doesn't even have any built-in fonts. You might think that an XNA program running on the phone can make use of the same native fonts as Silverlight programs, but this is not so. Silverlight uses vector-based TrueType fonts and XNA doesn't know anything about such exotic concepts. To XNA, everything is a bitmap, including fonts.

If you wish to use a particular font in your XNA program, that font must be embedded into the executable as a collection of bitmaps for each character. XNA Game Studio (which is integrated into Visual Studio) makes the actual process of font embedding very easy, but it raises some thorny legal issues. You can't legally distribute an XNA program unless you can also legally distribute the embedded font, and with most of the fonts distributed with Windows itself or Windows applications, this is not the case.

To help you out of this legal quandary, Microsoft licensed some fonts from Ascender Corporation specifically for the purpose of allowing you to embed them in your XNA programs. Here they are:

Kootenay	Lindsey
Miramonte	Pescadero
Miramonte Bold	**Pescadero Bold**
PERICLES	Segoe UI Mono
PERICLES LIGHT	**Segoe UI Mono Bold**

Notice that the Pericles font uses small capitals for lower-case letters, so it's probably suitable only for headings.

From the File menu of Visual Studio select New and Project. On the left of the dialog box, select Visual C# and XNA Game Studio 4.0. In the middle, select Windows Phone Game (4.0). Select a location and enter a project name of XnaHelloPhone.

Visual Studio creates two projects, one for the program and the other for the program's content. XNA programs usually contain lots of content, mostly bitmaps and 3D models, but fonts as well. To add a font to this program, right-click the Content project (labeled "XnaHelloPhoneContent (Content)" and from the pop-up menu choose Add and New Item. Choose Sprite Font, leave the filename as SpriteFont1.spritefont, and click Add.

The word "sprite" is common in game programming and usually refers to a small bitmap that can be moved very quickly, much like the sprites you might encounter in an enchanted forest. In XNA, even fonts are sprites.

You'll see SpriteFont1.spritefont show up in the file list of the Content directory, and you can edit an extensively commented XML file describing the font.

XNA Project: XnaHelloPhone   File: **SpriteFont1.spritefont** (complete w/o comments)

```xml
<XnaContent xmlns:Graphics="Microsoft.Xna.Framework.Content.Pipeline.Graphics">
  <Asset Type="Graphics:FontDescription">
    <FontName>Segoe UI Mono</FontName>
    <Size>14</Size>
    <Spacing>0</Spacing>
    <UseKerning>true</UseKerning>
    <Style>Regular</Style>
    <CharacterRegions>
      <CharacterRegion>
        <Start>&#32;</Start>
        <End>&#126;</End>
      </CharacterRegion>
    </CharacterRegions>
  </Asset>
</XnaContent>
```

Within the *FontName* tags you'll see Segoe UI Mono, but you can change that to one of the other fonts I listed earlier. If you want Pericles Light, put the whole name in there, but if you want Miramonte Bold or Pescadero Bold or Segoe UI Mono Bold, use just Miramonte or Pescadero or Segoe UI Mono, and enter the word Bold between the Style tags. You can use Bold for the other fonts as well, but for the other fonts, bold will be synthesized, while for Miramonte or Pescadero or Segoe UI Mono, you'll get the font actually designed for bold.

The *Size* tags indicate the point size of the font. In XNA as in Silverlight, you deal almost exclusively with pixel coordinates and dimensions, but the conversion between points and pixels used within XNA is based on 96 DPI displays. The point size of 14 becomes a pixel size of 18-2/3 within your XNA program. This is very close to the 15-point and 20-pixel "normal" *FontSize* in Silverlight for Windows Phone.

The *CharacterRegions* section of the file indicates the ranges of hexadecimal Unicode character encodings you need. The default setting from 0x32 through 0x126 includes all the non-control characters of the ASCII character set.

The filename of SpriteFont1.spritefont is not very descriptive. I like to rename it to something that describes the actual font; if you're sticking with the default font settings, you can rename it to Segoe14.spritefont. If you look at the properties for this file—right-click the filename and select Properties—you'll see an Asset Name that is also the filename without the extension: Segoe14. This Asset Name is what you use to refer to the font in your program to load the font. If you want to confuse yourself, you can change the Asset Name independently of the filename.

In its initial state, the XNAHelloPhone project contains two C# code files: Program.cs and Game1.cs. The first is very simple and turns out to be irrelevant for Windows Phone 7 games! A preprocessor directive enables the *Program* class only if a symbol of WINDOWS or XBOX is defined. When compiling Windows Phone programs, the symbol WINDOWS_PHONE is defined instead.

For most small games, you'll be spending all your time in the Game1.cs file. The *Game1* class derives from *Game* and in its pristine state it defines two fields: *graphics* and *spriteBatch*. To those two fields I want to add three more:

XNA Project: XnaHelloPhone   File: Game1.cs (excerpt showing fields)

```
namespace XnaHelloPhone
{
    public class Game1 : Microsoft.Xna.Framework.Game
    {
        GraphicsDeviceManager graphics;
        SpriteBatch spriteBatch;
        string text = "Hello, Windows Phone 7!";
        SpriteFont segoe14;
        Vector2 textPosition;
        ...
    }
}
```

These three new fields simply indicate the text that the program will display, the font it will use to display it, and the position of the text on the screen. That position is specified in pixel coordinates relative to the upper-left corner of the display. The *Vector2* structure has two fields named *X* and *Y* of type *float*. For performance purposes, all floating-point values in XNA are single-precision. (Silverlight is all double-precision.) The *Vector2* structure is often used for two-dimensional points, sizes, and even vectors.

When the game is run on the phone, the *Game1* class is instantiated and the *Game1* constructor is executed. This standard code is provided for you:

XNA Project: XnaHelloPhone   File: Game1.cs (excerpt)

```
public Game1()
{
    graphics = new GraphicsDeviceManager(this);
    Content.RootDirectory = "Content";

    // Frame rate is 30 fps by default for Windows Phone.
    TargetElapsedTime = TimeSpan.FromTicks(333333);
}
```

The first statement initializes the *graphics* field. In the second statement, *Content* is a property of *Game* of type *ContentManager*, and *RootDirectory* is a property of that class.

Setting this property to "Content" is consistent with the Content directory that is currently storing the 14-point Segoe font. The third statement sets a time for the program's game loop, which governs the pace at which the program updates the video display. The Windows Phone 7 screen is refreshed at 30 frames per second.

After *Game1* is instantiated, a *Run* method is called on the *Game1* instance, and the base *Game* class initiates the process of starting up the game. One of the first steps is a call to the *Initialize* method, which a *Game* derivative can override. XNA Game Studio generates a skeleton method to which I won't add anything:

XNA Project: XnaHelloPhone   File: Game1.cs (excerpt)

```
protected override void Initialize()
{
    base.Initialize();
}
```

The *Initialize* method is not the place to load the font or other content. That comes a little later when the base class calls the *LoadContent* method.

XNA Project: XnaHelloPhone   File: Game1.cs (excerpt)

```
protected override void LoadContent()
{
    spriteBatch = new SpriteBatch(GraphicsDevice);

    segoe14 = this.Content.Load<SpriteFont>("Segoe14");
    Vector2 textSize = segoe14.MeasureString(text);
    Viewport viewport = this.GraphicsDevice.Viewport;

    textPosition = new Vector2((viewport.Width - textSize.X) / 2,
                               (viewport.Height - textSize.Y) / 2);

}
```

The first statement in this method is provided for you. You'll see shortly how this *spriteBatch* object is used to shoot sprites out to the display.

The other statements are ones I've added, and you'll notice I tend to preface property names like *Content* and *GraphicsDevice* with the keyword *this* to remind myself that they're properties and not a static class. As I mentioned, the *Content* property is of type *ContentManager*. The generic *Load* method allows loading content into the program, in this case content of type *SpriteFont*. The name in quotation marks is the Asset Name as indicated in the content's properties. This statement stores the loaded font in the *segoe14* field of type *SpriteFont*.

In XNA, sprites (including text strings) are usually displayed by specifying the pixel coordinates relative to the upper-left corner or the sprite relative to the upper-left corner of the display. To calculate these coordinates, it's helpful to know both the screen size and the size of the text when displayed with a particular font.

The *SpriteFont* class has a very handy method named *MeasureString* that returns a *Vector2* object with the size of a particular text string in pixels. (For the 14-point Segoe UI Mono font, which has an equivalent height of 18-2/3 pixels, the *MeasureString* call returns a height of 28 pixels.)

An XNA program generally uses the *Viewport* property of the *GraphicsDevice* class to obtain the size of the screen. This is accessible through the *GraphicsDevice* property of *Game* and provides *Width* and *Height* properties.

It is then straightforward to calculate *textPosition*—the point relative to the upper-left corner of the viewport where the upper-left corner of the text string is to be displayed.

The initialization phase of the program has now concluded, and the real action begins. The program enters the *game loop*. In synchronization with the 30 frame-per-second refresh rate of the video display, two methods in your program are called: *Update* followed by *Draw*. Back and forth: *Update, Draw, Update, Draw, Update, Draw*…. (It's actually somewhat more complicated than this if the *Update* method requires more than 1/30th of a second to complete, but I'll discuss these timing issues in more detail in a later chapter.)

In the *Draw* method you want to draw on the display. But that's *all* you want to do. If you need to perform some calculations in preparation for drawing, you should do those in the *Update* method. The *Update* method prepares the program for the *Draw* method. Very often an XNA program will be moving sprites around the display based on user input. For the phone, this user input mostly involves fingers touching the screen. All handling of user input should also occur during the *Update* method. You'll see an example in Chapter 3.

You should write your *Update* and *Draw* methods so that they execute as quickly as possible. That's rather obvious, I guess, but here's something very important that might not be so obvious:

You should avoid code in *Update* and *Draw* that routinely allocates memory from the program's local heap. Eventually the .NET garbage collector will want to reclaim some of this memory, and while the garbage collector is doing its job, your game might stutter a bit. Throughout the chapters on XNA programming, you'll see techniques to avoid allocating memory from the heap.

Your *Draw* methods probably won't contain any questionable code; it's usually in the *Update* method where trouble lurks. Avoid any *new* expressions involving classes. These always cause memory allocation. Instantiating a structure is fine, however, because structure instances are stored on the stack and not in the heap. (XNA uses structures rather than classes for many types of objects you'll often need to create in *Update*.) But heap allocations can also occur without explicit *new* expressions. For example, concatenating two strings creates another string on the heap. If you need to perform string manipulation in *Update*, you should use *StringBuilder*. Conveniently, XNA provides methods to display text using *StringBuilder* objects.

In XnaHelloPhone, however, the *Update* method is trivial. The text displayed by the program is anchored in one spot. All the necessary calculations have already been performed in the *LoadContent* method. For that reason, the *Update* method will be left simply as XNA Game Studio originally created it:

XNA Project: **XnaHelloPhone**   File: **Game1.cs** (excerpt)

```
protected override void Update(GameTime gameTime)
{
    if (GamePad.GetState(PlayerIndex.One).Buttons.Back == ButtonState.Pressed)
        this.Exit();

    base.Update(gameTime);
}
```

The default code uses the static *GamePad* class to check if the phone's hardware Back button has been pressed and uses that to exit the game.

Finally, there is the *Draw* method. The version created for you simply colors the background with a light blue:

XNA Project: **XnaHelloPhone**   File: **Game1.cs** (excerpt)

```
protected override void Draw(GameTime gameTime)
{
    GraphicsDevice.Clear(Color.CornflowerBlue);

    base.Draw(gameTime);
}
```

The color known as CornflowerBlue has achieved iconic status in the XNA programming community. When you're developing an XNA program, the appearance of the light blue screen is very comforting because it means the program has at least gotten as far as *Draw*. But if you want to conserve power on OLED displays, you want to go with darker backgrounds. In my revised version, I've compromised by setting the background to a darker blue. As in Silverlight, XNA supports the 140 colors that have come to be regarded as standard. The text is colored white:

XNA Project: **XnaHelloPhone**   File: **Game1.cs** (excerpt)

```
protected override void Draw(GameTime gameTime)
{
    GraphicsDevice.Clear(Color.Navy);

    spriteBatch.Begin();
    spriteBatch.DrawString(segoe14, text, textPosition, Color.White);
    spriteBatch.End();

    base.Draw(gameTime);
}
```

Sprites get out on the display by being bundled into a *SpriteBatch* object, which was created during the call to *LoadContent*. Between calls to *Begin* and *End* there can be multiple calls to *DrawString* to draw text and *Draw* to draw bitmaps. Those are the only options. This particular *DrawString* call references the font, the text to display, the position of the upper-left corner of the text relative to the upper-left corner of the screen, and the color. And here it is:

Oh, that's interesting! By default, Silverlight programs come up in portrait mode, but XNA programs come up in landscape mode. Let's turn the phone or emulator sideways:

Much better!

But this raises a question: Do Silverlight programs always run in portrait mode and XNA programs always run in landscape mode?

Is program biology destiny?

Chapter 2
Getting Oriented

By default, Silverlight programs for Windows Phone 7 run in portrait mode, and XNA programs run in landscape mode. This chapter discusses how to transcend those defaults and explores other issues involving screen sizes, element sizes, and events.

Silverlight and Dynamic Layout

If you run the SilverlightHelloPhone program from the last chapter, and you turn the phone or emulator sideways, you'll discover that the display doesn't change to accommodate the new orientation. That's easy to fix. In the root *PhoneApplicationPage* tag, of MainPage.xaml change the attribute

```
SupportedOrientations="Portrait"
```

to:

```
SupportedOrientations="PortraitOrLandscape"
```

SupportedOrientations is a property of *PhoneApplicationPage*. It's set to a member of the *SupportedPageOrientation* enumeration, either *Portrait*, *Landscape*, or *PortraitOrLandscape*.

Recompile. Now when you turn the phone or emulator sideways, the contents of the page shift around accordingly:

The *SupportedOrientations* property also allows you to restrict your program to *Landscape* if you need to.

This response to orientation really shows off dynamic layout in Silverlight. Everything has moved around and some elements have changed size. Silverlight originated in WPF and the desktop, so historically it was designed to react to changes in window sizes and aspect ratios. This facility carries well into the phone.

Two of the most important properties in working with dynamic layout are *HorizontalAlignment* and *VerticalAlignment*. In the last chapter, using these properties to center text in a Silverlight program was certainly easier than performing calculations based on screen size and text size that XNA required.

On the other hand, if you now needed to stack a bunch of text strings, you would probably find it straightforward in XNA, but not so obvious in Silverlight.

Rest assured that there are ways to organize elements in Silverlight. A whole category of elements called *panels* exist solely for that purpose. You can even position elements based on pixel coordinates, if that's your preference. But a full coverage of panels won't come until Chapter 9.

In the meantime, you can try putting multiple elements into the content grid. Normally a *Grid* organizes its content into cells identified by row and column, but this program puts nine *TextBlock* elements in a single-cell *Grid* to demonstrate the use of *HorizontalAlignment* and *VerticalAlignment* in nine different combinations:

Silverlight Project: SilverlightCornersAndEdges   File: MainPage.xaml

```
<Grid x:Name="ContentPanel" Grid.Row="1" Margin="12,0,12,0">
    <TextBlock Text="Top-Left"
               VerticalAlignment="Top"
               HorizontalAlignment="Left" />

    <TextBlock Text="Top-Center"
               VerticalAlignment="Top"
               HorizontalAlignment="Center" />

    <TextBlock Text="Top-Right"
               VerticalAlignment="Top"
               HorizontalAlignment="Right" />

    <TextBlock Text="Center-Left"
               VerticalAlignment="Center"
               HorizontalAlignment="Left" />

    <TextBlock Text="Center"
               VerticalAlignment="Center"
               HorizontalAlignment="Center" />

    <TextBlock Text="Center-Right"
               VerticalAlignment="Center"
               HorizontalAlignment="Right" />
```

```
    <TextBlock Text="Bottom-Left"
              VerticalAlignment="Bottom"
              HorizontalAlignment="Left" />

    <TextBlock Text="Bottom-Center"
              VerticalAlignment="Bottom"
              HorizontalAlignment="Center"  />

    <TextBlock Text="Bottom-Right"
              VerticalAlignment="Bottom"
              HorizontalAlignment="Right" />
  </Grid>
```

As with many of the simpler Silverlight programs in this book, I've set the *SupportedOrientations* property of *MainPage* to *PortraitOrLandscape*. And here it is turned sideways:

Although this screen appears to show all the combinations, the program does *not* actually show the *default* settings of the *HorizontalAlignment* and *VerticalAlignment* properties. The default settings are enumeration members named *Stretch*. If you try them out, you'll see that the *TextBlock* sits in the upper-left corner, just as with values of *Top* and *Left*. But what won't be so obvious is that the *TextBlock* occupies the entire interior of the *Grid*. The *TextBlock* has a transparent background (and you can't set an alternative) so it's a little difficult to tell the difference. But I'll demonstrate the effect in the next chapter.

Obviously the *HorizontalAlignment* and *VerticalAlignment* properties are very important in the layout system in Silverlight. So is *Margin*. Try adding a *Margin* setting to the first *TextBlock* in this program:

```
<TextBlock Text="Top-Left"
          VerticalAlignment="Top"
          HorizontalAlignment="Left"
          Margin="100" />
```

Now there's a 100-pixel breathing room between the *TextBlock* and the left and top edges of the client area. The *Margin* property is of type *Thickness*, a structure that has four properties named *Left*, *Top*, *Right*, and *Bottom*. If you specify only one number in XAML, that's used for all four sides. You can also specify two numbers like this:

```
Margin="100 200"
```

The first applies to the left and right; the second to the top and bottom. With four numbers

```
Margin="100 200 50 300"
```

they're in the order left, top, right, and bottom. Watch out: If the margins are too large, the text or parts of the text will disappear. Silverlight preserves the margins even at the expense of truncating the element.

If you set both *HorizontalAlignment* and *VerticalAlignment* to *Center*, and set *Margin* to four different numbers, you'll notice that the text is no longer visually centered in the content area. Silverlight bases the centering on the size of the element including the margins.

TextBlock also has a *Padding* property:

```
<TextBlock Text="Top-Left"
           VerticalAlignment="Top"
           HorizontalAlignment="Left"
           Padding="100 200" />
```

Padding is also of type *Thickness*, and when used with the *TextBlock*, *Padding* is visually indistinguishable from *Margin*. But they are definitely different: *Margin* is space on the outside of the *TextBlock*; *Padding* is space inside the *TextBlock* not occupied by the text itself. If you were using *TextBlock* for touch events (as I'll demonstrate in the next chapter), it would respond to touch in the *Padding* area but not the *Margin* area.

The *Margin* property is defined by *FrameworkElement*; in real-life Silverlight programming, almost everything gets a non-zero *Margin* property to prevent the elements from being jammed up against each other. The *Padding* property is rarer; it's defined only by *TextBlock*, *Border*, and *Control*.

It's possible to use *Margin* to position multiple elements within a single-cell *Grid*. It's not common—and there are better ways to do the job—but it is possible. I'll have an example in Chapter 5.

What's crucial to realize is what we're *not* doing. We're not explicitly setting the *Width* and *Height* of the *TextBlock* like in some antique programming environment:

```
<TextBlock Text="Top-Left"
           VerticalAlignment="Top"
           HorizontalAlignment="Left"
           Width="100"
           Height="50" />
```

You're second guessing the size of the *TextBlock* without knowing as much about the element as the *TextBlock* itself. In some cases, setting *Width* and *Height* is appropriate, but not here.

The *Width* and *Height* properties are of type *double*, and the default values are those special floating-point values called Not a Number or NaN. If you need to get the *actual* width and height of an element as it's rendered on the screen, access the properties named *ActualWidth* and *ActualHeight* instead. (But watch out: These values will have non-zero values only when the element has been rendered on the screen.)

Some useful events are also available for obtaining information involving element sizes. The *Loaded* event is fired when visuals are first arranged on the screen; *SizeChanged* is supported by elements to indicate when they've changed size; *LayoutUpdated* is useful when you want notification that a layout cycle has occurred, such as occurs when orientation changes.

The SilverlightWhatSize project demonstrates the use of the *SizeChanged* method by displaying the sizes of several elements in the standard page. It's not often that you need these precise sizes, but they might be of interest occasionally.

You can associate a particular event with an event handler right in XAML, but the actual event handler must be implemented in code. When you type an event name in XAML (such as *SizeChanged*) Visual Studio will offer to create an event handler for you. That's what I did with the *SizeChanged* event for the content grid:

SilverlightProject: SilverlightWhatSize   File: MainPage.xaml (excerpt)

```
<Grid x:Name="ContentPanel" Grid.Row="1" Margin="12,0,12,0"
      SizeChanged="ContentPanel_SizeChanged">
    <TextBlock Name="txtblk"
               HorizontalAlignment="Center"
               VerticalAlignment="Center" />
</Grid>
```

I also assigned the *TextBlock* property *Name* to "txtblk." The *Name* property plays a very special role in Silverlight. If you compile the program at this point and look inside MainPage.g.cs—the code file that the compiler generates based on the MainPage.xaml file— you'll see a bunch of fields in the *MainPage* class, among them a field named *txtblk* of type *TextBlock*:

```
internal System.Windows.Controls.TextBlock txtblk;
```

You'll also notice that this field is assigned from code in the *InitializeComponent* method:

```
this.txtblk = ((System.Windows.Controls.TextBlock)(this.FindName("txtblk")));
```

This means that anytime after the constructor in MainPage.xaml.cs calls *InitializeComponent*, any code in the *MainPage* class can reference that *TextBlock* element in the XAML file using the *txtblk* variable stored as a field in the class.

You'll notice that several of the elements in the MainPage.xaml file are assigned names with *x:Name* rather than *Name*. As used in XAML, these two attributes are basically equivalent. *Name* only works with elements (that is, instances of classes that derive from *FrameworkElement* because that's where the *Name* property is defined) but *x:Name* works with everything.

This means that code in the MainPage class in MainPage.xaml.cs has a field available named *ContentPanel* to reference the standard *Grid* that appears in MainPage.xaml, and similarly for the other elements in MainPage.xaml.

Assigning names to elements is one of two primary ways in which code and XAML interact. The second way is for the element defined in XAML to fire an event that is handled in code. Here's the handler for the *SizeChanged* event of the content grid as Visual Studio created it:

SilverlightProject: SilverlightWhatSize   File: **MainPage.xaml.cs** (excerpt)

```
private void ContentPanel_SizeChanged(object sender, SizeChangedEventArgs e)
{

}
```

I usually don't like the way Visual Studio creates these handlers. Normally I remove the keyword *private*, I rename the event handlers to start them with the word *On,* and I eliminate underscores. This one I'd call *OnContentPanelSizeChanged.* I also tend to change the event arguments from *e* to *args*.

But for this program I'll leave it as is. On entry to the method, the *sender* argument is the element that fired the event, in this case the *Grid* named *ContentPanel.* The second argument contains information specific to the event.

I added a body to this method that just sets the *Text* property of *txtblk* to a longish multi-line string:

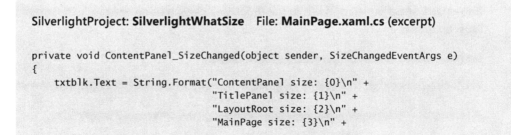

SilverlightProject: SilverlightWhatSize   File: **MainPage.xaml.cs** (excerpt)

```
private void ContentPanel_SizeChanged(object sender, SizeChangedEventArgs e)
{
    txtblk.Text = String.Format("ContentPanel size: {0}\n" +
                                "TitlePanel size: {1}\n" +
                                "LayoutRoot size: {2}\n" +
                                "MainPage size: {3}\n" +
```

```
                                           "Frame size: {4}",
                                           e.NewSize,
                                           new Size(TitlePanel.ActualWidth, TitlePanel.
   ActualHeight),

                                           new Size(LayoutRoot.ActualWidth, LayoutRoot.
   ActualHeight),

                                           new Size(this.ActualWidth, this.ActualHeight),
                                           Application.Current.RootVisual.RenderSize);

   }
```

The five items are of type *Size*, a structure with *Width* and *Height* properties. The size of the *ContentPanel* itself is available from the *NewSize* property of the event arguments. For the next three, I used the *ActualWidth* and *ActualHeight* properties.

Notice the last item. The static property *Application.Current* returns the *Application* object associated with the current process. This is the *App* object created by the program. It has a property named *RootVisual* that references the frame, but the property is defined to be of type *UIElement*. The *ActualWidth* and *ActualHeight* properties are defined by *FrameworkElement*, the class that derives from *UIElement*. Rather than casting, I chose to use a property of type *Size* that *UIElement* defines.

The first *SizeChanged* event occurs when the page is created and laid out, that is, when the content grid changes size from 0 to a finite value:

The 32-pixel difference between the *MainPage* size and the frame size accommodates the system tray at the top. You can prevent that tray from appearing while your application is running (and in effect, get access to the entire screen) by changing an attribute in the root element of MainPage.xaml from:

```
shell:SystemTray.IsVisible="True"
```

to

```
shell:SystemTray.IsVisible="False"
```

The syntax of this attribute might seem a little peculiar. *SystemTray* is a class in the *Microsoft .Phone.Shell* namespace and *IsVisible* is a property of that class, and both the class and property appear together because it's a special kind of property called an *attached property*.

The topmost *Grid* named *LayoutRoot* is the same size as *MainPage*. The vertical size of the *TitlePanel* (containing the two titles) and the vertical size of *ContentPanel* don't add up to the vertical size of *LayoutRoot* because of the 45-pixel vertical margin (17 pixels on the top and 28 pixels on the bottom) of the *TitlePanel*.

Subsequent *SizeChanged* events occur when something in the visual tree causes a size change, or when the phone changes orientation:

Notice that the frame doesn't change orientation. In the landscape view, the system tray takes away 72 pixels of width from *MainPage*.

Orientation Events

In many of the simpler Silverlight programs in this book, I'll set *SupportedOrientations* to *PortraitOrLandscape*, and try to write orientation-independent applications. For Silverlight programs that get text input, it's crucial for the program to be aligned with the hardware keyboard (if one exists) and the location of that keyboard can't be anticipated.

Obviously there is more to handling orientation changes than just setting the *SupportedOrientations* property! In some cases, you might want to manipulate your layout from code in the page class. If you need to perform any special handling, both *PhoneApplicationFrame* and *PhoneApplicationPage* include *OrientationChanged* events. *PhoneApplicationPage* supplements that event with a convenient and equivalent protected overridable method called *OnOrientationChanged*.

The *MainPage* class in the SilverlightOrientationDisplay project shows how to override *OnOrientationChanged*, but what it does with this information is merely to display the current orientation. The content grid in this project contains a simple *TextBlock*:

SilverlightProject: SilverlightOrientationDisplay   File: MainPage.xaml (excerpt)

```
<Grid x:Name="ContentPanel" Grid.Row="1" Margin="12,0,12,0">
    <TextBlock Name="txtblk"
               HorizontalAlignment="Center"
               VerticalAlignment="Center" />
</Grid>
```

Here's the complete code-behind file. The constructor initializes the *TextBlock* text with the current value of the *Orientation* property, which is a member of the *PageOrientation* enumeration:

SilverlightProject: SilverlightOrientationDisplay   File: MainPage.xaml.cs

```
using System.Windows.Controls;
using Microsoft.Phone.Controls;

namespace SilverlightOrientationDisplay
{
    public partial class MainPage : PhoneApplicationPage
    {
        public MainPage()
        {
            InitializeComponent();
            txtblk.Text = Orientation.ToString();
        }

        protected override void OnOrientationChanged(OrientationChangedEventArgs args)
        {
            txtblk.Text = args.Orientation.ToString();
            base.OnOrientationChanged(args);
        }
    }
}
```

The *OnOrientationChanged* method obtains the new value from the event arguments.

XNA Orientation

By default, XNA for Windows Phone is set up for a landscape orientation, perhaps to be compatible with other screens on which games are played. Both landscape orientations are supported, and the display will automatically flip around when you turn the phone from one landscape orientation to the other. If you prefer designing your game for a portrait display, it's easy to do that. In the constructor of the *Game1* class of XnaHelloPhone, try inserting the following statements:

```
graphics.PreferredBackBufferWidth = 320;
graphics.PreferredBackBufferHeight = 480;
```

The *back buffer* is the surface area on which XNA constructs the graphics you display in the *Draw* method. You can control both the size and the aspect ratio of this buffer. Because the buffer width I've specified here is smaller than the buffer height, XNA assumes that I want a portrait display:

Look at that! The back buffer I specified is not the same aspect ratio as the Windows Phone 7 display, so the drawing surface is letter-boxed! The text is larger because it's the same pixel size but now the display resolution has been reduced.

Although you may not be a big fan of the retro graininess of this particular display, you should seriously consider specifying a smaller back buffer if your game doesn't need the high resolution provided by the phone. Performance will improve and battery consumption will decrease. You can set the back buffer to anything from 240 × 240 up to 480 × 800 (for portrait mode) or 800 × 480 (for landscape). XNA uses the aspect ratio to determine whether you want portrait or landscape.

Setting a desired back buffer is also an excellent way to target a specific display dimension in code but allow for devices of other sizes that may come in the future.

By default the back buffer is 800 × 480, but it's actually not displayed at that size. It's scaled down a bit to accommodate the system tray. To get rid of the system tray (and possibly annoy your users who like to always know what time it is) you can set

```
graphics.IsFullScreen = true;
```

in the *Game1* constructor.

It's also possible to have your XNA games respond to orientation changes, but they'll definitely have to be restructured a bit. The simplest type of restructuring to accommodate orientation changes is demonstrated in the XnaOrientableHelloPhone project. The fields now include a *textSize* variable:

XNA Project: XnaOrientableHelloPhone   File: Game1.cs (excerpt showing fields)

```
public class Game1 : Microsoft.Xna.Framework.Game
{
    GraphicsDeviceManager graphics;
    SpriteBatch spriteBatch;
    string text = "Hello, Windows Phone 7!";
    SpriteFont segoe14;
    Vector2 textSize;
    Vector2 textPosition;
    . . .
}
```

The *Game1* constructor includes a statement that sets the *SupportedOrientations* property of the *graphics* field:

XNA Project: XnaOrientableHelloPhone   File: Game1.cs (excerpt)

```
public Game1()
{
    graphics = new GraphicsDeviceManager(this);
    Content.RootDirectory = "Content";
```

```
    // Allow portrait mode as well
    graphics.SupportedOrientations = DisplayOrientation.Portrait |
                                     DisplayOrientation.LandscapeLeft |
                                     DisplayOrientation.LandscapeRight;

    // Frame rate is 30 fps by default for Windows Phone.
    TargetElapsedTime = TimeSpan.FromTicks(333333);
}
```

You can also use *SupportedOrientation* to restrict the phone to just one of the two landscape orientations. The statement to support both portrait and landscape looks simple, but there are repercussions. When the orientation changes, the graphics device is effectively reset (which generates some events) and the back buffer dimensions are swapped. You can subscribe to the *OrientationChanged* event of the *GameWindow* class (accessible through the *Window* property) or you can check the *CurrentOrientation* property of the *GameWindow* object.

I chose a little different approach. Here's the new *LoadContent* method, which you'll notice obtains the text size and stores it as a field, but does not get the viewport.

XNA Project: XnaOrientableHelloPhone   File: Game1.cs (excerpt)

```
protected override void LoadContent()
{
    spriteBatch = new SpriteBatch(GraphicsDevice);
    segoe14 = this.Content.Load<SpriteFont>("Segoe14");
    textSize = segoe14.MeasureString(text);
}
```

Instead, the viewport is obtained during the *Update* method because the dimensions of the viewport reflect the orientation of the display.

XNA Project: XnaOrientableHelloPhone   File: Game1.cs (excerpt)

```
protected override void Update(GameTime gameTime)
{
    // Allows the game to exit
    if (GamePad.GetState(PlayerIndex.One).Buttons.Back == ButtonState.Pressed)
        this.Exit();

    Viewport viewport = this.GraphicsDevice.Viewport;
    textPosition = new Vector2((viewport.Width - textSize.X) / 2,
                               (viewport.Height - textSize.Y) / 2);
    base.Update(gameTime);
}
```

Whatever the orientation currently is, the *Update* method calculates a location for the text. The *Draw* method is the same as several you've seen before.

XNA Project: XnaOrientableHelloPhone   File: Game1.cs (excerpt)

```
protected override void Draw(GameTime gameTime)
{
    GraphicsDevice.Clear(Color.Navy);

    spriteBatch.Begin();
    spriteBatch.DrawString(segoe14, text, textPosition, Color.White);
    spriteBatch.End();

    base.Draw(gameTime);
}
```

Now the phone or emulator can be turned between portrait and landscape, and the display will switch as well.

If you need to obtain the size of the phone's display independent of any back buffers or orientation (but taking account of the system tray), that's available from the *ClientBounds* property of the *GameWindow* class, which you can access from the *Window* property of the *Game* class:

```
Rectangle clientBounds = this.Window.ClientBounds;
```

Simple Clocks (*Very* Simple Clocks)

So far in this chapter I've described two Silverlight events—*SizeChanged* and *OrientationChanged*—but used them in different ways. For *SizeChanged*, I associated the event with the event handler in XAML, but for *OrientationChanged*, I overrode the equivalent *OnOrientationChanged* method.

Of course, you can attach handlers to events entirely in code as well. One handy class for Silverlight programs is *DispatcherTimer*, which periodically nudges the program with a *Tick* event and lets the program do some work. A timer is essential for a clock program, for example.

The content grid of the SilverlightSimpleClock project contains just a centered *TextBlock*:

Silverlight Project: SilverlightSimpleClock   File: MainPage.xaml (excerpt)

```
<Grid x:Name="ContentPanel" Grid.Row="1" Margin="12,0,12,0">
    <TextBlock Name="txtblk"
               HorizontalAlignment="Center"
               VerticalAlignment="Center" />
</Grid>
```

Here's the entire code-behind file. Notice the *using* directive for the *System.Windows. Threading* namespace, which isn't included by default. That's the namespace where *DispatcherTimer* resides:

Silverlight Project: SilverlightSimpleClock   File: MainPage.xaml.cs

```
using System;
using System.Windows.Threading;
using Microsoft.Phone.Controls;

namespace SilverlightSimpleClock
{
    public partial class MainPage : PhoneApplicationPage
    {
        public MainPage()
        {
            InitializeComponent();

            DispatcherTimer tmr = new DispatcherTimer();
            tmr.Interval = TimeSpan.FromSeconds(1);
            tmr.Tick += OnTimerTick;
            tmr.Start();
        }

        void OnTimerTick(object sender, EventArgs args)
        {
            txtblk.Text = DateTime.Now.ToString();
        }
    }
}
```

The constructor initializes the *DispatcherTimer*, instructing it to call *OnTimerTick* once every second. The event handler simply converts the current time to a string to set it to the *TextBlock*.

Although *DispatcherTimer* is defined in the *System.Windows.Threading* namespace, the *OnTimerTick* method is called in the same thread as the rest of the program. If that was not the case, the program wouldn't be able to access the *TextBlock* directly. Silverlight elements and related objects are not thread safe, and they will prohibit access from threads that did not create them. I'll discuss the procedure for accessing Silverlight elements from secondary threads in Chapter 5.

The clock is yet another Silverlight program in this chapter that changes the *Text* property of a *TextBlock* dynamically during runtime. The new value shows up rather magically without any additional work. This is a very different from older graphical environments like Windows API programming or MFC programming, where a program draws "on demand," that is, when an area of a window becomes invalid and needs to be repainted, or when a program deliberately invalidates an area to force painting.

A Silverlight program often doesn't seem to draw at all! Deep inside of Silverlight is a visual composition layer that operates in a retained graphics mode and organizes all the visual elements into a composite whole. Elements such as *TextBlock* exist as actual entities inside this composition layer. At some point, *TextBlock* is rendering itself—and re-rendering itself when one of its properties such as *Text* changes—but what it renders is retained along with the rendered output of all the other elements in the visual tree.

In contrast, an XNA program is actively drawing during every frame of the video display. This is conceptually different from older Windows programming environments as well as Silverlight. It is very powerful, but I'm sure you know quite well what must also come with great power.

Sometimes an XNA program's display is static; the program might not need to update the display every frame. To conserve power, it is possible for the *Update* method to call the *SuppressDraw* method defined by the *Game* class to inhibit a corresponding call to *Draw*. The *Update* method will still be called 30 times per second because it needs to check for user input, but if the code in *Update* calls *SuppressDraw*, *Draw* won't be called during that cycle of the game loop. If the code in *Update* doesn't call *SuppressDraw*, *Draw* will be called.

An XNA clock program doesn't need a timer because a timer is effectively built into the normal game loop. However, the clock I want to code here won't display milliseconds so the display only needs to be updated every second. For that reason it uses the *SuppressDraw* method to inhibit superfluous *Draw* calls.

Here are the XnaSimpleClock fields:

XNA Project: XnaSimpleClock   File: Game1.cs (excerpt showing fields)

```
public class Game1 : Microsoft.Xna.Framework.Game
{
    GraphicsDeviceManager graphics;
    SpriteBatch spriteBatch;
    SpriteFont segoe14;
    Viewport viewport;
    Vector2 textPosition;
    StringBuilder text = new StringBuilder();
    DateTime lastDateTime;
    ...
}
```

Notice that instead of defining a field of type *string* named *text*, I've defined a *StringBuilder* instead. If you're creating new strings in your *Update* method for display during *Draw* (as this program will do), you should use *StringBuilder* to avoid the heap allocations associated with the normal *string* type. This program will only be creating a new string every second, so I really didn't need to use *StringBuilder* here, but it doesn't hurt to get accustomed to it. *StringBuilder* requires a *using* directive for the *System.Text* namespace.

Notice also the *lastDateTime* field. This is used in the *Update* method to determine if the displayed time needs to be updated.

The *LoadContent* method gets the font and the viewport of the display:

XNA Project: XnaSimpleClock   File: Game1.cs (excerpt)

```
protected override void LoadContent()
{
    spriteBatch = new SpriteBatch(GraphicsDevice);
    segoe14 = this.Content.Load<SpriteFont>("Segoe14");
    viewport = this.GraphicsDevice.Viewport;
}
```

The logic to compare two *DateTime* values to see if the time has changed is just a little tricky because *DateTime* objects obtained during two consecutive *Update* calls will *always* be different because they have will have different *Millisecond* fields. For this reason, a new *DateTime* is calculated based on the current time obtained from *DateTime.Now*, but subtracting the milliseconds:

XNA Project: XnaSimpleClock   File: Game1.cs (excerpt)

```csharp
protected override void Update(GameTime gameTime)
{
    // Allows the game to exit
    if (GamePad.GetState(PlayerIndex.One).Buttons.Back == ButtonState.Pressed)
        this.Exit();

    // Get DateTime with no milliseconds
    DateTime dateTime = DateTime.Now;
    dateTime = dateTime - new TimeSpan(0, 0, 0, 0, dateTime.Millisecond);

    if (dateTime != lastDateTime)
    {
        text.Remove(0, text.Length);
        text.Append(dateTime);
        Vector2 textSize = segoe14.MeasureString(text);
        textPosition = new Vector2((viewport.Width - textSize.X) / 2,
                                   (viewport.Height - textSize.Y) / 2);
        lastDateTime = dateTime;
    }
    else
    {
        SuppressDraw();
    }

    base.Update(gameTime);
}
```

At that point it's easy. If the time has changed, new values of *text*, *textSize*, and *textPosition* are calculated. Because *text* is a *StringBuilder* rather than a *string*, the old contents are removed and the new contents are appended. The *MeasureString* method of *SpriteFont* has an overload for *StringBuilder*, so that call looks exactly the same.

If the time has not changed, *SuppressDraw* is called. The result: *Draw* is called only once per second.

DrawString also has an overload for *StringBuilder*:

XNA Project: XnaSimpleClock   File: Game1.cs (excerpt)

```csharp
protected override void Draw(GameTime gameTime)
{
    GraphicsDevice.Clear(Color.Navy);

    spriteBatch.Begin();
    spriteBatch.DrawString(segoe14, text, textPosition, Color.White);
    spriteBatch.End();

    base.Draw(gameTime);
}
```

And here's the result:

SuppressDraw can be a little difficult to use—I've found it particularly tricky during the time that the program is first starting up—but it's one of the primary techniques used in XNA to reduce the power requirements of the program.

Chapter 3
An Introduction to Touch

Even for experienced Silverlight and XNA programmers, Windows Phone 7 comes with a feature that is likely to be new and unusual. The screen on the phone is sensitive to touch. And not like old touch screens that basically mimic a mouse, or the tablet screens that recognize handwriting.

The multi-touch screen on a Windows Phone 7 device can detect at least four simultaneous fingers. It is the interaction of these fingers that makes multi-touch so challenging for programmers. For this chapter, however, I have much a less ambitious goal. I want only to introduce the touch interfaces in the context of sample programs that respond to simple taps.

For testing critical multi-touch code, an actual Windows Phone 7 device is essential. In the interim, the phone emulator will respond to mouse activity and convert it to touch input. If you run the emulator under Windows 7 with a multi-touch display and a Windows 7 driver, you can also use touch directly on the emulator.

The programs in this chapter look much like the "Hello, Windows Phone 7!" programs in the first chapter, except that when you tap the text with your finger, it changes to a random color, and when you tap outside the area of the text, it goes back to white (or whatever color the text was when the program started up).

In a Silverlight program, touch input is obtained through events. In an XNA program, touch input comes through a static class polled during the *Update* method. One of the primary purposes of the XNA *Update* method is to check the state of touch input and make changes that affect what goes out to the screen during the *Draw* method.

Low-Level Touch Handling in XNA

The multi-touch input device is referred to in XNA as a *touch panel*. You use methods in the static *TouchPanel* class to obtain this input. Although you can obtain gestures, let's begin with the lower-level touch information.

It is possible (although not necessary) to obtain information about the multi-touch device itself by calling the static *TouchPanel.GetCapabilities* method. The *TouchPanelCapabilities* object returned from this method has two properties:

- *IsConnected* is *true* if the touch panel is available. For the phone, this will always be *true*.
- *MaximumTouchCount* returns the number of touch points, at least 4 for the phone.

For most purposes, you just need to use one of the other two static methods in *TouchPanel*. To obtain low-level touch input, you'll probably be calling this method during every call to *Update* after program initialization:

```
TouchCollection touchLocations = TouchPanel.GetState();
```

The *TouchCollection* is a collection of zero or more *TouchLocation* objects. *TouchLocation* has three properties:

- *State* is a member of the *TouchLocationState* enumeration: *Pressed, Moved, Released*.

- *Position* is a *Vector2* indicating the finger position relative to the upper-left corner of the viewport.

- *Id* is an integer identifying a particular finger from *Pressed* through *Released*.

If no fingers are touching the screen, the *TouchCollection* will be empty. When a finger first touches the screen, *TouchCollection* contains a single *TouchLocation* object with *State* equal to *Pressed*. On subsequent calls to *TouchPanel.GetState*, the *TouchLocation* object will have *State* equal to *Moved* even if the finger has not physically moved. When the finger is lifted from the screen, the *State* property of the *TouchLocation* object will equal *Released*. On subsequent calls to *TouchPanel.GetState*, the *TouchCollection* will be empty.

One exception: If the finger is tapped and released on the screen very quickly—that is, within a 1/30th of a second—it's possible that the *TouchLocation* object with *State* equal to *Pressed* will be followed with *State* equal to *Released* with no *Moved* states in between.

That's just one finger touching the screen and lifting. In the general case, multiple fingers will be touching, moving, and lifting from the screen independently of each other. You can track particular fingers using the *Id* property. For any particular finger, that *Id* will be the same from *Pressed*, through all the *Moved* values, to *Released*.

Very often when dealing with low-level touch input, you'll use a *Dictionary* object with keys based on the *Id* property to retain information for a particular finger.

TouchLocation also has a very handy method called *TryGetPreviousLocation*, which you call like this:

```
TouchLocation previousTouchLocation;
bool success = touchLocation.TryGetPreviousLocation(out previousTouchLocation);
```

Almost always, you will call this method when *touchLocation.State* is *Moved* because you can then obtain the previous location and calculate a difference. If *touchLocation.State* equals *Pressed*, then *TryGetPreviousLocation* will return *false* and *previousTouchLocation.State* will equal the enumeration member *TouchLocationState.Invalid*. You'll also get these results if you use the method on a *TouchLocation* that itself was returned from *TryGetPreviousLocation*.

The program I've proposed changes the text color when the user touches the text string, so the processing of *TouchPanel.GetStates* will be relatively simple. The program will examine only *TouchLocation* objects with *State* values of *Pressed*.

This project is called XnaTouchHello. Like the other XNA projects you've seen so far, it needs a font, which I've made a little larger so it provides a more substantial touch target. A few more fields are required:

XNA Project: XnaTouchHello   File: Game1.cs (excerpt showing fields)

```
public class Game1 : Microsoft.Xna.Framework.Game
{
    GraphicsDeviceManager graphics;
    SpriteBatch spriteBatch;

    Random rand = new Random();
    string text = "Hello, Windows Phone 7!";
    SpriteFont segoe36;
    Vector2 textSize;
    Vector2 textPosition;
    Color textColor = Color.White;
    ...

}
```

The *LoadContent* method is similar to earlier versions except that *textSize* is saved as a field because it needs to be accessed in later calculations:

XNA Project: XnaTouchHello   File: Game1.cs (excerpt)

```
protected override void LoadContent()
{
    spriteBatch = new SpriteBatch(GraphicsDevice);

    segoe36 = this.Content.Load<SpriteFont>("Segoe36");
    textSize = segoe36.MeasureString(text);
    Viewport viewport = this.GraphicsDevice.Viewport;
    textPosition = new Vector2((viewport.Width - textSize.X) / 2,
                               (viewport.Height - textSize.Y) / 2);
}
```

As is typical with XNA programs, much of the "action" occurs in the *Update* method. The method calls *TouchPanel.GetStates* and then loops through the collection of *TouchLocation* objects to find only those with *State* equal to *Pressed*.

XNA Project: XnaTouchHello   File: **Game1.cs** (excerpt)

```
protected override void Update(GameTime gameTime)
{
    if (GamePad.GetState(PlayerIndex.One).Buttons.Back == ButtonState.Pressed)
        this.Exit();

    TouchCollection touchLocations = TouchPanel.GetState();

    foreach (TouchLocation touchLocation in touchLocations)
    {
        if (touchLocation.State == TouchLocationState.Pressed)
        {
            Vector2 touchPosition = touchLocation.Position;

            if (touchPosition.X >= textPosition.X &&
                touchPosition.X < textPosition.X + textSize.X &&
                touchPosition.Y >= textPosition.Y &&
                touchPosition.Y < textPosition.Y + textSize.Y)
            {
                textColor = new Color((byte)rand.Next(256),
                                      (byte)rand.Next(256),
                                      (byte)rand.Next(256));
            }
            else
            {
                textColor = Color.White;
            }
        }
    }

    base.Update(gameTime);
}
```

If the *Position* is inside the rectangle occupied by the text string, the *textColor* field is set to a random RGB color value using one of the constructors of the *Color* structure. Otherwise, *textColor* is set to *Color.White*.

The *Draw* method looks very similar to the versions you've seen before, except that the text color is a variable:

XNA Project: XnaTouchHello   File: **Game1.cs** (excerpt)

```
protected override void Draw(GameTime gameTime)
{
    this.GraphicsDevice.Clear(Color.Navy);

    spriteBatch.Begin();
    spriteBatch.DrawString(segoe36, text, textPosition, textColor);
```

```
        spriteBatch.End();

        base.Draw(gameTime);
    }
```

One problem you might notice is that touch is not quite as deterministic as you might like. Even when you touch the screen with a single finger, the finger might make contact with the screen in more than one place. In some cases, the same *foreach* loop in *Update* might set *textColor* more than once!

The XNA Gesture Interface

The *TouchPanel* class also includes gesture recognition, which is demonstrated by the XnaTapHello project. The fields of this project are the same as those in XnaTouchHello, but the *LoadContent* method is a little different:

XNA Project: XnaTapHello   File: Game1.cs (excerpt)

```
protected override void LoadContent()
{
    spriteBatch = new SpriteBatch(GraphicsDevice);

    segoe36 = this.Content.Load<SpriteFont>("Segoe36");
    textSize = segoe36.MeasureString(text);
    Viewport viewport = this.GraphicsDevice.Viewport;
    textPosition = new Vector2((viewport.Width - textSize.X) / 2,
                               (viewport.Height - textSize.Y) / 2);

    TouchPanel.EnabledGestures = GestureType.Tap;
}
```

Notice the final statement. *GestureType* is an enumeration with members *Tap*, *DoubleTap*, *Flick*, *Hold*, *Pinch*, *PinchComplete*, *FreeDrag*, *HorizontalDrag*, *VerticalDrag*, and *DragComplete*, defined as bit flags so you can combine the ones you want with the C# bitwise OR operator.

The *Update* method is very different.

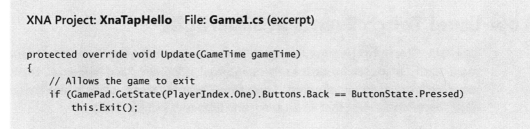

XNA Project: XnaTapHello   File: Game1.cs (excerpt)

```
protected override void Update(GameTime gameTime)
{
    // Allows the game to exit
    if (GamePad.GetState(PlayerIndex.One).Buttons.Back == ButtonState.Pressed)
        this.Exit();
```

```
while (TouchPanel.IsGestureAvailable)
{
    GestureSample gestureSample = TouchPanel.ReadGesture();

    if (gestureSample.GestureType == GestureType.Tap)
    {
        Vector2 touchPosition = gestureSample.Position;

        if (touchPosition.X >= textPosition.X &&
            touchPosition.X < textPosition.X + textSize.X &&
            touchPosition.Y >= textPosition.Y &&
            touchPosition.Y < textPosition.Y + textSize.Y)
        {
            textColor = new Color((byte)rand.Next(256),
                                  (byte)rand.Next(256),
                                  (byte)rand.Next(256));
        }
        else
        {
            textColor = Color.White;
        }
    }
}

base.Update(gameTime);
}
```

Although this program is interested in only one type of gesture, the code is rather generalized. If a gesture is available, it is returned from the *TouchPanel.ReadGesture* method as an object of type *GestureSample*. Besides the *GestureType* and *Position* used here, a *Delta* property provides movement information in the form of a *Vector2* object. For some gestures (such as *Pinch*), the *GestureSample* also reports the status of a second touch point with *Position2* and *Delta2* properties.

The *Draw* method is the same as the previous program, but you'll find that the program behaves a little differently from the first one: In the first program, the text changes color when the finger touches the screen; in the second, the color change occurs when the finger lifts from the screen. The gesture recognizer needs to wait until that time to determine what type of gesture it is.

Low-Level Touch Events in Silverlight

Like XNA, Silverlight also supports two different programming interfaces for working with multi-touch, which can be most easily categorized as low-level and high-level. The low-level interface is based around the static *Touch.FrameReported* event, which is very similar to the XNA *TouchPanel* except that it's an event and it doesn't include gestures.

The high-level interface consists of three events defined by the *UIElement* class: *ManipulationStarted*, *ManipulationDelta*, and *ManipulationCompleted*. The *Manipulation* events, as they're collectively called, consolidate the interaction of multiple fingers into movement and scaling factors.

The core of the low-level touch interface in Silverlight is a class called *TouchPoint*, an instance of which represents a particular finger touching the screen. *TouchPoint* has four get-only properties:

- *Action* of type *TouchAction*, an enumeration with members *Down*, *Move*, and *Up*.
- *Position* of type *Point*, relative to the upper-left corner of a particular element. Let's call this element the *reference* element.
- *Size* of type *Size*. This is supposed to represent the touch area (and, hence, finger pressure, more or less) but Windows Phone 7 doesn't return useful values.
- *TouchDevice* of type *TouchDevice*.

The *TouchDevice* object has two get-only properties:

- *Id* of type *int*, used to distinguish between fingers. A particular finger is associated with a unique *Id* for all events from *Down* through *Up*.
- *DirectlyOver* of type *UIElement*, the topmost element underneath the finger.

As you can see, the Silverlight *TouchPoint* and *TouchDevice* objects give you mostly the same information as the XNA *TouchLocation* object, but the *DirectlyOver* property of *TouchDevice* is often very useful for determining what element the user is touching.

To use the low-level touch interface, you install a handler for the static *Touch.FrameReported* event:

```
Touch.FrameReported += OnTouchFrameReported;
```

The *OnTouchFrameReported* method looks like this:

```
void OnTouchFrameReported(object sender, TouchFrameEventArgs args)
{
    . . .
}
```

The event handler gets all touch events throughout your application. The *TouchFrameEventArgs* object has a *TimeStamp* property of type *int*, plus three methods:

- *GetTouchPoints(refElement)* returns a *TouchPointCollection*
- *GetPrimaryTouchPoint(refElement)* returns one *TouchPoint*
- *SuspendMousePromotionUntilTouchUp()*

In the general case, you call *GetTouchPoints*, passing to it a reference element. The *TouchPoint* objects in the returned collection have *Position* properties relative to that element. You can pass *null* to *GetTouchPoints* to get *Position* properties relative to the upper-left corner of the application.

The reference element and the *DirectlyOver* element have no relationship to each other. The event always gets all touch activity for the entire program. Calling *GetTouchPoints* or *GetPrimaryTouchPoints* with a particular element does *not* limit the events to only those events involving that element. All that it does is cause the *Position* property to be calculated relative to that element. (For that reason, *Position* coordinates can easily be negative if the finger is to the left of or above the reference element.) The *DirectlyOver* element indicates the element under the finger.

A discussion of the second and third methods requires some background: The *Touch. FrameReported* event originated on Silverlight for the desktop, where it is convenient for the mouse logic of existing controls to automatically use touch. For this reason, touch events are "promoted" to mouse events.

But this promotion only involves the "primary" touch point, which is the activity of the first finger that touches the screen when no other fingers are touching the screen. If you don't want the activity of this finger to be promoted to mouse events, the event handler usually begins like this:

```
void OnTouchFrameReported(object sender, TouchFrameEventArgs args)
{
    TouchPoint primaryTouchPoint = args.GetPrimaryTouchPoint(null);

    if (primaryTouchPoint != null && primaryTouchPoint.Action == TouchAction.Down)
    {
        args.SuspendMousePromotionUntilTouchUp();
    }
    . . .
}
```

The *SuspendMousePromotionUntilTouchUp* method can only be called when a finger first touches the screen when no other fingers are touching the screen.

On Windows Phone 7, such logic presents something of a quandary. As written, it basically wipes out all mouse promotion throughout the application. If your phone application incorporates Silverlight controls that were originally written for mouse input but haven't been upgraded to touch, you're basically disabling those controls.

Of course, you can also check the *DirectlyOver* property to suspend mouse promotion selectively. But on the phone, no elements should be processing mouse input except for those controls that don't process touch input! So it might make more sense to *never* suspend mouse promotion.

I'll leave that matter for your consideration and your older mouse-handling controls. Meanwhile, the program I want to write is only interested in the primary touch point when it has a *TouchAction* of *Down*, so I can use that same logic.

The SilverlightTouchHello project has a *TextBlock* in the XAML file:Silverlight Project:

SilverlightTouchHello   File: **MainPage.xaml (excerpt)**

```
<Grid x:Name="ContentPanel" Grid.Row="1" Margin="12,0,12,0">
    <TextBlock Name="txtblk"
               Text="Hello, Windows Phone 7!"
               Padding="0 34"
               HorizontalAlignment="Center"
               VerticalAlignment="Center" />
</Grid>
```

Notice the *Padding* value. I know that the font displayed here has a *FontSize* property of 20 pixels, which actually translates into a *TextBlock* that is about 27 pixels tall. I also know that it's recommended that touch targets not be smaller than 9 millimeters. If the resolution of the phone display is 264 DPI, then 9 millimeters is 94 pixels. (The calculation is 9 millimeters divided by 25.4 millimeters to the inch, times 264 pixels per inch.) The *TextBlock* is short by 67 pixels. So I set a *Padding* value that puts 34 more pixels on both the top and bottom (but not the sides).

I used *Padding* rather than *Margin* because *Padding* is space *inside* the *TextBlock*. The *TextBlock* actually becomes larger than the text size would imply. *Margin* is space *outside* the *TextBlock*. It's not part of the *TextBlock* itself and is excluded for purposes of hit-testing.

Here's the complete code-behind file. The constructor of *MainPage* installs the *Touch. FrameReported* event handler.

Silverlight Project: **SilverlightTouchHello**   File: **MainPage.xaml.cs**

```
using System;
using System.Windows.Input;
using System.Windows.Media;
using Microsoft.Phone.Controls;

namespace SilverlightTouchHello
{
    public partial class MainPage : PhoneApplicationPage
    {
        Random rand = new Random();
        Brush originalBrush;

        public MainPage()
        {
            InitializeComponent();
            originalBrush = txtblk.Foreground;
            Touch.FrameReported += OnTouchFrameReported;
        }
```

```
        void OnTouchFrameReported(object sender, TouchFrameEventArgs args)
        {
            TouchPoint primaryTouchPoint = args.GetPrimaryTouchPoint(null);

            if (primaryTouchPoint != null && primaryTouchPoint.Action == TouchAction.
Down)
            {
                if (primaryTouchPoint.TouchDevice.DirectlyOver == txtblk)
                {
                    txtblk.Foreground = new SolidColorBrush(
                            Color.FromArgb(255, (byte)rand.Next(256),
                                                (byte)rand.Next(256),
                                                (byte)rand.Next(256)));
                }
                else
                {
                    txtblk.Foreground = originalBrush;
                }
            }
        }
    }
}
```

The event handler is only interested in primary touch points with an *Action* of *Down*. If the
DirectlyOver property is the element named *txtblk*, a random color is created. Unlike the
Color structure in XNA, the Silverlight *Color* structure doesn't have a constructor to set
a color from red, green, and blue values, but it does have a static *FromArgb* method that
creates a *Color* object based on alpha, red, green, and blue values, where alpha is opacity.
Set the alpha channel to 255 to get an opaque color. Although it's not obvious at all in the
XAML files, the *Foreground* property is actually of type *Brush*, an abstract class from which
SolidColorBrush descends.

If *DirectlyOver* is not *txtblk*, then the program doesn't change the color to white, because
that wouldn't work if the user chose a color theme of black text on a white background.
Instead, it sets the *Foreground* property to the brush originally set on the *TextBlock*. This is
obtained in the constructor.

The Manipulation Events

The high-level touch interface in Silverlight involves three events: *ManipulationStarted*,
ManipulationDelta, and *ManipulationCompleted*. These events don't bother with reporting
the activity of individual fingers. Instead, they consolidate the activity of multiple fingers into
translation and scaling operations. The events also accumulate velocity information, so while
they don't support inertia directly, they can be used to implement inertia.

The *Manipulation* events will receive more coverage in the chapters ahead. In this chapter I'm going to stick with *ManipulationStarted* just to detect contact of a finger on the screen, and I won't bother with what the finger does after that.

While *Touch.FrameReported* delivered touch information for the entire application, the *Manipulation* events are based on individual elements, so in SilverlightTapHello1, a *ManipulationStarted* event handler can be set on the *TextBlock*:

Silverlight Project: SilverlightTapHello1   File: MainPage.xaml (excerpt)

```
<Grid x:Name="ContentPanel" Grid.Row="1" Margin="12,0,12,0">
    <TextBlock Text="Hello, Windows Phone 7!"
               Padding="0 34"
               HorizontalAlignment="Center"
               VerticalAlignment="Center"
               ManipulationStarted="OnTextBlockManipulationStarted" />
</Grid>
```

The MainPage.xaml.cs contains this event handler:

Silverlight Project: SilverlightTapHello1   File: MainPage.xaml.cs (excerpt)

```
public partial class MainPage : PhoneApplicationPage
{
    Random rand = new Random();

    public MainPage()
    {
        InitializeComponent();
    }
    void OnTextBlockManipulationStarted(object sender,
                                        ManipulationStartedEventArgs args)
    {
        TextBlock txtblk = sender as TextBlock;

        Color clr = Color.FromArgb(255, (byte)rand.Next(256),
                                        (byte)rand.Next(256),
                                        (byte)rand.Next(256));

        txtblk.Foreground = new SolidColorBrush(clr);

        args.Complete();
    }
}
```

The event handler is able to get the element generating the message from the *sender* argument. That will always be the *TextBlock*. The *TextBlock* is also available from the *args. OriginalSource* property and the *args.ManipulationContainer* property.

Notice the call to the *Complete* method of the event arguments at the end. This is not required but effectively tells the system that further *Manipulation* events involving this finger won't be necessary.

This program is flawed: If you try it out, you'll see that it works only partially. Touching the *TextBlock* changes the text to a random color. But if you touch outside the *TextBlock*, the text does *not* go back to white. Because this event was set on the *TextBlock*, the event handler is called only when the user touches the *TextBlock*. No other *Manipulation* events are processed by the program.

A program that functions correctly according to my original specification needs to get touch events occurring *anywhere* on the page. A handler for the *ManipulationStarted* event needs to be installed on *MainPage* rather than just on the *TextBlock*.

Although that's certainly possible, there's actually an easier way. The *UIElement* class defines all the *Manipulation* events. But the *Control* class (from which *MainPage* derives) supplements those events with protected virtual methods. You don't need to install a handler for the *ManipulationStarted* event on *MainPage*; instead you can override the *OnManipulationStarted* virtual method.

This approach is implemented in the SilverlightTapHello2 project. The XAML file doesn't refer to any events but gives the *TextBlock* a name so that it can be referred to in code:

Silverlight Project: SilverlightTapHello2   File: MainPage.xaml (excerpt)

```
<Grid x:Name="ContentPanel" Grid.Row="1" Margin="12,0,12,0">
    <TextBlock Name="txtblk"
               Text="Hello, Windows Phone 7!"
               Padding="0 34"
               HorizontalAlignment="Center"
               VerticalAlignment="Center" />
</Grid>
```

The *MainPage* class overrides the *OnManipulationStarted* method:

Silverlight Project: SilverlightTapHello2   File: MainPage.xaml.cs (excerpt)

```
public partial class MainPage : PhoneApplicationPage
{
    Random rand = new Random();
    Brush originalBrush;

    public MainPage()
    {
        InitializeComponent();
        originalBrush = txtblk.Foreground;
    }
```

```
    protected override void OnManipulationStarted(ManipulationStartedEventArgs args)
    {
        if (args.OriginalSource == txtblk)
        {
            txtblk.Foreground = new SolidColorBrush(
                        Color.FromArgb(255, (byte)rand.Next(256),
                                            (byte)rand.Next(256),
                                            (byte)rand.Next(256)));
        }
        else
        {
            txtblk.Foreground = originalBrush;
        }

        args.Complete();
        base.OnManipulationStarted(args);
    }
}
```

In the *ManipulationStartedEventArgs* a property named *OriginalSource* indicates where this event began—in other words, the topmost element that the user tapped. If this equals the *txtblk* object, the method creates a random color for the *Foreground* property. If not, then the *Foreground* property is set to the original brush.

In this *OnManiulationStarted* method we're handling events for *MainPage*, but that *OriginalSource* property tells us the event actually originated lower in the visual tree. This is part of the benefit of the Silverlight feature known as *routed event handling*.

Routed Events

In Microsoft Windows programming, keyboard and mouse input always go to particular controls. Keyboard input always goes to the control with the input focus. Mouse input always goes to the topmost enabled control under the mouse pointer. Stylus and touch input is handled similarly to the mouse. But sometimes this is inconvenient. Sometimes the control underneath needs the user-input more than the control on top.

To be a bit more flexible, Silverlight implements a system called *routed event handling*. Most user input events—including the three *Manipulation* events—do indeed originate using the same paradigm as Windows. The *Manipulation* events originate at the topmost enabled element touched by the user. However, if that element is not interested in the event, the event then goes to that element's parent, and so forth up the visual tree ending at the *PhoneApplicationFrame* element. Any element along the way can grab the input and do something with it, and also inhibit further progress of the event up the tree.

This is why you can override the *OnManipulationStarted* method in *MainPage* and also get manipulation events for the *TextBlock*. By default the *TextBlock* isn't interested in those events.

The event argument for the *ManipulationStarted* event is *ManipulationStartedEventArgs*, which derives from *RoutedEventArgs*. It is *RoutedEventArgs* that defines the *OriginalSource* property that indicates the element on which the event began.

But this suggests another approach that combines the two techniques shown in SilverlightTapHello1 and SilverlightTapHello2. Here's the XAML file of SilverlightTapHello3:

Silverlight Project: SilverlightTapHello3   File: MainPage.xaml (excerpt)

```xml
<Grid x:Name="ContentPanel" Grid.Row="1" Margin="12,0,12,0">
    <TextBlock Name="txtblk"
               Text="Hello, Windows Phone 7!"
               Padding="0 34"
               HorizontalAlignment="Center"
               VerticalAlignment="Center"
               ManipulationStarted="OnTextBlockManipulationStarted" />
</Grid>
```

The *TextBlock* has a *Name* as in the first program. A handler for the *ManipulationStarted* event is set on the *TextBlock* as in the first program. Both the event handler and an override of *OnManipulationStarted* appear in the code-behind file:

Silverlight Project: SilverlightTapHello3   File: MainPage.xaml.cs (excerpt)

```csharp
public partial class MainPage : PhoneApplicationPage
{
    Random rand = new Random();
    Brush originalBrush;

    public MainPage()
    {
        InitializeComponent();
        originalBrush = txtblk.Foreground;
    }

    void OnTextBlockManipulationStarted(object sender,
                                        ManipulationStartedEventArgs args)
    {
        txtblk.Foreground = new SolidColorBrush(
                Color.FromArgb(255, (byte)rand.Next(256),
                                    (byte)rand.Next(256),
                                    (byte)rand.Next(256)));
        args.Complete();
        args.Handled = true;
    }
```

```
protected override void OnManipulationStarted(ManipulationStartedEventArgs args)
{
    txtblk.Foreground = originalBrush;

    args.Complete();
    base.OnManipulationStarted(args);
}
}
```

The logic has been split between the two methods, making the whole thing rather more elegant, I think. The *OnTextBlockManipulationStarted* method only gets events when the *TextBlock* is touched. The *OnManipulationStarted* event gets all events for *MainPage*.

At first there might seem to be a bug here. After *OnTextBlockManipulationStarted* is called, the event continues to travel up the visual tree and *OnManipulationStarted* sets the color back to white. But that's not what happens: The crucial statement that makes this work right is this one at the end of the *OnTextBlockManipulationStarted* handler for the *TextBlock*:

```
args.Handled = true;
```

That statement says that the event has now been handled and it should *not* travel further up the visual tree. Remove that statement and the *TextBlock* never changes from its initial color—at least not long enough to see.

Some Odd Behavior?

Now try this. In many of the Silverlight programs I've shown so far, I've centered the *TextBlock* within the content grid by setting the following two attributes:

```
HorizontalAlignment="Center"
VerticalAlignment="Center"
```

Delete them from SilverlightTapHello3, and recompile and run the program. The text appears at the upper-left corner of the *Grid*. But now if you touch *anywhere* within the large area below the *TextBlock*, the text will change to a random color, and only by touching the title area above the text can you change it back to white.

By default the *HorizontalAlignment* and *VerticalAlignment* properties are set to enumeration values called *Stretch*. The *TextBlock* is actually filling the *Grid*. You can't see it, of course, but the fingers don't lie.

With other elements—those that display bitmaps, for example—this stretching effect is much less subtle.

Chapter 4
Bitmaps, Also Known as Textures

Aside from text, one of the most common objects to appear in both Silverlight and XNA applications is the *bitmap*, formally defined as a two-dimensional array of bits corresponding to the pixels of a graphics display device.

In Silverlight, a bitmap is sometimes referred to as an *image*, but that's mostly a remnant of the Windows Presentation Foundation, where the word *image* refers to both bitmaps and vector-based drawings. In both WPF and Silverlight, the *Image* element displays bitmaps but the *Image* element is not the bitmap itself.

In XNA, a bitmap has a data type of *Texture2D* and hence is often referred to as a *texture*, but that term is mostly related to 3D programming where bitmaps are used to cover surfaces of 3D solids. In XNA 2D programming, bitmaps are often used as sprites.

Bitmaps are also used to symbolize your application on the phone. A new XNA or Silverlight project in Visual Studio results in the creation of three bitmaps for various purposes.

The native Windows bitmap format has an extension of BMP but it's become less popular in recent years as compressed formats have become widespread. At this time, the three most popular bitmap formats are probably:

- JPEG (Joint Photography Experts Group)
- PNG (Portable Network Graphics)
- GIF (Graphics Interchange File)

XNA supports all three (and more). Silverlight supports only JPEG and PNG. (And if you're like most Silverlight programmers, you'll not always remember this simple fact and someday wonder why your Silverlight program simply refuses to display a GIF or a BMP.)

The compression algorithms implemented by PNG and GIF do not result in the loss of any data. The original bitmap can be reconstituted exactly. For that reason, these are often referred to as "lossless" compression algorithms.

JPEG implements a "lossy" algorithm by discarding visual information that is less perceptible by human observers. This type of compression works well for real-world images such as photographs, but is less suitable for bitmaps that derive from text or vector-based images, such as architectural drawings or cartoons.

Both Silverlight and XNA allow manipulating bitmaps at the pixel level for generating bitmaps—or altering existing bitmaps—interactively or algorithmically. This chapter will focus more on the techniques of obtaining bitmaps from various sources, including the program itself, the Web, the phone's built-in camera, and the phone's photo library.

XNA Texture Drawing

Because XNA 2D programming is almost entirely a process of moving sprites around the screen, you might expect that loading and drawing bitmaps in an XNA program is fairly easy, and you would be correct.

The first project is called XnaLocalBitmap, so named because this bitmap will be stored as part of the program's content. To add a new bitmap to the program's content project, right-click the XnaLocalBitmapContent project name, select Add and then New Item, and then Bitmap File. You can create the bitmap right in Visual Studio.

Or, you can create the bitmap in an external program, as I did. Windows Paint is often convenient, so for this exercise I created the following bitmap with a dimension of 320 pixels wide and 160 pixels high:

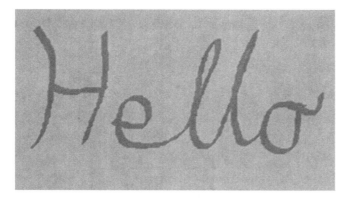

I saved it under the name Hello.png.

To add this file as part of the program's content, right-click the XnaLocalBitmapContent project in Visual Studio, select Add and Existing Item, and then navigate to the file. Once the file shows up, you can right-click it to display Properties, and you'll see that it has an Asset Name of "Hello."

The goal is to display this bitmap centered on the screen. Define a field in the Game1.cs file to store the *Texture2D* and another field for the position:

XNA Project: **XnaLocalBitmap**   File: **Game1.cs** (excerpt showing fields)

```
public class Game1 : Microsoft.Xna.Framework.Game
{
    GraphicsDeviceManager graphics;
    SpriteBatch spriteBatch;
    Texture2D helloTexture;
    Vector2 position;
    ...
}
```

Both fields are set during the *LoadContent* method. Use the same generic method to load the *Texture2D* as you use to load a *SpriteFont*. The *Texture2D* class has properties named *Width* and *Height* that provide the dimensions of the bitmap in pixels. As with the programs that centered text in the Chapter 1, the *position* field indicates the pixel location on the display that corresponds to the upper-left corner of the bitmap:

XNA Project: **XnaLocalBitmap**   File: **Game1.cs** (excerpt)

```
protected override void LoadContent()
{
    spriteBatch = new SpriteBatch(GraphicsDevice);
    helloTexture = this.Content.Load<Texture2D>("Hello");
    Viewport viewport = this.GraphicsDevice.Viewport;
    position = new Vector2((viewport.Width - helloTexture.Width) / 2,
                          (viewport.Height - helloTexture.Height) / 2);
}
```

The *SpriteBatch* class has seven *Draw* methods to render bitmaps. This one is certainly the simplest:

XNA Project: **XnaLocalBitmap**   File: **Game1.cs** (excerpt)

```
protected override void Draw(GameTime gameTime)
{
    GraphicsDevice.Clear(Color.Navy);

    spriteBatch.Begin();
    spriteBatch.Draw(helloTexture, position, Color.White);
    spriteBatch.End();

    base.Draw(gameTime);
}
```

The final argument to Draw is a color that can be used to attenuate the existing colors in the bitmap. Use *Color.White* if you want the bitmap's colors to display without any alteration.

And here it is:

The Silverlight *Image* Element

The equivalent program in Silverlight is even simpler. Let's create a project named SilverlightLocalBitmap. First create a directory in the project to store the bitmap. This isn't strictly required but it makes for a tidier project. Programmers usually name this directory Images or Media or Assets depending on the types of files that might be stored there. Right-click the project name and choose Add and then New Folder. Let's name it Images. Then right-click the folder name and choose Add and Existing Item. Navigate to the Hello. png file. (If you've created a different bitmap on your own, keep in mind that Silverlight supports only JPEG and PNG files.)

From the Add button choose either Add or Add as Link. If you choose Add, a copy will be made and the file will be physically copied into a subdirectory of the project. If you choose Add as Link, only a file reference will be retained with the project but the file will still be copied into the executable.

The final step: Right-click the bitmap filename and display Properties. Note that the Build Action is Resource. It's possible to change that Build Action to Content, but let's leave it for now and I'll discuss the difference shortly.

In Silverlight, you use the *Image* element to display bitmaps just as you use the *TextBlock* element to display text. Set the *Source* property of *Image* to the folder and filename of the bitmap within the project:

Silverlight Project: **SilverlightLocalBitmap**   File: **MainPage.xaml** (excerpt)

```
<Grid x:Name="ContentPanel" Grid.Row="1" Margin="12,0,12,0">
    <Image Source="Images/Hello.png" />
</Grid>
```

The display looks a little different than the XNA program, and it's not just the titles. By default, the *Image* element expands or contracts the bitmap as much as possible to fill its container (the content grid) while retaining the correct aspect ratio. This is most noticeable if you set the *SupportedOrientations* attribute of the *PhoneApplicationPage* start tag to *PortraitOrLandscape* and turn the phone sideways:

If you want to display the bitmap in its native pixel size, you can set the *Stretch* property of Image to *None*:

```
<Image Source="Images/Hello.png"
       Stretch="None" />
```

Images Via the Web

One feature that's really nice about the *Image* element is that you can set the *Source* property to a URL, such as in this Silverlight project:

Silverlight Project: **SilverlightWebBitmap**   File: **MainPage.xaml** (excerpt)

```
<Grid x:Name="ContentPanel" Grid.Row="1" Margin="12,0,12,0">
    <Image Source="http://www.charlespetzold.com/Media/HelloWP7.jpg" />
</Grid>
```

Here it is:

This is certainly easy enough, and pulling images off the Web rather than binding them into the application certainly keeps the size of the executable down. But an application running on Windows Phone 7 is not guaranteed to have an Internet connection, and you're undoubtedly associated with other problems associated with downloading. The *Image* element has two events named *ImageOpened* and *ImageFailed* that you can use to determine if the download was successful or not.

For Windows Phone 7 programs that display a lot of bitmaps, you need to do some hard thinking. You can embed the bitmaps into the executable and have their access guaranteed, or you can save space and download them when necessary.

In XNA, downloading a bitmap from the Web is not quite as easy, but a .NET class named *WebClient* makes the job relatively painless. It's somewhat easier to use than the common alternative (*HttpWebRequest* and *HttpWebResponse*) and is often the preferred choice for downloading individual items.

You can use *WebClient* to download either strings (commonly XML files) or binary objects. The actual transfer occurs asynchronously and then *WebClient* calls a method in your program to indicate completion or failure. This method call is in your program's thread, so you get the benefit of an asynchronous data transfer without explicitly dealing with secondary threads.

To use *WebClient* in an XNA program, you'll need to add a reference to the System.Net library: In the Solution Explorer, under the project name, right click References and select Add Reference. In the .NET table, select System.Net. (Silverlight programs get a reference to System.Net automatically.)

The Game1.cs file of the XnaWebBitmap project also requires a *using* directive for the *System .Net* namespace. The program defines the same fields as the earlier program:

XNA Project: XnaWebBitmap File: Game1.cs (excerpt showing fields)

```
public class Game1 : Microsoft.Xna.Framework.Game
{
    GraphicsDeviceManager graphics;
    SpriteBatch spriteBatch;
    Texture2D helloTexture;
    Vector2 position;
    . . .
}
```

The *LoadContent* method creates an instance of *WebClient*, sets the callback method, and then initiates the transfer:

XNA Project: XnaWebBitmap File: Game1.cs (excerpt)

```
protected override void LoadContent()
{
    spriteBatch = new SpriteBatch(GraphicsDevice);

    WebClient webClient = new WebClient();
    webClient.OpenReadCompleted += OnWebClientOpenReadCompleted;
    webClient.OpenReadAsync(new Uri("http://www.charlespetzold.com/Media/HelloWP7.
jpg"));
}
```

The *OnWebClientOpenReadCompleted* method is called when the entire file has been downloaded. You'll want to check if the download hasn't been cancelled and that no error has been reported. If everything is OK, the *Result* property of the event arguments is of type *Stream*. You can use that *Stream* with the static *Texture2D.FromStream* method to create a *Texture2D* object:

```
XNA Project: XnaWebBitmap   File: Game1.cs (excerpt)

void OnWebClientOpenReadCompleted(object sender, OpenReadCompletedEventArgs args)
{
    if (!args.Cancelled && args.Error == null)
    {
        helloTexture = Texture2D.FromStream(this.GraphicsDevice, args.Result);
        Viewport viewport = this.GraphicsDevice.Viewport;
        position = new Vector2((viewport.Width - helloTexture.Width) / 2,
                               (viewport.Height - helloTexture.Height) / 2);
    }
}
```

The *Texture2D.FromStream* method supports JPEG, PNG, and GIF.

By default, the *AllowReadStreamBuffering* property of *WebClient* is *true*, which means that the entire file will have been downloaded when the *OpenReadCompleted* event is raised. The *Stream* object available in the *Result* property is actually a memory stream, except that it's an instance of a class internal to the .NET libraries rather than *MemoryStream* itself.

If you set *AllowReadStreamBuffering* to *false*, then the *Result* property will be a network stream. The *Texture2D* class will not allow you to read from that stream on the main program thread.

Normally the *LoadContent* method of a *Game* derivative is called before the first call to the *Update* or *Draw* method, but it is essential to remember that a gap of time will separate *LoadContent* from the *OnWebClientOpenReadCompleted* method. During that time an asynchronous read is occurring, but the *Game1* class is proceeding as normal with calls to *Update* and *Draw*. For that reason, you should only attempt to access the *Texture2D* object when you know that it's valid:

```
XNA Project: XnaWebBitmap   File: Game1.cs (excerpt)

protected override void Draw(GameTime gameTime)
{
    GraphicsDevice.Clear(Color.Navy);

    if (helloTexture != null)
    {
        spriteBatch.Begin();
        spriteBatch.Draw(helloTexture, position, Color.White);
        spriteBatch.End();
    }

    base.Draw(gameTime);
}
```

In a real program, you'd also want to provide some kind of notification to the user if the bitmap could not be downloaded.

Image and ImageSource

Although you can certainly use *WebClient* in a *Silverlight* application, it's not generally necessary with bitmaps because the bitmap-related classes already implement asynchronous downloading.

However, once you begin investigating the *Image* element, it may seem a little confusing. The *Image* element is not the bitmap; the *Image* element merely displays the bitmap. In the uses you've seen so far, the *Source* property of *Image* has been set to a relative file path or a URL:

```
<Image Source="Images/Hello.png" />
<Image Source="http://www.charlespetzold.com/Media/HelloWP7.jpg" />
```

You might have assumed that this *Source* property was of type *string*. Sorry, not even close! You're actually seeing XAML syntax that hides some extensive activity behind the scenes. The *Source* property is really of type *ImageSource*, an abstract class from which derives *BitmapSource*, another abstract class but one that defines a method named *SetSource* that allows loading the bitmap from a *Stream* object.

From *BitmapSource* derives *BitmapImage*, which supports a constructor that accepts a *Uri* object and also includes a *UriSource* property of type *Uri*. The SilverlightTapToDownload1 project mimics a program that needs to download a bitmap whose URL is known only at runtime. The XAML contains an *Image* element with no bitmap to display:

Silverlight Project: SilverlightTapToDownload1   File: MainPage.xaml (excerpt)

```
<Grid x:Name="ContentPanel" Grid.Row="1" Margin="12,0,12,0">
    <Image Name="img" />
</Grid>
```

BitmapImage requires a *using* directive for the *System.Windows.Media.Imaging* namespace. When *MainPage* gets a tap, it creates a *BitmapImage* from the *Uri* object and sets that to the *Source* property of the *Image*:

Silverlight Project: SilverlightTapToDownload1   File: MainPage.xaml.cs (excerpt)

```
protected override void OnManipulationStarted(ManipulationStartedEventArgs args)
{
    Uri uri = new Uri("http://www.charlespetzold.com/Media/HelloWP7.jpg");
    BitmapImage bmp = new BitmapImage(uri);
    img.Source = bmp;

    args.Complete();
    args.Handled = true;
    base.OnManipulationStarted(args);
}
```

Remember to tap the screen to initiate the download!

The *BitmapImage* class defines *ImageOpened* and *ImageFailed* events (which the *Image* element also duplicates) and also includes a *DownloadProgess* event.

If you want to explicitly use *WebClient* in a Silverlight program, you can do that as well, as the next project demonstrates. The SilverlightTapToDownload2.xaml file is the same as SilverlightTapToDownload1.xaml. The code-behind file uses *WebClient* much like the earlier XNA program:

```
Silverlight Project: SilverlightTapToDownload2   File: MainPage.xaml.cs (excerpt)

protected override void OnManipulationStarted(ManipulationStartedEventArgs args)
{
    WebClient webClient = new WebClient();
    webClient.OpenReadCompleted += OnWebClientOpenReadCompleted;
    webClient.OpenReadAsync(new Uri("http://www.charlespetzold.com/Media/HelloWP7.
jpg"));

    args.Complete();
    args.Handled = true;
    base.OnManipulationStarted(args);
}

void OnWebClientOpenReadCompleted(object sender, OpenReadCompletedEventArgs args)
{
    if (!args.Cancelled && args.Error == null)
    {
        BitmapImage bmp = new BitmapImage();
        bmp.SetSource(args.Result);
        img.Source = bmp;
    }
}
```

Notice the use of *SetSource* to create the bitmap from the *Stream* object.

Loading Local Bitmaps from Code

In a Silverlight program, you've seen that a bitmap added to the project as a resource is bound into the executable. It's so customary to reference that local bitmap directly from XAML that very few experienced Silverlight programmers could tell you offhand how to do it in code. The SilverlightTapToLoad project shows you how.

Like the other Silverlight programs in this chapter, the SilverlightTapToLoad project contains an *Image* element in its content grid. The Hello.png bitmap is stored in the Images directory and has a Build Action of Resource.

The MainPage.xaml.cs file requires a *using* directive for the *System.Windows.Media.Imaging* namespace for the *BitmapImage* class. Another *using* directive for *System.Windows.Resources* is required for the *StreamResourceInfo* class.

When the screen is tapped, the event handler accesses the resource using the static *GetResourceStream* method defined by the *Application* class:

Silverlight Project: SilverlightTapToLoad   File: MainPage.xaml.cs

```
protected override void OnManipulationStarted(ManipulationStartedEventArgs args)
{
    Uri uri = new Uri("/SilverlightTapToLoad;component/Images/Hello.png", UriKind
.Relative);
    StreamResourceInfo resourceInfo = Application.GetResourceStream(uri);
    BitmapImage bmp = new BitmapImage();
    bmp.SetSource(resourceInfo.Stream);
    img.Source = bmp;

    args.Complete();
    args.Handled = true;
    base.OnManipulationStarted(args);
}
```

Notice how complicated that URL is! It begins with the name of the program followed by a semicolon, followed by the word "component" and then the folder and filename of the file. If you change the Build Action of the Hello.png file to Content rather than Resource, you can simplify the syntax considerably:

```
Uri uri = new Uri("Images/Hello.png", UriKind.Relative);
```

What's the difference?

Navigate to the *Bin/Debug* subdirectory of the Visual Studio project and find the SilverlightTapToLoad.xap file that contains your program. If you rename it the file to a ZIP extension you can look inside. The bulk of the file will be SilverlightTapToLoad.dll, the compiled binary.

In both cases, the bitmap is obviously stored somewhere within the XAP file. The difference is this:

- With a Build Action of Resource for the bitmap, it is stored inside the SilverlightTapToLoad.dll file along with the compiled program

- With a Build Action of Content, the bitmap is stored external to the SilverlightTapToLoad.dll file but within the XAP file, and when you rename the XAP file to a ZIP file, you can see the *Images* directory and the file.

Which is better?

In a document entitled "Creating High Performance Silverlight Applications for Windows Phone," Microsoft has recommending using a Build Action of Content rather than Resource for assets included in your application to minimize the size of the binary and startup time. However, if these assets are in a Silverlight library that the program references, then it is better for them to be embedded in the binary with a Build Action of Resource.

If you have a number of images in your program, and you don't want to include them all in the XAP file, but you're nervous about downloading the images, why not do a little of both? Include low resolution (or highly compressed) images in the XAP file, but download better versions asynchronously while the application is running.

Capturing from the Camera

Besides embedding bitmaps in your application or accessing them from the web, Windows Phone 7 also allows you to acquire images from the built-in camera.

Your application has no control over the camera itself. For reasons of security, your program cannot arbitrarily snap a picture, or "see" what's coming through the camera lens. Your application basically invokes a standard camera utility, the user points and shoots, and the picture is returned back to your program.

The classes you use for this job are in the *Microsoft.Phone.Tasks* namespace, which contains several classes referred to as *choosers* and *launchers*. Conceptually, these are rather similar, except that choosers return data to your program but launchers do not.

The *CameraCaptureTask* is derived from the generic *ChooserBase* class which defines a *Completed* event and a *Show* method. Your program attaches a handler for the *Completed* event and calls *Show*. When the *Completed* event handler is called, the *PhotoResult* event argument contains a *Stream* object to the photo. From there, you already know what to do.

Like the earlier programs in this chapter, the SilverlightTapToShoot program contains an *Image* element in the content grid of its MainPage.xaml file. Here's the entire code-behind file:

Silverlight Project: SilverlightTapToShoot   File: MainPage.xaml.cs

```
using System.Windows.Input;
using System.Windows.Media.Imaging;
using Microsoft.Phone.Controls;
using Microsoft.Phone.Tasks;

namespace SilverlightTapToShoot
{
```

```
public partial class MainPage : PhoneApplicationPage
{
    CameraCaptureTask camera = new CameraCaptureTask();;

    public MainPage()
    {
        InitializeComponent();

        camera.Completed += OnCameraCaptureTaskCompleted;
    }

    protected override void OnManipulationStarted(ManipulationStartedEventArgs
args)
    {
        camera.Show();

        args.Complete();
        args.Handled = true;
        base.OnManipulationStarted(args);
    }

    void OnCameraCaptureTaskCompleted(object sender, PhotoResult args)
    {
        if (args.TaskResult == TaskResult.OK)
        {
            BitmapImage bmp = new BitmapImage();
            bmp.SetSource(args.ChosenPhoto);
            img.Source = bmp;
        }
    }
}
}
```

You can run this program on the phone emulator. When you tap the emulator screen, the call to *Show* causes the camera task to start up and you'll navigate to a page that resembles the actual camera. You can "shoot" a photo by tapping an icon in the upper-right corner of the screen. The simulated "photo" just looks like a large white square with a small black square inside one of the edges. Then you need to click the Accept button.

You can also run this program on the phone itself, of course, but not when the phone is tethered to the PC and the Zune software is running. After deploying the application to the phone using Visual Studio, you'll need to close the Zune software before testing the program.

If you need to use Visual Studio to debug an application that uses the camera while the application is running on the phone, you can use a little command-line program called WPDTPTConnect32.exe or WPDTPTConnect64.exe (depending on whether your development machine is 32-bit or 64-bit). These program is an alternative to the Zune software for allowing the Visual Studio debugger to control your program as it's running on the phone. The Zune software must be closed before you use these programs.

In either case, when you press the Accept button, the camera goes away and the program's *OnCameraCaptureTaskCompleted* method takes over. It creates a *BitmapImage* object, sets the input stream from *args.ChoosenPhoto*, and then sets the *BitmapImage* object to the *Image* element, displaying the photo on the screen.

The whole process seems fairly straightforward. Conceptually it seems as if the program is spawning the camera process, and then resuming control when that camera process terminates.

However, the Windows Phone 7 documentation that I'm consulting warns that this is not the case. There's something else going on that is not so evident at first and which you will probably find somewhat unnerving.

When the SilverlightTapToShoot program calls the *Show* method on the *CameraCaptureTask* object, the SilverlightTapToShoot program is terminated. (Not immediately, though. The *OnManipulationStarted* method is allowed to return back to the program, and a couple other events are fired, but then the program is definitely terminated.)

The camera utility then runs. When the camera utility has done its job, the SilverlightTapToShoot program is re-executed. It's a new instance of the program. The program starts up from the beginning, the *MainPage* constructor is eventually called which sets the *Completed* event of the *CameraCaptureTask* to *OnCameraCaptureTaskCompleted*, and then that method is called.

For these reasons, the documentation advises that when you use a chooser or launcher such as *CameraCaptureTask*, the object must be defined as a field, and the handler for the *Completed* event must be attached in the program's constructor, and as late in the constructor as possible because once the handler is attached when the program starts up again, it will be called.

This termination and re-execution of your program is a characteristic of Windows Phone 7 programming call *tombstoning*. When the program is terminated as the camera task begins, sufficient information is retained by the phone operating system to start the program up again when the camera finishes. However, not enough information is retained to restore the program entirely to its pre-tombstone state. That's your responsibility.

Running a launcher or chooser is one way tombstoning can occur. But it also occurs when the user leaves your program by pressing the Start button on the phone. Eventually the user could return to your program by pressing the Back button, and your program needs to be re-executed from its tombstoned state. Tombstoning also takes place when a lack of activity on the phone causes it to go into a lock state.

Tombstoning does *not* occur when your program is running and the user presses the Back button. The Back button simply terminates the program normally.

When tombstoning occurs, obviously you'll want to save some of the state of your program so you can restore that state when the program starts up again, and obviously Windows Phone 7 has facilities to help you out. That's in Chapter 6.

With all that said, in later versions of the Windows Phone 7 operating system, including the one I'm using as I'm finishing the chapters for this book, I am not seeing tombstoning occur when using *CameraCaptureTask*. But it doesn't hurt to prepare for it.

The Phone's Photo Library

As you take pictures with the phone and synchronize your phone with the PC, the phone accumulates a photo library. A program running on the phone can access this library in one of two ways:

- From the perspective of your program, the *PhotoChooserTask* is much like the *CameraCaptureTask* except it takes the user to the photo library and allows the user to choose one photo, which is then returned to the program.

- The XNA namespace *Microsoft.Xna.Framework.Media* has a *MediaLibrary* and related classes that let a program obtain collections of all the photos stored in the photo library, and present these to the user.

I'm going to show you these two approaches with two programs. Just for variety (and to demonstrate how to use XNA classes in a Silverlight program), I'll use XNA for the first approach and Silverlight for the second.

You can run these two programs on the phone emulator. The emulator includes a small collection of photos specifically for testing programs such as these. When testing the programs on the actual phone, however, the phone must be untethered from the PC or the Zune software must be closed, because the Zune software won't allow simultaneous access to the phone's photo library. After you close Zune, you can run WPDTPTConnect32.exe or WPDTPTConnect64. exe program to allow Visual Studio to debug the program running on the phone.

The XnaTapToBrowse program requires a *using* directive for *Microsoft.Phone.Tasks*. It creates a *PhotoChooserTask* object along with the other fields:

Silverlight Project: XnaTapToBrowse   File: Game1.cs (excerpt showing fields)

```
public class Game1 : Microsoft.Xna.Framework.Game
{
    GraphicsDeviceManager graphics;
    SpriteBatch spriteBatch;
    Texture2D texture;
    PhotoChooserTask photoChooser = new PhotoChooserTask();
    ...
}
```

In compliance with the recommendations of the documentation, the class attaches a handler for the *Completed* event in the constructor:

Silverlight Project: XnaTapToBrowse   **File: Game1.cs (excerpt)**

```
public Game1()
{
    graphics = new GraphicsDeviceManager(this);
    Content.RootDirectory = "Content";

    // Frame rate is 30 fps by default for Windows Phone.
    TargetElapsedTime = TimeSpan.FromTicks(333333);

    TouchPanel.EnabledGestures = GestureType.Tap;
    photoChooser.Completed += OnPhotoChooserCompleted;
}
```

As usual, the *Update* method checks for user input. If a tap has occurred, the method calls the *Show* event of the *PhotoChooserTask* object:

Silverlight Project: XnaTapToBrowse   **File: Game1.cs (excerpt)**

```
protected override void Update(GameTime gameTime)
{
    // Allows the game to exit
    if (GamePad.GetState(PlayerIndex.One).Buttons.Back == ButtonState.Pressed)
        this.Exit();

    while (TouchPanel.IsGestureAvailable)
        if (TouchPanel.ReadGesture().GestureType == GestureType.Tap)
            photoChooser.Show();

    base.Update(gameTime);
}

void OnPhotoChooserCompleted(object sender, PhotoResult args)
{
    if (args.TaskResult == TaskResult.OK)
        texture = Texture2D.FromStream(this.GraphicsDevice, args.ChosenPhoto);
}
```

The handler for the *Completed* event then creates a *Texture2D* from the stream available from the *ChosenPhoto* property. The *Draw* override doesn't attempt to render this object until it's available:

Silverlight Project: XnaTapToBrowse   File: Game1.cs (excerpt)

```
protected override void Draw(GameTime gameTime)
{
    GraphicsDevice.Clear(Color.Navy);

    if (texture != null)
    {
        spriteBatch.Begin();
        spriteBatch.Draw(texture, this.GraphicsDevice.Viewport.Bounds, Color.White);
        spriteBatch.End();
    }

    base.Draw(gameTime);
}
```

I'm using a slight variation of the *Draw* method of *SpriteBatch* here. Rather than provide a position for the *Texture2D* in the second argument, I'm providing a whole rectangle equal to the size of the viewport. This causes the photo to expand (or, more likely, shrink) in size, very possibly distorting the image by not taking account of the original aspect ratio. More sophisticated code can handle those problems, of course.

The SilverlightAccessLibrary program requires a reference to the Microsoft.Xna.Framework DLL, and you'll probably get a warning about including an XNA library in your Silverlight program. It's OK! The content area in the MainPage.xaml file contains both a bitmap-less *Image* and a text-less *TextBlock* in the *Grid*:

Silverlight Project: SilverlightAccessLibrary   File: MainPage.xaml (excerpt)

```
<Grid x:Name="ContentPanel" Grid.Row="1" Margin="12,0,12,0">
    <Image Name="img" />

    <TextBlock Name="txtblk"
               TextWrapping="Wrap"
               TextAlignment="Center"
               VerticalAlignment="Bottom" />
</Grid>
```

Rather than present the entire photo library to the user (a task that would be a little difficult with only the rudimentary Silverlight layout elements I've described so far), the program picks one at random, and picks another when the user taps the screen:

Silverlight Project: SilverlightAccessLibrary   File: MainPage.xaml.cs (excerpt)

```
public partial class MainPage : PhoneApplicationPage
{
    MediaLibrary mediaLib = new MediaLibrary();
    Random rand = new Random();

    public MainPage()
    {
        InitializeComponent();
        GetRandomPicture();
    }

    protected override void OnManipulationStarted(ManipulationStartedEventArgs args)
    {
        GetRandomPicture();

        args.Complete();
        base.OnManipulationStarted(args);
    }

    void GetRandomPicture()
    {
        PictureCollection pictures = mediaLib.Pictures;

        if (pictures.Count > 0)
        {
            int index = rand.Next(pictures.Count);
            Picture pic = pictures[index];

            BitmapImage bmp = new BitmapImage();
            bmp.SetSource(pic.GetImage());
            img.Source = bmp;

            txtblk.Text = String.Format("{0}\n{1}\n{2}",
                                    pic.Name, pic.Album.Name, pic.Date);
        }
    }
}
```

The XNA *MediaLibrary* class is instantiated as a field. In the *GetRandomPicture* method, the program obtains a *PictureCollection* object from the *MediaLibrary* class and picks one at random. The *Picture* object has a *GetImage* method that returns a stream, and a *Name*, *Album*, and *Data* information that the program displays in the overlaying *TextBlock*.

A Windows Phone 7 program can also save a bitmap back into the library. All such bitmaps go into a special album called Saved Pictures. I'll show you how to do that in Chapters 14 and 22.

Chapter 5
Sensors and Services

This chapter covers two of the facilities in Windows Phone 7 that provide information about the outside world. With the user's permission, the location service lets your application obtain the phone's location on the earth in the traditional geographic coordinates of longitude and latitude, whereas the accelerometer tells your program which way is down.

The accelerometer and location service are related in that neither of them will work very well in outer space.

Although the accelerometer and the location service are ostensibly rather easy, this chapter also explores issues involved with working with secondary threads of execution, handling asynchronous operations, and accessing web services.

Accelerometer

Windows Phones contain an accelerometer—a small hardware device that essentially measures force, which elementary physics tells us is proportional to acceleration. When the phone is held still, the accelerometer responds to the force of gravity, so the accelerometer can tell your application the direction of the Earth relative to the phone.

A simulation of a bubble level is an archetypal application that makes use of an accelerometer, but the accelerometer can also provide a basis for interactive animations. For example, you might pilot a messenger bike through the streets of Manhattan by tilting the phone left or right to indicate steering.

The accelerometer also responds to sudden movements such as shakes or jerks, useful for simulations of dice or some other type of randomizing activity. Coming up with creative uses of the accelerometer is one of the many challenges of phone development.

It is convenient to represent the accelerometer output as a vector in three-dimensional space. Vectors are commonly written in boldface, so the acceleration vector can be symbolized as (x, y, z). XNA defines a three-dimensional vector type; Silverlight does not.

While a three-dimensional point (x, y, z) indicates a particular location in space, the vector (x, y, z) encapsulates instead a direction and a magnitude. Obviously the point and the vector are related: The direction of the vector (x, y, z) is the direction from the point $(0, 0, 0)$ to the point (x, y, z). But the vector (x, y, z) is definitely not the line from $(0, 0, 0)$ to (x, y, z). It's only the direction of that line.

The magnitude of the vector **(x, y, z)** is calculable from the three-dimensional form of the Pythagorean Theorem:

$Magnitude = \sqrt{x^2 + y^2 + z^2}$

For working with the accelerometer, you can imagine the phone as defining a three-dimensional coordinate system. No matter how the phone is oriented, the positive Y axis points from the bottom of the phone (with the buttons) to the top, the positive X axis points from left to right,

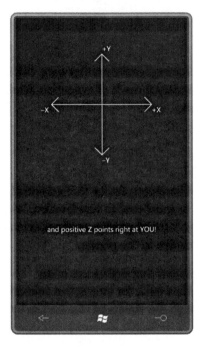

This is a traditional three-dimensional coordinate system, the same coordinate system used in XNA 3D programming. It's termed a *right-hand* coordinate system: Point the index finger of your right hand to increasing X, the middle finger to increase Y, and your thumb points to increasing Z. Or, curve the fingers of your right hand from the positive X axis to the positive Y axis. Your thumb again points to increasing Z.

This coordinate system remains fixed relative to the phone regardless how you hold the phone, and regardless of the orientation of any programs running on the phone. In fact, as you might expect, the accelerometer is the basis for performing orientation changes of Windows Phone 7 applications.

When the phone is still, the accelerometer vector points towards the Earth. The magnitude is 1, meaning 1 *g*, which is the force of gravity on the earth's surface. When holding your phone in the upright position, the acceleration vector is **(0, –1, 0)**, that is, straight down.

Turn the phone 90° counter-clockwise (called landscape left) and the acceleration vector becomes **(–1, 0, 0)**, upside down it's **(0, 1, 0)**, and another 90° counter-clockwise turn brings you to the landscape right orientation and an accelerometer value of **(1, 0, 0)**. Sit the phone down on the desk with the display facing up, and the acceleration vector is **(0, 0, –1)**. (That final value is what the Windows Phone 7 emulator always reports.)

Of course, the acceleration vector will *rarely* be those exact values, and even the magnitude won't be exact. For a still phone, the magnitude may vary by a few percentage points with different orientations. When you visit the Moon with your Windows Phone 7, you can expect acceleration vector magnitudes in the region of 0.17 but limited cell phone reception.

I've been describing values of the acceleration vector when the device is still. The acceleration vector can point in other directions (and the magnitude can become larger or smaller) when the phone is accelerating, that is, gaining or losing velocity. For example, if you jerk the phone to the left, the acceleration vector points to the right but only when the device is gaining velocity. As the velocity stabilizes, the acceleration vector again registers only gravity. When you decelerate this jerk to the left, the acceleration vector goes to the left briefly as the device comes to a stop.

If the phone is in free fall, the magnitude of the accelerometer vector should theoretically go down to zero.

To use the accelerometer, you'll need a reference to the Microsoft.Devices.Sensors library, and a *using* directive for the *Microsoft.Devices.Sensors* namespace. In WMAppManifest.xml, you need

```
<Capability Name="ID_CAP_SENSORS" />
```

This is set by default.

In your program you create an instance of the *Accelerometer* class, set an event handler for the *ReadingChanging* event, and call *Start*.

And then it gets a little tricky. Let's take a look at a project named SilverlightAccelerometer. that simply displays the current reading in its content grid. A centered *TextBlock* is defined in the XAML file:

Silverlight Project: **SilverlightAccelerometer**   File: **MainPage.xaml** (excerpt)

```
<Grid x:Name="ContentPanel" Grid.Row="1" Margin="12,0,12,0">
    <TextBlock Name="txtblk"
               HorizontalAlignment="Center"
               VerticalAlignment="Center" />
</Grid>
```

This is a program that will display the accelerometer vector throughout its lifetime, so it creates the *Accelerometer* class in its constructor and calls *Start*:

Silverlight Project: SilverlightAccelerometer   File: MainPage.xaml.cs (excerpt)

```
public MainPage()
{
    InitializeComponent();

    Accelerometer acc = new Accelerometer();
    acc.ReadingChanged += OnAccelerometerReadingChanged;

    try
    {
        acc.Start();
    }
    catch (Exception exc)
    {
        txtblk.Text = exc.Message;
    }
}
```

The documentation warns that calling *Start* might raise an exception, so the program protects itself against that eventuality. The *Accelerometer* also supports *Stop* and *Dispose* methods, but this program doesn't make use of them. A *State* property is also available if you need to know if the accelerometer is available and what it's currently doing.

A *ReadingChanged* event is accompanied by the *AccelerometerReadingEventArgs* event arguments. The object has properties named *X*, *Y*, and *Z* of type *double* and *TimeStamp* of type *DateTimeOffset*. In the SilverlightAccelerometer program, the job of the event handler is to format this information into a string and set it to the *Text* property of the *TextBlock*.

The catch here is that the event handler (in this case *OnAccelerometerReadingChanged*) is called on a different thread of execution, and this means it must be handled in a special way.

A little background: All the user-interface elements and objects in a Silverlight application are created and accessed in a main thread of execution often called the *user interface thread* or the *UI thread*. These user-interface objects are not thread safe; they are not built to be accessed simultaneously from multiple threads. For this reason, Silverlight will not allow you to access a user-interface object from a non-UI thread.

This means that the *OnAccelerometerReadingChanged* method cannot directly access the *TextBlock* element to set a new value to its *Text* property.

Fortunately, there's a solution involving a class named *Dispatcher* defined in the *System. Windows.Threading* namespace. Through the *Dispatcher* class, you can post jobs from a non-UI thread on a queue where they are later executed by the UI thread. This process sounds complex, but from the programmer's perspective it's fairly easy because these jobs take the form of simple method calls.

An instance of this *Dispatcher* is readily available. The *DependencyObject* class defines a property named *Dispatcher* of type *Dispatcher*, and many Silverlight classes derive from *DependencyObject*. Instances of all of these classes can be accessed from non-UI threads because they all have *Dispatcher* properties. You can use any *Dispatcher* object from any *DependencyObject* derivative created in your UI thread. They are all the same.

The *Dispatcher* class defines a method named *CheckAccess* that returns *true* if you can access a particular user interface object from the current thread. (The *CheckAccess* method is also duplicated by *DependencyObject* itself.) If an object can't be accessed from the current thread, then *Dispatcher* provides two versions of a method named *Invoke* that you use to post the job to the UI thread.

The SilverlightAccelerometer project implements a syntactically elaborate version of the code, but then I'll show you how to chop it down in size.

The verbose version requires a delegate and a method defined in accordance with that delegate. The delegate (and method) should have no return value, but as many arguments as you need to do the job, in this case the job of setting a string to the *Text* property of a *TextBlock*:

Project: **SilverlightAccelerometer**   File: **MainPage.xaml.cs** (excerpt)

```
delegate void SetTextBlockTextDelegate(TextBlock txtblk, string text);

void SetTextBlockText(TextBlock txtblk, string text)
{
    txtblk.Text = text;
}
```

The *OnAccelerometerReadingChanged* is responsible for calling *SetTextBlockText*. It first makes use of *CheckAccess* to see if it can just call the *SetTextBlockText* method directly. If not, then the handler calls the *BeginInvoke* method. The first argument is an instantiation of the delegate with the *SetTextBlockText* method; this is followed by all the arguments that *SetTextBlockText* requires:

Project: **SilverlightAccelerometer**   File: **MainPage.xaml.cs** (excerpt)

```
void OnAccelerometerReadingChanged(object sender, AccelerometerReadingEventArgs args)
{
    string str = String.Format("X = {0:F2}\n" +
                               "Y = {1:F2}\n" +
```

```
                        "Z = {2:F2}\n\n" +
                        "Magnitude = {3:F2}\n\n" +
                        "{4}",
                        args.X, args.Y, args.Z,
                        Math.Sqrt(args.X * args.X + args.Y * args.Y +
                                              args.Z * args.Z),
                        args.Timestamp);

    if (txtblk.CheckAccess())
    {
        SetTextBlockText(txtblk, str);
    }
    else
    {
        txtblk.Dispatcher.BeginInvoke(new SetTextBlockTextDelegate(SetTextBlockText),
                        txtblk, str);

    }
}
```

This is not too bad, but the need for the code to jump across threads has necessitated an additional method and a delegate. Is there a way to do the whole job right in the event handler?

Yes! The *BeginInvoke* method has an overload that accepts an *Action* delegate, which defines a method that has no return value and no arguments. You can create an anonymous method right in the *BeginInvoke* call. The complete code following the creation of the string object looks like this:

```
if (txtblk.CheckAccess())
{
    txtblk.Text = str;
}
else
{
    txtblk.Dispatcher.BeginInvoke(delegate()
    {
        txtblk.Text = str;
    });
}
```

The anonymous method begins with the keyword *delegate* and concludes with the curly brace following the method body. The empty parentheses following the *delegate* keyword are not required.

The anonymous method can also be defined using a lambda expression:

```
if (txtblk.CheckAccess())
{
    txtblk.Text = str;
}
```

```
else
{
    txtblk.Dispatcher.BeginInvoke(() =>
    {
        txtblk.Text = str;
    });
}
```

The duplicated code that sets the *Text* property of *TextBlock* to *str* looks a little ugly here (and would be undesirable if it involved more than just one statement), but you don't really need to call *CheckAccess*. You can just call *BeginInvoke* and nothing bad will happen even if you are calling it from the UI thead.

The Windows Phone 7 emulator doesn't contain any actual accelerometer, so it always reports a value of (0, 0, –1), which indicates the phone is lying on a flat surface. The program only makes sense when running on an actual phone:

The values here indicate the phone is roughly upright but tilted back a bit, which is a very natural orientation in actual use.

A Simple Bubble Level

One handy tool found in any workshop is a bubble level, also called a spirit level. A little bubble always floats to the top of a liquid, so it visually indicates whether something is parallel or orthogonal to the earth, or tilted in some way.

The XnaAccelerometer project includes a 48-by-48 pixel bitmap named Bubble.bmp that consists of a red circle:

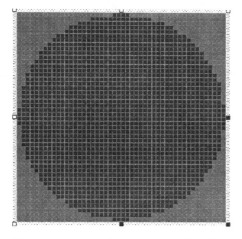

The magenta on the corners makes those areas of the bitmap transparent when XNA renders it.

As with the Silverlight program, you'll need a reference to the Microsoft.Devices.Sensors library and a using directive for the *Microsoft.Devices.Sensors* namespace.

The fields in the *Game1* class mostly involve variables necessary to position that bitmap on the screen:

XNA Project: XnaAccelerometer   File: Game1.cs (excerpt showing fields)

```
public class Game1 : Microsoft.Xna.Framework.Game
{
    const float BUBBLE_RADIUS_MAX = 25;
    const float BUBBLE_RADIUS_MIN = 12;

    GraphicsDeviceManager graphics;
    SpriteBatch spriteBatch;

    Vector2 screenCenter;
    float screenRadius;        // less BUBBLE_RADIUS_MAX

    Texture2D bubbleTexture;
    Vector2 bubbleCenter;
    Vector2 bubblePosition;
    float bubbleScale;

    Vector3 accelerometerVector;
    object accelerometerVectorLock = new object();
    …

}
```

Towards the bottom you'll see a field named *accelerometerVector* of type *Vector3*. The
OnAccelerometerReadingChanged event handler will store a new value in that field, and
the *Update* method will utilize the value in calculating a position for a bitmap.

OnAccelerometerReadingChanged and *Update* run in separate threads. One is setting the
field; the other is accessing the field. This is no problem if the field is set or accessed in
a single machine code instruction. That would be the case if *Vector3* were a class, which is
a reference type and basically referenced with something akin to a pointer. But *Vector3* is
a structure (a value type) consisting of three properties of type *float*, each of which occupies
four bytes, for a total of 12 bytes or 96 bits. Setting or accessing this *Vector3* field requires
this many bits to be transferred.

A Windows Phone 7 device contains at least a 32-bit ARM processor, and a brief glance at
the ARM instruction set does not reveal any machine code that would perform a 12-byte
memory transfer in one instruction. This means that the accelerometer thread storing a new
Vector3 value could be interrupted midway in the process by the *Update* method in the
program's main thread when it retrieves that value. The resultant value might have *X*, *Y*, and
Z values mixed up from two readings.

While that could hardly be classified as a catastrophe in this program, let's play it entirely safe
and use the C# *lock* statement to make sure the *Vector3* value is stored and retrieved by the
two threads without interruption. That's the purpose of the *accelerometerVectorLock* variable
among the fields.

I chose to create the *Accelerometer* object and set the event handler in the *Initialize* method:

XNA Project: XnaAccelerometer   File: Game1.cs (excerpt)

```
protected override void Initialize()
{
    Accelerometer accelerometer = new Accelerometer();
    accelerometer.ReadingChanged += OnAccelerometerReadingChanged;

    try
    {
        accelerometer.Start();
    }
    catch
    {
    }

    base.Initialize();
}

void OnAccelerometerReadingChanged(object sender, AccelerometerReadingEventArgs args)
{
```

```
    lock (accelerometerVectorLock)
    {
        accelerometerVector = new Vector3((float)args.X, (float)args.Y, (float)
args.Z);
    }
}
```

Notice that the event handler uses the *lock* statement to set the *accelerometerVector* field. That prevents code in the *Update* method from accessing the field during this short duration.

The *LoadContent* method loads the bitmap used for the bubble and initializes several variables used for positioning the bitmap:

XNA Project: **XnaAccelerometer**   File: **Game1.cs (excerpt)**

```
protected override void LoadContent()
{
    spriteBatch = new SpriteBatch(GraphicsDevice);

    Viewport viewport = this.GraphicsDevice.Viewport;
    screenCenter = new Vector2(viewport.Width / 2, viewport.Height / 2);
    screenRadius = Math.Min(screenCenter.X, screenCenter.Y) - BUBBLE_RADIUS_MAX;

    bubbleTexture = this.Content.Load<Texture2D>("Bubble");
    bubbleCenter = new Vector2(bubbleTexture.Width / 2, bubbleTexture.Height / 2);
}
```

When the *X* and *Y* properties of accelerometer are zero, the bubble is displayed in the center of the screen. That's the reason for both *screenCenter* and *bubbleCenter*. The *screenRadius* value is the distance from the center when the magnitude of the *X* and *Y* components is 1.

The *Update* method safely access the *accelerometerVector* field and calculates *bubblePosition* based on the *X* and *Y* components. It might seem like I've mixed up the *X* and *Y* components in the calculation, but that's because the default screen orientation is portrait in XNA, so it's opposite the coordinates of the acceleration vector. Because both landscape modes are supported by default, it's also necessary to multiply the acceleration vector values by –1 when the phone has been tilted into the *LandscapeRight* mode:

XNA Project: **XnaAccelerometer**   File: **Game1.cs (excerpt)**

```
protected override void Update(GameTime gameTime)
{
    // Allows the game to exit
    if (GamePad.GetState(PlayerIndex.One).Buttons.Back == ButtonState.Pressed)
        this.Exit();
```

```
    Vector3 accVector;

    lock (accelerometerVectorLock)
    {
        accVector = accelerometerVector;
    }

    int sign = this.Window.CurrentOrientation ==
                              DisplayOrientation.LandscapeLeft ? 1 : -1;

    bubblePosition = new Vector2(screenCenter.X + sign * screenRadius * accVector.Y,
                        screenCenter.Y + sign * screenRadius * accVector.X);
    float bubbleRadius = BUBBLE_RADIUS_MIN + (1 - accVector.Z) / 2 *
                        (BUBBLE_RADIUS_MAX - BUBBLE_RADIUS_MIN);
    bubbleScale = bubbleRadius / (bubbleTexture.Width / 2);

    base.Update(gameTime);
}
```

In addition, a *bubbleScale* factor is calculated based on the *Z* component of the vector. The idea is that the bubble is largest when the screen is facing up and smallest when the screen is facing down, as if the screen is really one side of a rectangular pool of liquid that extends below the phone, and the size of the bubble indicates how far it is from the surface.

The *Draw* override uses a long version of the *Draw* method of *SpriteBatch*.

XNA Project: XnaAccelerometer   File: **Game1.cs (excerpt)**

```
protected override void Draw(GameTime gameTime)
{
    GraphicsDevice.Clear(Color.Navy);

    spriteBatch.Begin();
    spriteBatch.Draw(bubbleTexture, bubblePosition, null, Color.White, 0,
                    bubbleCenter, bubbleScale, SpriteEffects.None, 0);
    spriteBatch.End();
    base.Draw(gameTime);
}
```

Notice the *bubbleScale* argument, which scales the bitmap to a particular size. The center of scaling is provided by the previous argument to the method, *bubbleCenter*. That point is also aligned with the *bubblePosition* value relative to the screen.

The program doesn't look like much, and is even more boring running on the emulator. Here's an indication that the phone is roughly upright and tilted back a bit:

You'll discover that the accelerometer is very jittery and cries out for some data smoothing. I'll discuss this and other accelerometer-related issues in Chapter 12.

Geographic Location

With the user's permission, a Windows Phone 7 program can obtain the geographic location of the phone using a technique called Assisted-GPS or A-GPS.

The most accurate method of determining location is accessing signals from Global Positioning System (GPS) satellites. However, GPS can be slow. It doesn't work well in cities or indoors, and it's considered expensive in terms of battery use. To work more cheaply and quickly, an A-GPS system can attempt to determine location from cell-phone towers or the network. These methods are faster and more reliable, but less accurate.

The core class involved in location detection is *GeoCoordinateWatcher*. You'll need a reference to the System.Device assembly and a *using* direction for the *System.Device. Location* namespace. The WMAppManifest.xml file requires the tag:

```
<Capability Name="ID_CAP_LOCATION" />
```

This is included by default.

The *GeoCoordinateWatcher* constructor optionally takes a member of the *GeoPositionAccuracy* enumeration:

- *Default*
- *High*

After creating a *GeoCoordinateWatcher* object, you'll want to install a handler for the *PositionChanged* event and call *Start*. The *PositionChanged* event delivers a *GeoCoordinate* object that has eight properties:

- *Latitude*, a *double* between –90 and 90 degrees
- *Longitude*, a *double* between –180 and 180 degrees
- *Altitude* of type *double*
- *HorizontalAccuracy* and *VerticalAccuracy* of type *double*
- *Course*, a *double* between 0 and 360 degrees
- *Speed* of type *double*
- *IsUnknown*, a Boolean that is *true* if the *Latitude* or *Longitude* is not a number

If the application does not have permission to get the location, then *Latitude* and *Longitude* will be *Double.NaN*, and *IsUnknown* will be *true*.

In addition, *GeoCoordinate* has a *GetDistanceTo* method that calculates the distance between two *GeoCoordinate* objects.

I'm going to focus on the first two properties, which together are referred to as *geographic coordinates* to indicate a point on the surface of the Earth. Latitude is the angular distance from the equator. In common usage, latitude is an angle between 0 and 90 degrees and followed with either N or S meaning north or south. For example, the latitude of New York City is approximately 40°N. In the *GeoCoordinate* object, latitudes north of the equator are positive values and south of the equator are negative values, so that 90° is the North Pole and –90° is the South Pole.

All locations with the same latitude define a *line of latitude*. Along a particular line of latitude, longitude is the angular distance from the Prime Meridian, which passes through the Royal Observatory at Greenwich England. In common use, longitudes are either east or west. New York City is 74°W because it's west of the Prime Meridian. In a *GeoCoordinate* object, positive longitude values denote east and negative values are west. Longitude values of 180 and –180 meet up at the International Date Line.

Although the *System.Device.Location* namespace includes classes that use the geographic coordinates to determine civic address (streets and cities), these are not implemented in the initial release of Windows Phone 7.

The XnaLocation project simply displays numeric values.

XNA Project: XnaLocation   File: Game1.cs (excerpt showing fields)

```
public class Game1 : Microsoft.Xna.Framework.Game
{
    GraphicsDeviceManager graphics;
    SpriteBatch spriteBatch;
    SpriteFont segoe14;
    string text = "Obtaining location...";
    Viewport viewport;
    Vector2 textPosition;
    …
}
```

As with the accelerometer, I chose to create and initialize the *GeoCoordinateWatcher* in the *Initialize* override. The event handler is called in the same thread, so nothing special needs to be done to format the results in a string:

XNA Project: XnaLocation   File: Game1.cs (excerpt)

```
protected override void Initialize()
{
    GeoCoordinateWatcher geoWatcher = new GeoCoordinateWatcher();
    geoWatcher.PositionChanged += OnGeoWatcherPositionChanged;
    geoWatcher.Start();

    base.Initialize();
}

void OnGeoWatcherPositionChanged(object sender,
                         GeoPositionChangedEventArgs<GeoCoordinate> args)
{
    text = String.Format("Latitude: {0:F3}\r\n" +
                         "Longitude: {1:F3}\r\n" +
                         "Altitude: {2}\r\n\r\n" +
                         "{3}",
                         args.Position.Location.Latitude,
                         args.Position.Location.Longitude,
                         args.Position.Location.Altitude,
                         args.Position.Timestamp);
}
```

The *LoadContent* method simply obtains the font and saves the *Viewport* for later text positioning:

XNA Project: XnaLocation   File: Game1.cs (excerpt)

```
protected override void LoadContent()
{
    spriteBatch = new SpriteBatch(GraphicsDevice);
    segoe14 = this.Content.Load<SpriteFont>("Segoe14");
    viewport = this.GraphicsDevice.Viewport;
}
```

The size of the displayed string could be different depending on different values. That's why the position of the string is calculated from its size and the *Viewport* values in the *Update* method:

XNA Project: XnaLocation   File: Game1.cs (excerpt)

```
protected override void Update(GameTime gameTime)
{
    // Allows the game to exit
    if (GamePad.GetState(PlayerIndex.One).Buttons.Back == ButtonState.Pressed)
        this.Exit();

    Vector2 textSize = segoe14.MeasureString(text);
    textPosition = new Vector2((viewport.Width - textSize.X) / 2,
                               (viewport.Height - textSize.Y) / 2);
    base.Update(gameTime);
}
```

The *Draw* method is trivial:

XNA Project: XnaLocation   File: Game1.cs (excerpt)

```
protected override void Draw(GameTime gameTime)
{
    GraphicsDevice.Clear(Color.Navy);

    spriteBatch.Begin();
    spriteBatch.DrawString(kootenay14, text, textPosition, Color.White);
    spriteBatch.End();

    base.Draw(gameTime);
}
```

Because the *GeoCoordinateWatcher* is left running for the duration of the program, it should update the location as the phone is moved. Here's where I live:

With the phone emulator, however, the *GeoCoordinateWatcher* program might not work. With some beta software releases of Windows Phone 7 development tools, the Accelerometer always returned the coordinates of a spot in Princeton, New Jersey, perhaps as a subtle reference to the college where Alan Turing earned his PhD.

Using a Map Service

Of course, most people curious about their location prefer to see a map rather than numeric coordinates. The Silverlight demonstration of the location service displays a map that comes to the program in the form of bitmaps.

In a real phone application, you'd probably be using Bing Maps, particularly considering the existence of a Bing Maps Silverlight Control tailored for the phone. Unfortunately, making use of Bing Maps in a program involves opening a developer account, and getting a maps key and a credential token. This is all free and straightforward but it doesn't work well for a program that will be shared among all the readers of a book.

For that reason, I'll be using an alternative that doesn't require keys or tokens. This alternative is Microsoft Research Maps, which you can learn all about at *msrmaps.com*. The aerial images are provided by the United States Geological Survey (USGS). Microsoft Research Maps makes these images available through a web service called MSR Maps Service, but still sometimes referred to by its old name of TerraService.

The downside is that the images are not quite state-of-the-art and the service doesn't always seem entirely reliable.

MSR Maps Service is a SOAP (Simple Object Access Protocol) service with the transactions described in a WSDL (Web Services Description Language) file. Behind the scenes, all the transactions between your program and the web service are in the form of XML files. However, to avoid programmer anguish, generally the WSDL file is used to generate a *proxy*, which is a collection of classes and structures that allow your program to communicate with the web service with method calls and events.

You can generate this proxy right in Visual Studio. Here's how I did it: I first created an Windows Phone 7 project in Visual Studio called SilverlightLocationMapper. In the Solution Explorer, I right-clicked the project name and selected Add Service Reference. In the Address field I entered the URL of the MSR Maps Service WSDL file: *http://MSRMaps.com/ TerraService2.asmx*.

(You might wonder if the URL should be *http://msrmaps.com/TerraService2.asmx?WSDL* because that's how WSDL files are often referenced. That address will actually seem to work at first, but you'll get files containing obsolete URLs.)

After you've entered the URL in the Address field, press Go. Visual Studio will access the site and report back what it finds. There will be one service, called by the old name of TerraService.

Next you'll want to enter a name in the Namespace field to replace the generic ServiceReference1. I used MsrMapsService and pressed OK.

You'll then see MsrMapsService show up under the project in the Solution Explorer. If you click the little Show All Files icon at the top of the Solution Explorer, you can view the generated files. In particular, nested under MsrMapsService and Reference.svcmap, you'll see Reference.cs, a big file (over 4000 lines) with a namespace of XnaLocationMapper. MsrMapsService, which combines the original project name and the name you selected for the web service.

This Reference.cs file contains all the classes and structures you need to access the web service, and which are documented on the *msrmaps.com* web site. To access these classes in your program, add a *using* direction:

```
using SilverlightLocationMapper.MsrMapsService;
```

You also need a reference to the System.Device assembly and *using* directives for the *System.Device.Location*, *System.IO*, and *System.Windows.Media.Imaging* namespacess.

In the MainPage.xaml file, I left the *SupportedOrientations* property at its default setting of *Portrait*, I removed the page title to free up more space, and I moved the title panel below the content grid just in case there was a danger of something spilling out of the content grid and obscuring the title. Moving the title panel below the content grid in the XAML file ensures that it will be visually on top.

Here's the content grid:

Silverlight Project: **SilverlightLocationMapper**   File: **MainPage.xaml** (excerpt)

```
<Grid x:Name="ContentPanel" Grid.Row="1" Margin="12,0,12,0">
    <TextBlock Name="statusText"
               HorizontalAlignment="Center"
               VerticalAlignment="Center"
               TextWrapping="Wrap" />

    <Image Source="Images/usgslogoFooter.png"
           Stretch="None"
           HorizontalAlignment="Right"
           VerticalAlignment="Bottom" />
</Grid>
```

The *TextBlock* is used to display status and (possibly) errors; the *Image* displays a logo of the United States Geological Survey.

The map bitmaps will be inserted between the *TextBlock* and *Image* so they obscure the *TextBlock* but the *Image* remains on top.

The code-behind file has just two fields, one for the *GeoCoordinateWatcher* that supplies the location information, and the other for the proxy class created when the web service was added:

Silverlight Project: **SilverlightLocationMapper**   File: **MainPage.xaml.cs** (excerpt)

```
public partial class MainPage : PhoneApplicationPage
{
    GeoCoordinateWatcher geoWatcher = new GeoCoordinateWatcher();
    TerraServiceSoapClient proxy = new TerraServiceSoapClient();
    ...
}
```

You use the proxy by calling its methods, which make network requests. All these methods are asynchronous. For each method you call, you must also supply a handler for a completion event that is fired when the information you requested has been transferred to your application.

The completion event is accompanied by event arguments: a *Cancelled* property of type *bool*, an *Error* property that is *null* if there is no error, and a *Result* property that depends on the request.

I wanted the process to begin after the program was loaded and displayed, so I set a handler for the *Loaded* event. That *Loaded* handler sets the handlers for the two completion events I'll require of the proxy, and also starts up the *GeoCoordinateWatcher*:

Silverlight Project: SilverlightLocationMapper   File: MainPage.xaml.cs (excerpt)

```
public MainPage()
{
    InitializeComponent();
    Loaded += OnMainPageLoaded;
}

void OnMainPageLoaded(object sender, RoutedEventArgs args)
{
    // Set event handlers for TerraServiceSoapClient proxy
    proxy.GetAreaFromPtCompleted += OnProxyGetAreaFromPtCompleted;
    proxy.GetTileCompleted += OnProxyGetTileCompleted;

    // Start GeoCoordinateWatcher going
    statusText.Text = "Obtaining geographic location...";
    geoWatcher.PositionChanged += OnGeoWatcherPositionChanged;
    geoWatcher.Start();
}
```

When coordinates are obtained, the following *OnGeoWatcherPositionChanged* method is called. This method begins by turning off the *GeoCoordinateWatcher*. The program is not equipped to continuously update the display, so it can't do anything with any additional location information. It appends the longitude and latitude to the *TextBlock* called *ApplicationTitle* displayed at the top of the screen.

Silverlight Project: SilverlightLocationMapper   File: MainPage.xaml.cs (excerpt)

```
void OnGeoWatcherPositionChanged(object sender,
                         GeoPositionChangedEventArgs<GeoCoordinate> args)
{
    // Turn off GeoWatcher
    geoWatcher.PositionChanged -= OnGeoWatcherPositionChanged;
    geoWatcher.Stop();

    // Set coordinates to title text
    GeoCoordinate coord = args.Position.Location;
    ApplicationTitle.Text += ": " + String.Format("{0:F2}°{1} {2:F2}°{3}",
                                    Math.Abs(coord.Latitude),
                                    coord.Latitude > 0 ? 'N' : 'S',
                                    Math.Abs(coord.Longitude),
                                    coord.Longitude > 0 ? 'E' : 'W');
```

```
    // Query proxy for AreaBoundingBox
    LonLatPt center = new LonLatPt();
    center.Lon = args.Position.Location.Longitude;
    center.Lat = args.Position.Location.Latitude;

    statusText.Text = "Accessing Microsoft Research Maps Service...";
    proxy.GetAreaFromPtAsync(center, 1, Scale.Scale16m,
(int)ContentPanel.ActualWidth,

(int)ContentPanel.ActualHeight);
}
```

The method concludes by making its first call to the proxy. The *GetAreaFromPtAsync* call requires a longitude and latitude as a center point, but some other information as well. The second argument is 1 to get an aerial view and 2 for a map (as you'll see at the end of this chapter). The third argument is the desired scale, a member of the *Scale* enumeration. The member I've chosen means that each pixel of the returned bitmaps is equivalent to 16 meters.

Watch out: Some scaling factors—in particular, *Scale2m*, *Scale8m*, and *Scale32m*—result in GIF files being returned. Remember, remember, remember that Silverlight doesn't do GIF! For the other scaling factors, JPEGS are returned.

The final arguments to *GetAreaFromPtAsync* are the width and height of the area you wish to cover with the map.

All the bitmaps you get back from the MSR Maps Service are 200 pixels square. Almost always, you'll need multiple bitmaps to tile a complete area. For example, if the last two arguments to *GetAreaFromPtAsync* are 400 and 600, you'll need 6 bitmaps to tile the area.

Well, actually not: An area of 400 pixels by 600 pixels will require 12 bitmaps, 3 horizontally and 4 vertically.

Here's the catch: These bitmaps aren't specially created when a program requests them. They already exist on the server in all the various scales. The geographic coordinates where these bitmaps begin and end are fixed. So if you want to cover a particular area of your display with a tiled map, and you want the center of this area to be precisely the coordinate you specify, the existing tiles aren't going to fit exactly. You want sufficient tiles to cover your area, but the tiles around the boundary are going to hang over the edges.

What you get back from the *GetAreaFromPtAsync* call (in the following *OnProxyGetAreaFromPtCompleted* method) is an object of type *AreaBoundingBox*. This is a rather complex structure that nonetheless has all the information required to request the individual tiles you need and then assemble them together in a grid.

Silverlight Project: SilverlightLocationMapper   File: **MainPage.xaml.cs (excerpt)**

```
void OnProxyGetAreaFromPtCompleted(object sender, GetAreaFromPtCompletedEventArgs
args)
{
    if (args.Error != null)
    {
        statusText.Text = args.Error.Message;
        return;
    }

    statusText.Text = "Getting map tiles...";

    AreaBoundingBox box = args.Result;
    int xBeg = box.NorthWest.TileMeta.Id.X;
    int yBeg = box.NorthWest.TileMeta.Id.Y;
    int xEnd = box.NorthEast.TileMeta.Id.X;
    int yEnd = box.SouthWest.TileMeta.Id.Y;

    // Loop through the tiles
    for (int x = xBeg; x <= xEnd; x++)
        for (int y = yBeg; y >= yEnd; y--)
        {
            // Create Image object to display tile
            Image img = new Image();
            img.Stretch = Stretch.None;
            img.HorizontalAlignment = HorizontalAlignment.Left;
            img.VerticalAlignment = VerticalAlignment.Top;
            img.Margin = new Thickness((x - xBeg) * 200 -
box.NorthWest.Offset.XOffset,
                                        (yBeg - y) * 200 -
box.NorthWest.Offset.YOffset,
                                        0, 0);

            // Insert after TextBlock but before Image with logo
            ContentPanel.Children.Insert(1, img);

            // Define the tile ID
            TileId tileId = box.NorthWest.TileMeta.Id;
            tileId.X = x;
            tileId.Y = y;

            // Call proxy to get the tile (Notice that Image is user object)
            proxy.GetTileAsync(tileId, img);
        }
}
```

I won't discuss the intricacies of *AreaBoundingBox* because it's more or less documented on the *msrmaps.com* web site, and I was greatly assisted by some similar logic on the site written for Windows Forms (which I suppose dates it a bit).

Notice that the loop creates each *Image* object to display each tile. Each of these *Image* objects has the same *Stretch*, *HorizontalAlignment*, and *VerticalAlignment* properties, but a different *Margin*. This *Margin* is how the individual tiles are positioned within the content grid. The *XOffset* and *YOffset* values cause the tiles to hang off the top and left edges of the content grid. The content grid doesn't clip its contents, so these tiles possibly extend to the top of the program's page.

Notice also that each *Image* object is passed as a second argument to the proxy's *GetTileAsync* method. This is called the *UserState* argument. The proxy doesn't do anything with this argument except return it as the *UserState* property of the completion arguments, as shown here:

Silverlight Project: **SilverlightLocationManager**   File: **MainPage.xaml.cs (excerpt)**

```
void OnProxyGetTileCompleted(object sender, GetTileCompletedEventArgs args)
{
    if (args.Error != null)
    {
        return;
    }

    Image img = args.UserState as Image;
    BitmapImage bmp = new BitmapImage();
    bmp.SetSource(new MemoryStream(args.Result));
    img.Source = bmp;
}
```

That's how the method links up the particular bitmap tile with the particular *Image* element already in place in the content grid.

It is my experience that in most cases, the program doesn't get all the tiles it requests. If you're very lucky—and you happen to be running the program somewhere in my neighborhood—your display might look like this:

If you change the second argument of the *proxy.GetAreaFromPtAsync* call from a 1 to a 2, you get back images of an actual map rather than an aerial view:

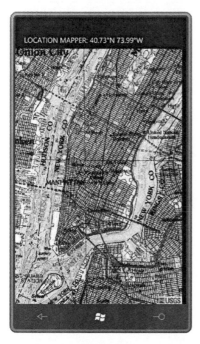

It has a certain retro charm—and I love the watercolor look—but I'm afraid that modern users are accustomed to something just a little more 21st century.

Chapter 6
Issues in Application Architecture

A Silverlight application for Windows Phone 7 consists of several standard classes:

- an *App* class that derives from *Application*;
- an instance of the *PhoneApplicationFrame* class; and
- one or more classes that derive from *PhoneApplicationPage*.

This chapter is partially about the "or more" of that last item. The programs you've seen so far have consisted of a single class named *MainPage* that derives from *PhoneApplicationPage*. In more complex applications, you might want to have multiple pages and allow the user to navigate among them, much like navigating among Web pages.

Page navigation would seem to be an advanced Silverlight programming topic, and a topic that applies only to Silverlight programming rather than XNA programming. However, there are issues involved with navigation that are related to the very important topic of *tombstoning*, which is what happens to your Windows Phone 7 application when the user navigates to another application through the phone's Start screen. Tombstoning is very much an issue that also affects XNA programmers.

Basic Navigation

The SilverlightSimpleNavigation project begins as usual with a *MainPage* class, and as usual I set the two *TextBlock* elements for the titles:

Silverlight Project: SilverlightSimpleNavigation   File: MainPage.xaml (excerpt)

```
<StackPanel x:Name="TitlePanel" Grid.Row="0" Margin="12,17,0,28">
    <TextBlock x:Name="ApplicationTitle" Text="SIMPLE NAVIGATION" ... />
    <TextBlock x:Name="PageTitle" Text="main page" ... />
</StackPanel>
```

The content area of MainPage.xaml contains only a *TextBlock* that sets a handler for its *ManipulationStarted* event:

Silverlight Project: SilverlightSimpleNavigation   File: MainPage.xaml (excerpt)

```
<Grid x:Name="ContentPanel" Grid.Row="1" Margin="12,0,12,0">
    <TextBlock Text="Navigate to 2nd Page"
               HorizontalAlignment="Center"
               VerticalAlignment="Center"
               Padding="0 34"
               ManipulationStarted="OnTextBlockManipulationStarted" />
</Grid>
```

Notice the *Text* property on the *TextBlock*: "Navigate to 2nd page." The code-behind file contains the handler for *ManipulationStarted* but also overrides the *OnManipulationStarted* method for the whole page:

Silverlight Project: SilverlightSimpleNavigation   File: MainPage.xaml.cs (excerpt)

```
public partial class MainPage : PhoneApplicationPage
{
    Random rand = new Random();

    public MainPage()
    {
        InitializeComponent();
    }

    void OnTextBlockManipulationStarted(object sender, ManipulationStartedEventArgs
args)
    {
        this.NavigationService.Navigate(new Uri("/SecondPage.xaml",
UriKind.Relative));

        args.Complete();
        args.Handled = true;
    }

    protected override void OnManipulationStarted(ManipulationStartedEventArgs args)
    {
        ContentPanel.Background = new SolidColorBrush(
            Color.FromArgb(255, (byte)rand.Next(255),
                                (byte)rand.Next(255),
                                (byte)rand.Next(255)));

        base.OnManipulationStarted(args);
    }
}
```

If you touch anywhere on the page outside of the *TextBlock*, the background of the *ContentPanel* is set to a random color. Touch the *TextBlock*, and the handler accesses the *NavigationService* property of the page. This is an object of type *NavigationService* that contains properties, methods, and events related to navigation, including the crucial *Navigate* method:

```
this.NavigationService.Navigate(new Uri("/SecondPage.xaml", UriKind.Relative));
```

The argument is an object of type *Uri*. Notice the slash in front of SecondPage.xaml, and notice the use of *UriKind.Relative* to indicate a URI relative to MainPage.xaml.

I created a second page in the SilverlightSimpleNavigation project by right-clicking the project name in the Visual Studio solution explorer, and selecting Add and New Item. From the Add New Item dialog box, I picked Windows Phone Portrait Page and gave it a name of SecondPage.xaml.

This process creates not only SecondPage.xaml but also the code-behind file SecondPage.cs. The two SecondPage files are virtually identical to the two MainPage files that Visual Studio customarily creates. Like *MainPage*, *SecondPage* derives from *PhoneApplicationPage*.

I gave the titles In SecondPage.xaml the same application name as FirstPage.xaml but a page title of "second page":

Silverlight Project: SilverlightSimpleNavigation   File: SecondPage.xaml (excerpt)

```
<StackPanel x:Name="TitlePanel" Grid.Row="0" Margin="12,17,0,28">
    <TextBlock x:Name="ApplicationTitle" Text="SIMPLE NAVIGATION" ... />
    <TextBlock x:Name="PageTitle" Text="second page" ... />
</StackPanel>
```

The content area of SecondPage.xaml is very much like MainPage.xaml but the *TextBlock* reads "Go Back to 1st Page":

Silverlight Project: SilverlightSimpleNavigation   File: SecondPage.xaml (excerpt)

```
<Grid x:Name="ContentPanel" Grid.Row="1" Margin="12,0,12,0">
    <TextBlock Text="Go Back to 1st Page"
               HorizontalAlignment="Center"
               VerticalAlignment="Center"
               Padding="0 34"
               ManipulationStarted="OnTextBlockManipulationStarted" />
</Grid>
```

The code-behind file of the *SecondPage* class is also very much like the *FirstPage* class:

Silverlight Project: **SilverlightSimpleNavigation**   File: **SecondPage.xaml.cs** (excerpt)

```
public partial class SecondPage : PhoneApplicationPage
{
    Random rand = new Random();

    public SecondPage()
    {
        InitializeComponent();
    }

    void OnTextBlockManipulationStarted(object sender, ManipulationStartedEventArgs
args)
    {
        this.NavigationService.GoBack();

        args.Complete();
        args.Handled = true;
    }

    protected override void OnManipulationStarted(ManipulationStartedEventArgs args)
    {
        ContentPanel.Background = new SolidColorBrush(
            Color.FromArgb(255, (byte)rand.Next(255),
                                (byte)rand.Next(255),
                                (byte)rand.Next(255)));

        base.OnManipulationStarted(args);
    }
}
```

Once again, when you touch anywhere on the page except the *TextBlock*, the background changes to a random color. When you touch the *TextBlock*, the handler calls another method of *NavigationService*:

```
this.NavigationService.GoBack();
```

This call causes the program to go back to the page that navigated to SecondPage.xaml, in this case, MainPage.xaml. Take a look at the *Navigate* call in MainPage.cs again:

```
this.NavigationService.Navigate(new Uri("/SecondPage.xaml", UriKind.Relative));
```

Navigation in a Silverlight program is based around XAML files in much the same way that navigation in a traditional Web environment is based around HTML files. The actual instance of the *SecondPage* class is created behind the scenes. The *PhoneApplicationFrame* instance in the application handles many of the actual mechanics of navigation, but the public interface of *PhoneApplicationFrame* also involves *Uri* objects and XAML files rather than instances of *PhoneApplicationPage* derivatives.

Let's run the program. The program begins with the main page, and you can touch the screen to change the color:

Now touch the *TextBlock* that says "Navigate to 2nd Page" and the second page comes into view:

You can touch that screen to change to a different color:

Now touch the *TextBlock* that says "Go Back to 1st Page". (Alternatively, you can press the phone's hardware Back button.) You'll be whisked back to the main page with the color just as you left it:

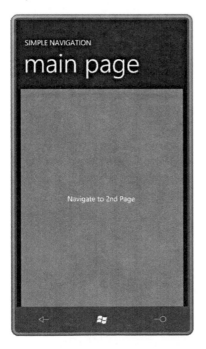

Now touch the *TextBlock* again to navigate to the second page:

The background is black. The second page does *not* display the color you set when you last visited the second page. This is very obviously a brand new instance of the *SecondPage* class.

The navigation system in Silverlight for Windows Phone is based around the metaphor of the last-in-first-out data structure called the *stack*. I'll sometimes refer to the page calling *Navigate* as the *source* page and the page being navigated to as the *destination* page. When the source page calls *Navigate*, the source page is put on the stack and a new instance of the destination page is created and displayed. When a page calls *GoBack*—or when the user presses the phone's hardware Back button—that page is abandoned, and the page at the top of the stack is popped off and displayed.

Within a Silverlight application, the phone's Back button performs the same function as a call to *GoBack* except if you're at the initial page of the program, in which case the hardware Back button terminates the application.

Try this: Replace the *GoBack* call in SecondPage.xaml.cs with the following:

```
this.NavigationService.Navigate(new Uri("/MainPage.xaml", UriKind.Relative));
```

This is not the same as the *GoBack* call. You won't go back to the original instance of *MainPage*. This call causes *SecondPage* to navigate to a *new* instance of *MainPage*, and if you keep pressing the *TextBlock* on each on the pages, you'll build up a whole stack of alternating *MainPage* and *SecondPage* instances, each of which can have its own unique color. You'll need to use the hardware Back button on the phone to back up through all these pages and finally terminate the application.

Navigate and *GoBack* are the two basic methods of *NavigationService*, and it's unlikely you'll need to use anything beyond these for your applications. Keep in mind that you're coding for a phone, and it doesn't make a lot of sense to have very complex navigation schemes within your program without also some way of reminding the user how the current page was arrived at and how to unwind the process.

Perhaps the most important use of secondary pages in a Silverlight application for the phone is to serve as dialog boxes. When a program needs some information from the user, it navigates to a new page to collection that information. The user enters the information, and then goes back to the main page.

Passing Data to Pages

The possible use of pages as dialog boxes provokes two questions:

- How do I pass data from a source page to a destination page?
- How do I return data when going back to the original page?

Interestingly, a facility is provided specifically for the first item but not for the second. I'll show you this facility and then look at more generalized solutions to the second problem.

The following project is called SilverlightPassData. It is very much like the first project in this chapter except that when *MainPage* navigates to *SecondPage*, it provides *SecondPage* with its current background color, and *SecondPage* initializes itself with that color.

Here's the content area of MainPage.xaml, the same as in the previous program:

Silverlight Project: SilverlightPassData   File: MainPage.xaml (excerpt)

```
<Grid x:Name="ContentPanel" Grid.Row="1" Margin="12,0,12,0">
    <TextBlock Text="Navigate to 2nd Page"
               HorizontalAlignment="Center"
               VerticalAlignment="Center"
               Padding="0 34"
               ManipulationStarted="OnTextBlockManipulationStarted" />
</Grid>
```

I won't show you the *OnManipulationStarted* override because it's the same as in the previous program, but the *ManipulationStarted* event handler for the *TextBlock* is a bit enhanced:

Silverlight Project: **SilverlightPassData**   File: **MainPage.xaml.cs** (excerpt)

```
void OnTextBlockManipulationStarted(object sender, ManipulationStartedEventArgs args)
{
    string destination = "/SecondPage.xaml";

    if (ContentPanel.Background is SolidColorBrush)
    {
        Color clr = (ContentPanel.Background as SolidColorBrush).Color;
        destination += String.Format("?Red={0}&Green={1}&Blue={2}",
                                     clr.R, clr.G, clr.B);
    }

    this.NavigationService.Navigate(new Uri(destination, UriKind.Relative));

    args.Complete();
    args.Handled = true;
}
```

If the *Background* brush of the *ContentPanel* is a *SolidColorBrush*, then the handler gets the *Color* and formats the red, green, and blue values into a string that is appended to the name of the destination page. The URI now looks something like this:

"/SecondPage.xaml?Red=244&Green=43&Blue=91"

You'll recognize this as a common format of an HTML query string.

The SilverlightPassData project also contains a *SecondPage* class that is the same as the one in the first project except that the code-behind file contains an override of the *OnNavigatedTo* method:

Silverlight Project: **SilverlightPassData**   File: **SecondPage.xaml.cs** (excerpt)

```
protected override void OnNavigatedTo(NavigationEventArgs args)
{
    IDictionary<string, string> parameters = this.NavigationContext.QueryString;

    if (parameters.ContainsKey("Red"))
    {
        byte R = Byte.Parse(parameters["Red"]);
        byte G = Byte.Parse(parameters["Green"]);
        byte B = Byte.Parse(parameters["Blue"]);

        ContentPanel.Background =
            new SolidColorBrush(Color.FromArgb(255, R, G, B));
    }

    base.OnNavigatedTo(args);
}
```

You'll need a *using* directive for the *System.Windows.Navigation* namespace for the *NavigationEventArgs* class.

The *OnNavigatedTo* method is defined by *Page*, the class from which *PhoneApplicationPage* derives. The method is called right after the page has been created. When *OnNavigatedTo* is called, the page's constructor has already executed, of course, but not much else has happened.

The destination class can access the query strings used to invoke the page through the page's *NavigationContext* property. This property is of type *NavigationContext*, a class that has only one public property named *QueryString*, which returns a dictionary that I've saved in a variable called *parameters*. The code here assumes that if the "Red" query string is present, the "Blue" and "Green" must exist as well. It passes all the strings to the *Byte.Parse* method and reconstructs the color.

Now as you navigate from *MainPage* to *SecondPage*, the background color remains the same. As you go back, however, that's not the case. There is no built-in facility like the query string to return data from one page to another.

Sharing Data Among Pages

Keep in mind that all the pages in your program have convenient access to the *App* class that derives from *Application*. The static *Application.Current* property returns the *Application* object associated with the program, and you can simply cast that to *App*. This means that you can use the *App* class for storing data you want to share among multiple pages of the application.

In the SilverlightShareData project, I defined a simple public property in the *App* class:

Silverlight Project: **SilverlightShareData**   File: **App.xaml.cs** (excerpt)

```
public partial class App : Application
{
    // public property for sharing data among pages
    public Color? SharedColor { set; get; }

    . . .

}
```

I defined this property of type nullable *Color* rather than just *Color* for those cases where a *SolidColorBrush* has not been set on the *Background* property of *ContentPanel*. In those cases, the *Background* property is *null* and there shouldn't be a *Color* stored in this property. If the property were of type *Color*, then a *Color* would be stored by default; that *Color* value would be transparent black, and that's wrong. Even non-transparent black is wrong if the user has selected the Light color scheme.

Much of the program remains the same, except that when you touch the *TextBlock* in *MainPage*, the handler first attempts to save a color in the new *App* class property before navigating to *SecondPage*:

Silverlight Project: SilverlightShareData   File: MainPage.xaml.cs (excerpt)

```
void OnTextBlockManipulationStarted(object sender, ManipulationStartedEventArgs args)
{
    if (ContentPanel.Background is SolidColorBrush)
        (Application.Current as App).SharedColor =
                        (ContentPanel.Background as SolidColorBrush).Color;

    this.NavigationService.Navigate(new Uri("/SecondPage.xaml", UriKind.Relative));

    args.Complete();
    args.Handled = true;
}
```

The *OnNavigatedTo* override in *SecondPage* than accesses that property:

Silverlight Project: SilverlightShareData   File: SecondPage.xaml.cs (excerpt)

```
protected override void OnNavigatedTo(NavigationEventArgs args)
{
    Color? sharedColor = (Application.Current as App).SharedColor;

    if (sharedColor != null)
        ContentPanel.Background =
                new SolidColorBrush(sharedColor.Value);

    base.OnNavigatedTo(args);
}
```

Similarly, when you press the *TextBlock* on *SecondPage*, the handler saves whatever color the background now happens to be back in the *App* class before calling *GoBack*:

Silverlight Project: SilverlightShareData   File: SecondPage.xaml.cs (excerpt)

```
void OnTextBlockManipulationStarted(object sender, ManipulationStartedEventArgs args)
{
    if (ContentPanel.Background is SolidColorBrush)
        (Application.Current as App).SharedColor =
                        (ContentPanel.Background as SolidColorBrush).Color;

    this.NavigationService.GoBack();
```

```
        args.Complete();
        args.Handled = true;
    }
```

The *MainPage* class also overrides *OnNavigatedTo* so it too can retrieve the stored color and set it to the background of the grid:

Silverlight Project: SilverlightShareData   File: MainPage.xaml.cs (excerpt)

```
protected override void OnNavigatedTo(NavigationEventArgs args)
{
    Color? sharedColor = (Application.Current as App).SharedColor;

    if (sharedColor != null)
        ContentPanel.Background =
                new SolidColorBrush(sharedColor.Value);

    base.OnNavigatedTo(args);
}
```

Now as you navigate between the pages they always share the same color.

Using the *App* class as a repository for shared data among pages is so convenient that you might find yourself using it exclusively. But you should really consider more structured solutions that involve only the pages navigating between each other and not some third-party class like *App*.

Besides the *OnNavigatedTo* virtual method, *Page* also defines an *OnNavigatedFrom* method, which at first seems much less useful. After all, a page knows that it's navigating from itself because it's just called *Navigate* or *GoBack*.

However, both *OnNavigatedFrom* and *OnNavigatedTo* have event arguments of type *NavigationEventArgs*, which defines two properties: *Uri* of type *Uri*, and *Content* of type *object*. These always indicate the page being navigated to.

For example, *MainPage* calls *Navigate* with an argument of "/SecondPage.xaml". The *OnNavigatedFrom* method in *MainPage* is called with event arguments with a *Uri* property indicating "/SecondPage.xaml" and a *Content* property of type *SecondPage*. This is the newly created instance of *SecondPage* that is about to be displayed, and this is the most convenient way to obtain that instance. The *OnNavigatedTo* method of *SecondPage* is then called with the same event arguments indicating a *Uri* of "/SecondPage.xaml" and the *SecondPage* object.

Similarly, when *SecondPage* calls *GoBack*, its *OnNavigatedFrom* method is called with event arguments that include a *Uri* property indicating "/MainPage.xaml" and a *Content* property with the *MainPage* instance. The *OnNavigatedTo* method of *MainPage* is then called with those same event arguments.

This means that during the *OnNavigatedFrom* method, a class has an opportunity to set a property or call a method in the class of the destination page.

Let's look at an example called SilverlightInsertData. The project has two pages named *MainPage* and *SecondPage* and the XAML files are the same as those you've already seen. The *MainPage* class doesn't have any logic to randomly change its color. Instead, it uses *SecondPage* to obtain a color for it. You can think of *SecondPage* as a dialog box that returns a random color to *MainPage*.

Here's most of the code-behind file in *MainPage*:

Silverlight Project: SilverlightInsertData   File: MainPage.xaml.cs (excerpt)

```
public partial class MainPage : PhoneApplicationPage
{
    public MainPage()
    {
        InitializeComponent();
    }

    public Color? ReturnedColor { set; get; }

    void OnTextBlockManipulationStarted(object sender, ManipulationStartedEventArgs args)
    {
        this.NavigationService.Navigate(new Uri("/SecondPage.xaml", UriKind.Relative));

        args.Complete();
        args.Handled = true;
    }
    ...
}
```

Notice the *ReturnedColor* property, of type nullable *Color* just like the property in the *App* class in the previous program.

Here's the *SecondPage* code-behind file:

Silverlight Project: SilverlightInsertData   File: SecondPage.xaml.cs (excerpt)

```
public partial class SecondPage : PhoneApplicationPage
{
    Random rand = new Random();

    public SecondPage()
    {
        InitializeComponent();
    }
```

```
    void OnTextBlockManipulationStarted(object sender, ManipulationStartedEventArgs
args)
    {
        this.NavigationService.GoBack();

        args.Complete();
        args.Handled = true;
    }

    protected override void OnManipulationStarted(ManipulationStartedEventArgs args)
    {
        ContentPanel.Background = new SolidColorBrush(
            Color.FromArgb(255, (byte)rand.Next(255),
                                (byte)rand.Next(255),
                                (byte)rand.Next(255)));

        base.OnManipulationStarted(args);
    }

    protected override void OnNavigatedFrom(NavigationEventArgs args)
    {
        if (ContentPanel.Background is SolidColorBrush)
        {
            Color clr = (ContentPanel.Background as SolidColorBrush).Color;

            if (args.Content is MainPage)
                (args.Content as MainPage).ReturnedColor = clr;
        }

        base.OnNavigatedFrom(e);
    }
}
```

As in the previous programs, *SecondPage* changes its background to a random color
when touched, and calls *GoBack* when the *TextBlock* is touched. The new code is in the
OnNavigatedFrom override, which is called shortly after the class calls *GoBack*. If there's
a valid *SolidColorBrush* available, the method checks if it's navigating to an object of type
MainPage. If so, then it saves the *Color* object in the *ReturnedColor* property of *MainPage*.

MainPage can retrieve the value of that property in its *OnNavigatedTo* override:

Silverlight Project: SilverlightInsertData   File: MainPage.xaml.cs (excerpt)

```
public partial class MainPage : PhoneApplicationPage
{
    ...
    protected override void OnNavigatedTo(NavigationEventArgs args)
    {
        if (ReturnedColor != null)
```

```
            ContentPanel.Background =
                    new SolidColorBrush(ReturnedColor.Value);

        base.OnNavigatedTo(args);
    }
}
```

In a sense, *MainPage* invokes *SecondPage* to obtain a *Color* value, just like a real dialog box. But if you navigate to *SecondPage* subsequent times, it always starts out with a black screen (or white if you've selected the Light color theme).

Interestingly, *SecondPage* can't initialize itself from any property in *MainPage* because the *OnNavigatedTo* call that *SecondPage* receives doesn't reference the source page. To work in a symmetrical manner, *SecondPage* would need to define its own public *Color* property, and *MainPage* would need to initialize that property in its own *OnNavigatedFrom* override.

You might consider a little variation on this program where *SecondPage* defines the *ReturnedColor* property. When *MainPage* navigates to *SecondPage* the *OnNavigatedFrom* method in *MainPage* is called, and the method saves the instance of *SecondPage* being navigated to in a field in *MainPage*. When *SecondPage* is finished, it saves the *Color* value in its *ReturnedColor* property and calls *GoBack*. The *OnNavigatedTo* method in *MainPage* is then called. *MainPage* can use the *SecondPage* instance saved as a field to access the *ReturnedColor* property.

This scheme sounds fine, but it won't always work. The problem is that *MainPage* can't be assured that the *SecondPage* instance it navigates to will be the same *SecondPage* instance that navigates back to *MainPage*. You'll have a better sense of this problem soon.

Retaining Data across Instances

Every time *MainPage* navigates to *SecondPage*, it's a different instance of *SecondPage*. That's why *SecondPage* always starts out the same. It's always a new instance.

If we want *SecondPage* to "remember" the last color it was set to, something outside of *SecondPage* must be responsible for saving that data. That could be *MainPage*.

Or, *SecondPage* could save its state in *isolated storage*. Isolated storage is much like regular disk storage. To access it, you use classes in the *System.IO.IsolatedStorage* namespace. Every Windows Phone 7 application has access to isolated storage but only to files that the application itself has created. Isolated storage allows an application to save data between multiple executions, and is ideal for saving application settings.

I'll present examples of isolated storage later in this chapter.

A third solution is provided by a class named *PhoneApplicationService*, defined in the *Microsoft.Phone.Shell* namespace. An instance of *PhoneApplicationService* is created in the standard App.xaml file:

```
<Application.ApplicationLifetimeObjects>
    <!--Required object that handles lifetime events for the application-->
    <shell:PhoneApplicationService
        Launching="Application_Launching" Closing="Application_Closing"
        Activated="Application_Activated" Deactivated="Application_Deactivated"/>
</Application.ApplicationLifetimeObjects>
```

Following the *PhoneApplicationService* tag are four events being associated with handlers; you'll see examples of these events later in this chapter. Don't create a new *PhoneApplicationService*. You can obtain this existing *PhoneApplicationService* with the static *PhoneApplicationService.Current* property.

PhoneApplicationService contains a property named *State*, which is a dictionary that lets you save and restore data. This *State* property is of type *IDictionary<string, object>*. You store objects in this dictionary using text keys. This data is only retained while the application is running, so it's not suitable for application settings that must be preserved between multiple executions of a program. Data retained by the applicaton only when it's running is sometimes known as "transient" data.

Any object you store in this *State* dictionary must be serializable, that is, it must be possible to convert the object into XML, and recreate the object from XML. It must have a public parameterless constructor, and all its public properties must either be serializable or be of types that have *Parse* methods to convert the strings back to objects.

It's not always obvious what objects are serializable and which ones are not. When I first started experimenting, I tried to store *SolidColorBrush* objects in the *State* dictionary. The program raised an exception that said "Type 'System.Windows.Media.Transform' cannot be serialized." It took awhile to remember that *Brush* has a property named *Transform* of type *Transform*, an abstract class. I had to serialize the *Color* instead.

Let's modify the previous program so that *SecondPage* uses this *State* property. In the SilverlightRetainData project, everything is the same except for a *using* directive for the *Microsoft.Phone.Shell* namespace and two overrides in *SecondPage*. Here they are:

Silverlight Project: **SilverlightRetainData**   File: **SecondPage.xaml.cs** (excerpt)

```
protected override void OnNavigatedFrom(NavigationEventArgs args)
{
    if (ContentPanel.Background is SolidColorBrush)
    {
        Color clr = (ContentPanel.Background as SolidColorBrush).Color;
```

```
            if (args.Content is MainPage)
                (args.Content as MainPage).ReturnedColor = clr;

            // Save color
            PhoneApplicationService.Current.State["Color"] = clr;
        }

        base.OnNavigatedFrom(args);
    }

    protected override void OnNavigatedTo(NavigationEventArgs args)
    {
        // Retrieve color
        if (PhoneApplicationService.Current.State.ContainsKey("Color"))
        {
            Color clr = (Color)PhoneApplicationService.Current.State["Color"];
            ContentPanel.Background = new SolidColorBrush(clr);
        }

        base.OnNavigatedTo(args);
    }
```

During the *OnNavigatedFrom* call, if there's a valid *Color* object available, then it's saved in the *State* dictionary with a key of "Color":

```
PhoneApplicationService.Current.State["Color"] = clr;
```

During the *OnNavigatedTo* override, if the key exists, then the *Color* value is loaded from the dictionary and *SolidColorBrush* is made from the *Color*. The key will not exist if you've just started running the program and you've navigated to *SecondPage* for the first time. But on subsequent navigations to *SecondPage*, the page is restored to the color you last set.

Every time you exit the program by pressing the Back button on the main page, the *State* dictionary is discarded with the rest of the *PhoneApplicationService*. This *State* dictionary is only suitable for saving transient data that a program needs to retain while it's running. If you need to save data between multiple executions of a program, use isolated storage.

Now try this: Navigate to *SecondPage*. Touch the screen to change the color. Now press the phone's hardware Start button. You've left the SilverlightRetainData program. From the phone's start screen, you can navigate to other programs, but eventually you'll want to press the phone's Back button to return to the SilverlightRetainData program and *SecondPage*. The color is still there.

Now go back to *MainPage*. The color you set in *SecondPage* is displayed. From *MainPage*, press the phone's hardware Start button, leaving the program. Navigate around a bit if you want but eventually start pressing the Back button to come back to SilverlightRetainData and *MainPage*.

Lo and behold, the screen has lost its color! What happened?

The Multitasking Ideal

Over the past few decades, it's been a common desire that our personal computers be able to do more than one thing at a time. But when user interfaces are involved, multitasking is never quite as seamless as we'd like. The Terminate-and-Stay-Resident (TSR) programs of MS-DOS and the cooperative multitasking of early Windows were only the first meager attempts in an ongoing struggle. In theory, process switching is easy. But sharing resources—including the screen and a handful of various input devices—is very hard.

While the average user might marvel at the ability of modern Windows to juggle many different applications at once, we programmers still wrestle with the difficulties of multitasking— carefully coding our UI threads to converse amicably with our non-UI threads, always on the lookout for the hidden treachery of asynchronous operations.

Every new application programming interface we encounter makes a sort of awkward accommodation with the ideals of multitasking, and as we become familiar with the API we also become accustomed to this awkward accommodation, and eventually we might even consider this awkward accommodation to be a proper solution to the problem.

On Windows Phone 7, that awkward accommodation is known as *tombstoning*.

Task Switching on the Phone

We want our phones to be much like our other computers. We want to have a lot of applications available. We want to start up a particular application as soon as we conceive a need for it. While that application is running, we want it to be as fast as possible and have access to unlimited resources. But we want this application to coexist with other running applications because we want to be able to jump among multiple applications running on the machine.

Arbitrarily jumping among multiple running applications is somewhat impractical on the phone. It would require some kind of display showing all the currently running applications, much like the Windows taskbar. Either this taskbar would have to be constantly visible—taking valuable screen space away from the active applications—or a special button or command would need to be assigned to display the taskbar or task list.

Instead, Windows Phone 7 manages multiple active applications by implementing a stack. In a sense, this application stack extends the page stack within a single Silverlight program. You can think of the phone as an old-fashioned web browser with no tab feature and no Forward button. But it does have a Back button and it also has a Start button, which brings you to the Start screen and allows you to launch a new program.

Suppose you choose to launch a program called Analyze. You work a little with Analyze and then decide you're finished. You press the Back button. The Analyze program is terminated and you're back at the Start screen. That's the simple scenario.

Later you decide you need to run Analyze again. While you're using Analyze, you need to check something on the Web. You press the Start button to get to the Start screen and select Internet Explorer. While you're browsing, you remember you haven't played any games recently. You press the Start button, select Backgammon and play a little of that. While playing Backgammon, you wonder about the odds of a particular move, so you press the Start button again and run Calc. Then you feel guilty about not doing any work, so you press the Start button again and run Draft.

Draft is a Silverlight program with multiple pages. From the main page, you navigate to several other pages.

Now start pressing the Back button. You go backwards through all the pages in the page stack of the Draft, then Draft is terminated as you go back to Calc. Calc still displays the remnants of your work, and Calc is terminated as you go back to Backgammon, which shows a game in progress, and Backgammon is terminated as you go back to Internet Explorer, and again you go backwards through any Web pages you may have navigated through, and IE is terminated as you go back to Analyze, and Analyze is terminated as you go back to the Start screen. The stack is now empty.

This type of navigation is a good compromise for small devices, and it's consistent with users' experiences in web browsing. The stack is conceptually very simple: The Start button pushes the current application on the stack so a new application can be run; the Back button terminates the current application and pops one off the top of the stack.

However, the limited resources of the phone convinced the Windows Phone 7 developers that applications on the stack should have as minimum a footprint as possible. For this reason, an application put on the stack does not continue plugging away at work. It's not even put into a suspended state of some sort. Something more severe than that happens. The process is actually terminated. When this terminated program comes off the stack, it is then re-executed from scratch.

This is tombstoning. The application is killed but then allowed to come back to life.

You've probably seen enough movies to know that re-animating a corpse can be a very scary proposition. Almost always the hideous thing that arises out of the filthy grave is not the clean and manicured loved one who went in.

The trick here is to persuade the disinterred program to look and feel much the same as when it was last alive and the user interacted with it. This process is a collaboration between you and Windows Phone 7. The phone gives you the tools (events and a place to put some data); your job is to use the tools to restore your program to a presentable state. Ideally the user should have no idea that it's a completely new process.

For some applications, resurrection doesn't have to be 100% successful. We all have experience with navigating among Web pages to know what's acceptable and what's not.

For example, suppose you visit a long Web page, and you scroll down a ways, then you navigate to another page. When you go back to the original page, it's not too upsetting if it's lost your place and you're back at the top of the page.

On the other hand, if you've just spent 10 minutes filling out a large form, you definitely do *not* want to see all your work gone after another page tells you that you've made one tiny error.

Let's nail down some terminology that's consistent with some events I'll discuss later:

- When an application is run from the Start screen, it is said to be *launched*.

- When an application is terminated as a result of the Back button, it is *closed*.

- When the program is running and the user presses the Start button, the program is said to be *deactivated*, even though it really is quite dead. This is the tombstoned state.

- When a program comes out of tombstoning as the user navigates back to it, it is said to be *activated*, even though it's really starting up from scratch.

Page State

The *SilverlightFlawedTombstoning* project is a simple Silverlight program with just one page. The program responds to taps on the screen by changing the background of *ContentGrid* to a random color, and displaying the total number of taps in its page title. Everything of interest happens in the code-behind file:

Silverlight Project: SilverlightFlawedTombstoning   File: MainPage.xaml.cs (excerpt)

```
public partial class MainPage : PhoneApplicationPage
{
    Random rand = new Random();
    int numTaps = 0;

    public MainPage()
    {
        InitializeComponent();
        UpdatePageTitle(numTaps);
    }

    protected override void OnManipulationStarted(ManipulationStartedEventArgs args)
    {
        ContentPanel.Background =
            new SolidColorBrush(Color.FromArgb(255, (byte)rand.Next(256),
                                                    (byte)rand.Next(256),
                                                    (byte)rand.Next(256)));

        UpdatePageTitle(++numTaps);
```

```
        args.Complete();
        base.OnManipulationStarted(args);
    }

    void UpdatePageTitle(int numTaps)
    {
        PageTitle.Text = String.Format("{0} taps total", numTaps);
    }
}
```

The little *UpdatePageTitle* method is called from both the program's constructor (where it always results in displaying a value of 0) and from the *OnManipulationStarted* override.

Build and deploy the program to the phone or phone emulator by pressing F5 (or selecting Start Debugging from the Debug menu). Arrange Visual Studio so you can see the Output window. When the program starts up, tap the screen several times to change the color and bump up the tap count. Now press the phone's Start button. You can see from Visual Studio that two threads in the program end and the program has terminated, but to the phone the program has actually been deactivated and tombstoned.

Now press the Back button to return to the program. You'll see a blank screen with the word "Resuming…" and the Output window in Visual Studio shows libraries being loaded. That's the program coming back to life.

However, when the program comes back into view, you'll see that the color and the number of taps have been lost. All your hard work! Totally gone! This is not a good way for a program to emerge from tombstoning. It is this state data that we want to preserve when the program is flat-lined.(Now you may see why the approach I described after the SilverlightInsertData program would not always work. That scheme involved saving the instance of *SecondPage* when *MainPage* navigated to that page. But if the user goes to the Start screen from *SecondPage* and then returned, that would be a new instance of *SecondPage* and not the one that *FrontPage* saved.)

An excellent opportunity to save and reload state data for a page is through overrides of the *OnNavigatedTo* and *OnNavigatedFrom* methods defined by the *Page* class from which *PhoneApplicationPage* derives. As you've seen, these methods are called when a page is brought into view by being loaded by the frame, and when the page is detached from the frame.

Using these methods is particularly appropriate if your Silverlight application will have multiple pages that the user can navigate among. You've already discovered that a new instance of *PhoneApplicationPage* is created every time a user navigates to a page, so you'll probably want to save and reload page state data for normal navigation anyway. By overriding *OnNavigatedTo* and *OnNavigatedFrom* you're effectively solving two problems with one solution.

Although Windows Phone 7 leaves much of the responsibility for restoring a tombstoned application to the program itself, it will cause the correct page to be loaded on activation, so it's possible that a page-oriented Silverlight program that saves and restores page state data using the *State* property of *PhoneApplicationSerivce* class during *OnNavigatedTo* and *OnNavigatedFrom* will need no special processing for tombstoning. The phone operating system preserves this *State* property during the time a program is deactivated and tombstoned, but gets rid of it when the program closes and is terminated for real.

The code-behind file for SilverlightBetterTombstoning includes a *using* directive for *Microsoft.Phone.Shell* and uses this *State* dictionary. Here's the complete class:

Silverlight Project: **SilverlightBetterTombstoning**   File: **MainPage.xaml.cs (excerpt)**

```
public partial class MainPage : PhoneApplicationPage
{
    Random rand = new Random();
    int numTaps = 0;
    PhoneApplicationService appService = PhoneApplicationService.Current;

    public MainPage()
    {
        InitializeComponent();
        UpdatePageTitle(numTaps);
    }

    protected override void OnManipulationStarted(ManipulationStartedEventArgs args)
    {
        ContentPanel.Background =
            new SolidColorBrush(Color.FromArgb(255, (byte)rand.Next(256),
                                                    (byte)rand.Next(256),
                                                    (byte)rand.Next(256)));
        UpdatePageTitle(++numTaps);

        args.Complete();
        base.OnManipulationStarted(args);
    }

    void UpdatePageTitle(int numTaps)
    {
        PageTitle.Text = String.Format("{0} taps total", numTaps);
    }

    protected override void OnNavigatedFrom(NavigationEventArgs args)
    {
        appService.State["numTaps"] = numTaps;

        if (ContentPanel.Background is SolidColorBrush)
        {
            appService.State["backgroundColor"] =
                        (ContentPanel.Background as SolidColorBrush).Color;
        }

        base.OnNavigatedFrom(args);
    }
```

```
    protected override void OnNavigatedTo(NavigationEventArgs args)
    {
        // Load numTaps
        if (appService.State.ContainsKey("numTaps"))
        {
            numTaps = (int)appService.State["numTaps"];
            UpdatePageTitle(numTaps);
        }

        // Load background color
        object obj;

        if (appService.State.TryGetValue("backgroundColor", out obj))
            ContentPanel.Background = new SolidColorBrush((Color)obj);

        base.OnNavigatedTo(args);
    }
}
```

Notice the *appService* field set to *PhoneApplicationService.Current*. That's just for convenience for accessing the *State* property. You can use the long *PhoneApplicationService.Current.State* instead if you prefer.

Storing items in the *State* dictionary is easier than getting them out. The syntax:

```
appService.State["numTaps"] = numTaps;
```

replaces an existing item if the "numTaps" key exists, or adds a new item if the key does not exist. Saving the background color is a little trickier: By default the *Background* property of *ContentPanel* is *null*, so the code checks for a non-*null* value before attempting to save the *Color* property.

To get items out of the dictionary, you can't use similar syntax. You'll raise an exception if the key does not exist. (And these keys will *not* exist when the application is launched.) The *OnNavigatedTo* method shows two different standard ways of accessing the items: The first checks if the dictionary contains the key; the second uses *TryGetValue*, which returns *true* if the key exists.

In a real program, you'll probably want to use *string* variables for the keys to avoid accidently typing inconsistent values. (If your typing is impeccable, don't worry about the multiple identical strings taking up storage: Strings are interned, and identical strings are consolidated into one.) You'll probably also want to write some standard routines that perform these jobs.

Try running this program like you ran the earlier one: Press F5 to deploy it to the phone or phone emulator from Visual Studio. Tap the screen a few times. Press the Start button as if you're going to start a new program. Visual Studio indicates that the process has terminated. Now press the Back button. When the program resumes the settings have been saved and the corpse looks as good as new!

As you experiment, you'll discover that the settings are saved when the application is tombstoned (that is, when you navigate away from the application with the Start button and then return) but not when a new instance starts up from the Start list. This is correct behavior. The operating system discards the *State* dictionary when the program terminates for real. The State dictionary is only for transient data and not for data that affects other instances of the same application.

If you want some similar data shared among all instances of a program, you probably want to implement what's often called *application settings*. You can do that as well.

Isolated Storage

Every program installed on Windows Phone 7 has access to its own area of permanent disk storage referred to as *isolated storage*, which the program can access using classes in the *System.IO.IsolatedStorage* namespace. Whole files can be read and written to in isolated storage, and I'll show you how to do that in the program that concludes this chapter. For the program that following I'm going to focus instead on a special use of isolated storage for storing application settings. The *IsolatedStorageSettings* class exists specifically for this purpose.

For application settings, you should be thinking in terms of the whole application rather than a particular page. Perhaps some of the application settings apply to multiple pages. Hence, a good place to deal with these application settings is in the program's *App* class.

Not coincidentally, it is the App.xaml file that creates a *PhoneApplicationService* object (the same *PhoneApplicationService* object used for saving transient data) and assigns event handlers for four events:

```
<shell:PhoneApplicationService Launching="Application_Launching"
                               Closing="Application_Closing"
                               Activated="Application_Activated"
                               Deactivated="Application_Deactivated"/>
```

The *Launching* event is fired when the program is first executed from the Start screen. The *Deactivated* event occurs when the program is tombstoned, and the *Activated* event occurs when the program is resurrected from tombstoning. The *Closing* event occurs when the program is really terminated, probably by the user pressing the Back button.

So, when a program starts up, it gets either a *Launching* event or an *Activated* event (but never both), depending whether it's being started from the Start screen or coming out of a tombstoned state. When a program ends, it gets either a *Deactivated* event or a *Closing* event, depending whether it's being tombstoned or terminated for real.

A program should load application settings during the *Launching* event and save them in response to the *Closing* event. That much is obvious. But a program should also save application settings during the *Deactivated* event because the program really doesn't know if it will ever be resurrected. And if it is resurrected, it should load application settings during the *Activated* event because otherwise it won't know about those settings.

Conclusion: application settings should be loaded during the *Launching* and *Activated* events and saved during the *Deactivated* and *Closing* events.

For the SilverlightIsolatedStorage program, I decided that the number of taps should continue to be treated as transient data—part of the state of the page. But the background color should be an application setting and shared among all instances.

In App.xaml.cs I defined the following public property:

Silverlight Project: SilverlightIsolatedStorage   File: App.xaml.cs (excerpt)

```
public partial class App : Application
{
    // Application settings
    public Brush BackgroundBrush { set; get; }
    ...
}
```

Conceivably this can be one of many application settings that are accessible throughout the application.

App.xaml.cs already has empty event handlers for all the *PhoneApplicationService* events. I gave each handler a body consisting of a single method call:

Silverlight Project: SilverlightIsolatedStorage   File: App.xaml.cs (excerpt)

```
private void Application_Launching(object sender, LaunchingEventArgs e)
{
    LoadSettings();
}

private void Application_Activated(object sender, ActivatedEventArgs e)
{
    LoadSettings();
}

private void Application_Deactivated(object sender, DeactivatedEventArgs e)
{
    SaveSettings();
}

private void Application_Closing(object sender, ClosingEventArgs e)
{
    SaveSettings();
}
```

Here are the *LoadSettings* and *SaveSettings* methods. Both methods obtain an *IsolatedStorageSettings* object. Like the *State* property of *PhoneApplicationService*, the *IsolatedStorageSettings* object is a dictionary. One method in the program loads (and the other saves) the *Color* property of the *BackgroundBrush* property with code that is similar to what you saw before.

Silverlight Project: SilverlightIsolatedStorage   File: App.xaml.cs (excerpt)

```
void LoadSettings()
{
    IsolatedStorageSettings settings = IsolatedStorageSettings.ApplicationSettings;

    Color clr;

    if (settings.TryGetValue<Color>("backgroundColor", out clr))
        BackgroundBrush = new SolidColorBrush(clr);
}

void SaveSettings()
{
    IsolatedStorageSettings settings = IsolatedStorageSettings.ApplicationSettings;

    if (BackgroundBrush is SolidColorBrush)
    {
        settings["backgroundColor"] = (BackgroundBrush as SolidColorBrush).Color;
        settings.Save();
    }
}
```

And finally, here's the new MainPage.xaml.cs file. This file—and any other class in the program—can get access to the *App* object using the static *Application.Current* property and casting it to an *App*. The constructor of *MainPage* obtains the *BackgroundBrush* property from the *App* class, and the *OnManipulationStarted* method sets that *BackgroundBrush* property.

Silverlight Project: SilverlightIsolatedStorage   File: MainPage.xaml.cs (excerpt)

```
public partial class MainPage : PhoneApplicationPage
{
    Random rand = new Random();
    int numTaps = 0;
    PhoneApplicationService appService = PhoneApplicationService.Current;

    public MainPage()
    {
        InitializeComponent();
        UpdatePageTitle(numTaps);
```

```
            // Access App class for isolated storage setting
            Brush brush = (Application.Current as App).BackgroundBrush;

            if (brush != null)
                ContentPanel.Background = brush;
        }

        protected override void OnManipulationStarted(ManipulationStartedEventArgs args)
        {
            SolidColorBrush brush =
                new SolidColorBrush(Color.FromArgb(255, (byte)rand.Next(256),
                                                        (byte)rand.Next(256),
                                                        (byte)rand.Next(256)));
            ContentPanel.Background = brush;

            // Save to App class for isolated storage setting
            (Application.Current as App).BackgroundBrush = brush;

            UpdatePageTitle(++numTaps);

            args.Complete();
            base.OnManipulationStarted(args);
        }

        void UpdatePageTitle(int numTaps)
        {
            PageTitle.Text = String.Format("{0} taps total", numTaps);
        }

        protected override void OnNavigatedFrom(NavigationEventArgs args)
        {
            appService.State["numTaps"] = numTaps;

            base.OnNavigatedFrom(args);
        }

        protected override void OnNavigatedTo(NavigationEventArgs args)
        {
            // Load numTaps
            if (appService.State.ContainsKey("numTaps"))
            {
                numTaps = (int)appService.State["numTaps"];
                UpdatePageTitle(numTaps);
            }
        }
    }
}
```

Because that background color has been upgraded from transient page data to an application setting, references to it have been removed in the *OnNavigatedFrom* and *OnNavigatedTo* overrides.

Xna Tombstoning and Settings

XNA applications aren't normally built around pages like Silverlight applications. If you wanted, however, you could certainly implement your own page-like structure within an XNA program. You'll recall that the state of the phone's Back button is checked during every call to the standard *Update* override. You can use this logic for navigational purposes as well as for terminating the program. But that's something I'll let you work out on your own.

An XNA program can also make use of the same *PhoneApplicationService* class used by Silverlight programs for saving transient state information during tombstoning. An XNA program can also use this class to install handlers for the four *PhoneApplicationService* events: *Launching*, *Activated*, *Deactivated*, and *Closing.* You'll need references both to the Microsoft.Phone library (for *PhoneApplicationService* itself) and System.Windows (for the *IApplicationService* interface that *PhoneApplicationService* implements). Within the Game1.cs file you'll want a *using* directive for *Microsoft.Phone.Shell.*

In the constructor of the *Game1* class you can obtain the *PhoneApplicationService* instance associated with the application through the static *PhoneApplicationService.Current* property.

The *Game* class also defines a couple handy virtual methods named *OnActivated* and *OnDeactivated* that are also useful for handling tombstoning. The *OnActivated* method is called during launching and re-activation, and *OnDeactivated* is called during deactivation and program closing, much like the *OnNavigatedTo* and *OnNavigatedFrom* virtual methods of a Silverlight page.

In the XnaTombstoning program that concludes this chapter I've tried to mimic the functionality and structure of the SilverlightIsolatedStorage program. The program uses the *PhoneApplicationService* events for saving and restoring application settings (a *Color*), and overrides of the *OnDeactivated* and *OnActivated* events for retaining transient data (the number of taps).

But I went a little further in providing a more generalized solution for application settings. I gave the *XnaTombstoning* project a dedicated *Settings* class that uses the more generalized features of isolated storage that involve real files rather than just simple settings. You'll need a reference to System.Xml.Serialization library for this class as well *using* directives for the *System.IO, System.IO.IsolatedStorage,* and *System.Xml.Serialization* namespaces.

Silverlight Project: XnaTombstoning   File: Settings.cs (excerpt)

```
public class Settings
{
    const string filename = "settings.xml";
```

```
    // Application settings
    public Color BackgroundColor { set; get; }

    public Settings()
    {
        BackgroundColor = Color.Navy;
    }

    public void Save()
    {
        IsolatedStorageFile storage = IsolatedStorageFile.GetUserStoreForApplication();
        IsolatedStorageFileStream stream = storage.CreateFile(filename);
        XmlSerializer xml = new XmlSerializer(GetType());
        xml.Serialize(stream, this);
        stream.Close();
        stream.Dispose();
    }

    public static Settings Load()
    {
        IsolatedStorageFile storage = IsolatedStorageFile.GetUserStoreForApplication();
        Settings settings;

        if (storage.FileExists(filename))
        {
            IsolatedStorageFileStream stream =
                    storage.OpenFile("settings.xml", FileMode.Open);
            XmlSerializer xml = new XmlSerializer(typeof(Settings));
            settings = xml.Deserialize(stream) as Settings;
            stream.Close();
            stream.Dispose();
        }
        else
        {
            settings = new Settings();
        }

        return settings;
    }
}
```

The idea here is that an instance of this *Settings* class itself is serialized and saved in isolated storage in the *Save* method, and then retrieved from isolated storage and deserialized in the *Load* method. Notice that the *Load* method is static and returns an instance of the *Settings* class.

When an instance of this *Settings* class is serialized, all its public properties are serialized. This class has exactly one public property of type *Color* named *BackgroundColor* but it would be very easy to add more properties to this class as the application develops and gets more sophisticated.

In the *Save* method, the area of isolated storage reserved for this application is obtained from the static *IsolatedStorageFile.GetUserStoreForApplication* method. This method returns an object of type *IsolatedStorageFile* but the name is a little misleading. This *IsolatedStorageFile* object is closer in functionality to a *file system* than a *file*. You use the object to maintain directories, and to create and open files. A call to *CreateFile* returns an *IsolatedStorageFileStream* which here is used with an *XmlSerializer* object to serialize and save the file.

The *Load* method is a bit more complex because it's possible that the program is being run for the very first time and the settings.xml file does not exist. In that case, the *Load* method creates a new instance of *Settings*.

Notice the constructor that initializes the properties to their default values, which in this case only involves the single public property named *BackgroundColor*. If you add a second public property for another application setting at some point, you'll want to also specify a default value of that property in the constructor. The first time you run the new version of the program, that new property will be initialized in the constructor, but the *Load* method will retrieve a file that doesn't have that property, so the new version smoothly integrates with the previous version.

Here's another consideration: This scheme only works if the properties representing application settings are serializable. For a more complex program, that might not be the case. For objects that are not serializable but still must be saved to isolated storage, you can still include a property for that object in this file but you'll want to flag that property definition with the *[XmlIgnore]* attribute. The property will be ignored for serialization purposes. Instead you'll need to handle that property with special code in the *Save* and *Load* methods.

The remainder of the XnaTombstoning project lets you tap the screen and responds by displaying a new random background color and a count of the number of taps. The background color is treated as an application setting (as is evident by its inclusion in the *Settings* class) and the number of taps is a transient setting.

Here's an excerpt of the *Game1* class showing the fields, constructor, and *PhoneApplicationService* events:

Silverlight Project: XnaTombstoning   File: Game1.cs (excerpt)

```
public class Game1 : Microsoft.Xna.Framework.Game
{
    GraphicsDeviceManager graphics;
    SpriteBatch spriteBatch;

    Settings settings;
    SpriteFont segoe14;
```

```
            Viewport viewport;
            Random rand = new Random();
            StringBuilder text = new StringBuilder();
            Vector2 position;
            int numTaps = 0;

            public Game1()
            {
                graphics = new GraphicsDeviceManager(this);
                Content.RootDirectory = "Content";

                // Frame rate is 30 fps by default for Windows Phone.
                TargetElapsedTime = TimeSpan.FromTicks(333333);

                TouchPanel.EnabledGestures = GestureType.Tap;

                PhoneApplicationService appService = PhoneApplicationService.Current;
                appService.Launching += OnAppServiceLaunching;
                appService.Activated += OnAppServiceActivated;
                appService.Deactivated += OnAppServiceDeactivated;
                appService.Closing += OnAppServiceClosing;
            }

            ...

            void OnAppServiceLaunching(object sender, LaunchingEventArgs args)
            {
                settings = Settings.Load();
            }

            void OnAppServiceActivated(object sender, ActivatedEventArgs args)
            {
                settings = Settings.Load();
            }

            void OnAppServiceDeactivated(object sender, DeactivatedEventArgs args)
            {
                settings.Save();
            }

            void OnAppServiceClosing(object sender, ClosingEventArgs args)
            {
                settings.Save();
            }
        }
```

A *Settings* object named *settings* is saved as a field. The constructor attaches handlers for the four events of *PhoneApplicationService* and it is in the handlers for these events that the application settings are saved and loaded.

The *LoadContent* override contains nothing surprising:

Silverlight Project: XnaTombstoning   File: Game1.cs (excerpt)

```
protected override void LoadContent()
{
    spriteBatch = new SpriteBatch(GraphicsDevice);
    segoe14 = this.Content.Load<SpriteFont>("Segoe14");
    viewport = this.GraphicsDevice.Viewport;
}
```

The *Update* method reads taps, updates the *numTaps* field, determines a new random color, and also prepares a *StringBuilder* object for displaying the number of taps:

Silverlight Project: XnaTombstoning   File: Game1.cs (excerpt)

```
protected override void Update(GameTime gameTime)
{
    // Allows the game to exit
    if (GamePad.GetState(PlayerIndex.One).Buttons.Back == ButtonState.Pressed)
        this.Exit();

    while (TouchPanel.IsGestureAvailable)
        if (TouchPanel.ReadGesture().GestureType == GestureType.Tap)
        {
            numTaps++;
            settings.BackgroundColor =  new Color((byte)rand.Next(255),
                                                  (byte)rand.Next(255),
                                                  (byte)rand.Next(255));
        }

    text.Remove(0, text.Length);
    text.AppendFormat("{0} taps total", numTaps);
    Vector2 textSize = segoe14.MeasureString(text.ToString());
    position = new Vector2((viewport.Width - textSize.X) / 2,
                          (viewport.Height - textSize.Y) / 2);

    base.Update(gameTime);
}
```

Notice that the new color is saved not as a field, but as the *BackgroundColor* property of the *Settings* instance. That property is then referenced in the *Draw* override:

Silverlight Project: XnaTombstoning   File: Game1.cs (excerpt)

```
protected override void Draw(GameTime gameTime)
{
    GraphicsDevice.Clear(settings.BackgroundColor);

    spriteBatch.Begin();
    spriteBatch.DrawString(segoe14, text, position, Color.White);
    spriteBatch.End();

    base.Draw(gameTime);
}
```

The transient value of the *numTaps* field is saved to and restored from the *State* dictionary of the *PhoneApplicationService* in overrides of *OnActivated* and *OnDeactivated*:

Silverlight Project: XnaTombstoning   File: Game1.cs (excerpt)

```
protected override void OnActivated(object sender, EventArgs args)
{
    if (PhoneApplicationService.Current.State.ContainsKey("numTaps"))
        numTaps = (int)PhoneApplicationService.Current.State["numTaps"];

    base.OnActivated(sender, args);
}

protected override void OnDeactivated(object sender, EventArgs args)
{
    PhoneApplicationService.Current.State["numTaps"] = numTaps;
    base.OnDeactivated(sender, args);
}
```

It might seem a little arbitrary to save and restore application settings in one set of event handlers, and save and restore transient settings in another set of overrides to virtual methods, and in a practical sense it is arbitrary. The program will get a call to *OnActivated* about the same time the *Launching* and *Activated* events are fired, and a call to *OnDeactivated* about the same time the *Deactivated* and *Closing* events are fired. The differentiation is more conceptual in that *OnActivated* and *OnDeactivated* are associated with the *Game* instance, so they should be used for properties associated with the game rather than overall application settings.

It's possible that you'll need to save an unserializable object as a transient setting, but because it's not serializable, you can't use the *State* dictionary of the *PhoneApplicationService* class. You'll need to use isolated storage for such an object, but you don't want to accidently retrieve that object and reuse it when the program is run again. In this case, you'll use a flag in the *State* dictionary indicating whether you need to load the transient object from isolated storage.

Testing and Experimentation

Programmers at Microsoft who have been writing Windows Phone 7 applications longer than many of us report that dealing with tombstoning can be one of the trickier aspects of phone development. The techniques I've shown you in this chapter illustrate a good starting point but all applications will have slightly different requirements. Surely you'll want to do a lot of testing in your own programs, and it always helps to know exactly what methods of a program are being called and in what order. For this job, the *Debug.WriteLine* method of the *System.Diagnostics* namespace can be very helpful.

Part II
XNA

Chapter 7
Principles of Movement

Much of the core of an XNA program is dedicated to moving sprites around the screen. Sometimes these sprites move under user control; at other times they move on their own volition as if animated by some internal vital force. Instead of moving real sprites, you can instead move some text, and text is what I'll be sticking with for this entire chapter. The concepts and strategies involved in moving text around the screen are the same as those in moving sprites.

A particular text string seems to move around the screen when it's given a different position in the *DrawString* method during subsequent calls of the *Draw* method in *Game*. In Chapter 1, you'll recall, the *textPosition* variable was simply assigned a fixed value during the *LoadContent* method. This code puts the text in the center of the screen:

```
Vector2 textSize = segoe14.MeasureString(text);
Viewport viewport = this.GraphicsDevice.Viewport;
textPosition = new Vector2((viewport.Width - textSize.X) / 2,
                           (viewport.Height - textSize.Y) / 2);
```

Most of the programs in this chapter recalculate *textPosition* during every call to *Update* so the text is drawn in a different location during the *Draw* method. Usually nothing fancy will be happening; the text will simply be moved from the top of the screen down to the bottom, and then back up to the top, and down again. Lather, rinse, repeat.

I'm going to begin with a rather "naïve" approach to moving text, and then refine it. If you're not accustomed to thinking in terms of vectors or parametric equations, my refinements will at first seem to make the program more complex, but you'll see that the program actually becomes simpler and more flexible.

The Naïve Approach

For this first attempt at text movement, I want to try something simple. I'm just going to move the text up and down vertically so the movement is entirely in one dimension. All we have to worry about is increasing and decreasing the *Y* coordinate of *textPosition*.

If you want to play along, you can create a Visual Studio project named NaiveTextMovement and add the 14-point Segoe UI Mono font to the Content directory. The fields in the *Game1* class are defined like so:

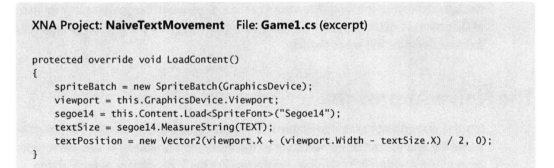

XNA Project: NaiveTextMovement   File: Game1.cs (excerpt showing fields)

```
public class Game1 : Microsoft.Xna.Framework.Game
{
    const float SPEED = 240f;           // pixels per second
    const string TEXT = "Hello, Windows Phone 7!";

    GraphicsDeviceManager graphics;
    SpriteBatch spriteBatch;
    SpriteFont segoe14;
    Viewport viewport;
    Vector2 textSize;
    Vector2 textPosition;
    bool isGoingUp = false;
        . . .
    }
}
```

Nothing should be too startling here. I've defined both the SPEED and TEXT as constants. The SPEED is set at 240 pixels per second. The Boolean *isGoingUp* indicates whether the text is currently moving down the screen or up the screen.

The *LoadContent* method is very familiar from the program in Chapter 1 except that the viewport is saved as a field:

XNA Project: NaiveTextMovement   File: Game1.cs (excerpt)

```
protected override void LoadContent()
{
    spriteBatch = new SpriteBatch(GraphicsDevice);
    viewport = this.GraphicsDevice.Viewport;
    segoe14 = this.Content.Load<SpriteFont>("Segoe14");
    textSize = segoe14.MeasureString(TEXT);
    textPosition = new Vector2(viewport.X + (viewport.Width - textSize.X) / 2, 0);
}
```

Notice that this *textPosition* centers the text horizontally but positions it at the top of the screen. As is usual with most XNA programs, all the real calculational work occurs during the *Update* method:

XNA Project: NaiveTextMovement   File: Game1.cs (excerpt)

```
protected override void Update(GameTime gameTime)
{
    if (GamePad.GetState(PlayerIndex.One).Buttons.Back == ButtonState.Pressed)
        this.Exit();

    if (!isGoingUp)
    {
        textPosition.Y += SPEED * (float)gameTime.ElapsedGameTime.TotalSeconds;
        if (textPosition.Y + textSize.Y > viewport.Height)
        {
            float excess = textPosition.Y + textSize.Y - viewport.Height;
            textPosition.Y -= 2 * excess;
            isGoingUp = true;
        }
    }
    else
    {
        textPosition.Y -= SPEED * (float)gameTime.ElapsedGameTime.TotalSeconds;

        if (textPosition.Y < 0)
        {
            float excess = - textPosition.Y;
            textPosition.Y += 2 * excess;
            isGoingUp = false;
        }
    }

    base.Update(gameTime);
}
```

The *GameTime* argument to *Update* has two crucial properties of type *TimeSpan*: *TotalGameTime* and *ElapsedGameTime*. This "game time" might not exactly keep pace with real time. There are some approximations involved so that animations are smoothly paced. But it's close. *TotalGameTime* reflects the length of time since the game was started; *ElapsedGameTime* is the time since the previous *Update* call. In general, *ElapsedGameTime* will always equal the same value—33-1/3 milliseconds reflecting the 30 Hz refresh rate of the phone's video display.

You can use either *TotalGameTime* or *ElapsedGameTime* to pace movement. In this example, on the first call to *Update*, the *textPosition* has been calculated so the text is positioned on the upper edge of the screen and *isGoingUp* is false. The code increments *textPosition.Y* based on the product of SPEED (which is in units of pixels per second) and the total seconds that have elapsed since the last *Update* call, which will actually be 1/30th second.

It could be that performing this calculation moves the text too far—for example, partially beyond the bottom of the screen. This can be detected if the vertical text position plus the height of the text is greater than the *Bottom* property of the viewport heigh. In that case I calculate something I call *excess*. This is the distance that the vertical text position has exceeded the boundary of the display. I compensate with two times that—as if the text has bounced off the bottom and is now *excess* pixels above the bottom of the screen. At that point, *isGoingUp* is set to *true*.

The logic for moving up is (as I like to say) the same but completely opposite. The actual *Draw* override is simple:

XNA Project: **NaiveTextMovement**   File: **Game1.cs** (excerpt)

```
protected override void Draw(GameTime gameTime)
{
    GraphicsDevice.Clear(Color.Navy);

    spriteBatch.Begin();
    spriteBatch.DrawString(segoe14, TEXT, textPosition, Color.White);
    spriteBatch.End();

    base.Draw(gameTime);
}
```

The big problem with this naïve approach is that it doesn't incorporate any mathematical tools that would allow us to do something a little more complex—for example, move the text diagonally rather than just in one dimension.

What's missing from the NaiveTextMovement program is any concept of direction that would allow escaping from horizontal or vertical movement. What we need are vectors.

A Brief Review of Vectors

A vector is a mathematical entity that encapsulates both a direction and a magnitude. Very often a vector is symbolized by a line with an arrow. These three vectors have the same direction but different magnitudes:

These three vectors have the same magnitude but different directions:

These three vectors have the same magnitude and the same direction, and hence are considered to be identical:

A vector has no location, so even if these three vectors seem to be in different locations and, perhaps for that reason, somewhat distinct, they really aren't in any location at all.

A point has no magnitude and no dimension. A point is *just* location. In two-dimensional space, a point is represented by a number pair (x, y) to represent a horizontal distance and a vertical distance from an origin $(0, 0)$:

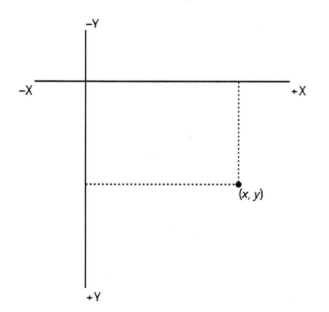

The figure shows increasing values of Y going down for consistency with the two-dimensional coordinate system in XNA. (XNA 3D is different.)

A vector has magnitude and dimension but no location., but like the point a vector is represented by the number pair (*x, y*) except that it's usually written in boldface like **(*x, y*)** to indicate a vector rather than a point.

How can it be that two-dimensional points and two-dimensional vectors are both represented in the same way? Consider two points (*x1, y1*) and (*x2, y2*), and a line from the first point to the second:

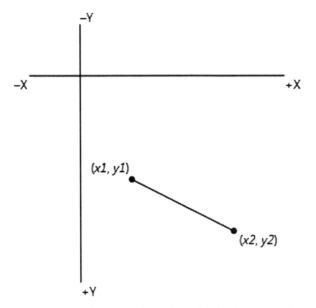

That line has the same length and is in the same direction as a line from the origin to (*x2 – x1, y2 – y1*):

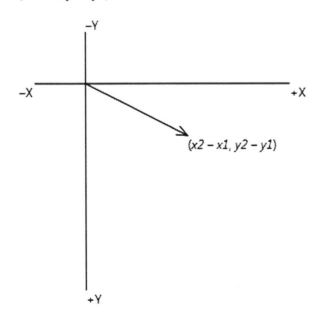

That magnitude and direction define the vector **(x2 – x1, y2 – y1)**.

For that reason, XNA uses the same *Vector2* structure to store two-dimensional coordinate points and two-dimensional vectors. (There is also a *Point* structure in XNA but the *X* and *Y* fields are integers.)

For the vector **(x, y)**, the magnitude is the length of the line from the point (0, 0) to the point (x, y). You can determine the length of the line and the vector using the Pythagorean Theorem, which has the honor of being the most useful tool in computer graphics programming:

$$length = \sqrt{x^2 + y^2}$$

The *Vector2* structure defines a *Distance* method that will perform this calculation for you. *Vector2* also includes a *DistanceSquared* method, which despite the longer name, is actually a simpler calculation. It is very likely that the *Vector2* structure implements *DistanceSquared* like this:

```
public float DistanceSquare()
{
    return x * x + y * y;
}
```

The *Distance* method is then based on *DistanceSquared*:

```
public float Distance()
{
    return (float)Math.Sqrt(DistanceSquare());
}
```

If you only need to compare magnitudes between two vectors, use *DistanceSquared* because it's faster. In the context of working with *Vector2* objects, the terms "length" and "distance" and "magnitude" can be used interchangeably.

Because you can represent points, vectors, and sizes with the same *Vector2* structure, the structure provides plenty of flexibility for performing arithmetic calculations. It's up to you to perform these calculations with some degree of intelligence. For example, suppose *point1* and *point2* are both objects of type *Vector2* but you're using them to represent points. It makes no sense to add those two points together, although *Vector2* will allow you to do so. But it makes lot of sense to *subtract* one point from another to obtain a vector:

```
Vector2 vector = point2 - point1;
```

The operation just subtracts the *X* values and the *Y* values; the vector is in the direction from *point1* to *point2* and its magnitude is the distance between those points. It is also common to add a vector to a point:

```
Vector2 point2 = point1 + vector;
```

This operation obtains a point that is a certain distance and in a certain direction from another point. You can multiply a vector by a single number. If *vector* is an object of type *Vector2*, then

```
vector *= 5;
```

is equivalent to:

```
vector.X *= 5;
vector.Y *= 5;
```

The operation effectively increases the magnitude of the vector by a factor of 5. Similarly you can divide a vector by a number. If you divide a vector by the vector's length, then the resultant length becomes 1. This is known as a *normalized* vector, and *Vector2* has a *Normalize* method specifically for that purpose. The statement:

```
vector.Normalize();
```

is equivalent to

```
vector /= vector.Distance();
```

Often more conveniently, the static *Vector.Normalize* method creates a normalized vector from another vector:

```
Vector normalizedVector = Vector.Normalize(vector)
```

A normalized vector represents just a direction without magnitude, but it can be multiplied by a number to give it that length.

If *vector* has a certain length and direction, then –*vector* has the same length but the opposite direction. I'll make use of this operation in the next program coming up.

The direction of a vector **(x, y)** is the direction from the point (0, 0) to the point (x, y). You can convert that direction to an angle with the second most useful tool in computer graphics programming, the *Math.Atan2* method:

```
float angle = (float)Math.Atan2(vector.Y, vector.X);
```

Notice that the Y component is specified first. The angle is in radians—remember that there are 2π radians to 360 degrees—measured clockwise from the positive X axis.

If you have an angle in radians, you can obtain a normalized vector from it like so:

```
Vector2 vector = new Vector2((float)Math.Cos(angle),
                             (float)Math.Sin(angle));
```

The *Vector2* structure has four static properties: *Vector2.Zero* returns a *Vector2* object with both X and Y set to zero. That's actually an invalid vector because it has no direction, but it's useful for representing a point at the origin. *Vector2.UnitX* is the normalized vector **(1, 0)**, i.e., pointing right in the direction of the positive X axis, and *Vector2.UnitY* is the vector **(0, 1)** pointing up *Vector2.One* is the point (1, 1) or the vector **(1, 1)**, which is useful if you're using the *Vector2* for horizontal and vertical scaling factors (as I do later in this chapter.)

Moving Sprites with Vectors

That little refresher course should provide enough knowledge to revamp the text-moving program to use vectors. This Visual Studio project is called VectorTextMovement. Here are the fields:

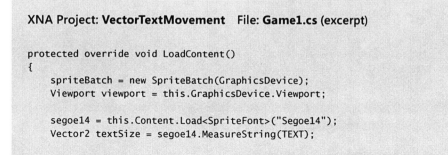

```
XNA Project: VectorTextMovement   File: Game1.cs (excerpt showing fields)

public class Game1 : Microsoft.Xna.Framework.Game
{
    const float SPEED = 240f;            // pixels per second
    const string TEXT = "Hello, Windows Phone 7!";

    GraphicsDeviceManager graphics;
    SpriteBatch spriteBatch;
    SpriteFont segoe14;
    Vector2 midPoint;
    Vector2 pathVector;
    Vector2 pathDirection;
    Vector2 textPosition;
    ...
}
```

The text will be moved between two points (called *position1* and *position2* in the *LoadContent* method), and the *midPoint* field will store the point midway between those two points. The *pathVector* field is the vector from *position1* to *position2*, and *pathDirection* is *pathVector* normalized.

The *LoadContent* method calculates and initializes all these fields:

```
XNA Project: VectorTextMovement   File: Game1.cs (excerpt)

protected override void LoadContent()
{
    spriteBatch = new SpriteBatch(GraphicsDevice);
    Viewport viewport = this.GraphicsDevice.Viewport;

    segoe14 = this.Content.Load<SpriteFont>("Segoe14");
    Vector2 textSize = segoe14.MeasureString(TEXT);
```

```
    Vector2 position1 = new Vector2(viewport.Width - textSize.X, 0);
    Vector2 position2 = new Vector2(0, viewport.Height - textSize.Y);
    midPoint = Vector2.Lerp(position1, position2, 0.5f);

    pathVector = position2 - position1;
    pathDirection = Vector2.Normalize(pathVector);
    textPosition = position1;
}
```

The starting point is *position1*, which puts the text in the upper-right corner. The *position2* point is the lower-left corner. The calculation of *midPoint* makes use of the static *Vector2.Lerp* method, which stands for Linear intERPolation. If the third argument is 0, *Vector2.Lerp* returns its first argument; if the third argument is 1, *Vector2.Lerp* returns its second argument, and for values in between, the method performs a linear interpolation. *Lerp* is probably overkill for calculating a midpoint: All that's really necessary is to average the two *X* values and the two *Y* values.

Note that *pathVector* is the entire vector from *position1* to *position2* while *pathDirection* is the same vector normalized. The method concludes by initializing *textPosition* to *position1*. The use of these fields should become apparent in the *Update* method:

XNA Project: VectorTextMovement   **File: Game1.cs (excerpt)**

```
protected override void Update(GameTime gameTime)
{
    if (GamePad.GetState(PlayerIndex.One).Buttons.Back == ButtonState.Pressed)
        this.Exit();

    float pixelChange = SPEED * (float)gameTime.ElapsedGameTime.TotalSeconds;
    textPosition += pixelChange * pathDirection;

    if ((textPosition - midPoint).LengthSquared() > (0.5f * pathVector).
LengthSquared())
    {
        float excess = (textPosition - midPoint).Length()- (0.5f * pathVector).
Length();
        pathDirection = -pathDirection;
        textPosition += 2 * excess * pathDirection;
    }

    base.Update(gameTime);
}
```

The first time *Update* is called, *textPosition* equals *position1* and *pathDirection* is a normalized vector from *position1* to *position2*. This is the crucial calculation:

```
textPosition += pixelChange * pathDirection;
```

Multiplying the normalized *pathDirection* by *pixelChange* results in a vector that is in the same direction as *pathDirection* but with a length of *pixelChange*. The *textPosition* point is increased by this amount.

After a few seconds of *textPosition* increases, *textPosition* will go beyond *position2*. That can be detected when the length of the vector from *midPoint* to *textPosition* is greater than the length of half the *pathVector*. The direction must be reversed: *pathDirection* is set to the negative of itself, and *textPosition* is adjusted for the bounce.

Notice there's no longer a need to determine if the text is moving up or down. The calculation involving *textPosition* and *midPoint* works for both cases. Also notice that the *if* statement performs a comparison based on *LengthSquared* but the calculation of *excess* requires the actual *Length* method. Because the *if* clause is calculated for every *Update* call, it's good to try to keep the code efficient. The length of half the *pathVector* never changes, so I could have been even more efficient by storing *Length* or *LengthSquared* (or both) as fields.

The *Draw* method is the same as before:

```
XNA Project: VectorTextMovement   File: Game1.cs (excerpt)

protected override void Draw(GameTime gameTime)
{
    GraphicsDevice.Clear(Color.Navy);

    spriteBatch.Begin();
    spriteBatch.DrawString(segoe14, TEXT, textPosition, Color.White);
    spriteBatch.End();

    base.Draw(gameTime);
}
```

Working with Parametric Equations

It is well known that when the math or physics professor says "Now let's introduce a new variable to simplify this mess," no one really believes that the discussion is heading towards a simpler place. But it's very often true, and it's the whole rationale behind parametric equations. Into a seemingly difficult system of formulas a new variable is introduced that is often simply called *t*, as if to suggest *time*. The value of *t* usually ranges from 0 to 1 (although that's just a convention) and other variables are calculated based on *t*. Amazingly enough, simplicity often results.

Let's think about the problem of moving text around the screen in terms of a "lap." One lap consists of the text moving from the upper-right corner (*position1*) to the lower-left corner (*position2*) and back up to *position1*.

How long does that lap take? We can easily calculate the lap time based on the regular speed in pixels-per-second and the length of the lap, which is twice the magnitude of the vector called *pathVector* in the previous program, and which was calculated as *position2 – position1*.

Once we know the speed in laps per second, it should be easy to calculate a *tLap* variable ranging from 0 to 1, where 0 is the beginning of the lap and 1 is the end, at which point *tLap* starts over again at 0. From *tLap* we can get *pLap*, which is a relative position on the lap ranging from 0 (the top or *position1*) to 1 (the bottom or *position2*). From *pLap*, calculating *textPosition* should also be easy. The following table shows the relationship between these three variables:

tLap:	0	0.5	1
pLap:	0	1	0
textPosition:	position1	position2	position1

Probably right away we can see that

```
textPosition = position1 + pLap * pathVector;
```

where *pathVector* (as in the previous program) equals *position2* minus *position1*. The only really tricky part is the calculation of *pLap* based on *tLap*.

The ParametricTextMovement project contains the following fields:

XNA Project: ParametricTextMovement   **File: Game1.cs (excerpt showing fields)**

```
public class Game1 : Microsoft.Xna.Framework.Game
{
    const float SPEED = 240f;              // pixels per second
    const string TEXT = "Hello, Windows Phone 7!";

    GraphicsDeviceManager graphics;
    SpriteBatch spriteBatch;
    SpriteFont segoe14;
    Vector2 position1;
    Vector2 pathVector;
    Vector2 textPosition;
    float lapSpeed;                        // laps per second
    float tLap;
    ...
}
```

The only new variables here are *lapSpeed* and *tLap*. As is now customary, most of the variables are set during the *LoadContent* method:

XNA Project: ParametricTextMovement   File: **Game1.cs** (excerpt)

```
protected override void LoadContent()
{
    spriteBatch = new SpriteBatch(GraphicsDevice);
    Viewport viewport = this.GraphicsDevice.Viewport;

    segoe14 = this.Content.Load<SpriteFont>("Segoe14");
    Vector2 textSize = segoe14.MeasureString(TEXT);
    position1 = new Vector2(viewport.Width - textSize.X, 0);
    Vector2 position2 = new Vector2(0, viewport.Height - textSize.Y);
    pathVector = position2 - position1;

    lapSpeed = SPEED / (2 * pathVector.Length());
}
```

In the calculation of *lapSpeed*, the numerator is in units of pixels-per-second. The denominator is the length of the entire lap, which is two times the length of *pathVector*; therefore the denominator is in units of pixels-per-lap. Dividing pixels-per-second by pixels-per-lap give you a speed in units of laps-per-second.

One of the big advantages of this parametric technique is the sheer elegance of the *Update* method:

XNA Project: ParametricTextMovement   File: **Game1.cs** (excerpt)

```
protected override void Update(GameTime gameTime)
{
    if (GamePad.GetState(PlayerIndex.One).Buttons.Back == ButtonState.Pressed)
        this.Exit();

    tLap += lapSpeed * (float)gameTime.ElapsedGameTime.TotalSeconds;
    tLap %= 1;
    float pLap = tLap < 0.5f ? 2 * tLap : 2 - 2 * tLap;
    textPosition = position1 + pLap * pathVector;

    base.Update(gameTime);
}
```

The *tLap* field is incremented by the *lapSpeed* times the elapsed time in seconds. The second calculation removes any integer part, so if *tLap* is incremented to 1.1 (for example), it gets bumped back down to 0.1.

I will agree the calculation of *pLap* from *tLap*—which is a transfer function of sorts—looks like an indecipherable mess at first. But if you break it down, it's not too bad: If *tLap* is less than 0.5, then *pLap* is twice *tLap*, so for *tLap* from 0 to 0.5, *pLap* goes from 0 to 1. If *tLap* is greater than or equal to 0.5, *tLap* is doubled and subtracted from 2, so for *tLap* from 0.5 to 1, *pLap* goes from 1 back down to 0.

The *Draw* method remains the same:

```
XNA Project: ParametricTextMovement   File: Game1.cs (excerpt)

protected override void Draw(GameTime gameTime)
{
    GraphicsDevice.Clear(Color.Navy);

    spriteBatch.Begin();
    spriteBatch.DrawString(segoe14, TEXT, textPosition, Color.White);
    spriteBatch.End();

    base.Draw(gameTime);
}
```

There are some equivalent ways of performing these calculations. Instead of saving *pathVector* as a field you could save *position2*. Then during the *Update* method you would calculate *textPosition* using the *Vector2.Lerp* method:

```
textPosition = Vector2.Lerp(position1, position2, pLap);
```

In *Update*, instead of calculating an increment to *tLap*, you can calculate *tLap* directly from the *TotalGameState* of the *GameTime* argument and keep the variable local:

```
float tLap = (lapSpeed * (float)gameTime.TotalGameTime.TotalSeconds) % 1;
```

Fiddling with the Transfer Function

I want to change one statement in the ParametricTextMovement program and improve the program enormously by making the movement of the text more natural and fluid. Can it be done? Of course!

Earlier I showed you the following table:

tLap:	0	0.5	1
pLap:	0	1	0
textPosition:	position1	position2	position1

In the ParametricTextMovement project I assumed that the transfer function from *tLap* to *pLap* would be linear, like so:

```
float pLap = tLap < 0.5f ? 2 * tLap : 2 - 2 * tLap;
```

But it doesn't have to be linear. The VariableTextMovement project is the same as ParametricTextMovent except for the calculation of *pLap*, which is now:

```
float pLap = (1 - (float)Math.Cos(tLap * MathHelper.TwoPi)) / 2;
```

When *tLap* is 0, the cosine is 1 and *pLap* is 0. When *tLap* is 0.5, the argument to the cosine function is π radians (180 degrees). The cosine is –1, it's subtracted from 1 and the result is divided by 2, so the result is 1. And so forth. But the difference is dramatic: The text now slows down as it approaches the corners and then speeds up as it moves away.

You can also try a couple others. This one slows down only when it reaches the bottom:

```
float pLap = (float)Math.Sin(tLap * Math.PI);
```

At the top of the screen it's at full velocity and seems to ricochet off the edge of the screen. This one's just the opposite and seems more like a bouncing ball slowed down by gravity at the top:

```
float pLap = 1 - Math.Abs((float)Math.Cos(tLap * Math.PI));
```

So you see that it's true: Using parametric equations not only simplifies the code but makes it much more amenable to enhancements.

Scaling the Text

If you've glanced at the documentation of the *SpriteBatch* class, you've seen five other versions of the *DrawString* method. Until now I've been using this one:

```
DrawString(spriteFont, text, position, color);
```

There are also these two:

```
DrawString(spriteFont, text, position, color, rotation, origin, uniformScale, effects,
layerDepth);
```

```
DrawString(spriteFont, text, position, color, rotation, origin, vectorScale, effects,
layerDepth);
```

The other three versions of *DrawString* are the same except the second argument is a *StringBuilder* rather than a *string*. If you're displaying text that frequently changes, you might want to switch to *StringBuilder* to avoid lots of memory allocations from the local heap.

The additional arguments to these longer versions of *DrawString* are primarily for rotating, scaling, and flipping the text. The exception is the last argument, which is a *float* value that indicates how multiple sprites should be arranged from front (0) to back (1). I won't be using that argument in connection with *DrawString*.

The penultimate argument is a member of the *SpriteEffects* enumeration: The default is *None*. The *FlipHorizontally* and *FlipVertically* members both create mirror images but don't change the location of the text:

SpriteEffects.None

ꙅ꙰Ɉɔɘꟻꟻɘ꙰ɘɈiɿqƨ

ꙅ꙰Ɉɔɘꟻꟻɘ꙰ɘɈiɿqƨ

The alternatives are really the same just flipped 180° from each other.

The argument labeled *origin* is a point with a default value of (0, 0). This argument is used for three related purposes:

- It is the point relative to the text string that is aligned with the *position* argument relative to the screen.

- It is the center of rotation. The *rotation* argument is a clockwise angle in radians.

- It is the center of scaling. Scaling can be specified with either a single number, which scales equally in the horizontal and vertical directions to maintain the correct aspect ratio, or a *Vector2*, which allows unequal horizontal and vertical scaling. (Sometimes these two modes of scaling are called isotropic—equal in all directions—and anisotropic.)

If you use one of the longer versions of *DrawString* and aren't interested in scaling, do not set that argument to zero! Text or a sprite scaled to a zero dimension will not show up on the screen and you'll spend many hours trying to figure out what went wrong. (I speak from experience.) If you don't want any scaling, set the argument to 1 or the static property *Vector2.One*.

The very first XNA program in this book calculated *textPosition* based on the dimensions of the screen and the dimensions of the text:

```
textPosition = new Vector2((viewport.Width - textSize.X) / 2,
                           (viewport.Height - textSize.Y) / 2);
```

The *textPosition* is the point on the screen where the upper-left corner of the text is to be aligned. With the longer versions of *DrawString*, some alternatives become possible. For example:

```
textPosition = new Vector2(viewport.Width / 2, viewport.Height / 2);
origin = new Vector2(textSize.X / 2, textSize.Y / 2);
```

Now the *textPosition* is set to the center of the screen and *origin* is set to the center of the text. This *DrawString* call uses those two variables to put the text in the center of the screen:

```
spriteBatch.DrawString(segoe14, TEXT, textPosition, Color.White,
                       0, origin, 1, SpriteEffects.None, 0);
```

The *textPosition* could be set to the lower-right corner of the screen, and *origin* could be set to the lower-right corner of the text:

```
textPosition = new Vector2(viedwport.Width, viewport.Height);
origin = new Vector2(textSize.X, textSize.Y);
```

Now the text will be positioned in the lower-right corner of the screen.

Rotation and scaling are always relative to a point. This is most obvious with rotation, as anyone who's ever explored the technology of propeller beanies will confirm. But scaling is also relative to a point. As an object grows or shrinks in size, one point remains anchored; that's the point indicated by the *origin* argument to *DrawString*. (The point could actually be outside the area of the scaled object.)

The ScaleTextToViewport project displays a text string in its center and expands it out to fill the viewport. As with the other programs, it includes a font. Here are the fields:

XNA Project: **ScaleTextToViewport**   File: **Game1.cs (excerpt showing fields)**

```
public class Game1 : Microsoft.Xna.Framework.Game
{
    const float SPEED = 0.5f;            // laps per second
    const string TEXT = "Hello, Windows Phone 7!";

    GraphicsDeviceManager graphics;
    SpriteBatch spriteBatch;
    SpriteFont segoe14;
    Vector2 textPosition;
    Vector2 origin;
    Vector2 maxScale;
    Vector2 scale;
    float tLap;
    ...
}
```

The "lap" in this program is a complete cycle of scaling the text up and then back down to normal. During this lap, the *scale* field will vary between *Vector2.One* and *maxScale*.

The *LoadContent* method sets the *textPosition* field to the center of the screen, the *origin* field to the center of the text, and *maxScale* to the maximum scaling factor necessary to fill the screen with the text. All alignment, rotation, and scaling are based on both the center of the text and the center of the screen.

XNA Project: ScaleTextToViewport   File: **Game1.cs** (excerpt)

```
protected override void LoadContent()
{
    spriteBatch = new SpriteBatch(GraphicsDevice);
    Viewport viewport = this.GraphicsDevice.Viewport;

    segoe14 = this.Content.Load<SpriteFont>("Segoe14");
    Vector2 textSize = segoe14.MeasureString(TEXT);
    textPosition = new Vector2(viewport.Width / 2, viewport.Height / 2);
    origin = new Vector2(textSize.X / 2, textSize.Y / 2);
    maxScale = new Vector2(viewport.Width / textSize.X, viewport.Height / textSize.Y);
}
```

As in the previous couple programs, *tLap* repetitively cycles from 0 through 1. During this single lap, the *pLap* variable goes from 0 to 1 and back to 0, where 0 means unscaled and 1 means maximally scaled. The *Vector2.Lerp* method calculates *scale* based on *pLap*.

XNA Project: ScaleTextToViewport   File: **Game1.cs** (excerpt)

```
protected override void Update(GameTime gameTime)
{
    if (GamePad.GetState(PlayerIndex.One).Buttons.Back == ButtonState.Pressed)
        this.Exit();

    tLap = (SPEED * (float)gameTime.TotalGameTime.TotalSeconds) % 1;
    float pLap = (1 - (float)Math.Cos(tLap * MathHelper.TwoPi)) / 2;
    scale = Vector2.Lerp(Vector2.One, maxScale, pLap);

    base.Update(gameTime);
}
```

The *Draw* method uses one of the long versions of *DrawString* with the *textPosition*, *angle*, and *origin* calculated during *LoadContent*, and the *scale* calculated during *Update*:

XNA Project: ScaleTextToViewport   File: **Game1.cs** (excerpt)

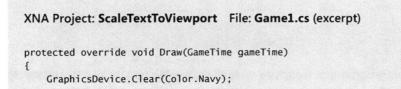

```
protected override void Draw(GameTime gameTime)
{
    GraphicsDevice.Clear(Color.Navy);
```

```
        spriteBatch.Begin();
        spriteBatch.DrawString(segoe14, TEXT, textPosition, Color.White,
                            0, origin, scale, SpriteEffects.None, 0);
        spriteBatch.End();

        base.Draw(gameTime);
    }
```

As you run this program, you'll notice that the vertical scaling doesn't make the top and bottom of the text come anywhere close to the edges of the screen. The reason is that *MeasureString* returns a vertical dimension based on the maximum text height for the font, which includes space for descenders, possible diacritical marks, and a little breathing room as well.

It should also be obvious that you're dealing with a bitmap font here:

The display engine tries to smooth out the jaggies but it's debatable whether the fuzziness is an improvement. If you need to scale text and maintain smooth vector outlines, that's a job for Silverlight. Or, you can start with a large font size and always scale down.

Two Text Rotation Programs

Let's conclude this chapter with two programs that rotate text.

It would be fairly simple to write a program that just rotates text around its center, but let's try something just a little more challenging. Let's gradually speed up the rotation and then stop it when a finger touches the screen. After the finger is released, the rotation should start up slowly again and then get faster. As the speed in revolutions per second approaches the refresh rate of the video display (or some integral fraction thereof), the rotating text should seem to slow down, stop, and reverse. That will be fun to see as well.

A little background about working with acceleration: One of the most common forms of acceleration we experience in day-to-day life involves objects in free-fall. In a vacuum on the surface of the Earth, the effect of gravity produces an acceleration of a constant 32 feet per second per second, or, as it's often called, 32 feet per second squared:

$$a = 32\frac{ft}{sec^2}$$

The seemingly odd units of "feet per second per second" really means that every second, the velocity increases by 32 feet per second. At any time t in seconds, the velocity is given by the simple formula:

$$v(t) = at$$

where a is 32 feet per second squared. When the acceleration in units of feet per second squared is multiplied by a time, the result has units of feet per second, which is a velocity. At 0 seconds, the velocity is 0. At 1 second the velocity is 32 feet per second. At 2 seconds the velocity is 64 feet per second, and so forth.

The distance an object in free fall travels is given by the formula:

$$x(t) = \tfrac{1}{2}at^2$$

Rudimentary calculus makes this family of formulas comprehensible: The velocity is the derivative of the distance, and the acceleration is the derivative of the velocity. In this formula, the acceleration is multiplied by a time squared, so the units reduce to feet. At the end of one second the velocity of an object in free fall is up to 32 feet per second but because the free-fall started at a zero velocity, the object has only traveled a distance of 16 feet. By the end of two seconds, it's gone 64 feet.

In the TouchToStopRotation project, velocity is in units of revolutions per second and acceleration in units of revolutions per second squared. The program requires an additional *using* directive for *System.Text*.

XNA Project: TouchToStopRevolution   File: Game1.cs (excerpt showing fields)

```
public class Game1 : Microsoft.Xna.Framework.Game
{
    const float ACCELERATION = 1;       // revs per second squared
    const float MAXSPEED = 30;          // revs per second
    const string TEXT = "Hello, Windows Phone 7!";

    GraphicsDeviceManager graphics;
    SpriteBatch spriteBatch;
    SpriteFont segoe14;
```

```
    Vector2 textPosition;
    Vector2 origin;
    Vector2 statusPosition;
    float speed;
    float angle;
    StringBuilder strBuilder = new StringBuilder();
    ...

}
```

The MAXSPEED constant is set at 30 revolutions per second, which is the same as the frame rate. As the spinning text reaches that speed, it should appear to stop. The ACCELERATION is 1 revolution per second squared, which means that every second, the velocity increases by 1 revolution per second. At the end of the first second, the speed is 1 revolution per second. At the end of the second second, the speed is 2 revolutions per second. Velocity gets to MAXSPEED at the end of 30 seconds.

The fields include a *speed* variable and a *StringBuilder*, which I'll use for displaying the current velocity on the screen at *statusPosition*. The *LoadContent* method prepares most of these fields:

XNA Project: **TouchToStopRevolution**   File: **Game1.cs (excerpt)**

```
protected override void LoadContent()
{
    spriteBatch = new SpriteBatch(GraphicsDevice);
    Viewport viewport = this.GraphicsDevice.Viewport;
    textPosition = new Vector2(viewport.Width / 2, viewport.Height / 2);

    segoe14 = this.Content.Load<SpriteFont>("Segoe14");
    Vector2 textSize = segoe14.MeasureString(TEXT);
    origin = new Vector2(textSize.X / 2, textSize.Y / 2);
    statusPosition = new Vector2(viewport.Width - textSize.X,
                                 viewport.Height - textSize.Y);
}
```

The *Update* method increases *speed* based on the acceleration, and then increases *angle* based on the new *speed* value.

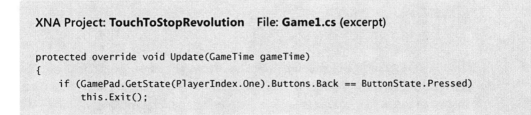

XNA Project: **TouchToStopRevolution**   File: **Game1.cs (excerpt)**

```
protected override void Update(GameTime gameTime)
{
    if (GamePad.GetState(PlayerIndex.One).Buttons.Back == ButtonState.Pressed)
        this.Exit();
```

```
        if (TouchPanel.GetState().Count == 0)
        {
            speed += ACCELERATION * (float)gameTime.ElapsedGameTime.TotalSeconds;
            speed = Math.Min(MAXSPEED, speed);
            angle += MathHelper.TwoPi * speed * (float)gameTime.ElapsedGameTime.
TotalSeconds;
            angle %= MathHelper.TwoPi;
        }
        else
        {
            if (speed == 0)
                SuppressDraw();

            speed = 0;
        }
        strBuilder.Remove(0, strBuilder.Length);
        strBuilder.AppendFormat(" {0:F1} revolutions/second", speed);

        base.Update(gameTime);
    }
```

If *TouchPanel.GetState()* returns a collection containing anything—that is, if anything is touching the screen—then *speed* is set back to zero. Moreover, the next time *Update* is called and something is still touching the screen, then *SuppressDraw* is called. So by touching the screen you're not only inhibiting the rotation of the text, but you're saving power as well.

Also notice the use of *StringBuilder* to update the status field. The *Draw* method is similar to those in previous programs but with two calls to *DrawString*:

XNA Project: **TouchToStopRevolution**   File: **Game1.cs (excerpt)**

```
protected override void Draw(GameTime gameTime)
{
    GraphicsDevice.Clear(Color.Navy);

    spriteBatch.Begin();
    spriteBatch.DrawString(segoe14, strBuilder, statusPosition, Color.White);
    spriteBatch.DrawString(segoe14, TEXT, textPosition, Color.White,
                        angle, origin, 1, SpriteEffects.None, 0);
    spriteBatch.End();

    base.Draw(gameTime);
}
```

For the final program in this chapter, I went back to a default origin of the upper-left corner of the text. But I wanted that upper-left corner of the text string to crawl around the inside perimeter of the display, and I also wanted the text to be fully visible at all times. That implies that the text rotates 90 degrees as it makes it way past each corner. Here's the text maneuvering around the lower-right corner of the display:

The program is called TextCrawl, and the fields should look mostly familiar at this point:

XNA Project: TextCrawl   File: Game1.cs (excerpt showing fields)

```
public class Game1 : Microsoft.Xna.Framework.Game
{
    const float SPEED = 0.1f;            // laps per second
    const string TEXT = "Hello, Windows Phone 7!";

    GraphicsDeviceManager graphics;
    SpriteBatch spriteBatch;
    SpriteFont segoe14;
    Viewport viewport;
    Vector2 textSize;
    Vector2 textPosition;
    float tCorner;           // height / perimeter
    float tLap;
    float angle;
    ...
}
```

The *tLap* variable goes from 0 to 1 as the text makes its way counter-clockwise around the perimeter. To help figure out what side it's currently on, I also define *tCorner*. If *tLap* is less than *tCorner*, the text is on the left edge of the display; if *tLap* is greater than *tCorner* but less than 0.5, it's on the bottom of the display, and so forth. The *LoadContent* method is nothing special:

XNA Project: TextCrawl   File: Game1.cs (excerpt)

```
protected override void LoadContent()
{
    spriteBatch = new SpriteBatch(GraphicsDevice);
```

```
        viewport = this.GraphicsDevice.Viewport;
        tCorner = 0.5f * viewport.Height / (viewport.Width + viewport.Height);
        segoe14 = this.Content.Load<SpriteFont>("Segoe14");
        textSize = segoe14.MeasureString(TEXT);
    }
```

The *Update* method is the real monster, I'm afraid. The objective here is to calculate a *textPosition* and *angle* for the eventual call to *DrawString*.

XNA Project: TextCrawl   File: Game1.cs (excerpt)

```
protected override void Update(GameTime gameTime)
{
    if (GamePad.GetState(PlayerIndex.One).Buttons.Back == ButtonState.Pressed)
        this.Exit();

    tLap = (tLap + SPEED * (float)gameTime.ElapsedGameTime.TotalSeconds) % 1;

    if (tLap < tCorner)              // down left side of screen
    {
        textPosition.X = 0;
        textPosition.Y = (tLap / tCorner) * viewport.Height;
        angle = -MathHelper.PiOver2;

        if (textPosition.Y < textSize.X)
            angle += (float)Math.Acos(textPosition.Y / textSize.X);
    }
    else if (tLap < 0.5f)            // across bottom of screen
    {
        textPosition.X = ((tLap - tCorner) / (0.5f - tCorner)) * viewport.Width;
        textPosition.Y = viewport.Height;
        angle = MathHelper.Pi;

        if (textPosition.X < textSize.X)
            angle += (float)Math.Acos(textPosition.X / textSize.X);
    }
    else if (tLap < 0.5f + tCorner) // up right side of screen
    {
        textPosition.X = viewport.Width;
        textPosition.Y = (1 - (tLap - 0.5f) / tCorner) * viewport.Height;
        angle = MathHelper.PiOver2;

        if (textPosition.Y + textSize.X > viewport.Height)
            angle += (float)Math.Acos((viewport.Height - textPosition.Y) /
textSize.X);
    }
    else                            // across top of screen
    {
        textPosition.X = (1 - (tLap - 0.5f - tCorner) / (0.5f - tCorner)) * viewport.
Width;
```

```
        textPosition.Y = 0;
        angle = 0;

        if (textPosition.X + textSize.X > viewport.Width)
            angle += (float)Math.Acos((viewport.Width - textPosition.X) / textSize.X);
    }

    base.Update(gameTime);
}
```

As I was developing this code, I found it convenient to concentrate on getting the first three statements in each *if* and *else* block working correctly. These statements simply move the upper-left corner of the text string counter-clockwise around the inside perimeter of the display. The initial calculation of *angle* ensures that the top of the text is flush against the edge. Only when I got all that working was I ready to attack the code that alters *angle* for the movement around the corners. A couple simple drawings convinced me that the inverse cosine was the right tool for the job. After all that work in *Update*, the *Draw* method is trivial:

XNA Project: TextCrawl   File: Game1.cs (excerpt)

```
protected override void Draw(GameTime gameTime)
{
    GraphicsDevice.Clear(Color.Navy);

    spriteBatch.Begin();
    spriteBatch.DrawString(segoe14, TEXT, textPosition, Color.White,
                        angle, Vector2.Zero, 1, SpriteEffects.None, 0);
    spriteBatch.End();

    base.Draw(gameTime);
}
```

In the next chapter you'll see how to make sprites travel along curves.

Chapter 8
Textures and Sprites

I promised that learning how to use XNA to move text around the screen would provide a leg up in the art of moving regular bitmap sprites. This relationship becomes very obvious when you begin examining the *Draw* methods supported by the *SpriteBatch*. The *Draw* methods have almost the same arguments as *DrawString* but work with bitmaps rather than text. In this chapter I'll examine techniques for moving and turning sprites, particularly along curves.

The *Draw* Variants

Both the *Game* class and the *SpriteBatch* class have methods named *Draw*. Despite the identical names, the two methods are not genealogically related through a class hierarchy. In a class derived from *Game* you override the *Draw* method so that you can call the *Draw* method of *SpriteBatch*. This latter *Draw* method comes in seven different versions. The simplest one is:

```
Draw(Texture2D texture, Vector2 position, Color color)
```

The first argument is a *Texture2D*, which is basically a bitmap. A *Texture2D* is potentially a little more complex than an ordinary bitmap because it could have multiple "mipmap" levels. (These represent the same image but at different resolutions to allow the image to be displayed at a variety of sizes.) The *Texture2D* objects that I'll be discussing there are plain old bitmaps. Professional game developers often use specialized tools to create these bitmaps, but I'm going to use Paint because it's readily available. After you create these bitmaps, you add them to the content of the XNA project, and then load them into your program the same way you load a font.

The second argument to *Draw* indicates where the bitmap is to appear on the display. By default, the *position* argument indicates the point on the display where the upper-left corner of the texture is to appear.

The *Color* argument is used a little differently than with *DrawString* because the texture itself can contain color information. The argument is referred to in the documentation as a "color channel modulation," and it serves as a filter through which to view the bitmap.

Conceptually, every pixel in the bitmap has a one-byte red value, a one-byte green value, and a one-byte blue value (ignoring alpha for the moment). When the bitmap is displayed by *Draw*, these red, green, and blue colors values are effectively multiplied by the one-byte red, green, and blue values of the *Color* argument to *Draw*, and the results are divided by 255 to bring them back in the range of 0 to 255. That's what's used to color that pixel.

For example, suppose your texture has lots of color information and you wish all those colors to be preserved on the display. Use a value of *Color.White* in the *Draw* method.

Now suppose you want to draw that same texture but darker. Perhaps the sun is setting in your game world. Use some gray color value in the *Draw* method. The darker the gray, the darker the texture will appear. If you use *Color.Black*, the texture will appear as a silhouette with no color.

Suppose your texture is all white and you wish to display it as blue. Use *Color.Blue* in the *Draw* method. You can display the same all-white texture in a variety of colors. (I'll do precisely that in the first sample program in this chapter.)

If your texture is yellow (a combination of red and green) and you use *Color.Green* in the *Draw* method, it will be displayed as green. If you use *Color.Red* in the *Draw* method it will be displayed as red. If you use *Color.Blue* in the *Draw* method, it will turn black. The argument to *Draw* can only attenuate or suppress color. You cannot get colors that aren't in the texture to begin with.

The second version of the *Draw* method is:

```
Draw(Texture2D texture, Rectangle destination, Color color)
```

Instead of a *Vector2* to indicate the position of the texture, you use a *Rectangle*, which is the combination of a point (the upper-left corner), a width, and a height. If the width and height of the *Rectangle* don't match the width and height of the texture, the texture will be scaled to the size of the *Rectangle*. The original aspect ratio is ignored.

If you only want to display a rectangular subset of the texture, you can use one of the two slightly expanded versions of the *Draw* method:

```
Draw(Texture2D texture, Vector2 position, Rectangle? source, Color color)
Draw(Texture2D texture, Rectangle destination, Rectangle? source, Color color)
```

The third arguments are nullable *Rectangle* objects. If you set this argument to *null*, the result is the same as using one of the first two versions of *Draw*. Otherwise you can specify a pixel subset of the image.

The next two versions of *Draw* have five additional arguments that you'll recognize from the *DrawString* methods:

```
Draw(Texture2D texture, Vector2 position, Rectangle? source, Color color,
     float rotation, Vector2 origin, float scale, SpriteEffects effects, float depth)

Draw(Texture2D texture, Vector2 position, Rectangle? source, Color color,
     float rotation, Vector2 origin, Vector2 scale, SpriteEffects effects, float depth)
```

As with *DrawString*, the *rotation* angle is in radians, measured clockwise. The *origin* is a point in the texture that is to be aligned with the *position* argument. You can scale uniformly with a single *float* or differently in the horizontal and vertical directions with a *Vector2*. The *SpriteEffects* enumeration lets you flip an image horizontally or vertically to get its mirror image. The last argument allows overriding the defaults for layering multiple textures on the screen.

Finally, there's also a slightly shorter longer version where the second argument is a destination rectangle:

```
spriteBatch.Draw(Texture2D texture, Rectangle destination, Rectangle? source, Color color,
                 float rotation, Vector2 origin, SpriteEffects effects, float depth)
```

Notice there's no separate scaling argument because scaling in this one is handled through the *destination* argument.

Within the *Draw* method of your *Game* class, you use the *SpriteBatch* object like so:

```
spriteBatch.Begin();
spriteBatch.Draw ...
spriteBatch.End();
```

Within the *Begin* and *End* calls, you can have any number of calls to *Draw* and *DrawString*. The *Draw* calls can reference the same texture. You can also have multiple calls to *Begin* followed by *End* with *Draw* and *DrawString* in between.

Another Hello Program?

If you're tired of "hello, world" programs by now, I've got some bad news. But this time I'll compose a very blocky rendition of the word "HELLO" using two different bitmaps—a vertical bar and a horizontal bar. The letter "H" will be two vertical bars and one horizontal bar. The "O" at the end will look like a rectangle.

And then, when you tap the screen, all 15 bars will fly apart in random directions and then come back together. Sound like fun?

If you were creating the FlyAwayHello program in scratch, the first step would be to add content to the Content directory—not a font this time but two bitmaps called HorzBar.png and VertBar.png. You can create these right in Visual Studio or in Paint. By default, Paint creates an all-white bitmap for you. That's ideal! All I want you to do is change the size. Click the Paint Button menu (upper-left below the title bar) and select Properties. Change the size to 45 pixels wide and 5 pixels high. (The exact dimensions really don't matter; the program is coded to be a little flexible.) It's most convenient to save the file right in the Content directory of the project under the name HorzBar.png. Now change the size to 5 pixels wide and 75 pixels high. Save under the name VertBar.png.

Although the bitmaps are now in the proper directory, the XNA project doesn't know of their existence. In Visual Studio, right click the Content directory and choose Add Existing Item. You can select both PNG files and add them to the project.

I'm going to use a little class called *SpriteInfo* to keep track of the 15 textures required for forming the text. If you're creating the project from scratch, right-click the project name, and select Add and then New Item (or select Add New Item from the main Project menu). From the dialog box select Class and give it the name SpriteInfo.cs.

XNA Project: **FlyAwayHello**   File: **SpriteInfo.cs** (complete)

```csharp
using Microsoft.Xna.Framework;
using Microsoft.Xna.Framework.Graphics;

namespace FlyAwayHello
{
    public class SpriteInfo
    {
        public static float InterpolationFactor { set; get; }

        public Texture2D Texture2D { protected set; get; }
        public Vector2 BasePosition { protected set; get; }
        public Vector2 PositionOffset { set; get; }
        public float MaximumRotation { set; get; }

        public SpriteInfo(Texture2D texture2D, int x, int y)
        {
            Texture2D = texture2D;
            BasePosition = new Vector2(x, y);
        }

        public Vector2 Position
        {
            get
            {
                return BasePosition + InterpolationFactor * PositionOffset;
            }
        }

        public float Rotation
        {
            get
            {
                return InterpolationFactor * MaximumRotation;
            }
        }
    }
}
```

The required constructor stores a *Texture2D* along with positioning information. This is how each sprite is initially positioned to spell out the word "HELLO." Later in the "fly away" animation, the program sets the *PositionOffset* and *MaximumRotation* properties. The *Position* and *Rotation* properties perform calculations based on the static *InterpolationFactor*, which can range from 0 to 1.

Here are the fields of the *Game1* class:

XNA Project: FlyAwayHello   File: **Game1.cs (excerpt showing fields)**

```
public class Game1 : Microsoft.Xna.Framework.Game
{
    static readonly TimeSpan ANIMATION_DURATION = TimeSpan.FromSeconds(5);
    const int CHAR_SPACING = 5;

    GraphicsDeviceManager graphics;
    SpriteBatch spriteBatch;
    Viewport viewport;
    List<SpriteInfo> spriteInfos = new List<SpriteInfo>();
    Random rand = new Random();
    bool isAnimationGoing;
    TimeSpan animationStartTime;
    ...
}
```

This program initiates an animation only when the user taps the screen, so I'm handling the timing just a little differently than in earlier programs, as I'll demonstrate in the *Update* method.

The *LoadContent* method loads the two *Texture2D* objects using the same generic *Load* method that previous programs used to load a *SpriteFont*. Enough information is now available to create and initialize all *SpriteInfo* objects:

XNA Project: FlyAwayHello   File: **Game1.cs (excerpt)**

```
protected override void LoadContent()
{
    spriteBatch = new SpriteBatch(GraphicsDevice);
    viewport = this.GraphicsDevice.Viewport;

    Texture2D horzBar = Content.Load<Texture2D>("HorzBar");
    Texture2D vertBar = Content.Load<Texture2D>("VertBar");

    int x = (viewport.Width - 5 * horzBar.Width - 4 * CHAR_SPACING) / 2;
    int y = (viewport.Height - vertBar.Height) / 2;
    int xRight = horzBar.Width - vertBar.Width;
    int yMiddle = (vertBar.Height - horzBar.Height) / 2;
    int yBottom = vertBar.Height - horzBar.Height;

    // H
    spriteInfos.Add(new SpriteInfo(vertBar, x, y));
    spriteInfos.Add(new SpriteInfo(vertBar, x + xRight, y));
    spriteInfos.Add(new SpriteInfo(horzBar, x, y + yMiddle));
```

```
    // E
    x += horzBar.Width + CHAR_SPACING;
    spriteInfos.Add(new SpriteInfo(vertBar, x, y));
    spriteInfos.Add(new SpriteInfo(horzBar, x, y));
    spriteInfos.Add(new SpriteInfo(horzBar, x, y + yMiddle));
    spriteInfos.Add(new SpriteInfo(horzBar, x, y + yBottom));

    // LL
    for (int i = 0; i < 2; i++)
    {
        x += horzBar.Width + CHAR_SPACING;
        spriteInfos.Add(new SpriteInfo(vertBar, x, y));
        spriteInfos.Add(new SpriteInfo(horzBar, x, y + yBottom));
    }

    // O
    x += horzBar.Width + CHAR_SPACING;
    spriteInfos.Add(new SpriteInfo(vertBar, x, y));
    spriteInfos.Add(new SpriteInfo(horzBar, x, y));
    spriteInfos.Add(new SpriteInfo(horzBar, x, y + yBottom));
    spriteInfos.Add(new SpriteInfo(vertBar, x + xRight, y));
}
```

The *Update* method is responsible for keeping the animation going. If the *isAnimationGoing* field is *false*, it checks for a new finger pressed on the screen.

XNA Project: FlyAwayHello   File: Game1.cs (excerpt)

```
protected override void Update(GameTime gameTime)
{
    if (GamePad.GetState(PlayerIndex.One).Buttons.Back == ButtonState.Pressed)
        this.Exit();

    if (isAnimationGoing)
    {
        TimeSpan animationTime = gameTime.TotalGameTime - animationStartTime;
        double fractionTime = (double)animationTime.Ticks /
                                            ANIMATION_DURATION.Ticks;

        if (fractionTime >= 1)
        {
            isAnimationGoing = false;
            fractionTime = 1;
        }

        SpriteInfo.InterpolationFactor = (float)Math.Sin(Math.PI * fractionTime);
    }
    else
    {
        TouchCollection touchCollection = TouchPanel.GetState();
```

```
        bool atLeastOneTouchPointPressed = false;

        foreach (TouchLocation touchLocation in touchCollection)
            atLeastOneTouchPointPressed |=
                touchLocation.State == TouchLocationState.Pressed;

        if (atLeastOneTouchPointPressed)
        {
            foreach (SpriteInfo spriteInfo in spriteInfos)
            {
                float r1 = (float)rand.NextDouble() - 0.5f;
                float r2 = (float)rand.NextDouble() - 0.5f;
                float r3 = (float)rand.NextDouble();

                spriteInfo.PositionOffset = new Vector2(r1 * viewport.Width,
                                                        r2 * viewport.Height);
                spriteInfo.MaximumRotation = 2 * (float)Math.PI * r3;
            }
            animationStartTime = gameTime.TotalGameTime;
            isAnimationGoing = true;
        }
    }
    base.Update(gameTime);
}
```

When the animation begins, the *animationStartTime* is set from the *TotalGameTime* property of *GameTime*. During subsequent calls, *Update* compares that value with the new *TotalGameTime* and calculates an interpolation factor. The *InterpolationFactor* property of *SpriteInfo* is static so it need be set only once to affect all the *SpriteInfo* instances. The *Draw* method loops through the *SpriteInfo* objects to access the *Position* and *Rotation* properties:

XNA Project: FlyAwayHello   File: Game1.cs (excerpt)

```
protected override void Draw(GameTime gameTime)
{
    GraphicsDevice.Clear(Color.Navy);
    spriteBatch.Begin();

    foreach (SpriteInfo spriteInfo in spriteInfos)
    {
        spriteBatch.Draw(spriteInfo.Texture2D, spriteInfo.Position, null,
            Color.Lerp(Color.Blue, Color.Red, SpriteInfo.InterpolationFactor),
            spriteInfo.Rotation, Vector2.Zero, 1, SpriteEffects.None, 0);
    }

    spriteBatch.End();
    base.Draw(gameTime);
}
```

The *Draw* call also uses *SpriteInfo.InterpolationFactor* to interpolate between blue and red for coloring the bars. Notice that the *Color* structure also has a *Lerp* method. The text is normally blue but changes to red as the pieces fly apart.

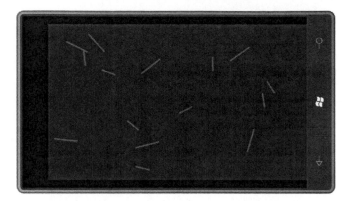

That call to *Draw* could actually be part of *SpriteInfo*. *SpriteInfo* could define its own *Draw* method with an argument of type *SpriteBatch*, and then pass its own *Texture2D, Position*, and *Rotation* properties to the *Draw* method of the *SpriteBatch*:

```
public void Draw(SpriteBatch spriteBatch)
{
    spriteBatch.Draw(Texture2D, Position, null,
                     Color.Lerp(Color.Blue, Color.Red, InterpolationFactor),
                     Rotation, Vector2.Zero, 1, SpriteEffects.None, 0);
}
```

The loop in the *Draw* override of the *Game1* glass then looks like this:

```
foreach (SpriteInfo spriteInfo in spriteInfos)
{
    spriteInfo.Draw(spriteBatch);
}
```

This is a common technique and allows *SpriteInfo* to have fewer public properties.

Driving Around the Block

For the remainder of this chapter I want to focus on techniques to maneuver a sprite around some kind of path. To make it more "realistic," I commissioned my wife Deirdre to make a little race-car in Paint:

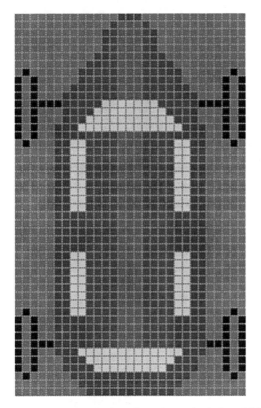

The car is 48 pixels tall and 29 pixels in width. Notice the magenta background: If you want part of an image to be transparent in an XNA scene, you can use a 32-bit bitmap format that supports transparency, such as PNG. Each pixel in this format has 8-bit red, green, and blue components but also an 8-bit alpha channel for transparency. (I'll explore this format in the next chapter.) The Paint program in Windows does not support bitmap transparency, alas, but you can use magenta instead. In Paint, create magenta by setting the red and blue values to 255 and green to 0.

In each of the projects in this chapter, this image is stored as the file car.png as part of the project's content. The first project is called CarOnRectangularCourse and demonstrates a rather clunky approach to driving a car around the perimeter of the screen. Here are the fields:

XNA Project: **CarOnRectangularCourse**   File: **Game1.cs** (excerpt showing fields)

```
public class Game1 : Microsoft.Xna.Framework.Game
{
    const float SPEED = 100;            // pixels per second
    GraphicsDeviceManager graphics;
    SpriteBatch spriteBatch;
```

```
    Texture2D car;
    Vector2 carCenter;
    Vector2[] turnPoints = new Vector2[4];
    int sideIndex = 0;
    Vector2 position;
    float rotation;
    ...
}
```

The *turnPoints* array stores the four points near the corners of the display where the car makes a sharp turn. Calculating these points is one of the primary activities of the *LoadContent* method, which also loads the *Texture2D* and initializes other fields:

XNA Project: CarOnRectangularCourse   File: Game1.cs (excerpt)

```
protected override void LoadContent()
{
    spriteBatch = new SpriteBatch(GraphicsDevice);
    car = this.Content.Load<Texture2D>("car");
    carCenter = new Vector2(car.Width / 2, car.Height / 2);
    float margin = car.Width;
    Viewport viewport = this.GraphicsDevice.Viewport;
    turnPoints[0] = new Vector2(margin, margin);
    turnPoints[1] = new Vector2(viewport.Width - margin, margin);
    turnPoints[2] = new Vector2(viewport.Width - margin, viewport.Height - margin);
    turnPoints[3] = new Vector2(margin, viewport.Height - margin);
    position = turnPoints[0];
    rotation = MathHelper.PiOver2;
}
```

I use the *carCenter* field as the *origin* argument to the *Draw* method, so that's the point on the car that aligns with a point on the course defined by the four members of the *turnPoints* array. The *margin* value makes this course one car width from the edge of the display; hence the car is really separated from the edge of the display by half its width.

I described this program as "clunky" and the *Update* method proves it:

XNA Project: CarOnRectangularCourse   File: Game1.cs (excerpt)

```
protected override void Update(GameTime gameTime)
{
    if (GamePad.GetState(PlayerIndex.One).Buttons.Back == ButtonState.Pressed)
        this.Exit();

    float pixels = SPEED * (float)gameTime.ElapsedGameTime.TotalSeconds;
```

```
    switch (sideIndex)
    {
        case 0:          // top
            position.X += pixels;

            if (position.X > turnPoints[1].X)
            {
                position.X = turnPoints[1].X;
                position.Y = turnPoints[1].Y + (position.X - turnPoints[1].X);
                rotation = MathHelper.Pi;
                sideIndex = 1;
            }
            break;

        case 1:          // right
            position.Y += pixels;

            if (position.Y > turnPoints[2].Y)
            {
                position.Y = turnPoints[2].Y;
                position.X = turnPoints[2].X - (position.Y - turnPoints[2].Y);
                rotation = -MathHelper.PiOver2;
                sideIndex = 2;
            }
            break;

        case 2:          // bottom
            position.X -= pixels;

            if (position.X < turnPoints[3].X)
            {
                position.X = turnPoints[3].X;
                position.Y = turnPoints[3].Y + (position.X - turnPoints[3].X);
                rotation = 0;
                sideIndex = 3;
            }
            break;

        case 3:          // left
            position.Y -= pixels;

            if (position.Y < turnPoints[0].Y)
            {
                position.Y = turnPoints[0].Y;
                position.X = turnPoints[0].X - (position.Y - turnPoints[0].Y);
                rotation = MathHelper.PiOver2;
                sideIndex = 0;
            }
            break;
    }
    base.Update(gameTime);
}
```

This is the type of code that screams out "There's got to be a better way!" Elegant it is not, and not very versatile either. But before I take a stab at a more flexible approach, here's the entirely predictable *Draw* method that incorporates the updated *position* and *rotation* values calculated during *Update*:

XNA Project: **CarOnRectangularCourse**   File: **Game1.cs** (excerpt)

```
protected override void Draw(GameTime gameTime)
{
    GraphicsDevice.Clear(Color.Blue);

    spriteBatch.Begin();
    spriteBatch.Draw(car, position, null, Color.White, rotation,
                     carCenter, 1, SpriteEffects.None, 0);
    spriteBatch.End();

    base.Draw(gameTime);
}
```

Movement Along a Polyline

The code in the previous program will work for any rectangle whose corners are stored in the *turnPoints* array, but it won't work for any arbitrary collection of four points, or more than four points. In computer graphics, a collection of points that describe a series of straight lines is often called a *polyline*, and it would be nice to write some code that makes the car travel along any arbitrary polyline.

The next project, called CarOnPolylineCourse, includes a class named *PolylineInterpolator* that does precisely that. Let me show you the *Game1* class first, and then I'll describe the *PolylineInterpolator* class that makes it all possible. Here are the fields:

XNA Project: **CarOnPolylineCourse**   File: **Game1.cs** (excerpt showing fields)

```
public class Game1 : Microsoft.Xna.Framework.Game
{
    const float SPEED = 0.25f;            // laps per second
    GraphicsDeviceManager graphics;
    SpriteBatch spriteBatch;
    Texture2D car;
    Vector2 carCenter;
    PolylineInterpolator polylineInterpolator = new PolylineInterpolator();
    Vector2 position;
    float rotation;
    ...
}
```

You'll notice a speed in terms of laps, and the instantiation of the mysterious *PolylineInterpolator* class. The *LoadContent* method is very much like that in the previous project except instead of adding points to an array called *turnPoints*, it adds them to a *Vertices* property of the *PolylineInterpolator* class:

XNA Project: CarOnPolylineCourse   File: Game1.cs (excerpt)

```
protected override void LoadContent()
{
    spriteBatch = new SpriteBatch(GraphicsDevice);
    car = this.Content.Load<Texture2D>("Car");
    carCenter = new Vector2(car.Width / 2, car.Height / 2);
    float margin = car.Width;
    Viewport viewport = this.GraphicsDevice.Viewport;

    polylineInterpolator.Vertices.Add(
            new Vector2(car.Width, car.Width));
    polylineInterpolator.Vertices.Add(
            new Vector2(viewport.Width - car.Width, car.Width));
    polylineInterpolator.Vertices.Add(
            new Vector2(car.Width, viewport.Height - car.Width));
    polylineInterpolator.Vertices.Add(
            new Vector2(viewport.Width - car.Width, viewport.Height - car.Width));
    polylineInterpolator.Vertices.Add(
            new Vector2(car.Width, car.Width));
}
```

Also notice that the method adds the beginning point in again at the end, and that these points don't exactly describe the same course as the previous project. The previous project caused the car to travel from the upper-left to the upper-right down to lower-right and across to the lower-left and back up to upper-left. The order here goes from upper-left to upper-right but then diagonally down to lower-left and across to lower-right before another diagonal trip up to the beginning. This is precisely the kind of versatility the previous program lacked.

As with the programs in the last chapter that used parametric equations, the *Update* method is now so simple it makes you want to weep:

XNA Project: CarOnPolylineCourse   File: Game1.cs (excerpt)

```
protected override void Update(GameTime gameTime)
{
    if (GamePad.GetState(PlayerIndex.One).Buttons.Back == ButtonState.Pressed)
        this.Exit();

    float t = (SPEED * (float)gameTime.TotalGameTime.TotalSeconds) % 1;
    float angle;
```

```
        position = polylineInterpolator.GetValue(t, false, out angle);
        rotation = angle + MathHelper.PiOver2;

        base.Update(gameTime);
    }
```

As usual, *t* is calculated to range from 0 to 1, where 0 indicates the beginning of the course in the upper-left corner of the screen, and *t* approaches 1 as it's heading towards that initial position again. This *t* is passed directly to the *GetValue* method of *PolylineInterpolator*, which returns a *Vector2* value somewhere along the polyline.

As an extra bonus, the last argument of *GetValue* allows obtaining an *angle* value that is the tangent of the polyline at that point. This angle is measured clockwise relative to the positive X axis. For example, when the car is travelling from the upper-left corner to the upper-right, *angle* is 0. When the car is travelling from the upper-right corner to the lower-left, the angle is somewhere between $\pi/2$ and π, depending on the aspect ratio of the screen. The car in the bitmap is facing up so it needs to be rotated an additional $\pi/2$ radians.

The *Draw* method is the same as before:

XNA Project: CarOnPolylineCourse   File: Game1.cs (excerpt)

```
protected override void Draw(GameTime gameTime)
{
    GraphicsDevice.Clear(Color.Blue);

    spriteBatch.Begin();
    spriteBatch.Draw(car, position, null, Color.White, rotation,
                        carCenter, 1, SpriteEffects.None, 0);
    spriteBatch.End();

    base.Draw(gameTime);
}
```

Here's the car heading towards the lower-left corner:

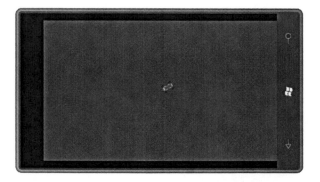

For demonstration purposes, the *PolylineInterpolator* class sacrifices efficiency for simplicity. Here's the entire class:

XNA Project: CarOnPolylineCourse File: **PolylineInterpolator.cs** (complete)

```
using System;
using System.Collections.Generic;
using Microsoft.Xna.Framework;

namespace CarOnPolylineCourse
{
    public class PolylineInterpolator
    {
        public PolylineInterpolator()
        {
            Vertices = new List<Vector2>();
        }

        public List<Vector2> Vertices { protected set; get; }

        public float TotalLength()
        {
            float totalLength = 0;

            // Notice looping begins at index 1
            for (int i = 1; i < Vertices.Count; i++)
            {
                totalLength += (Vertices[i] - Vertices[i - 1]).Length();
            }
            return totalLength;
        }

        public Vector2 GetValue(float t, bool smooth, out float angle)
        {
            if (Vertices.Count == 0)
            {
                return GetValue(Vector2.Zero, Vector2.Zero, t, smooth, out angle);
            }

            else if (Vertices.Count == 1)
            {
                return GetValue(Vertices[0], Vertices[0], t, smooth, out angle);
            }

            if (Vertices.Count == 2)
            {
                return GetValue(Vertices[0], Vertices[1], t, smooth, out angle);
            }

            // Calculate total length
            float totalLength = TotalLength();
            float accumLength = 0;
```

```
        // Notice looping begins at index 1
        for (int i = 1; i < Vertices.Count; i++)
        {
            float prevLength = accumLength;
            accumLength += (Vertices[i] - Vertices[i - 1]).Length();

            if (t >= prevLength / totalLength && t <= accumLength / totalLength)
            {
                float tPrev = prevLength / totalLength;
                float tThis = accumLength / totalLength;
                float tNew = (t - tPrev) / (tThis - tPrev);

                return GetValue(Vertices[i - 1], Vertices[i],
                                tNew, smooth, out angle);
            }
        }

        return GetValue(Vector2.Zero, Vector2.Zero, t, smooth, out angle);
    }

    Vector2 GetValue(Vector2 vertex1, Vector2 vertex2, float t,
                     bool smooth, out float angle)
    {
        angle = (float)Math.Atan2(vertex2.Y - vertex1.Y, vertex2.X - vertex1.X);

        return smooth ? Vector2.SmoothStep(vertex1, vertex2, t) :
                        Vector2.Lerp(vertex1, vertex2, t);
    }
  }
}
```

The single *Vertices* property allows you to define a collection of *Vector2* objects that define the polyline. If you want the polyline to end up where it started, you need to explicitly duplicate that point. All the work occurs during the *GetValue* method. At that time, the method determines the total length of the polyline. It then loops through the vertices and accumulates their lengths, finding the pair of vertices whose accumulated length straddles the *t* value. These are passed to the private *GetValue* method to perform the linear interpolation using *Vector2.Lerp*, and to calculate the tangent angle with the graphics programmer's second BFF, *Math.Atan2*.

But wait: There's also a Boolean argument to *GetValue* that causes the method to use *Vector2.SmoothStep* rather than *Vector2.Lerp*. You can try out this alternative by replacing this call in the *Update* method of *Game1*:

```
position = polylineInterpolator.GetValue(t, false, out angle);
```

with this one:

```
position = polylineInterpolator.GetValue(t, true, out angle);
```

The "smooth step" interpolation is based on a cubic, and causes the car to slow down as it approaches one of the vertices, and speed up afterwards. It still makes an abrupt and unrealistic turn but the speed change is quite nice.

What I don't like about the *PolylineInterpolator* class is its inefficiency. *GetValue* needs to make several calls to the *Length* method of *Vector2*, which of course involves a square-root calculation. It would be nice for the class to retain the total length and the accumulated length at each vertex so it could simply re-use that information on successive *GetValue* calls. As written, the class can't do that because it has no knowledge when *Vector2* values are added to or removed from the *Vertices* collection. One possibility is to make that collection private, and to only allow a collection of points to be submitted in the class's constructor. Another approach is to replace the *List* with an *ObservableCollection*, which provides an event notification when objects are added and removed.

The Elliptical Course

The most unrealistic behavior of the previous program involves the turns. Real cars slow down to turn around corners, but they actually travel along a curved path to change direction. To make the previous program more realistic, the corners would have to be replaced by curves. These curves could be approximated with polylines, but the increasing number of polylines would then require *PolylineInterpolator* to be restructured for better performance.

Instead, I'm going to go off on a somewhat different tangent and drive the car around a traditional *oval* course, or to express it more mathematically, an *elliptical* course.

Let's look at some math. A circle centered on the point (0, 0) with a radius of R consists of all points (x, y) where

$$x^2 + y^2 = R^2$$

An ellipse has two radii. If these are parallel to the horizontal and vertical axes, they are sometimes called R_x and R_y, and the ellipse formula is:

$$\left(\frac{x}{R_x}\right)^2 + \left(\frac{x}{R_x}\right)^2 = 1$$

For our purposes, it is more convenient to represent the ellipse in the parametric form. In these two equations, x and y are functions of the angle α, which ranges from 0 to 2π:

$$x = R_x \cos\alpha$$

$$y = R_y \sin\alpha$$

When the ellipse is centered around the point (*Cx, Cy*), the formulas become:

$$x = C_x + R_x \cos\alpha$$
$$y = C_y + R_y \cos\alpha$$

If we also want to introduce a variable *t*, where *t* goes from 0 to 1, the formulas are:

$$x(t) = C_x + R_x \cos(2\pi t)$$
$$y(t) = C_y + R_y \sin(2\pi t)$$

And these will be ideal for our purpose. As *t* goes from 0 to 1, the car goes around the lap once. But how do we rotate the car so it appears to be travelling in a tangent to this ellipse? For that job, the differential calculus comes to the rescue. First, take the derivatives of the parametric equations:

$$x'(t) = -R_x \sin(2\pi t)$$
$$y'(t) = R_y \cos(2\pi t)$$

In physical terms, these equations represent the instantaneous change in direction in the X direction and Y direction, respectively. To turn that into a tangent angle, simply apply the ever useful *Math.Atan2*.

And now we're ready to code. Here are the fields:

XNA Project: CarOnOvalCourse   File: Game1.cs (excerpt showing fields)

```
public class Game1 : Microsoft.Xna.Framework.Game
{
    const float SPEED = 0.25f;           // laps per second
    GraphicsDeviceManager graphics;
    SpriteBatch spriteBatch;
    Texture2D car;
    Vector2 carCenter;
    Point ellipseCenter;
    float ellipseRadiusX, ellipseRadiusY;
    Vector2 position;
    float rotation;
    . . .
}
```

The fields include the three items required for the parametric equations for the ellipse: the center and the two radii. These are determined during the *LoadContent* method based on the dimensions of the available area of the screen:

XNA Project: **CarOnOvalCourse**   File: **Game1.cs (excerpt)**

```
protected override void LoadContent()
{
    spriteBatch = new SpriteBatch(GraphicsDevice);
    car = this.Content.Load<Texture2D>("car");
    carCenter = new Vector2(car.Width / 2, car.Height / 2);
    Viewport viewport = this.GraphicsDevice.Viewport;
    ellipseCenter = viewport.Bounds.Center;
    ellipseRadiusX = viewport.Width / 2 - car.Width;
    ellipseRadiusY = viewport.Height / 2 - car.Width;
}
```

Notice that the *Update* method below calculates two angles. The first, called *ellipseAngle*, is based on *t* and determines where on the ellipse the car is located. This is the angle passed to the parametric equations for the ellipse, to obtain the position as a combination of *x* and *y*:

XNA Project: **CarOnOvalCourse**   File: **Game1.cs (excerpt)**

```
protected override void Update(GameTime gameTime)
{
    if (GamePad.GetState(PlayerIndex.One).Buttons.Back == ButtonState.Pressed)
        this.Exit();

    float t = (SPEED * (float)gameTime.TotalGameTime.TotalSeconds) % 1;
    float ellipseAngle = MathHelper.TwoPi * t;
    float x = ellipseCenter.X + ellipseRadiusX * (float)Math.Cos(ellipseAngle);
    float y = ellipseCenter.Y + ellipseRadiusY * (float)Math.Sin(ellipseAngle);
    position = new Vector2(x, y);

    float dxdt = -ellipseRadiusX * (float)Math.Sin(ellipseAngle);
    float dydt = ellipseRadiusY * (float)Math.Cos(ellipseAngle);
    rotation = MathHelper.PiOver2 + (float)Math.Atan2(dydt, dxdt);

    base.Update(gameTime);
}
```

The second angle that *Update* calculates is called *rotation*. This is the angle that governs the orientation of the car. The *dxdt* and *dydt* variables are the derivatives of the parametric equations that I showed earlier. The *Math.Atan2* method provides the rotation angle relative to the positive X axis, and this must be rotated another 90 degrees for the original orientation of the bitmap.

By this time, you can probably recite *Draw* by heart:

```
XNA Project: CarOnOvalCourse    File: Game1.cs (excerpt)

protected override void Draw(GameTime gameTime)
{
    GraphicsDevice.Clear(Color.Blue);

    spriteBatch.Begin();
    spriteBatch.Draw(car, position, null, Color.White, rotation,
                     carCenter, 1, SpriteEffects.None, 0);
    spriteBatch.End();

    base.Draw(gameTime);
}
```

A Generalized Curve Solution

For movement along curves that are not quite convenient to express in parametric equations, XNA itself provides a generalized solution based around the *Curve* and *CurveKey* classes defined in the *Microsoft.Xna.Framework* namespace.

The *Curve* class contains a property named *Keys* of type *CurveKeyCollection*, a collection of *CurveKey* objects. Each *CurveKey* object allows you to specify a number pair of the form (*Position*, *Value*). Both the *Position* and *Value* properties are of type *float*. Then you pass a position to the *Curve* method *Evaluate*, and it returns an interpolated value.

But it's all rather confusing because—as the documentation indicates—the *Position* property of *CurveKey* is almost always a *time*, and the *Value* property is very often a *position*, or more accurately, one *coordinate* of a position. If you want to use *Curve* to interpolate between points in two-dimensional space, you need two instances of *Curve*—one for the X coordinate and the other for Y. These *Curve* instances are treated very much like parametric equations.

Suppose you want the car to go around a path that looks like an infinity sign, and let's assume that we're going to approximate the infinity sign with two adjacent circles. (The technique I'm going to show you will allow you to move those two circles apart at a later time if you'd like.)

Draw dots every 45 degrees on these two circles:

If the radius of each circle is 1 unit, the entire figure is 4 units wide and 2 units tall. The X coordinates of these dots (going from left to right) are the values 0, 0.293, 1, 0.707, 2, 2.293, 3, 3.707, and 4, and the Y coordinates (going from top to bottom) are the values 0, 0.293, 1, 1.707, and 2. The value 0.707 is simply the sine and cosine of 45 degrees, and 0.293 is one minus that value.

Let's begin at the point on the far left, and let's travel clockwise around the first circle. At the center of the figure, let's switch to going counter-clockwise around the second circle to form an infinity sign and finish with the same dot we started with. The X values are:

0, 0.293, 1, 1.707, 2, 2.293, 3, 3.707, 4, 3.707, 3, 2.293, 2, 1.707, 1, 0.293, 0

If we're using values of t ranging from 0 to 1 to drive around the infinity sign, then the first value corresponds to a t of 0, and the last (which is the same) to a t of 1. For each value, t is incremented by 1/16 or 0.0625. The Y values are:

1, 0.293, 0, 0.293, 1, 1.707, 2, 1.707, 1, 0.293, 0, 0.293, 1, 1.707, 2, 1.707, 1

We are now ready for some coding. Here are the fields for the CarOnInfinityCourse project:

XNA Project: CarOnInfinityCourse   File: Game1.cs (excerpt showing fields)

```
public class Game1 : Microsoft.Xna.Framework.Game
{
    const float SPEED = 0.1f;          // laps per second
    GraphicsDeviceManager graphics;
    SpriteBatch spriteBatch;
    Viewport viewport;
    Texture2D car;
    Vector2 carCenter;
    Curve xCurve = new Curve();
    Curve yCurve = new Curve();
    Vector2 position;
    float rotation;
    ...
}
```

Notice the two *Curve* objects, one for X coordinates and the other for Y. Because the initialization of these objects use precisely the coordinates I described above and don't require accessing any resources or program content, I decided to use the *Initialize* override for this work.

XNA Project: **CarOnInfinityCourse**   File: **Game1.cs** (excerpt)

```
protected override void Initialize()
{
    float[] xValues = { 0, 0.293f, 1, 1.707f, 2, 2.293f, 3, 3.707f,
                        4, 3.707f, 3, 2.293f, 2, 1.707f, 1, 0.293f };
    float[] yValues = { 1, 0.293f, 0, 0.293f, 1, 1.707f, 2, 1.707f,
                        1, 0.293f, 0, 0.293f, 1, 1.707f, 2, 1.707f };

    for (int i = -1; i < 18; i++)
    {
        int index = (i + 16) % 16;
        float t = 0.0625f * i;
        xCurve.Keys.Add(new CurveKey(t, xValues[index]));
        yCurve.Keys.Add(new CurveKey(t, yValues[index]));
    }
    xCurve.ComputeTangents(CurveTangent.Smooth);
    yCurve.ComputeTangents(CurveTangent.Smooth);
    base.Initialize();
}
```

The *xValues* and *yValues* arrays only have 16 values; they don't include the last point that duplicates the first. Rather oddly (you may think), the *for* loop goes from –1 through 17 but the modulo 16 operation ensures that the arrays are indexed from 0 through 15. The end result is that the *Keys* collections of *xCurve* and *yCurve* get coordinates associated with *t* values of –0.0625, 0, 0.0625, 0.0125, …, 0.875, 0.9375, 1, and 1.0625, which are apparently two more points than is necessary to make this thing work right.

These extra points are necessary for the *ComputeTangents* calls following the *for* loop. The *Curve* class performs a type of interpolation called a cubic Hermite spline, also called a *cspline*. Consider two points *pt1* and *pt2*. The cspline interpolates between these two points based not only on *pt1* and *pt2* but also on assumed tangents of the curve at *pt1* and *pt2*. You can specify these tangents to the *Curve* object yourself as part of the *CurveKeys* objects, or you can have the *Curve* object calculate tangents for you based on adjoining points. That is the approach I've taken by the two calls to *ComputeTangents*. With an argument of *CurveTangent.Smooth*, the *ComputeTangents* method uses not only the two adjacent points, but the points on either side. It's really just a simple weighted average but it's better than the alternatives.

The *Curve* and *CurveKey* classes have several other options, but the approach I've taken seemed to offer the best results with the least amount of work. (And isn't that what programming is all about?)

The *LoadContent* method needs to load the car and get its center point:

XNA Project: CarOnInfinityCourse File: **Game1.cs** (excerpt)

```
protected override void LoadContent()
{
    spriteBatch = new SpriteBatch(GraphicsDevice);
    viewport = this.GraphicsDevice.Viewport;
    car = this.Content.Load<Texture2D>("Car");
    carCenter = new Vector2(car.Width / 2, car.Height / 2);
}
```

Now it's time for *Update*. The method calculates *t* based on *TotalGameTime*. The *Curve* class defines a method named *Evaluate* that can accept this *t* value directly; this is how the program obtains interpolated X and Y coordinates. However, all the data in the two *Curve* objects are based on a maximum X coordinate of 4 and a Y coordinate of 2. For this reason, *Update* calls a little method I've supplied named *GetValue* that scales the values based on the size of the display.

XNA Project: CarOnInfinityCourse File: **Game1.cs** (excerpt)

```
protected override void Update(GameTime gameTime)
{
    if (GamePad.GetState(PlayerIndex.One).Buttons.Back == ButtonState.Pressed)
        this.Exit();

    float t = (SPEED * (float)gameTime.TotalGameTime.TotalSeconds) % 1;
    float x = GetValue(t, true);
    float y = GetValue(t, false);
    position = new Vector2(x, y);

    rotation = MathHelper.PiOver2 + (float)
        Math.Atan2(GetValue(t + 0.001f, false) - GetValue(t - 0.001f, false),
                   GetValue(t + 0.001f, true) - GetValue(t - 0.001f, true));

    base.Update(gameTime);
}

float GetValue(float t, bool isX)
{
    if (isX)
        return xCurve.Evaluate(t) * (viewport.Width - 2 * car.Width) / 4 + car.Width;

    return yCurve.Evaluate(t) * (viewport.Height - 2 * car.Width) / 2 + car.Width;
}
```

After calculating the *position* field, we have a little bit of a problem because the *Curve* class is missing an essential method: the method that provides the tangent of the spline. Tangents are required by the *Curve* class to *calculate* the spline, but after the spline is calculated, the class doesn't provide access to the tangents of the spline itself!

That's the purpose of the other four calls to *GetValue*. Small values are added to and subtracted from *t* to approximate the derivative and allow *Math.Atan2* to calculate the *rotation* angle.

Once again, *Draw* is trivial:

XNA Project: CarOnInfinityCourse   File: Game1.cs (excerpt)

```
protected override void Draw(GameTime gameTime)
{
    GraphicsDevice.Clear(Color.Blue);

    spriteBatch.Begin();
    spriteBatch.Draw(car, position, null, Color.White, rotation,
                carCenter, 1, SpriteEffects.None, 0);
    spriteBatch.End();

    base.Draw(gameTime);
}
```

If you want the *Curve* class to calculate the tangents used for calculating the spline (as I did in this program) it is essential to give the class sufficient points, not only beyond the range of points you wish to interpolate between, but enough so that these calculated tangents are more or less accurate. I originally tried defining the infinity course with points on the two circles every 90 degrees, and it didn't work well at all.

Chapter 9
Dynamic Textures

The most common way for an XNA program to obtain a *Texture2D* object is by loading it as program content. In Chapter 4 you also saw how a program can create a *Texture2D* from a *Stream* object using the static *Texture2D.FromSteam* method. This *Stream* object can reference a bitmap downloaded over the internet, or a picture stored in the user's photo library, or a photo just snapped by the phone's camera.

It is also possible to create a *Texture2D* object entirely in code using this constructor:

```
Texture2D texture = new Texture2D(this.GraphicsDevice, width, height);
```

The *width* and *height* arguments are integers that indicate the desired size of the *Texture2D* in pixels; this size cannot be changed after the *Texture2D* is created. The total number of pixels in the bitmap is easily calculated as *width * height*. The result is a bitmap filled with zeros. So now the big question is: How do you get actual stuff onto the surface of this bitmap?

You have two ways:

- Draw on the bitmap surface just as you draw on the video display.
- Algorithmically manipulate the actual pixel bits that make up the bitmap.

You can use these two techniques separately, or in combination with each other. You can also begin with an existing image, and modify it using these techniques.

The Render Target

Strictly speaking, you actually *can't* use the first of the two techniques with a *Texture2D* object. You need to create an instance of a class that derives from *Texture2D* called *RenderTarget2D*:

```
RenderTarget2D renderTarget = new RenderTarget2D(this.GraphicsDevice, width, height);
```

As with any code that references the *GraphicsDevice* property of the *Game* class, you'll want to wait until the *LoadContent* method to create any *Texture2D* or *RenderTarget2D* objects your program needs. You'll usually be storing the objects in fields so you can display them later on in the *Draw* override.

The idea behind the *RenderTarget2D* is fairly simple but understanding it requires some background:

As you know, normally during the *Draw* override of the *Game* class, your program draws to the video display. You can set the entire video display to a particular color by calling the *Clear* method of the *GraphicsDevice* object associated with your game:

```
this.GraphicsDevice.Clear(Color.CornflowerBlue);
```

You can draw *Texture2D* objects and text strings on the display using a *SpriteBatch* object:

```
spriteBatch.Begin();
spriteBatch.Draw(...);
spriteBatch.DrawString(...);
spriteBatch.End();
```

This *SpriteBatch* object is routinely created in the *LoadContent* override. It is associated with the *GraphicsDevice* object because a *GraphicsDevice* object is required in its constructor:

```
spriteBatch = new SpriteBatch(this.GraphicsDevice);
```

The calls to the *Clear* method of the *GraphicsDevice* and the *Draw* and *DrawString* methods of *SpriteBatch* actually draw on a bitmap called the *back buffer*, the contents of which are then transferred to the video display. You can discover some information about the back buffer through the *PresentationParameters* property of *GraphicsDevice*. If your program is running on a large-screen phone and you haven't indicated that you want a non-default size for the back buffer, you'll discover that the *BackBufferWidth* and *BackBufferHeight* properties of *PresentationParameters* indicate 800 and 480, respectively.

PresentationParameters also defines *BackBufferFormat* property set to set to a member of the *SurfaceFormat* enumeration. The format indicates both the number of bits in each pixel and how these bits represent color. For Windows Phone 7 devices, you'll discover that this *BackBufferFormat* property equals *SurfaceFormat.Bgr565*. This means that each pixel is 16 bits wide with 5 bits used for red and blue, and 6 bits for green in the following bit configuration:

RRRRRGGGGGGBBBBB

Green gets an extra bit because green is in the center of the spectrum of electromagnetic radiation that is visible to the human eye—the primary to which humans are most sensitive.

If you've ever seen any color gradients displayed on a Windows Phone 7 device—and if not, there's one coming up in this chapter—you've probably noticed that they aren't as smooth as gradients on common desktop displays. Video display adapters in common use on the desktop use 8 bits for each primary. The 5 or 6 bits for each primary in the Windows Phone 7 video display is insufficient to represent the color gradations that most humans can perceive. It is very likely that Windows Phone devices of the future will move beyond 16-bit color.

It is possible for an XNA program to temporarily replace the normal back buffer in the *GraphicsDevice* object with an object of type *RenderTarget2D*:

```
this.GraphicsDevice.SetRenderTarget(renderTarget);
```

You can then draw on this *RenderTarget2D* in the same way you draw on the back buffer. After you're finished drawing, you disassociate the *RenderTarget2D* from the *GraphicsDevice* with another call to *SetRenderTarget* with a *null* argument:

```
this.GraphicsDevice.SetRenderTarget(null);
```

Now the *GraphicsDevice* is back to normal.

If you're creating a *RenderTarget2D* that remains the same for the duration of the program, you'll generally perform this entire operation during the *LoadContent* override. If the *RenderTarget2D* needs to change, you can also draw on the bitmap during the *Update* override. Because *RenderTarget2D* derives from *Texture2D* you can display the *RenderTarget2D* on the screen during your *Draw* override just as you display any other *Texture2D* image.

Of course, you're not limited to one *RenderTarget2D* object. If you have a complex series of images that form some kind of animation, you can create a series of *RenderTarget2D* objects that you then display in sequence as a kind of movie.

Suppose you want to display something that looks like this:

That's a bunch of text strings all saying "Windows Phone 7" rotated around a center point with colors that vary between cyan and yellow. Of course, you can have a loop in the *Draw* override that makes 32 calls to the *DrawString* method of *SpriteBatch*, but if you assemble those text strings on a single bitmap, you can reduce the *Draw* override to just a single call to the *Draw* method of *SpriteBatch*. Moreover, it becomes easier to treat this assemblage of text strings as a single entity, and then perhaps rotate it like a pinwheel.

That's the idea behind the PinwheelText program. The program's content includes the 14-point Segoe UI Mono *SpriteFont*, but a *SpriteFont* object is not included among the program's fields, nor is the text itself:

XNA Project: PinwheelText   **File: Game1.cs** (excerpt showing fields)

```
public class Game1 : Microsoft.Xna.Framework.Game
{
    GraphicsDeviceManager graphics;
    SpriteBatch spriteBatch;

    Vector2 screenCenter;
    RenderTarget2D renderTarget;
    Vector2 textureCenter;
    float rotationAngle;
    ...
}
```

The *LoadContent* method is the most involved part of the program, but it only results in setting the *screenCenter*, *renderTarget*, and *textureCenter* fields. The *segoe14* and *textSize* variables set early on in the method are normally saved as fields but here they're only required locally:

XNA Project: PinwheelText   **File: Game1.cs** (excerpt)

```
protected override void LoadContent()
{
    // Create a new SpriteBatch, which can be used to draw textures.
    spriteBatch = new SpriteBatch(GraphicsDevice);

    // Get viewport info
    Viewport viewport = this.GraphicsDevice.Viewport;
    screenCenter = new Vector2(viewport.Width / 2, viewport.Height / 2);

    // Load font and get text size
    SpriteFont segoe14 = this.Content.Load<SpriteFont>("Segoe14");
    string text = " Windows Phone 7";
    Vector2 textSize = segoe14.MeasureString(text);

    // Create RenderTarget2D
    renderTarget =
        new RenderTarget2D(this.GraphicsDevice, 2 * (int)textSize.X,
                                                2 * (int)textSize.X);

    // Find center
    textureCenter = new Vector2(renderTarget.Width / 2,
                                renderTarget.Height / 2);
```

```
        Vector2 textOrigin = new Vector2(0, textSize.Y / 2);

        // Set the RenderTarget2D to the GraphicsDevice
        this.GraphicsDevice.SetRenderTarget(renderTarget);

        // Clear the RenderTarget2D and render the text
        this.GraphicsDevice.Clear(Color.Transparent);
        spriteBatch.Begin();

        for (float t = 0; t < 1; t += 1f / 32)
        {
            float angle = t * MathHelper.TwoPi;
            Color clr = Color.Lerp(Color.Cyan, Color.Yellow, t);
            spriteBatch.DrawString(segoe14, text, textureCenter, clr,
                                angle, textOrigin, 1, SpriteEffects.None, 0);
        }

        spriteBatch.End();

        // Restore the GraphicsDevice back to normal
        this.GraphicsDevice.SetRenderTarget(null);
    }
```

The *RenderTarget2D* is created with a width and height that is twice the width of the text string. The *RenderTarget2D* is set into the *GraphicsDevice* with a call to *SetRenderTarget* and then cleared to a transparent color with the *Clear* method. At this point a sequence of calls on the *SpriteBatch* object renders the text 32 times on the *RenderTarget2D*. The *LoadContent* call concludes by restoring the *GraphicsDevice* to the normal back buffer.

The *Update* method calculates a rotation angle for the resultant bitmap so it rotates 360° every eight seconds:

XNA Project: PinwheelText   File: Game1.cs (excerpt)

```
protected override void Update(GameTime gameTime)
{
    // Allows the game to exit
    if (GamePad.GetState(PlayerIndex.One).Buttons.Back == ButtonState.Pressed)
        this.Exit();

    rotationAngle =
        (MathHelper.TwoPi * (float) gameTime.TotalGameTime.TotalSeconds / 8) %
                                        MathHelper.TwoPi;
    base.Update(gameTime);
}
```

As promised, the *Draw* override can then treat that *RenderTarget2D* as a normal *Texture2D* in a single *Draw* call on the *SpriteBatch*. All 32 text strings seem to rotate in unison:

XNA Project: PinwheelText   **File: Game1.cs (excerpt)**

```
protected override void Draw(GameTime gameTime)
{
    GraphicsDevice.Clear(Color.Navy);

    spriteBatch.Begin();
    spriteBatch.Draw(renderTarget, screenCenter, null, Color.White,
                  rotationAngle, textureCenter, 1, SpriteEffects.None, 0);
    spriteBatch.End();

    base.Draw(gameTime);
}
```

The FlyAwayHello program in the previous chapter loaded two white bitmaps as program content. That wasn't really necessary. The program could have created those two bitmaps as *RenderTarget2D* objects and then just colored them white with a few simple statements. In FlyAwayHello you can replace these two statements in *LoadContent*:

```
Texture2D horzBar = Content.Load<Texture2D>("HorzBar");
Texture2D vertBar = Content.Load<Texture2D>("VertBar");
```

with these:

```
RenderTarget2D horzBar = new RenderTarget2D(this.GraphicsDevice, 45, 5);
this.GraphicsDevice.SetRenderTarget(horzBar);
this.GraphicsDevice.Clear(Color.White);
this.GraphicsDevice.SetRenderTarget(null);

RenderTarget2D vertBar = new RenderTarget2D(this.GraphicsDevice, 5, 75);
this.GraphicsDevice.SetRenderTarget(vertBar);
this.GraphicsDevice.Clear(Color.White);
this.GraphicsDevice.SetRenderTarget(null);
```

Yes, I know there's more code involved, but you no longer need the two bitmap files as program content, and if you ever wanted to change the sizes of the bitmaps, doing it in code is trivial.

The DragAndDraw program coming up lets you draw multiple solid-color rectangles by dragging your finger on the screen. Every time you touch and drag along the screen a new rectangle is drawn with a random color. Yet the entire program uses only one *RenderTarget2D* object containing just one white pixel!

That single *RenderTarget2D* object is stored as a field, along with a collection of *RectangleInfo* objects that will describe each drawn rectangle:

XNA Project: DragAndDraw   File: Game1.cs (excerpt showing fields)

```
public class Game1 : Microsoft.Xna.Framework.Game
{
    GraphicsDeviceManager graphics;
    SpriteBatch spriteBatch;

    struct RectangleInfo
    {
        public Vector2 point1;
        public Vector2 point2;
        public Color color;
    }

    List<RectangleInfo> rectangles = new List<RectangleInfo>();
    Random rand = new Random();
    RenderTarget2D tinyTexture;
    bool isDragging;

    public Game1()
    {
        graphics = new GraphicsDeviceManager(this);
        Content.RootDirectory = "Content";

        // Frame rate is 30 fps by default for Windows Phone.
        TargetElapsedTime = TimeSpan.FromTicks(333333);

        // Enable dragging gestures
        TouchPanel.EnabledGestures = GestureType.FreeDrag |
                                     GestureType.DragComplete;
    }
    ...
}
```

Notice also that the bottom of the *Game1* constructor enables two touch gestures, *FreeDrag* and *DragComplete*. These are gestures that correspond to touching the screen, dragging the finger (whatever which way), and lifting.

The *LoadContent* method creates the tiny *RenderTarget2D* object and colors it white:

XNA Project: DragAndDraw   File: Game1.cs (excerpt)

```
protected override void LoadContent()
{
    // Create a new SpriteBatch, which can be used to draw textures.
    spriteBatch = new SpriteBatch(GraphicsDevice);

    // Create a white 1x1 bitmap
    tinyTexture = new RenderTarget2D(this.GraphicsDevice, 1, 1);
```

```
        this.GraphicsDevice.SetRenderTarget(tinyTexture);
        this.GraphicsDevice.Clear(Color.White);
        this.GraphicsDevice.SetRenderTarget(null);
    }
```

The *Update* method handles the drag gestures. As you might recall from Chapter 3, the static *TouchPanel* class supports both low-level touch input and high-level gesture recognition. I'm using the gesture support in this program.

If gestures are enabled, then gestures are available when *TouchPanel.IsGestureAvailable* is *true*. You can then call *TouchPanel.ReadGesture* to return an object of type *GestureSample*. *TouchPanel.IsGestureAvailable* returns *false* when no more gestures are available during this particular *Update* call.

For this program, the *GestureType* property of *GestureSample* will be one of the two enumeration members, *GestureType.FreeDrag* or *GestureType.DragComplete*. The *FreeDrag* type indicates that the finger has touched the screen or is moving around the screen. *DragComplete* indicates that the finger has lifted.

For the *FreeDrag* gesture, two other properties of *GestureSample* are valid: *Position* is a *Vector2* object that indicates the current position of the finger relative to the screen; *Delta* is also a *Vector2* object that indicates the difference between the current position of the finger and the position of the finger in the last *FreeDrag* sample. (I don't use the *Delta* property in this program.) These properties are not valid with the *DragComplete* gesture.

The program maintains an *isDragging* field to help it discern when a finger first touches the screen and when a finger is moving around the screen, both of which are *FreeDrag* gestures:

XNA Project: DragAndDraw   File: Game1.cs (excerpt)

```
protected override void Update(GameTime gameTime)
{
    // Allows the game to exit
    if (GamePad.GetState(PlayerIndex.One).Buttons.Back == ButtonState.Pressed)
        this.Exit();

    while (TouchPanel.IsGestureAvailable)
    {
        GestureSample gesture = TouchPanel.ReadGesture();

        switch (gesture.GestureType)
        {
            case GestureType.FreeDrag:
                if (!isDragging)
                {
                    RectangleInfo rectInfo = new RectangleInfo();
```

```
                    rectInfo.point1 = gesture.Position;
                    rectInfo.point2 = gesture.Position;
                    rectInfo.color = new Color(rand.Next(256),
                                               rand.Next(256),
                                               rand.Next(256));
                    rectangles.Add(rectInfo);
                    isDragging = true;
                }
                else
                {
                    RectangleInfo rectInfo = rectangles[rectangles.Count - 1];
                    rectInfo.point2 = gesture.Position;
                    rectangles[rectangles.Count - 1] = rectInfo;
                }
                break;

            case GestureType.DragComplete:
                if (isDragging)
                    isDragging = false;
                break;
        }
    }
    base.Update(gameTime);
}
```

If *isDragging* is *false*, then a finger is first touching the screen and the program creates a new *RectangleInfo* object and adds it to the collection. At this time, the *point1* and *point2* fields of *RectangleInfo* are both set to the point where the finger touched the screen, and *color* is a random *Color* value.

With subsequent *FreeDrag* gestures, the *point2* field of the most recent *RectangleInfo* in the collection is re-set to indicate the current position of the finger. With *DragComplete*, nothing more needs to be done and the *isDragging* field is set to *false*.

In the *Draw* override (shown below), the program calls the *Draw* method of *SpriteBatch* once for each *RectangleInfo* object in the collection, in each case using the version of *Draw* that expands the *Texture2D* to the size of a *Rectangle* destination:

```
Draw(Texture2D texture, Rectangle destination, Color color)
```

The first argument is always the 1 × 1 white *RenderTarget2D* called *tinyTexture*, and the last argument is the random color stored in the *RectangleInfo* object.

The *Rectangle* argument to *Draw* requires some massaging, however. Each *RectangleInfo* object contains two points named *point1* and *point2* that are opposite corners of the rectangle drawn by the user. But depending how the finger dragged across the screen, *point1* might be the upper-right corner and *point2* the lower-left corner, or *point1* the lower-right corner and *point2* the upper-left corner, or two other possibilities.

The *Rectangle* object passed to *Draw* requires a point indicating the upper-left corner with non-negative width and heights values. (Actually, *Rectangle* also accepts a point indicating the lower-right corner with width and height values that are both negative, but that little fact doesn't help simplify the logic.) That's the purpose of the calls to *Math.Min* and *Math.Abs*:

XNA Project: **DragAndDraw**   File: **Game1.cs (excerpt)**

```
protected override void Draw(GameTime gameTime)
{
    GraphicsDevice.Clear(Color.Navy);

    spriteBatch.Begin();

    foreach (RectangleInfo rectInfo in rectangles)
    {
        Rectangle rect =
            new Rectangle((int)Math.Min(rectInfo.point1.X, rectInfo.point2.X),
                          (int)Math.Min(rectInfo.point1.Y, rectInfo.point2.Y),
                          (int)Math.Abs(rectInfo.point2.X - rectInfo.point1.X),
                          (int)Math.Abs(rectInfo.point2.Y - rectInfo.point1.Y));

        spriteBatch.Draw(tinyTexture, rect, rectInfo.color);
    }

    spriteBatch.End();

    base.Draw(gameTime);
}
```

Here it is after I've drawn a couple rectangles:

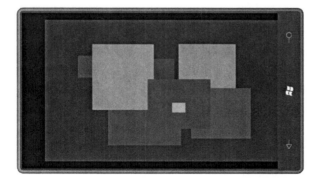

Preserving Render Target Contents

I mentioned earlier that the pixels in the Windows Phone 7 back buffer—and the video display itself—were only 16 bits wide. What is the color format of the bitmap created with *RenderTarget2D*?

By default, the *RenderTarget2D* is created with 32 bits per pixel—8 bits each for red, green, blue, and alpha—corresponding to the enumeration member *SurfaceFormat.Color*. I'll have more to say about this format before the end of this chapter, but this 32-bit color format is now commonly regarded as fairly standard. It is the only color format supported in Silverlight bitmaps, for example.

To maximize performance, you might want to create a *RenderTarget2D* or a *Texture2D* object that has the same pixel format as the back buffer and the display surface. Both classes support constructors that include arguments of type *SurfaceFormat* to indicate a color format.

For the PinwheelText program, creating a *RenderTarget2D* object with *SurfaceFormat. Bgr565* wouldn't work well. There's no alpha channel in this format so the background of the *RenderTarget2D* can't be transparent. The background would have to be specifically colored to match the background of the back buffer.

The following program creates a *RenderTarget2D* object that is not only the size of the back buffer but also the same color format. The program, however, is rather retro, and you might wonder what the point is.

Back in the early days of Microsoft Windows, particularly at trade shows where lots of computers were running, it was common to see programs that simply displayed a continuous series of randomly sized and colored rectangles. But the strategy of writing such a program using XNA is not immediately obvious. It makes sense to add a new rectangle to the mix during the *Update* method but you don't want to do it like the DragAndDraw program. The rectangle collection would increase by 30 rectangles every second, and by the end of an hour the *Draw* override would be trying to render over a hundred thousand rectangles every 33 milliseconds!

Instead, you probably want to build up the random rectangles on a *RenderTarget2D* that's the size of the back buffer. The rectangles you successively plaster on this *RenderTarget2D* can be based on the same 1 × 1 white bitmap used in DragAndDraw.

These two bitmaps are stored as fields of the RandomRectangles program together with a *Random* object:

XNA Project: RandomRectangles   File: Game1.cs (excerpt showing fields)

```
public class Game1 : Microsoft.Xna.Framework.Game
{
    GraphicsDeviceManager graphics;
    SpriteBatch spriteBatch;

    Random rand = new Random();
    RenderTarget2D tinyTexture;
    RenderTarget2D renderTarget;
    ...
}
```

The *LoadContent* method creates the two *RenderTarget2D* objects. The big one requires an extensive constructor, some arguments of which refer to features beyond the scope of this book:

XNA Project: RandomRectangles   File: Game1.cs (excerpt)

```
protected override void LoadContent()
{
    // Create a new SpriteBatch, which can be used to draw textures.
    spriteBatch = new SpriteBatch(GraphicsDevice);

    tinyTexture = new RenderTarget2D(this.GraphicsDevice, 1, 1);
    this.GraphicsDevice.SetRenderTarget(tinyTexture);
    this.GraphicsDevice.Clear(Color.White);
    this.GraphicsDevice.SetRenderTarget(null);

    renderTarget = new RenderTarget2D(
            this.GraphicsDevice,
            this.GraphicsDevice.PresentationParameters.BackBufferWidth,
            this.GraphicsDevice.PresentationParameters.BackBufferHeight,
            false,
            this.GraphicsDevice.PresentationParameters.BackBufferFormat,
            DepthFormat.None, 0, RenderTargetUsage.PreserveContents);
}
```

You can see the reference to the *BackBufferFormat* in the constructor, but also notice the last argument: the enumeration member *RenderTargetUsage.PreserveContents*. This is not the default option. Normally when a *RenderTarget2D* is set in a *GraphicsDevice*, the existing contents of the bitmap are ignored and essentially discarded. The *PreserveContents* option retains the existing render target data and allows each new rectangle to be displayed on top of all the previous rectangles.

The *Update* method determines some random coordinates and color values, sets the large *RenderTarget2D* object in the *GraphicsDevice*, and draws the tiny texture over the existing content with random *Rectangle* and *Color* values:

XNA Project: RandomRectangles   File: Game1.cs (excerpt)

```
protected override void Update(GameTime gameTime)
{
    // Allows the game to exit
    if (GamePad.GetState(PlayerIndex.One).Buttons.Back == ButtonState.Pressed)
        this.Exit();

    int x1 = rand.Next(renderTarget.Width);
    int x2 = rand.Next(renderTarget.Width);
    int y1 = rand.Next(renderTarget.Height);
    int y2 = rand.Next(renderTarget.Height);
```

```
        int r = rand.Next(256);
        int g = rand.Next(256);
        int b = rand.Next(256);
        int a = rand.Next(256);

        Rectangle rect = new Rectangle(Math.Min(x1, x2), Math.Min(y1, y2),
                                       Math.Abs(x2 - x1), Math.Abs(y2 - y1));
        Color clr = new Color(r, g, b, a);

        this.GraphicsDevice.SetRenderTarget(renderTarget);
        spriteBatch.Begin();
        spriteBatch.Draw(tinyTexture, rect, clr);
        spriteBatch.End();
        this.GraphicsDevice.SetRenderTarget(null);

        base.Update(gameTime);
    }
```

The *Draw* override simply displays that entire large *RenderTarget2D* on the display:

XNA Project: RandomRectangles   File: Game1.cs (excerpt)

```
protected override void Draw(GameTime gameTime)
{
    spriteBatch.Begin();
    spriteBatch.Draw(renderTarget, Vector2.Zero, Color.White);
    spriteBatch.End();

    base.Draw(gameTime);
}
```

After almost no time at all, the display looks something like this:

The colors used for the rectangles include a random alpha channel, so in general (as you can see) the rectangles are partially transparent. Interestingly enough, you can still get this transparency even if the rectangle being rendered has no alpha channel. Change the creation of *tinyTexture* to this:

```
tinyTexture = new RenderTarget2D(this.GraphicsDevice, 1, 1, false,
                        SurfaceFormat.Bgr565, DepthFormat.None);
```

Now *tinyTexture* itself is not capable of transparency, but it can still be rendered on the larger texture with a partially transparent color in the *Draw* call of *SpriteBatch*.

Drawing Lines

For developers coming from more mainstream graphical programming environments, it is startling to realize that XNA has no way of rendering simple lines and curves in 2D. In this chapter I'm going to show you two ways that limitation can be overcome.

Suppose you want to draw a red line between the points (x_1, y_1) and (x_2, y_2), and you want this line to have a 3-pixel thickness. First, create a *RenderTarget2D* that is 3 pixels high with a width equal to:

$$\sqrt{(x_2 - x_1)^2 + (y_2 - y_1)^2}$$

That's the length of the line between the two points. Now set the *RenderTarget2D* to the *GraphicsDevice*, clear it with *Color.Red*, and reset the *GraphicsDevice* back to normal.

During the *Draw* override, draw this bitmap to the screen using a position of (x_1, y_1) with an origin of (0, 1). That origin is the point within the *RenderTarget2D* that is aligned with the position argument. This line is supposed to have a 3-pixel thickness so the vertical center of the bitmap should be aligned with (x_1, y_1). In this *Draw* call you'll also need to apply a rotation equal to the angle from (x_1, y_1) to (x_2, y_2), which can be calculated with *Math.Atan2*.

Actually, you don't need a bitmap the size of the line. You can use a much smaller bitmap and apply a scaling factor. Probably the easiest bitmap size for this purpose is 2 pixels wide and 3 pixels high. That allows you to set an origin of (0, 1) in the *Draw* call, which means the point (0, 1) in the bitmap remains fixed. A horizontal scaling factor then enlarges the bitmap for the line length, and a vertical scaling factor handles the line thickness.

I have such a class in a XNA library project called Petzold.Phone.Xna. I created this project in Visual Studio by selecting a project type of Windows Phone Game Library (4.0). Here's the complete class I call *LineRenderer*:

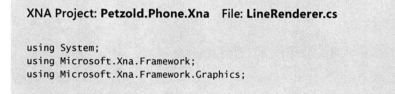

XNA Project: Petzold.Phone.Xna   File: LineRenderer.cs

```
using System;
using Microsoft.Xna.Framework;
using Microsoft.Xna.Framework.Graphics;
```

```
namespace Petzold.Phone.Xna
{
    public class LineRenderer
    {
        RenderTarget2D lineTexture;

        public LineRenderer(GraphicsDevice graphicsDevice)
        {
            lineTexture = new RenderTarget2D(graphicsDevice, 2, 3);

            graphicsDevice.SetRenderTarget(lineTexture);
            graphicsDevice.Clear(Color.White);
            graphicsDevice.SetRenderTarget(null);
        }

        public void DrawLine(SpriteBatch spriteBatch,
                             Vector2 point1, Vector2 point2,
                             float thickness, Color color)
        {
            Vector2 difference = point2 - point1;
            float length = difference.Length();
            float angle = (float)Math.Atan2(difference.Y, difference.X);
            spriteBatch.Draw(lineTexture, point1, null, color, angle,
                            new Vector2(0, 1),
                            new Vector2(length / 2, thickness / 3),
                            SpriteEffects.None, 0);
        }
    }
}
```

The constructor creates the small white *RenderTarget2D*. The *DrawLine* method requires an argument of type *SpriteBatch* and calls the *Draw* method on that object. Notice the scaling factor, which is the 7th argument to that *Draw* call. The width of the *RenderTarget2D* is 2 pixels, so horizontal scaling is half the length of the line. The height of the bitmap is 3 pixels, so the vertical scaling factor is the line thickness divided by 3. I chose a height of 3 so the line always straddles the geometric point regardless how thick it is.

To use this class in one of your programs, you'll first need to build the library project. Then, in any regular XNA project, you can right-click the References section in the Solution Explorer and select Add Reference. In the Add Reference dialog select the Browse label. Navigate to the directory with Petzold.Phone.Xna.dll and select it.

In the code file you'll need a *using* directive:

```
using Petzold.Phone.Xna;
```

You'll probably create a *LineRenderer* object in the *LoadContent* override and then call *DrawLine* in the *Draw* override, passing to it the *SpriteBatch* object you're using to draw other 2D graphics.

All of this is demonstrated in the TapForPolygon project. The program begins by drawing a triangle including lines from the center to each vertex. Tap the screen and it becomes a square, than again for a pentagon, and so forth:

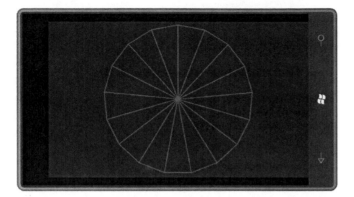

The *Game1* class has fields for the *LineRenderer* as well as a couple helpful variables.

XNA Project: TapForPolygon File: Game1.cs (excerpt showing fields)

```
public class Game1 : Microsoft.Xna.Framework.Game
{
    GraphicsDeviceManager graphics;
    SpriteBatch spriteBatch;

    LineRenderer lineRenderer;
    Vector2 center;
    float radius;
    int vertexCount = 3;

    public Game1()
    {
        graphics = new GraphicsDeviceManager(this);
        Content.RootDirectory = "Content";

        // Frame rate is 30 fps by default for Windows Phone.
        TargetElapsedTime = TimeSpan.FromTicks(333333);

        // Enable taps
        TouchPanel.EnabledGestures = GestureType.Tap;
    }
    . . .
}
```

Notice that the *Tap* gesture is enabled in the constructor. That *LineRenderer* is created in the *LoadContent* override:

```
XNA Project: TapForPolygon    File: Game1.cs (excerpt)

protected override void LoadContent()
{
    // Create a new SpriteBatch, which can be used to draw textures.
    spriteBatch = new SpriteBatch(GraphicsDevice);

    Viewport viewport= this.GraphicsDevice.Viewport;
    center = new Vector2(viewport.Width / 2, viewport.Height / 2);
    radius = Math.Min(center.X, center.Y) - 10;

    lineRenderer = new LineRenderer(this.GraphicsDevice);
}
```

The *Update* override is responsible for determining if a tap has occurred; if so, the *vertexCount* is incremented, going from (say) a hexadecagon to a heptadecagon as shown above.

```
XNA Project: TapForPolygon    File: Game1.cs (excerpt)

protected override void Update(GameTime gameTime)
{
    // Allows the game to exit
    if (GamePad.GetState(PlayerIndex.One).Buttons.Back == ButtonState.Pressed)
        this.Exit();

    while (TouchPanel.IsGestureAvailable)
        if (TouchPanel.ReadGesture().GestureType == GestureType.Tap)
            vertexCount++;

    base.Update(gameTime);
}
```

The lines—which are really just a single *RenderTarget2D* object stretched into long line-line shapes—are rendered in the *Draw* override. The *for* loop is based on the *vertexCount*; it draws two lines with every iteration: one from the center to the vertex and another from the previous vertex to the current vertex:

```
XNA Project: TapForPolygon    File: Game1.cs (excerpt)

protected override void Draw(GameTime gameTime)
{
    GraphicsDevice.Clear(Color.Navy);

    spriteBatch.Begin();

    Vector2 saved = new Vector2();
```

```
        for (int vertex = 0; vertex <= vertexCount; vertex++)
        {
            double angle = vertex * 2 * Math.PI / vertexCount;
            float x = center.X + radius * (float)Math.Sin(angle);
            float y = center.Y - radius * (float)Math.Cos(angle);
            Vector2 point = new Vector2(x, y);

            if (vertex != 0)
            {
                lineRenderer.DrawLine(spriteBatch, center, point, 3, Color.Red);
                lineRenderer.DrawLine(spriteBatch, saved, point, 3, Color.Red);
            }
            saved = point;
        }
        spriteBatch.End();

        base.Draw(gameTime);
    }
```

You don't have to use *LineRenderer* to draw lines on the video display. You can draw them on another *RenderTarget2D* objects. One possible application of the *LineRenderer* class used in this way is a "finger paint" program, where you draw free-form lines and curves with your finger. The next project is a very simple first stab at such a program. The lines you draw with your fingers are always red with a 25-pixel line thickness. Here are the fields and constructor (and please don't be too dismayed by the project name):

XNA Project: FlawedFingerPaint   File: Game1.cs (excerpt showing fields)

```
public class Game1 : Microsoft.Xna.Framework.Game
{
    GraphicsDeviceManager graphics;
    SpriteBatch spriteBatch;

    RenderTarget2D renderTarget;
    LineRenderer lineRenderer;

    public Game1()
    {
        graphics = new GraphicsDeviceManager(this);
        Content.RootDirectory = "Content";

        // Frame rate is 30 fps by default for Windows Phone.
        TargetElapsedTime = TimeSpan.FromTicks(333333);

        // Enable gestures
        TouchPanel.EnabledGestures = GestureType.FreeDrag;
    }
    ...
}
```

Notice that only the *FreeDrag* gesture is enabled. Each gesture will result in another short line being drawn that is connected to the previous line.

The *RenderTarget2D* object named *renderTarget* is used as a type of "canvas" on which you can paint with your fingers. It is created in the *LoadContent* method to be as large as the back buffer, and with the same color format, and preserving content:

XNA Project: FlawedFingerPaint   File: **Game1.cs** (excerpt)

```
protected override void LoadContent()
{
    // Create a new SpriteBatch, which can be used to draw textures.
    spriteBatch = new SpriteBatch(GraphicsDevice);

    renderTarget = new RenderTarget2D(
                    this.GraphicsDevice,
                    this.GraphicsDevice.PresentationParameters.BackBufferWidth,
                    this.GraphicsDevice.PresentationParameters.BackBufferHeight,
                    false,
                    this.GraphicsDevice.PresentationParameters.BackBufferFormat,
                    DepthFormat.None, 0, RenderTargetUsage.PreserveContents);

    this.GraphicsDevice.SetRenderTarget(renderTarget);
    this.GraphicsDevice.Clear(Color.Navy);
    this.GraphicsDevice.SetRenderTarget(null);

    lineRenderer = new LineRenderer(this.GraphicsDevice);
}
```

The *LoadContent* override also creates the *LineRenderer* object.

You'll recall that the *FreeDrag* gesture type is accompanied by a *Position* property that indicates the current location of the finger, and a *Delta* property, which is the difference between the current location of the finger and the previous location of the finger. That previous location can be calculated by subtracting *Delta* from *Position*, and those two points are used to draw a short line on the *RenderTarget2D* canvas:

XNA Project: FlawedFingerPaint   File: **Game1.cs** (excerpt)

```
protected override void Update(GameTime gameTime)
{
    // Allows the game to exit
    if (GamePad.GetState(PlayerIndex.One).Buttons.Back == ButtonState.Pressed)
        this.Exit();

    while (TouchPanel.IsGestureAvailable)
    {
        GestureSample gesture = TouchPanel.ReadGesture();
```

```
            if (gesture.GestureType == GestureType.FreeDrag &&
                gesture.Delta != Vector2.Zero)
            {

                this.GraphicsDevice.SetRenderTarget(renderTarget);
                spriteBatch.Begin();
                lineRenderer.DrawLine(spriteBatch,
                                       gesture.Position,
                                       gesture.Position - gesture.Delta,
                                       25, Color.Red);
                spriteBatch.End();
                this.GraphicsDevice.SetRenderTarget(null);
            }
        }
        base.Update(gameTime);
    }
```

The *Draw* override then merely needs to draw the canvas on the display:

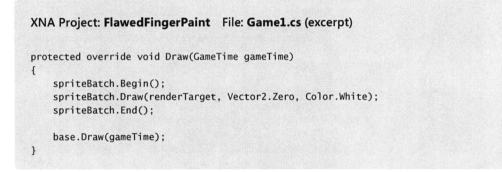

XNA Project: **FlawedFingerPaint**   File: **Game1.cs** (excerpt)

```
protected override void Draw(GameTime gameTime)
{
    spriteBatch.Begin();
    spriteBatch.Draw(renderTarget, Vector2.Zero, Color.White);
    spriteBatch.End();

    base.Draw(gameTime);
}
```

When you try this out, you'll find that it works really well in that you can quickly move your finger around the screen and you can draw a squiggly line:

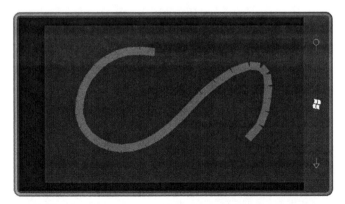

The only problem seems to be cracks in the figure, which become more severe as your finger makes fast sharp curves, and which justify the name of this project.

If you think about what's actually being rendered here, those cracks will make sense. You're really drawing rectangles between pairs of points, and if those rectangles are at angles to one another, then a sliver is missing:

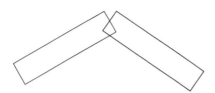

This is much less noticeable for thin lines, but becomes intolerable for thicker ones.

What can be done? Well, if the method displaying these rectangular textures knows that it's drawing a series of lines (called a *polyline* in graphics circles) it can increase the scaling factor of the bitmap a little more in the horizontal direction so they meet up at the outer corner rather than the center:

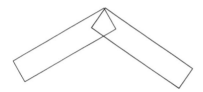

Getting this right requires calculations involving the angle between the two lines. And the technique has to be modified a bit for a finger painting program because you don't know what the next line will be at the time each line is rendered.

In environments that support line-drawing functions (such as Silverlight), problems such as these also exist with default line-drawing properties. However, in Silverlight it's possible to set rounded "caps" on the lines so they join very smoothly.

In XNA, putting rounded caps on the lines is probably best handled by manipulating the actual pixel bits.

Manipulating the Pixel Bits

Early in this chapter I showed you how to create a blank *Texture2D* object using one of its constructors:

```
Texture2D texture = new Texture2D(this.GraphicsDevice, width, height);
```

As with the back buffer and the *RenderTarget2D*, how the bits of each pixel correspond to a particular color is indicated by a member of the *SurfaceFormat* enumeration. A *Texture2D* created with this simple constructor will have a *Format* property of *SurfaceFormat.Color*, which means that every pixel consists of 4 bytes (or 32 bits) of data, one byte each for the red, green, and blue values and another byte for the alpha channel, which is the opacity of that pixel.

It is also possible (and very convenient) to treat each pixel as a 32-bit unsigned integer, which in C# is a *uint*. The colors appear in the 8-digit hexadecimal value of this *uint* like so:

AABBGGRR

Each letter represents four bits. If you have a *Texture2D* that you either loaded as content or created as shown above, and it has a *Format* property of *SurfaceFormat.Color*, you can obtain all the pixel bits of the bitmap by first creating an array of type *uint* large enough to encompass all the pixels:

```
uint[] pixels = new uint[texture.width * texture.height];
```

You then transfer all the pixels of the *Texture2D* into the array like so:

```
texture.GetData<uint>(pixels);
```

GetData is a generic method and you simply need to indicate the data type of the array. Overloads of *GetData* allow you to get pixels corresponding to a rectangular subset of the bitmap, or starting at an offset into the *pixels* array.

Because *RenderTarget2D* derives from *Texture2D* you can use this technique with *RenderTarget2D* objects as well.

You can also go the other way to transfer the data in the *pixels* array back into the bitmap:

```
texture.SetData<uint>(pixels);
```

The pixels in the *pixels* array are arranged by row beginning with the topmost row. The pixels in each row are arranged left by right. For a particular row *y* and column *x* in the bitmap, you can index the *pixels* array using a simple formula:

```
pixels[y * texture.width + x]
```

One exceptionally convenient property of the *Color* structure is *PackedValue*. This converts a *Color* object into a *uint* of the precise format required for this array, for example:

```
pixels[y * texture.width + x] = Color.Fuchsia.PackedValue;
```

In fact, *Color* and *uint* are so closely related that you can alternatively create a *pixels* array of type *Color*:

```
Color[] pixels = new Color[texture.Width * texture.Height];
```

You can then use this array with *GetData*

```
texture.GetData<Color>(pixels);
```

and *SetData*

```
texture.SetData<Color>(pixels);
```

and set individual pixels directly with *Color* values:

```
pixels[y * texture.width + x] = Color.AliceBlue;
```

All that's required is consistency.

You can create *Texture2D* objects in other color formats but the pixel array must have members of the correct size, for example *ushort* with *SurfaceFormat.Bgr565*. Consequently, none of the other formats are quite as easy to use as *SurfaceFormat.Color*, so that's what I'll be sticking with in this chapter.

Let's look at a simple example. Suppose you want a background to your game that consists of a gradient from blue at the left to red at the right. The GradientBackground project demonstrates how to create it. Here are the fields:

XNA Project: **GradientBackground**   File: **Game1.cs (excerpt showing fields)**

```
public class Game1 : Microsoft.Xna.Framework.Game
{
    GraphicsDeviceManager graphics;
    SpriteBatch spriteBatch;

    Rectangle viewportBounds;
    Texture2D background;
    ...
}
```

All the real work is done in the *LoadContent* override. The method creates a bitmap based on the *Viewport* size (but here using the *Bounds* property which has convenient integer dimensions), and fills it with data. The interpolation for the gradient is accomplished by the *Color.Lerp* method based on the *x* value:

XNA Project: **GradientBackground**   File: **Game1.cs (excerpt)**

```
protected override void LoadContent()
{
    spriteBatch = new SpriteBatch(GraphicsDevice);

    viewportBounds = this.GraphicsDevice.Viewport.Bounds;
    background = new Texture2D(this.GraphicsDevice, viewportBounds.Width,
                                                    viewportBounds.Height);

    Color[] pixels = new Color[background.Width * background.Height];
```

```
    for (int x = 0; x < background.Width; x++)
    {
        Color clr = Color.Lerp(Color.Blue, Color.Red,
                                (float)x / background.Width);

        for (int y = 0; y < background.Height; y++)
            pixels[y * background.Width + x] = clr;
    }
    background.SetData<Color>(pixels);
}
```

Don't forget to call *SetData* after filling the *pixels* array with data! It's pleasant to assume that there's some kind of behind-the-scenes binding between the *Texture2D* and the array, but there's really no such thing.

The *Draw* method simply draws the *Texture2D* like normal:

XNA Project: GradientBackground   File: Game1.cs (excerpt)

```
protected override void Draw(GameTime gameTime)
{
    spriteBatch.Begin();
    spriteBatch.Draw(background, viewportBounds, Color.White);
    spriteBatch.End();

    base.Draw(gameTime);
}
```

Here's the gradient:

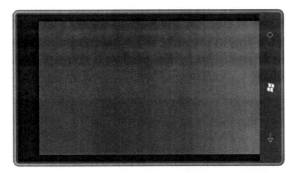

Although the code seems to imply hundreds of gradations between pure blue and pure red, the 16-bit color resolution of the Windows Phone 7 video display clearly shows 32 bands.

For this particular example, where the *Texture2D* is the same from top to bottom, it's not necessary to have quite so many rows. In fact, you can create the *background* object with just one row:

```
background = new Texture2D(this.GraphicsDevice, viewportBounds.Width, 1);
```

Because the other code in *LoadContent* is based on the *background.Width* and *background .Height* properties, nothing else needs to be changed (although the loops could certainly be simplified). In the *Draw* method, the bitmap is then stretched to fill the *Rectangle*:

```
spriteBatch.Draw(background, viewportBounds, Color.White);
```

Earlier in this chapter I created a 1 × 1 white *RenderTarget2D* using this code:

```
tinyTexture = new RenderTarget2D(this.GraphicsDevice, 1, 1);
this.GraphicsDevice.SetRenderTarget(tinyTexture);
this.GraphicsDevice.Clear(Color.White);
this.GraphicsDevice.SetRenderTarget(null);
```

You can do it with a *Texture2D* with only two lines of code that includes an in-line array:

```
tinyTexture = new Texture2D(this.GraphicsDevice, 1, 1);
tinyTexture.SetData<Color>(new Color[] { Color.White });
```

The Geometry of Line Drawing

To draw lines on a *Texture2D*, it would be convenient to directly set the pixels in the bitmap to render the line. For purposes of analysis and illustration, let's suppose you want to draw a line between *pt1* and *pt2*:

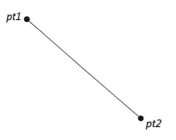

This geometric line has zero thickness, but a rendered line has a non-zero thickness, which we'll assume is *2R* pixels. (*R* stands for *radius*, and you'll understand why I'm thinking of it in those terms shortly.) You really want to draw a rectangle, where *pt1* and *pt2* are extended on each side by *R* pixels:

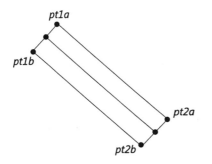

How are these corner points calculated? Well, it's really rather easy using vectors. Let's calculate the normalized vector from *pt1* to *pt2* and normalize it:

```
Vector2 vector = Vector2.Normalize(pt2 - pt1);
```

This vector must be rotated in increments of 90 degrees, and that's a snap. To rotate *vector* by 90 degrees clockwise, switch the X and Y coordinates while negating the Y coordinate:

```
Vector2 vect90 = new Vector2(-vector.Y, vector.X)
```

A vector rotated –90 degrees from *vector* is the negation of *vect90*.

If *vector* points from *pt1* to *pt2*, then the vector from *pt1* to *pt1a* (for example) is that vector rotated –90 degrees with a length of *R*. Then add that vector to *pt1* to get *pt1a*.

```
Vector2 pt1a = pt1 - R * vect90;
```

In a similar manner, you can also calculate *pt1b*, *pt2a*, and *pt2b*.

But as you saw before, the rectangle is not sufficient for thick lines that join at angles. To avoid those slivers seen earlier, you really need to draw rounded caps on these rectangles:

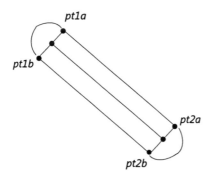

These are semi-circles of radius R centered on *pt1* and *pt2*.

At this point, we have derived an overall outline of the shape to draw for two successive points: A line from *pt1a* to *pt2a*, a semi-circle from *pt2a* to *pt2b*, another line from *pt2b* to *pt1b*, and another semi-circle from *pt1b* to *pt1a*. The goal is to find all pixels (x, y) in the interior of this outline.

When drawing vector outlines, parametric equations are ideal. When filling areas, it's best to go back to the standard equations that we learned in high school. You probably remember the equations for a line in slope-intercept form:

$$y = mx + b$$

where *m* is the slope of the line ("rise over run") and *b* is the value of *y* where the line intercepts the Y axis.

In computer graphics, however, areas are traditionally filled based on horizontal scan lines, also known as raster lines. (The terms come from television displays.) This straight line equation represents *x* as a function of *y*:

$$x = ay + b$$

For a line from *pt1* to *pt2*,

$$a = \frac{pt2.X - pt1.X}{pt2.Y - pt1.Y}$$

$$b = pt1.X - a \cdot pt1.Y$$

For any *y*, there is a point on the line that connects *pt1* and *pt2* if *y* is between *pt1.Y* and *pt2.Y*. The *x* value can then be calculated from the equations of the line.

Look at the previous diagram and imagine a horizontal scan line that crosses these two lines from *pt1a* to *pt2a*, and from *pt1b* to *pt2b*. For any *y*, we can calculate *xa* on the line from *pt1a* to *pt2a*, and *xb* on the line from *pt1b* to *pt2b*. For that scan line, the pixels that must be colored are those between (*xa, y*) and (*xb, y*). This can be repeated for all *y*.

This process gets a little messier for the rounded caps but not much messier. A circle of radius *R* centered on the origin consists of all points (*x, y*) that satisfy the equation:

$$x^2 + y^2 = R^2$$

For a circle centered on (*xc, yc*), the equation is:

$$(x - xc)^2 + (y - yc)^2 = R^2$$

Or for any *y*:

$$x = xc \pm \sqrt{R^2 - (y - yc)^2}$$

If the expression in the square root is negative, then *y* is outside the circle entirely. Otherwise, there are (in general) two values of *x* for each *y*. The only exception is when the square root is zero, that is, when *y* is exactly *R* units from *yc*, which are the top and bottom points of the circle.

We're dealing with a semicircle so it's a little more complex, but not much. Consider the semi-circle at the top of the diagram. The center is *pt1*, and the semicircle goes from *pt1b* to *pt1a*. The line from *pt1* to *pt1b* forms an angle *angle1* that can be calculated with *Math .Atan2*. Similarly for the line from *pt1* to *pt1a* there is an *angle2*. If the point (*x, y*) is on the circle as calculated above, it too forms an *angle* from the center *pt1*. If that angle is between *angle1* and *angle2*, then the point is on the semicircle. (This determination of "between" gets just a little messier because angles returned from *Math.Atan2* wrap around from π to $-\pi$.)

Now for any *y* we can examine both the two lines and the two semicircles and determine all points (*x*, *y*) that are on these four figures. At most, there will be only two such points—one where the scan line enters the figure and the other where it exits. For that scan line, all pixels between those two points can be filled.

The Petzold.Phone.Xna project contains several structures that help draw lines in a *Texture2D*. (I made them structures rather than classes because they will probably be frequently instantiated during *Update* calls.) All these structures implement this little interface:

XNA Project: Petzold.Phone.Xna   File: IGeometrySegment.cs

```
using System.Collections.Generic;

namespace Petzold.Phone.Xna
{
    public interface IGeometrySegment
    {
        void GetAllX(float y, IList<float> xCollection);
    }
}
```

For any *y* value the *GetAllX* method adds items to a collection of *x* values. In actual practice, with the structures in the library, often this collection will be returned empty. Sometimes it will contain one value, and sometimes two.

Here's the *LineSegment* structure:

XNA Project: Petzold.Phone.Xna   File: LineSegment.cs

```
using System.Collections.Generic;
using Microsoft.Xna.Framework;

namespace Petzold.Phone.Xna
{
    public struct LineSegment : IGeometrySegment
    {
        readonly float a, b;          // as in x = ay + b

        public LineSegment(Vector2 point1, Vector2 point2) : this()
        {
            Point1 = point1;
            Point2 = point2;

            a = (Point2.X - Point1.X) / (Point2.Y - Point1.Y);
            b = Point1.X - a * Point1.Y;
        }
```

```
        public Vector2 Point1 { private set; get; }
        public Vector2 Point2 { private set; get; }

        public void GetAllX(float y, IList<float> xCollection)
        {
            if ((Point2.Y > Point1.Y && y >= Point1.Y && y < Point2.Y) ||
                (Point2.Y < Point1.Y && y <= Point1.Y && y > Point2.Y))
            {
                xCollection.Add(a * y + b);
            }
        }
    }
}
```

Notice that the *if* statement in *GetAllX* checks that *y* is between *Point1.Y* and *Point2.Y*; it allows *y* values that equal *Point1.Y* but not those that equal *Point2.Y*. In other words, it defines the line to be all points from *Point1* (inclusive) up to but not including *Point2*. This caution about what points are included and excluded comes into play when multiple lines and arcs are connected; it helps avoid the possibility of having duplicate *x* values in the collection.

Also notice that no special consideration is given to horizontal lines, that is, lines where *Point1.Y* equals *Point2.Y* and where *a* equals infinity. If that is the case, then the *if* statement in the method is never satisfied. A scan line never crosses a horizontal boundary line.

The next structure is similar but for a generalized arc on the circumference of a circle:

XNA Project: Petzold.Phone.Xna   File: ArcSegment.cs

```
using System;
using System.Collections.Generic;
using Microsoft.Xna.Framework;

namespace Petzold.Phone.Xna
{
    public struct ArcSegment : IGeometrySegment
    {
        readonly double angle1, angle2;

        public ArcSegment(Vector2 center, float radius,
                          Vector2 point1, Vector2 point2) :
            this()
        {
            Center = center;
            Radius = radius;
            Point1 = point1;
            Point2 = point2;
            angle1 = Math.Atan2(point1.Y - center.Y, point1.X - center.X);
            angle2 = Math.Atan2(point2.Y - center.Y, point2.X - center.X);
        }
```

```
        public Vector2 Center { private set; get; }
        public float Radius { private set; get; }
        public Vector2 Point1 { private set; get; }
        public Vector2 Point2 { private set; get; }

        public void GetAllX(float y, IList<float> xCollection)
        {
            double sqrtArg = Radius * Radius - Math.Pow(y - Center.Y, 2);

            if (sqrtArg >= 0)
            {
                double sqrt = Math.Sqrt(sqrtArg);
                TryY(y, Center.X + sqrt, xCollection);
                TryY(y, Center.X - sqrt, xCollection);
            }
        }

        public void TryY(double y, double x, IList<float> xCollection)
        {
            double angle = Math.Atan2(y - Center.Y, x - Center.X);

            if ((angle1 < angle2 && (angle1 <= angle && angle < angle2)) ||
                (angle1 > angle2 && (angle1 <= angle || angle < angle2)))
            {
                xCollection.Add((float)x);
            }
        }
    }
}
```

The rather complex (but symmetrical) *if* clause in *TryY* accounts for the wrapping of angle values from π to −π. Notice also that the comparison of *angle* with *angle1* and *angle2* allows cases where *angle* equals *angle1* but not when *angle* equals *angle2*. It's allowing all angles from *angle1* (inclusive) up to but not including *angle2*.

For now, the final structure involved with line drawing represents a line with rounded caps:

XNA Project: **Petzold.Phone.Xna**   File: **RoundCappedLines.cs**

```
using System.Collections.Generic;
using Microsoft.Xna.Framework;

namespace Petzold.Phone.Xna
{
    public class RoundCappedLine : IGeometrySegment
    {
        LineSegment lineSegment1;
        ArcSegment arcSegment1;
        LineSegment lineSegment2;
        ArcSegment arcSegment2;
```

```
    public RoundCappedLine(Vector2 point1, Vector2 point2, float radius)
    {
        Point1 = point1;
        Point2 = point2;
        Radius = radius;

        Vector2 vector = point2 - point1;
        Vector2 normVect = vector;
        normVect.Normalize();

        Vector2 pt1a = Point1 + radius * new Vector2(normVect.Y, -normVect.X);
        Vector2 pt2a = pt1a + vector;
        Vector2 pt1b = Point1 + radius * new Vector2(-normVect.Y, normVect.X);
        Vector2 pt2b = pt1b + vector;

        lineSegment1 = new LineSegment(pt1a, pt2a);
        arcSegment1 = new ArcSegment(point2, radius, pt2a, pt2b);
        lineSegment2 = new LineSegment(pt2b, pt1b);
        arcSegment2 = new ArcSegment(point1, radius, pt1b, pt1a);
    }

    public Vector2 Point1 { private set; get; }
    public Vector2 Point2 { private set; get; }
    public float Radius { private set; get; }

    public void GetAllX(float y, IList<float> xCollection)
    {
        arcSegment1.GetAllX(y, xCollection);
        lineSegment1.GetAllX(y, xCollection);
        arcSegment2.GetAllX(y, xCollection);
        lineSegment2.GetAllX(y, xCollection);
    }
  }
}
```

This structure includes two *LineSegment* objects and two *ArcSegment* objects and defines them all based on the arguments to its own constructor. Implementing *GetAllX* is just a matter of calling the same method on the four components. It is the responsibility of the code calling *GetAllX* to ensure that the collection has previously been cleared. For *RoundCappedLines*, this method will return a collection with either one x value—a case that can be ignored for filling purposes—or two x values, in which case the pixels between those two x values can be filled.

Using these structures in an actual program is not as easy as using the *LineRenderer* class. The technique is demonstrated in the BetterFingerPaint project. The fields include a *Texture2D* on which to draw, the pixel array for that texture, and a reusable collection of *float* objects for passing to the line-drawing structures.

XNA Project: BetterFingerPaint   File: Game1.cs (excerpt showing fields)

```
public class Game1 : Microsoft.Xna.Framework.Game
{
    GraphicsDeviceManager graphics;
    SpriteBatch spriteBatch;

    Texture2D canvas;
    Color[] pixels;
    List<float> xCollection = new List<float>();

    public Game1()
    {
        graphics = new GraphicsDeviceManager(this);
        Content.RootDirectory = "Content";

        // Frame rate is 30 fps by default for Windows Phone.
        TargetElapsedTime = TimeSpan.FromTicks(333333);

        // Enable FreeDrag gestures
        TouchPanel.EnabledGestures = GestureType.FreeDrag;
    }
    ...
}
```

The *Game1* constructor enables the *FreeDrag* gesture, and as usual, those gestures are handled in the *Update* override shown below.

The *LoadContent* override creates this *Texture2D* to be the size of the screen and then initializes it with *Color.Navy* pixels:

XNA Project: BetterFingerPaint   File: Game1.cs (excerpt)

```
protected override void LoadContent()
{
    // Create a new SpriteBatch, which can be used to draw textures.
    spriteBatch = new SpriteBatch(GraphicsDevice);

    Rectangle viewportBounds = this.GraphicsDevice.Viewport.Bounds;
    canvas = new Texture2D(this.GraphicsDevice, viewportBounds.Width,
                                                viewportBounds.Height);

    pixels = new Color[canvas.Width * canvas.Height];

    for (int i = 0; i < pixels.Length; i++)
        pixels[i] = Color.Navy;

    canvas.SetData<Color>(pixels);
}
```

The key call in the *Update* override is to the *RoundCappedLine* constructor with the two points and the radius, which is half the line thickness. Following that, the routine can loop through all the Y values of the canvas, call the *GetAllX* method of the *RoundCappedLine* object, and then fill the area between the X values in the collection. However, the routine attempts to restrict looping and method calls to only X and Y values that could possibly be affected by the particular gesture.

XNA Project: BetterFingerPaint   File: Game1.cs (excerpt)

```
protected override void Update(GameTime gameTime)
{
    // Allows the game to exit
    if (GamePad.GetState(PlayerIndex.One).Buttons.Back == ButtonState.Pressed)
        this.Exit();

    bool canvasNeedsUpdate = false;
    int yMinUpdate = Int32.MaxValue, yMaxUpdate = 0;

    while (TouchPanel.IsGestureAvailable)
    {
        GestureSample gesture = TouchPanel.ReadGesture();

        if (gesture.GestureType == GestureType.FreeDrag &&
            gesture.Delta != Vector2.Zero)
        {
            Vector2 point1 = gesture.Position - gesture.Delta;
            Vector2 point2 = gesture.Position;
            float radius = 12;

            RoundCappedLine line = new RoundCappedLine(point1, point2, radius);

            int yMin = (int)(Math.Min(point1.Y, point2.Y) - radius - 1);
            int yMax = (int)(Math.Max(point1.Y, point2.Y) + radius + 1);

            yMin = Math.Max(0, Math.Min(canvas.Height, yMin));
            yMax = Math.Max(0, Math.Min(canvas.Height, yMax));

            for (int y = yMin; y < yMax; y++)
            {
                xCollection.Clear();
                line.GetAllX(y, xCollection);

                if (xCollection.Count == 2)
                {
                    int xMin = (int)(Math.Min(xCollection[0],
                                              xCollection[1]) + 0.5f);
                    int xMax = (int)(Math.Max(xCollection[0],
                                              xCollection[1]) + 0.5f);

                    xMin = Math.Max(0, Math.Min(canvas.Width, xMin));
                    xMax = Math.Max(0, Math.Min(canvas.Width, xMax));
```

```
                    for (int x = xMin; x < xMax; x++)
                    {
                        pixels[y * canvas.Width + x] = Color.Red;
                    }
                    yMinUpdate = Math.Min(yMinUpdate, yMin);
                    yMaxUpdate = Math.Max(yMaxUpdate, yMax);
                    canvasNeedsUpdate = true;
                }
            }
        }
    }

    if (canvasNeedsUpdate)
    {
        this.GraphicsDevice.Textures[0] = null;

        int height = yMaxUpdate - yMinUpdate;
        Rectangle rect = new Rectangle(0, yMinUpdate, canvas.Width, height);
        canvas.SetData<Color>(0, rect, pixels,
                    yMinUpdate * canvas.Width, height * canvas.Width);
    }
    base.Update(gameTime);
}
```

When all the gestures have been handled—and there may be more than one *FreeDrag* gesture during a single *Update* call—then the method has *yMinUpdate* and *yMaxUpdate* values indicating the rows that were affected by these particular gestures. These are used to construct a *Rectangle* object so that the *Texture2D* canvas is updated from the *pixels* array only where pixels have changed.

The simplest way to call *SetData* is like this:

```
texture.SetData<Color>(pixels);
```

This is an alternative:

```
texture.SetData<Color>(pixels, startIndex, count);
```

This call fills up the entire *Texture2D* from the *pixels* array but it begins at *startIndex* to index the array. The *count* argument must still be equal to the product of the pixel width and height of the *Texture2D*, and the array must have *count* values starting at *startIndex*. This variation might be useful if you're using the same *pixels* array for several small *Texture2D* objects.

The third variation is this:

```
texture.SetData<Color>(0, rectangle, pixels, startIndex, count);
```

The *rectangle* argument of type *Rectangle* restricts updating to a particular rectangle within the *Texture2D*. The *startIndex* still refers to an index of the *pixels* array but *count* must be equal to the product of the *rectangle* width and height. The method assumes that the *count* pixels beginning at *startIndex* are for that rectangular area.

If you're working with a single *pixels* array that corresponds to the entire *Texture2D*, and you want to restrict updating to a particular rectangular area, you don't have the flexibility to specify any rectangle you want because the rows of pixels in the *pixels* array are still based on the full width of the *Texture2D*. This means that the width of the rectangle must be the same as the width of the *Texture2D*. In short, you can only restrict the *SetData* call to one or more entire rows. That's why the code only retains *yMinUpdate* and *yMaxUpdate* and not the equivalent values for X.

In the *Update* method shown above you'll also see this call prior to calling *SetData*:

```
this.GraphicsDevice.Textures[0] = null;
```

This is sometimes necessary when calling *SetData* from the *Update* override if the particular *Texture2D* was the last thing displayed in the *Draw* method and it is still set in the *GraphicsDevice* object.

The *Draw* override is trivial:

XNA Project: **BetterFingerPaint**   File: **Game1.cs (excerpt)**

```
protected override void Draw(GameTime gameTime)
{
    spriteBatch.Begin();
    spriteBatch.Draw(canvas, Vector2.Zero, Color.White);
    spriteBatch.End();

    base.Draw(gameTime);
}
```

The really good news involves the display:

The strokes are solid with no cracks, and check out those nice rounded ends.

The BetterFingerPaint program will not let you draw with two fingers at once. To enhance the program for that feature while still using gestures would be somewhat messy. A single finger generates *FreeDrag* gestures while two fingers generate *Pinch* gestures, which include valid *Position2* and *Delta2* properties, but then the program would fail for three or simultaneous fingers.

To handle multiple fingers, it's necessary to go back to the low-level touch interface as shown in the following MultiFingerPaint project. Most of MultiFingerPaint is identical to BetterFingerPaint, but the constructor does *not* enable gestures:

XNA Project: **MultiFingerPaint**   File: **Game1.cs** (excerpt)

```
public Game1()
{
    graphics = new GraphicsDeviceManager(this);
    Content.RootDirectory = "Content";

    // Frame rate is 30 fps by default for Windows Phone.
    TargetElapsedTime = TimeSpan.FromTicks(333333);
}
```

I'll only show you part of the *Update* overrride because the rest is the same as before. The method essentially enumerates through the *TouchCollection* obtained from the *TouchPanel* *.GetState* call. This collection contains *TouchLocation* objects for multiple fingers touching the screen, moving, and lifting, but the program is only interested in moves. It doesn't even have to keep track of multiple fingers. All it needs to do is get a particular touch point, and the previous touch point for that finger from *TryGetPreviousLocation*, and draw a line between those points:

XNA Project: **MultiFingerPaint**   File: **Game1.cs** (excerpt)

```
protected override void Update(GameTime gameTime)
{
    // Allows the game to exit
    if (GamePad.GetState(PlayerIndex.One).Buttons.Back == ButtonState.Pressed)
        this.Exit();

    bool canvasNeedsUpdate = false;
    int yMinUpdate = Int32.MaxValue, yMaxUpdate = 0;

    TouchCollection touches = TouchPanel.GetState();

    foreach (TouchLocation touch in touches)
    {
```

```
        if (touch.State == TouchLocationState.Moved)
        {
            TouchLocation previousTouch;
            touch.TryGetPreviousLocation(out previousTouch);

            Vector2 point1 = previousTouch.Position;
            Vector2 point2 = touch.Position;
            float radius = 12;

            RoundCappedLine line = new RoundCappedLine(point1, point2, radius);
    ...
        }
```

And here it is with four fingers simultaneously:

Modifying Existing Images

You can modify an existing image by calling *GetData* on a "source" *Texture2D,* then algorithmically modifying the pixels and transferring them to a "destination" *Texture2D* with *SetData.* This is demonstrated in the RippleEffect project. The source *Texture2D* is a bitmap that I copied from my web site. The program modifies the pixels so the picture has waves that move horizontally across the image:

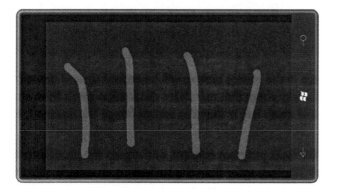

The fields of the program store the source ("src") and destination ("dst") *Texture2D* objects as well as the corresponding pixel arrays:

XNA Project: RippleEffect   File: Game1.cs (excerpt showing fields)

```
public class Game1 : Microsoft.Xna.Framework.Game
{
    GraphicsDeviceManager graphics;
    SpriteBatch spriteBatch;

    const int RIPPLE = 10;
    Texture2D srcTexture;
    Texture2D dstTexture;
    uint[] srcPixels;
    uint[] dstPixels;
    Vector2 position;


    ...
}
```

The constant indicates that pixels in the source bitmap will be moved up and down by 10 pixels. This is used both in the algorithm that calculates destination pixels from source pixels, and also to determine how much larger than the source image the destination image must be.

LoadContent loads the *srcTexture* from program content, and copies the pixels into the *srcPixels* array. The *dstTexture* is 20 pixels taller than the *srcTexture*; an array is allocated for the destination pixels but nothing is done with it yet:

XNA Project: RippleEffect   File: Game1.cs (excerpt)

```
protected override void LoadContent()
{
    // Create a new SpriteBatch, which can be used to draw textures.
    spriteBatch = new SpriteBatch(GraphicsDevice);

    srcTexture = this.Content.Load<Texture2D>("PetzoldTattoo");
    srcPixels = new uint[srcTexture.Width * srcTexture.Height];
    srcTexture.GetData<uint>(srcPixels);

    dstTexture = new Texture2D(this.GraphicsDevice,
                               srcTexture.Width,
                               srcTexture.Height + 2 * RIPPLE);
    dstPixels = new uint[dstTexture.Width * dstTexture.Height];

    Viewport viewport = this.GraphicsDevice.Viewport;
    position = new Vector2((viewport.Width - dstTexture.Width) / 2,
                          (viewport.Height - dstTexture.Height) / 2);
}
```

The goal during the *Update* method is to transfer pixels from *srcPixels* to *dstPixels* based on an algorithm that incorporates animation. The *dstPixels* array is then copied into *dstTexture* with *SetData*.

To transfer pixels from a source to a destination, two different approaches can be used:

- Loop through the source rows and columns. Get each source pixel. Figure out the corresponding destination row and column and store the pixel there.

- Loop through the destination rows and columns. Figure out the corresponding source row and column, get the pixel, and store it in the destination.

In the general case, the second approach is usually a bit harder than the first but that doesn't matter because it's the only one that guarantees that every pixel in the destination bitmap is set. That's why the *for* loops in the following method are based on *xDst* and *yDst*, the column and row of the destination bitmap. From these, *xSrc* and *xDst* are calculated. (In this particular algorithm, *xSrc* always equals *xDst*.)

The two pixel arrays can then be indexed with *dstIndex* and *srcIndex*. Although *dstIndex* will always be valid because it's based on valid *xDst* and *yDst* values, for some values *srcIndex* might not be valid. In those cases, I set the pixel referenced by *dstIndex* to a transparent value.

XNA Project: **RippleEffect**   File: **Game1.cs (excerpt)**

```
protected override void Update(GameTime gameTime)
{
    // Allows the game to exit
    if (GamePad.GetState(PlayerIndex.One).Buttons.Back == ButtonState.Pressed)
        this.Exit();

    float phase =
        (MathHelper.TwoPi * (float)gameTime.TotalGameTime.TotalSeconds) %
                                                            MathHelper.TwoPi;

    for (int xDst = 0; xDst < dstTexture.Width; xDst++)
    {
        int xSrc = xDst;
        float angle = phase - xDst * MathHelper.TwoPi / 100;
        int offset = (int)(RIPPLE * Math.Sin(angle));

        for (int yDst = 0; yDst < dstTexture.Height; yDst++)
        {
            int dstIndex = yDst * dstTexture.Width + xDst;
            int ySrc = yDst - RIPPLE + offset;
            int srcIndex = ySrc * dstTexture.Width + xSrc;

            if (ySrc < 0 || ySrc >= srcTexture.Height)
                dstPixels[dstIndex] = Color.Transparent.PackedValue;
            else
```

```
                    dstPixels[dstIndex] = srcPixels[srcIndex];
            }
        }
        this.GraphicsDevice.Textures[0] = null;
        dstTexture.SetData<uint>(dstPixels);

        base.Update(gameTime);
    }
```

In this *Update* override, the *srcTexture* is used solely to determine if *yDst* is beyond the bottom row of the bitmap; obviously I could have saved that number of rows and discarded the actual *srcTexture* image.

The *Update* override concludes with *dstTexture* being updated from the pixels in the *dstPixels* array and the *Draw* override simply displays that image:

XNA Project: RippleEffect   File: Game1.cs (excerpt)

```
protected override void Draw(GameTime gameTime)
{
    GraphicsDevice.Clear(Color.Navy);

    spriteBatch.Begin();
    spriteBatch.Draw(dstTexture, position, Color.White);
    spriteBatch.End();

    base.Draw(gameTime);
}
```

Although this program only modifies coordinates, similar programs could modify the actual color values of the pixels. It's also possible to base destination pixels on multiple source pixels for filtering effects.

But watch out for performance problems if you're calculating pixels and transferring data during every *Update* call. Both per-pixel processing and the *SetData* call require non-trivial time. The first version of this program ran fine on the phone emulator but bogged down to about two updates per second on the phone itself. I reduced the bitmap to 50% its original size (and ¼ the number of pixels) and that improved performance considerably.

In the next chapter, I'll show you how to calculate pixels algorithmically in a second thread of execution.

Chapter 10
From Gestures to Transforms

The primary means of user input to a Windows Phone 7 application is touch. A Windows Phone 7 device has a screen that supports at least four touch points, and applications must be written to accommodate touch in a way that feels natural and intuitive to the user.

As you've seen, XNA programmers have two basic approaches to obtaining touch input. With the low-level *TouchPanel.GetState* method a program can track individual fingers—each identified by an ID number—as they first touch the screen, move, and lift off. The *TouchPanel.ReadGesture* method provides a somewhat higher-level interface that allows rudimentary handling of inertia and two-finger manipulation in the form of "pinch" and "stretch" gestures.

Gestures and Properties

The various gestures supported by the *TouchPanel* class correspond to members of the *GestureType* enumeration:

- **Tap**—quickly touch and lift
- **DoubleTap**—the second of two successive taps
- **Hold**—press and hold for one second
- **FreeDrag**—move finger around the screen
- **HorizontalDrag**—horizontal component of *FreeDrag*
- **VerticalDrag**—vertical component of *FreeDrag*
- **DragComplete**—finger lifted from screen
- **Flick**—single-finger swiping movement
- **Pinch**—two fingers moving towards each other or apart
- **PinchComplete**—fingers lifted from screen

To receive information for particular gestures, the gestures must be enabled by setting the *TouchPanel.EnabledGestures* property. The program then obtains gestures during the *Update* override of the *Game* class in the form of *GestureSample* structures that include a *GestureType* property to identify the gesture.

GestureSample also defines four properties of type *Vector2*. None of these properties are valid for the *DragComplete* and *PinchComplete* types. Otherwise:

- *Position* is valid for all gestures except *Flick*.
- *Delta* is valid for all *Drag* gestures, *Pinch*, and *Flick*.
- *Position2* and *Delta2* are valid only for *Pinch*.

The *Position* property indicates the current position of the finger relative to the screen. The *Delta* property indicates the movement of the finger since the last position. For an object of type *GestureSample* named *gestureSample*,

```
Vector2 previousPosition = gestureSample.Position - gestureSample.Delta;
```

The *Delta* vector equals zero when the finger first touches the screen or when the finger is still.

Suppose you're only interested in dragging operations, and you enable the *FreeDrag* and *DragComplete* gestures. If you need to keep track of the complete distance a finger travels from the time it touches the screen to time it lifts, you can use one of two strategies: Either save the *Position* value from the first occurrence of *FreeDrag* after a *DragComplete* and compare that with the later *Position* values, or accumulate the *Delta* values in a running total.

Let's look at a simple program that lets the user drag a little bitmap around the screen. In the OneFingerDrag project the *Game1* class has fields to store a *Texture2D* and maintain its position:

XNA Project: OneFingerDrag   File: Game1.cs (excerpt showing fields)

```csharp
public class Game1 : Microsoft.Xna.Framework.Game
{
    GraphicsDeviceManager graphics;
    SpriteBatch spriteBatch;

    Texture2D texture;
    Vector2 texturePosition = Vector2.Zero;

    public Game1()
    {
        graphics = new GraphicsDeviceManager(this);
        Content.RootDirectory = "Content";

        // Frame rate is 30 fps by default for Windows Phone.
        TargetElapsedTime = TimeSpan.FromTicks(333333);

        TouchPanel.EnabledGestures = GestureType.FreeDrag;
    }
    ...
}
```

Notice the *FreeDrag* gesture enabled at the bottom of the constructor.

The *LoadContent* override loads the same *Texture2D* used in the RippleEffect project in the previous chapter:

XNA Project: **OneFingerDrag**   File: **Game1.cs** (excerpt)

```
protected override void LoadContent()
{
    // Create a new SpriteBatch, which can be used to draw textures.
    spriteBatch = new SpriteBatch(GraphicsDevice);

    texture = this.Content.Load<Texture2D>("PetzoldTattoo");
}
```

The *Update* override handles the *FreeDrag* gesture simply by adjusting the *texturePosition* vector by the *Delta* property of the *GestureSample*:

XNA Project: **OneFingerDrag**   File: **Game1.cs** (excerpt)

```
protected override void Update(GameTime gameTime)
{
    // Allows the game to exit
    if (GamePad.GetState(PlayerIndex.One).Buttons.Back == ButtonState.Pressed)
        this.Exit();

    while (TouchPanel.IsGestureAvailable)
    {
        GestureSample gesture = TouchPanel.ReadGesture();

        if (gesture.GestureType == GestureType.FreeDrag)
            texturePosition += gesture.Delta;
    }
    base.Update(gameTime);
}
```

Although *texturePosition* is a point and the *Delta* property of *GestureSample* is a vector, they are both *Vector2* values so they can be added.

The *while* loop might seem a little pointless in this program because we're only interested in a single gesture type. Couldn't it simply be an *if* statement? Actually, no. It is my experience that multiple gestures of the same type can be available during a single *Update* call.

The *Draw* override simply draws the *Texture2D* at the updated position:

XNA Project: OneFingerDrag   File: Game1.cs (excerpt)

```
protected override void Draw(GameTime gameTime)
{
    GraphicsDevice.Clear(Color.CornflowerBlue);

    spriteBatch.Begin();
    spriteBatch.Draw(texture, texturePosition, Color.White);
    spriteBatch.End();

    base.Draw(gameTime);
}
```

Initially the *Texture2D* is parked at the upper-left corner of the screen but by dragging your finger across the screen you can move it around:

You can actually drag your finger *anywhere* on the screen and the texture moves in response! The program doesn't check if the finger is actually sitting on the *Texture2D* but that's a fairly easy enhancement:

```
while (TouchPanel.IsGestureAvailable)
{
    GestureSample gesture = TouchPanel.ReadGesture();

    if (gesture.GestureType == GestureType.FreeDrag)
    {
        if (gesture.Position.X > texturePosition.X &&
            gesture.Position.X < texturePosition.X + texture.Width &&
            gesture.Position.Y > texturePosition.Y &&
            gesture.Position.Y < texturePosition.Y + texture.Height)
        {
            texturePosition += gesture.Delta;
        }
    }
}
```

You may not care for the way this logic works either. If you drag your finger across the screen in an area outside from the texture, the texture won't move, but if your finger then slides over the texture, it will start up. You'll probably want to drag the texture only if the first *FreeDrag* in a sequence is over the texture. If not, you'll want to ignore all *FreeDrag* gesture samples until a *DragComplete* occurs.

Scale and Rotate

Let's continue examining dragging gestures involving a simple figure, but using those gestures to implement scaling and rotation rather than movement. For the next three programs I'll position the *Texture2D* in the center of the screen, and it will remain in the center except that you can scale it or rotate it with a single finger.

The OneFingerScale project has a couple more fields than the previous program:

XNA Project: OneFingerScale   File: Game1.cs (excerpt showing fields)

```
public class Game1 : Microsoft.Xna.Framework.Game
{
    GraphicsDeviceManager graphics;
    SpriteBatch spriteBatch;

    Texture2D texture;
    Vector2 screenCenter;
    Vector2 textureCenter;
    Vector2 textureScale = Vector2.One;

    public Game1()
    {
        graphics = new GraphicsDeviceManager(this);
        Content.RootDirectory = "Content";

        // Frame rate is 30 fps by default for Windows Phone.
        TargetElapsedTime = TimeSpan.FromTicks(333333);

        TouchPanel.EnabledGestures = GestureType.FreeDrag;
    }
    ...
}
```

The program needs the center of the *Texture2D* because it uses a long version of the *Draw* call to *SpriteBatch* to include an origin argument. As you'll recall, the origin argument to Draw is the point in the *Texture2D* that is aligned with the position argument, and which also serves as the center of scaling and rotation.

Notice that the *textureScale* field is set to the vector **(1, 1)**, which means to multiply the width and height by 1. It's a common mistake to set scaling to zero, which tends to make graphical objects disappear from the screen.

All the uninitialized fields are set in the *LoadContent* override:

XNA Project: OneFingerScale   File: Game1.cs (excerpt)

```
protected override void LoadContent()
{
    // Create a new SpriteBatch, which can be used to draw textures.
    spriteBatch = new SpriteBatch(GraphicsDevice);

    Viewport viewport = this.GraphicsDevice.Viewport;
    screenCenter = new Vector2(viewport.Width / 2, viewport.Height / 2);

    texture = this.Content.Load<Texture2D>("PetzoldTattoo");
    textureCenter = new Vector2(texture.Width / 2, texture.Height / 2);
}
```

The handling of the *FreeDrag* gesture in the following *Update* override doesn't attempt to determine if the finger is over the bitmap. Because the bitmap is positioned in the center of the screen and it will be scaled to various degrees, that calculation is a little more difficult (although certainly not impossible.)

Instead, the *Update* override shows how to use the *Delta* property to determine the previous position of the finger, which is then used to calculate how far the finger has moved from the center of the texture (which is also the center of the screen) during this particular part of the entire gesture:

XNA Project: OneFingerScale   File: Game1.cs (excerpt)

```
protected override void Update(GameTime gameTime)
{
    // Allows the game to exit
    if (GamePad.GetState(PlayerIndex.One).Buttons.Back == ButtonState.Pressed)
        this.Exit();

    while (TouchPanel.IsGestureAvailable)
    {
        GestureSample gesture = TouchPanel.ReadGesture();

        if (gesture.GestureType == GestureType.FreeDrag)
        {
            Vector2 prevPosition = gesture.Position - gesture.Delta;

            float scaleX = (gesture.Position.X - screenCenter.X) /
                               (prevPosition.X - screenCenter.X);
            float scaleY = (gesture.Position.Y - screenCenter.Y) /
                               (prevPosition.Y - screenCenter.Y);

            textureScale.X *= scaleX;
```

```
            textureScale.Y *= scaleY;
        }
    }
    base.Update(gameTime);
}
```

For example, the center of the screen is probably the point (400, 240). Suppose during this particular part of the gesture, the *Position* property is (600, 200) and the *Delta* property is (20, 10). That means the previous position was (580, 190). In the horizontal direction, the distance of the finger from the center of the texture increased from 180 pixels (580 minus 400) to 200 pixels (600 minus 400) for a scaling factor of 200 divided by 180 or 1.11. In the vertical direction, the distance from the center decreased from 50 pixels (240 minus 190) to 40 pixels (240 minus 200) for a scaling factor of 40 divided by 80 or 0.80. The image increases in size by 11% in the horizontal direction and decreases by 20% in the vertical.

Therefore, multiply the X component of the scaling vector by 1.11 and the Y component by 0.80. As expected, that scaling factor shows up in the *Draw* override:

XNA Project: OneFingerScale   File: Game1.cs (excerpt)

```
protected override void Draw(GameTime gameTime)
{
    GraphicsDevice.Clear(Color.CornflowerBlue);

    spriteBatch.Begin();
    spriteBatch.Draw(texture, screenCenter, null, Color.White, 0,
                    textureCenter, textureScale, SpriteEffects.None, 0);
    spriteBatch.End();

    base.Draw(gameTime);
}
```

Probably the most rewarding way to play with this program is to "grab" the image at one of the corners and move that corner roughly towards or away from the center:

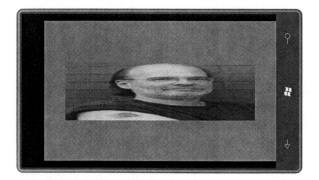

As you can see, there's nothing to prevent the image from losing its proper aspect ratio, as the calculations above imply. You can even—by sweeping your finger across the vertical center or horizontal center of the screen—cause the image to scale down to nothing!

In a real-life application, you probably want to put a lower limit on the scaling factor, perhaps 0.1 or 0.25, just to leave enough so the user can size it back up.

It's also likely that in some applications, you'll want to preserve the aspect ratio of the image. You'll want to derive just one scaling factor that applies to both horizontal and vertical scaling. It might seem reasonable to calculate separate scaling factors as shown in the OneFingerScale program and then just average them. But this is clearly wrong. If the user knows that a program preserves aspect ratio, the user will expect the image to scale appropriately with just a horizontal drag or a vertical drag.

You might consider calculating both scaling factors and taking the maximum. But that's not quite right either. You'll notice in OneFingerScale that when your finger is close to the center of the image, just a little movement is magnified into a large amount of scaling. If the finger is close to the center horizontally but far from the center vertically, then the scaling factors are different for equal horizontal and vertical finger movement.

Perhaps the best strategy is to examine the *Delta* property and determine whether the X or Y component has the greatest magnitude (apart from sign) and then use that for the scaling calculation. This is shown in the OneFingerUniformScale project.

The fields are the same as the previous program except that a *Vector2* scaling factor has been replaced with a *float*.

XNA Project: **OneFingerUniformScale**   File: **Game1.cs** (excerpt showing fields)

```
public class Game1 : Microsoft.Xna.Framework.Game
{
    GraphicsDeviceManager graphics;
    SpriteBatch spriteBatch;

    Texture2D texture;
    Vector2 screenCenter;
    Vector2 textureCenter;
    float textureScale = 1;
    . . .
}
```

The *LoadContent* override is exactly the same as the previous version, but the gesture handling in the *Update* override has become more extensive. The method checks whether the absolute value of the horizontal or vertical component of the *Delta* vector is largest, and also skips the calculation if they're both zero, which in the case when the user first touches a finger to the screen.

XNA Project: **OneFingerUniformScale**   File: **Game1.cs** (excerpt)

```
protected override void Update(GameTime gameTime)
{
    // Allows the game to exit
    if (GamePad.GetState(PlayerIndex.One).Buttons.Back == ButtonState.Pressed)
        this.Exit();

    while (TouchPanel.IsGestureAvailable)
    {
        GestureSample gesture = TouchPanel.ReadGesture();

        if (gesture.GestureType == GestureType.FreeDrag)
        {
            Vector2 prevPosition = gesture.Position - gesture.Delta;
            float scale = 1;

            if (Math.Abs(gesture.Delta.X) > Math.Abs(gesture.Delta.Y))
            {
                scale = (gesture.Position.X - screenCenter.X) /
                            (prevPosition.X - screenCenter.X);
            }
            else if (gesture.Delta.Y != 0)
            {
                scale = (gesture.Position.Y - screenCenter.Y) /
                            (prevPosition.Y - screenCenter.Y);
            }

            if (!float.IsInfinity(scale) && !float.IsNaN(scale))
            {
                textureScale = Math.Min(10,
                            Math.Max(0.25f, scale * textureScale));
            }
        }
    }
    base.Update(gameTime);
}
```

Another precaution implemented here is checking if the calculated value is infinite or not a number. This could be the case if the user touches the exact center of the screen resulting in division by zero. I've also clamped the overall scaling factor between 0.25 and 10, which are rather arbitrary values but still an important concept.

The *Draw* override is the same as in the previous program except that *textureScale* is a *float* rather than a *Vector2*:

XNA Project: OneFingerUniformScale   File: Game1.cs (excerpt)

```
protected override void Draw(GameTime gameTime)
{
    GraphicsDevice.Clear(Color.CornflowerBlue);

    spriteBatch.Begin();
    spriteBatch.Draw(texture, screenCenter, null, Color.White, 0,
                    textureCenter, textureScale, SpriteEffects.None, 0);
    spriteBatch.End();

    base.Draw(gameTime);
}
```

I set a maximum on *textureScale* after experimenting with an earlier version of the program. I touched the image very close to the center of the screen and a small movement expanded the image by a scaling factor of several hundred, where only two pixels of the image were visible on the screen! It's safe to say that's too much scaling.

It's possible for a program to ignore certain gestures that occur too close to a reference point. I do this in the next project.

Although single-finger scaling is somewhat unusual, single-finger rotation is very powerful and quite common—both on the computer screen and in real life. If your phone is sitting on the desk next to you, put your finger on a corner and pull it towards you. The phone probably rotates a bit relative to its center before being dragged.

Very often single-finger rotation is combined with regular dragging. Let's see how this works. The OneFingerRotation fields are somewhat similar to the previous programs:

XNA Project: OneFingerRotation   File: Game1.cs (excerpt showing fields)

```
public class Game1 : Microsoft.Xna.Framework.Game
{
    GraphicsDeviceManager graphics;
    SpriteBatch spriteBatch;

    Texture2D texture;
    Vector2 texturePosition;
    Vector2 textureCenter;
    float textureRotation;
    ...
}
```

The *LoadContent* override is similar as well The *texturePosition* field is initialized to be the center of the screen but this will change as the texture is dragged around the screen:

XNA Project: OneFingerRotation   File: Game1.cs (excerpt)

```
protected override void LoadContent()
{
    // Create a new SpriteBatch, which can be used to draw textures.
    spriteBatch = new SpriteBatch(GraphicsDevice);

    Viewport viewport = this.GraphicsDevice.Viewport;
    texturePosition = new Vector2(viewport.Width / 2, viewport.Height / 2);

    texture = this.Content.Load<Texture2D>("PetzoldTattoo");
    textureCenter = new Vector2(texture.Width / 2, texture.Height / 2);
}
```

The idea behind the *Update* method is to first examine the previous finger position and the new finger position relative to the center of the *Texture2D* at *texturePosition*. In *Update* I represent these two positions as vectors from that center called *oldVector* and *newVector*, and by "old" and "new" I mean "previous" and "current." If these two vectors are at different angles, then the *textureRotation* angle is altered by the difference in those angles.

Now we want to remove rotation from these finger positions. Anything left over should be applied to dragging the texture. The *oldVector* is recalculated so it has its original magnitude but now points in the same direction as *newVector*. A new delta value is recalculated from *newVector* and *oldVector* and this is used for dragging:

XNA Project: OneFingerRotation   File: Game1.cs (excerpt)

```
protected override void Update(GameTime gameTime)
{
    // Allows the game to exit
    if (GamePad.GetState(PlayerIndex.One).Buttons.Back == ButtonState.Pressed)
        this.Exit();

    while (TouchPanel.IsGestureAvailable)
    {
        GestureSample gesture = TouchPanel.ReadGesture();

        if (gesture.GestureType == GestureType.FreeDrag)
        {
            Vector2 delta = gesture.Delta;
            Vector2 newPosition = gesture.Position;
            Vector2 oldPosition = newPosition - delta;
```

```
            // Find vectors from center of bitmap to touch points
            Vector2 oldVector = oldPosition - texturePosition;
            Vector2 newVector = newPosition - texturePosition;

            // Avoid rotation if fingers are close to center
            if (newVector.Length() > 25 && oldVector.Length() > 25)
            {
                // Find angles from center of bitmap to touch points
                float oldAngle = (float)Math.Atan2(oldVector.Y, oldVector.X);
                float newAngle = (float)Math.Atan2(newVector.Y, newVector.X);

                // Adjust texture rotation angle
                textureRotation += newAngle - oldAngle;

                // Essentially rotate the old vector
                oldVector = oldVector.Length() / newVector.Length() * newVector;

                // Re-calculate delta
                delta = newVector - oldVector;
            }
            // Move texture
            texturePosition += delta;
        }
    }
    base.Update(gameTime);
}
```

The *Draw* override references that rotation angle but has a scaling factor equal to 1:

XNA Project: OneFingerRotation   File: Game1.cs (excerpt)

```
protected override void Draw(GameTime gameTime)
{
    GraphicsDevice.Clear(Color.CornflowerBlue);

    spriteBatch.Begin();
    spriteBatch.Draw(texture, texturePosition, null, Color.White,
                    textureRotation, textureCenter, 1, SpriteEffects.None, 0);
    spriteBatch.End();

    base.Draw(gameTime);
}
```

As you experiment with this, you'll find that the movement is very natural. You can grab the image at any point and drag it, and it's as if the image trails behind your finger just like when you use your finger to move the phone on your desk.

Of course, the most common form of scaling implemented in multi-touch applications involves two fingers in a pinching or stretching gesture, and in a sense, that isn't much more difficult than what you've already seen. I've been stretching and rotating relative to a reference point, and with two fingers it's similar except that the reference point is always the other finger.

For example, put two fingers on an on-screen object. If you keep one finger steady and move the other finger, you should expect all scaling and rotation to occur relative to the first finger. If that first finger is also moving, then whatever scaling and rotation it defines is relative to the second finger. If the two fingers move in the same direction, then normal dragging results.

The math is likely to get messy; fortunately XNA provides some very powerful tools to help out.

Matrix Transforms

Traditionally, two-dimensional graphical systems have supported operations called *transforms*. These are basically mathematical formulas that are applied to coordinates (x, y) to make new coordinates (x', y'). Although completely generalized transforms can potentially be very complex, two-dimensional graphics programming environments often restrict transforms to a subset called *affine* ("non-infinite") transforms, which are a slight superset of *linear* transforms.

Linear transforms of x and y look like this:

$$x' = a_x x + b_x y$$

$$y' = a_y x + b_y y$$

where the subscripted a and b are constants that define a particular transform. As you can see, x' and y' are both functions of x and y, but they are very simple functions. It's just multiplication by constants and adding the results; x and y aren't multiplied by each other, for example.

An affine translation adds in another constant that's not multiplied by anything:

$x' = a_x x + b_x y + c_x$

$y' = a_y x + b_y y + c_y$

Very often some of these constants are zero. If a_x and b_y are both 1, and b_x and a_y are both zero, then the formulas represent a type of transform known as *translation*:

$x' = x + c_x$

$y' = y + c_y$

This transform just causes a shift to another location—not unlike the OneFingerDrag program that started off this chapter.

If b_x and a_y are zero, and c_x and c_y are also zero, then the formulas represent *scaling*:

$x' = a_x x$

$y' = b_y y$

Coordinates are multiplied by factors to make objects larger or smaller.

The four multiplicative constants can be set to sines and cosines of a particular angle like so:

$x' = \cos(\ )x - \sin(\ )y$

$y' = \sin(\ )x - \cos(\ )y$

The formulas rotate the point around the origin by α degrees. Setting these four constants to other values not related by trigonometric functions cause a type of transform known as *skew*, which transforms a square into a parallelogram. But that's as strange as affine transforms get: Affine transforms never cause straight lines to become curves, or parallel lines to become non-parallel. As the name suggests, *affine* transforms don't cause coordinates to become infinite.

Translation, scaling, and rotation are the most common types of transforms, and they can be combined. To keep the math easy (well, *easier*) transforms are often represented as 3 × 3 matrices:

$$\begin{vmatrix} a_x & a_y & 0 \\ b_x & b_y & 0 \\ c_x & c_y & 1 \end{vmatrix}$$

A particular transform is applied to a point (x, y) by representing the point as a 1×3 matrix with a 1 in the third position and performing a matrix multiplication:

$$| x \ \ y \ \ 1 | \cdot \begin{vmatrix} a_x & a_y & 0 \\ b_x & b_y & 0 \\ c_x & c_y & 1 \end{vmatrix} = | x' \ y' \ 1 |$$

The identity matrix contains a diagonal of all 1's and results in no transform:

$$\begin{vmatrix} 1 & 0 & 0 \\ 0 & 1 & 0 \\ 0 & 0 & 1 \end{vmatrix}$$

Representing transforms with matrices is of great advantage when transforms are combined. Combining transforms is equivalent to multiplying matrices, and that's an operation that is well known. It is also well known that matrix multiplication is not commutative. The order of the multiplication makes a difference in the result.

For example, you might apply a scale transform to a graphical object to make it larger, and then apply a translate transform to move it. If you switch those two operations—perform the translation first and then the scaling—the result is different because you're effectively scaling the original translation factors as well.

Transforms in 2D space require a 3×3 matrix, and transforms in 3D space require a 4×4 matrix. There is a good reason why the matrix needs one more dimension that the coordinate space. It's all about translation. Translation is very basic and very desirable but it can't be represented with a linear transform that only applies factors to x and y. To represent translation as a linear transform, another dimension must be added. Translation in two dimensions in actually skew in three dimensions, and that's why the two-dimensional point is converted to a three-dimensional point with a Z value of 1 for multiplying by the matrix.

The third column of a two-dimensional affine transform matrix is always two zeroes and a 1 in the bottom right corner. That's what makes it an *affine* transform. (I'll discuss non-affine two-dimensional transforms towards the end of this chapter.)

After my big build-up, you'll probably be surprised to learn that XNA is unlike virtually all other graphical programming environments in that it does *not* support a structure that encapsulates a 3×3 transform matrix. In XNA matrices are used much more for 3D programming, so the XNA *Matrix* structure actually encapsulates a 4×4 matrix suitable for 3D graphics but a bit over-abundant for 2D graphics.

Although you can use the *Matrix* structure with 2D graphics—and it's very convenient for performing compound transforms—there is not much support for transforms in 2D drawing except a rather more extensive version of the *Begin* call of *SpriteBatch*:

```
spriteBatch.Begin(SpriteSortMode.Deferred, null, null, null, null, null, matrix);
```

If you use this form of the *Begin* call, then that *Matrix* object will affect all the *Draw* and *DrawString* calls until *End*. This can be very useful for applying a transform to a whole group of graphical objects.

You can also apply transforms to *Vector2* objects "manually" with several versions of the static *Vector2.Transform* method.

The *Matrix* structure supports very many static methods for creating *Matrix* objects that represent various types of transforms. These are all designed for 3D, but here's how you can use the most basic ones for 2D:

```
Matrix matrix = Matrix.CreateTranslation(xOffset, yOffset, 0);

Matrix matrix = Matrix.CreateScale(xScale, yScale, 1);

Matrix matrix = Matrix.CreateRotationZ(radians);
```

The last argument on the first two methods is normally set to the translation or scaling factor for the three-dimensional Z axis. Notice I've set the third argument in the second call to 1 rather than 0. A 0 will work for most purposes, but if you ever need to invert the matrix, a zero scaling factor is a real deal killer. Also notice that the third method name makes reference to the Z axis. The method needs to calculate rotation around the Z axis for rotation in the two-dimensional XY plane.

The *Matrix* structure supports arithmetical operators, so you can easily multiply matrices for compounding transforms. One of the most common reasons to multiply matrices is to represent scaling or rotation around a particular point.

Suppose you have a point stored as a *Vector2* object called *center*. You want to calculate a matrix that represents rotation by *angle* degrees but centered on that point. You begin with translation to move that center point to the origin, then you apply the rotation (or scaling) and then another translation to move the center back to where it was:

```
Matrix matrix = Matrix.CreateTranslation(-center.X, -center.Y, 0);
matrix *= Matrix.CreateRotationZ(angle);
matrix *= Matrix.CreateTranslation(center.X, center.Y, 0);
```

Notice the multiplication operators.

The *Matrix* structure in XNA has 16 public fields of type *float* representing all 16 cells of the 4 × 4 matrix. These have names that indicate their row and column position within the matrix:

$$\begin{vmatrix} M11 & M12 & M13 & M14 \\ M21 & M22 & M23 & M24 \\ M31 & M32 & M33 & M34 \\ M41 & M42 & M43 & M44 \end{vmatrix}$$

Rather than using the static methods of *Matrix* to create *Matrix* objects, you can set these fields individually (or set them all in a 16-argument constructor.) The subscripted constants that I used earlier correspond to these cells:

$$\begin{vmatrix} a_x & a_y & 0 & 0 \\ b_x & b_y & 0 & 0 \\ 0 & 0 & 1 & 1 \\ c_x & c_y & 0 & 1 \end{vmatrix}$$

The *M11* field is the horizontal scaling factor and *M22* is vertical scaling; *M41* is horizontal translation and *M42* is vertical translation. Or, you can rewrite the 2D affine transform formulas using the *Matrix* structure field names:

x' = M11 · x + M21 · y + M41

y' = M12 · x + M22 · y + M42

Knowing the relationship between these fields and transforms can aid in extracting information from the *Matrix* structure or implementing short cuts that don't involve creating new *Matrix* objects and multiplying them. I'll demonstrate some of these techniques in the pages ahead.

The *Pinch* Gesture

With the *Pinch* gesture, four *Vector2* properties of the *GestureSample* are valid: *Position*, *Delta*, *Position2*, and *Delta2*. The first two reflect the position and movement of one finger; the second two represent the second finger. This is ideal for scaling, although the actual mathematics are probably not immediately obvious.

Generally you'll want to support both *FreeDrag* and *Pinch* so the user can use one or two fingers. Then you need to decide whether to restrict scaling to uniform or non-uniform scaling, and whether rotation should be supported.

The DragAndPinch program handles both *FreeDrag* and *Pinch* gestures with non-uniform scaling and without rotation. As usual, these gestures are enabled in the constructor. The new field you'll see here is *Matrix* object initialized to the no-transform identity state with the static *Matrix.Identity* property:

XNA Project: **DragAndPinch**   File: **Game1.cs (excerpt showing fields)**

```
public class Game1 : Microsoft.Xna.Framework.Game
{
    GraphicsDeviceManager graphics;
    SpriteBatch spriteBatch;
```

```
    Texture2D texture;
    Matrix matrix = Matrix.Identity;

    public Game1()
    {
        graphics = new GraphicsDeviceManager(this);
        Content.RootDirectory = "Content";

        // Frame rate is 30 fps by default for Windows Phone.
        TargetElapsedTime = TimeSpan.FromTicks(333333);

        TouchPanel.EnabledGestures = GestureType.FreeDrag | GestureType.Pinch;
    }
    ...
}
```

The statement

```
Matrix matrix = Matrix.Identity;
```

is *not* the same as:

```
Matrix matrix = new Matrix();
```

Matrix is a structure, and like all structures its fields are initialized to zero values. A *Matrix* object with all zeroes is not good for anything since it completely obliterates anything it's applied to. A default do-nothing *Matrix* object should have all its diagonal cells set to 1, and that's what's provided by the *Matrix.Identity* property.

All dragging and pinching operations will be applied to the *matrix* field, which is then used in the *Draw* override.

The *LoadContent* method merely loads the *Texture2D*:

XNA Project: DragAndPinch   File: Game1.cs (excerpt)

```
protected override void LoadContent()
{
    // Create a new SpriteBatch, which can be used to draw textures.
    spriteBatch = new SpriteBatch(GraphicsDevice);

    texture = this.Content.Load<Texture2D>("PetzoldTattoo");
}
```

The *Update* override handles both *FreeDrag* and *Pinch*:

XNA Project: **DragAndPinch**   File: **Game1.cs (excerpt)**

```
protected override void Update(GameTime gameTime)
{
    // Allows the game to exit
    if (GamePad.GetState(PlayerIndex.One).Buttons.Back == ButtonState.Pressed)
        this.Exit();

    while (TouchPanel.IsGestureAvailable)
    {
        GestureSample gesture = TouchPanel.ReadGesture();

        switch (gesture.GestureType)
        {
            case GestureType.FreeDrag:
                matrix *= Matrix.CreateTranslation(gesture.Delta.X, gesture.Delta.Y, 0);
                break;

            case GestureType.Pinch:
                Vector2 oldPoint1 = gesture.Position - gesture.Delta;
                Vector2 newPoint1 = gesture.Position;
                Vector2 oldPoint2 = gesture.Position2 - gesture.Delta2;
                Vector2 newPoint2 = gesture.Position2;

                matrix *= ComputeScaleMatrix(oldPoint1, oldPoint2, newPoint2);
                matrix *= ComputeScaleMatrix(newPoint2, oldPoint1, newPoint1);
                break;
        }
    }
    base.Update(gameTime);
}
```

Notice that for *FreeDrag*, the method creates a new *Matrix* from the static *Matrix* *.CreateTranslation* method and multiplies it by the existing *matrix* field. You can replace that statement with the following:

```
matrix.M41 += gesture.Delta.X;
matrix.M42 += gesture.Delta.Y;
```

For the *Pinch* gesture, *Update* breaks down the data into "old" points and "new" points. When two fingers are both moving relative to each other, you can determine a composite scaling factor by treating the two fingers separately. Assume the first finger is fixed in position and the other is moving relative to it, and then the second finger is fixed in position and the first finger is moving relative to it. Each represents a separate scaling operation that you then multiply. In each case, you have a reference point (the fixed finger) and an old point and a new point (the moving finger).

To do this properly, for the first scaling operation the reference point should reflect the *old* position of the fixed finger, but for the second scaling factor you should use a reference point based on the *new* position of the fixed finger. That's the reason for the slightly asymmetrical calls to the *ComputeScaleMatrix* method shown above. Here's the method itself:

XNA Project: DragAndPinch   File: Game1.cs (excerpt)

```
Matrix ComputeScaleMatrix(Vector2 refPoint, Vector2 oldPoint, Vector2 newPoint)
{
    float scaleX = (newPoint.X - refPoint.X) / (oldPoint.X - refPoint.X);
    float scaleY = (newPoint.Y - refPoint.Y) / (oldPoint.Y - refPoint.Y);

    if (float.IsNaN(scaleX) || float.IsInfinity(scaleX) ||
        float.IsNaN(scaleY) || float.IsInfinity(scaleY) ||
        scaleX <= 0 || scaleY <= 0)
    {
        return Matrix.Identity;
    }

    scaleX = Math.Min(1.1f, Math.Max(0.9f, scaleX));
    scaleY = Math.Min(1.1f, Math.Max(0.9f, scaleY));

    Matrix matrix = Matrix.CreateTranslation(-refPoint.X, -refPoint.Y, 0);
    matrix *= Matrix.CreateScale(scaleX, scaleY, 1);
    matrix *= Matrix.CreateTranslation(refPoint.X, refPoint.Y, 0);

    return matrix;
}
```

That reference point plays two roles here: It is used to measure the increase or decrease in the position of the moving finger, and it is used to bracket the *Matrix.CreateScale* calls at the end to reflect scaling around a center point. You can replace those three calls at the end with the following:

```
Matrix matrix = Matrix.Identity;
matrix.M41 -= refPoint.X;
matrix.M42 -= refPoint.Y;

matrix *= Matrix.CreateScale(scaleX, scaleY, 1);

matrix.M41 += refPoint.X;
matrix.M42 += refPoint.Y;
```

The accumulated composite matrix is simply passed to the last argument of the *Begin* call of *spriteBatch* in the *Draw* override:

XNA Project: DragAndPinch   File: Game1.cs (excerpt)

```
protected override void Draw(GameTime gameTime)
{
    GraphicsDevice.Clear(Color.CornflowerBlue);
```

```
        spriteBatch.Begin(SpriteSortMode.Deferred, null, null, null, null, null, matrix);
        spriteBatch.Draw(texture, Vector2.Zero, Color.White);
        spriteBatch.End();

        base.Draw(gameTime);
    }
```

If you'd prefer to use the simpler form of the *Begin* call, you can extract the scaling and position information from the *Matrix* object and use them in the *Draw* call:

```
Vector2 scale = new Vector2(matrix.M11, matrix.M22);
Vector2 position = new Vector2(matrix.M41, matrix.M42);

spriteBatch.Begin();
spriteBatch.Draw(texture, position, null, Color.White, 0,
                 Vector2.Zero, scale, SpriteEffects.None, 0);
spriteBatch.End();
```

The *Matrix* structure also supports a *Decompose* method, which extracts scaling, rotation, and translation components. The rotation component is the form of a *Quaternion*, which is a very common tool for 3D rotation but never (to my knowledge) used in 2D graphics. Replace those *scale* and *position* calculations with the following:

```
Vector3 scale3;
Quaternion quaternion;
Vector3 translation3;

matrix.Decompose(out scale3, out quaternion, out translation3);

Vector2 scale = new Vector2(scale3.X, scale3.Y);
Vector2 position = new Vector2(translation3.X, translation3.Y);
```

Let's add both one and two-finger rotation support to the DragAndPinch program and call it DragPinchRotate. Everything is the same except for the *Update* override.

XNA Project: **DragPinchRotate**   File: **Game1.cs** (excerpt)

```
protected override void Update(GameTime gameTime)
{
    // Allows the game to exit
    if (GamePad.GetState(PlayerIndex.One).Buttons.Back == ButtonState.Pressed)
        this.Exit();

    while (TouchPanel.IsGestureAvailable)
    {
        GestureSample gesture = TouchPanel.ReadGesture();
```

```
        switch (gesture.GestureType)
        {
            case GestureType.FreeDrag:
                Vector2 newPoint = gesture.Position;
                Vector2 oldPoint = newPoint - gesture.Delta;
                Vector2 textureCenter = new Vector2(texture.Width / 2, texture.Height
/ 2);

                Vector2 refPoint = Vector2.Transform(textureCenter, matrix);

                matrix *= ComputeRotateAndTranslateMatrix(refPoint, oldPoint,
newPoint);
                break;

            case GestureType.Pinch:
                Vector2 oldPoint1 = gesture.Position - gesture.Delta;
                Vector2 newPoint1 = gesture.Position;
                Vector2 oldPoint2 = gesture.Position2 - gesture.Delta2;
                Vector2 newPoint2 = gesture.Position2;

                matrix *= ComputeScaleAndRotateMatrix(oldPoint1, oldPoint2,
newPoint2);
                matrix *= ComputeScaleAndRotateMatrix(newPoint2, oldPoint1,
newPoint1);
                break;
        }
    }
    base.Update(gameTime);
}
```

In the earlier program that demonstrated one-finger rotation, the *Texture2D* was always positioned at a point corresponding to its center, so the rotation reference point was always readily available. This *Texture2D* is positioned by the *Draw* call of *SpriteBatch* at the upper-left corner of the display, but its actual location is somewhere else based on the *Matrix* object.

For that reason, the *FreeDrag* logic expresses the center of the *Texture2D* relative to its upper-left corner as a *Vector2* value and then applies the current matrix transform to obtain a *refPoint* relative to the screen.

The *ComputeRotateAndTranslateMatrix* method that *Update* calls for the *FreeDrag* gesture is very similar to the previous one-finger rotation logic except that transforms are obtained and multiplied:

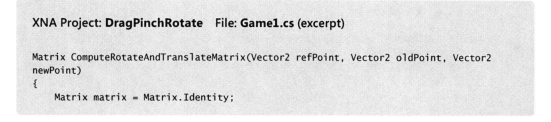

XNA Project: DragPinchRotate   File: Game1.cs (excerpt)

```
Matrix ComputeRotateAndTranslateMatrix(Vector2 refPoint, Vector2 oldPoint, Vector2
newPoint)
{
    Matrix matrix = Matrix.Identity;
```

```
        Vector2 delta = newPoint - oldPoint;
        Vector2 oldVector = oldPoint - refPoint;
        Vector2 newVector = newPoint - refPoint;

        // Avoid rotation if fingers are close to center
        if (newVector.Length() > 25 && oldVector.Length() > 25)
        {
            // Find angles from center of bitmap to touch points
            float oldAngle = (float)Math.Atan2(oldVector.Y, oldVector.X);
            float newAngle = (float)Math.Atan2(newVector.Y, newVector.X);

            // Calculate rotation matrix
            float angle = newAngle - oldAngle;
            matrix *= Matrix.CreateTranslation(-refPoint.X, -refPoint.Y, 0);
            matrix *= Matrix.CreateRotationZ(angle);
            matrix *= Matrix.CreateTranslation(refPoint.X, refPoint.Y, 0);

            // Essentially rotate the old vector
            oldVector = oldVector.Length() / newVector.Length() * newVector;

            // Re-calculate delta
            delta = newVector - oldVector;
        }
        // Include translation
        matrix *= Matrix.CreateTranslation(delta.X, delta.Y, 0);
        return matrix;
    }
```

Notice that the *Matrix.CreateRotationZ* call is sandwiched between two *Matrix
.CreateTranslation* calls to perform the rotation relative to the reference point, which is
the transformed center of the *Texture2D*. At the end, another *Matrix.CreateTranslation* call
handles the translation part of the gesture after rotation has been extracted.

Some of that same logic was merged into the *ComputeScaleMatrix* method from the
previous project for this new *ComputeScaleAndRotateMatrix* method that's called twice for
any *Pinch* gesture:

XNA Project: DragPinchRotate   File: Game1.cs (excerpt)

```
Matrix ComputeScaleAndRotateMatrix(Vector2 refPoint, Vector2 oldPoint, Vector2
newPoint)
{
    Matrix matrix = Matrix.Identity;
    Vector2 oldVector = oldPoint - refPoint;
    Vector2 newVector = newPoint - refPoint;

    // Find angles from reference point to touch points
    float oldAngle = (float)Math.Atan2(oldVector.Y, oldVector.X);
    float newAngle = (float)Math.Atan2(newVector.Y, newVector.X);
```

```
    // Calculate rotation matrix
    float angle = newAngle - oldAngle;
    matrix *= Matrix.CreateTranslation(-refPoint.X, -refPoint.Y, 0);
    matrix *= Matrix.CreateRotationZ(angle);
    matrix *= Matrix.CreateTranslation(refPoint.X, refPoint.Y, 0);

    // Essentially rotate the old vector
    oldVector = oldVector.Length() / newVector.Length() * newVector;
    float scale = 1;

    // Determine scaling from dominating delta
    if (Math.Abs(newVector.X - oldVector.X) > Math.Abs(newVector.Y - oldVector.Y))
        scale = newVector.X / oldVector.X;
    else
        scale = newVector.Y / oldVector.Y;

    // Calculate scaling matrix
    if (!float.IsNaN(scale) && !float.IsInfinity(scale) && scale > 0)
    {
        scale = Math.Min(1.1f, Math.Max(0.9f, scale));

        matrix *= Matrix.CreateTranslation(-refPoint.X, -refPoint.Y, 0);
        matrix *= Matrix.CreateScale(scale, scale, 1);
        matrix *= Matrix.CreateTranslation(refPoint.X, refPoint.Y, 0);
    }
    return matrix;
}
```

To scale uniformly, the method examines whether movement is dominant in the horizontal direction or vertical direction relative to the reference point, and that involves a comparison between the absolute values of the differences between *newVector* and *oldVector* (with the rotation component already extracted). Notice also how *Matrix.CreateScale* is sandwiched between two *Matrix.CreateTranslation* calls based on the reference points.

And now you can perform one-finger translation and rotation, and two-finger uniform scaling and rotation:

Although not explicitly included, a pair of fingers can also translate the image if the fingers move in the same direction.

Flick and Inertia

In the movie *Minority Report* (2002), Tom Cruise demonstrated how to flick an object off to one side of the computer screen, and the whole world said "Way cool!"

For the most part, implementing inertia in the touch interfaces of a program is your responsibility. XNA helps out just a little with the *Flick* gesture, which is generated when the user quickly sweeps a finger on the screen. The *Delta* property of the *GestureSample* object indicates the velocity of the finger in pixels per second. (That's what it's supposed to be, anyway. It actually seems to be closer to half the actual velocity.) The velocity is represented as a *Vector2*, so it indicates direction as well as magnitude.

There's no position information with the *Flick* gesture. It's basically the same no matter where you flick the screen. If you need to implement inertia based on finger position as well as velocity, you'll probably find yourself calculating velocity from *Drag* gestures by dividing the *Delta* values by the *ElapsedGameTime* property of the *GameTime* argument to *Update*.

To implement inertia, you need to continue moving an object based on an initial velocity and a deceleration value. If the velocity is in units pixels per second, the deceleration is probably in units of pixels per second squared. Every second, the velocity decreases by the deceleration value until the magnitude gets down to zero. For *Update* calls occurring every fraction of a second, the velocity decreases proportionally.

The FlickInertia project demonstrates a very simple implementation of inertia. The fields include *position*, *velocity*, and a deceleration constant:

XNA Project: FlickInertia   File: Game1.cs (excerpt showing fields)

```
public class Game1 : Microsoft.Xna.Framework.Game
{
    GraphicsDeviceManager graphics;
    SpriteBatch spriteBatch;

    const float DECELERATION = 1000; // pixels per second squared

    Texture2D texture;
    Vector2 position = Vector2.Zero;
    Vector2 velocity;
    SpriteFont segoe14;
    StringBuilder text = new StringBuilder();
```

```
    public Game1()
    {
        graphics = new GraphicsDeviceManager(this);
        Content.RootDirectory = "Content";

        // Frame rate is 30 fps by default for Windows Phone.
        TargetElapsedTime = TimeSpan.FromTicks(333333);

        TouchPanel.EnabledGestures = GestureType.Flick;
    }
    ...
}
```

The constructor enables only *Flick* gestures. The *LoadContent* override loads both the *Texture2D* and a font for displaying status information (position and velocity) on the screen:

XNA Project: FlickInertia   File: Game1.cs (excerpt)

```
protected override void LoadContent()
{
    // Create a new SpriteBatch, which can be used to draw textures.
    spriteBatch = new SpriteBatch(GraphicsDevice);

    texture = this.Content.Load<Texture2D>("PetzoldTattoo");
    segoe14 = this.Content.Load<SpriteFont>("Segoe14");
}
```

The *Update* override has several responsibilities. The first is to read the gesture and accumulate any additional velocity in the *velocity* field. If there's velocity in effect, the *velocity* vector is multiplied by the elapsed time in seconds to obtain a change in position. This is added to the *position* vector. The magnitude of the *velocity* vector must then be decreased by an amount based on the DECELERATION constant also multiplied by the elapsed time in seconds. Finally, a *StringBuilder* is formatted to display the two vectors:

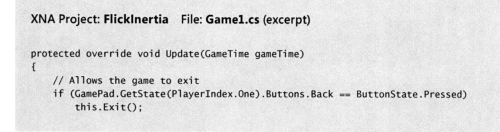

XNA Project: FlickInertia   File: Game1.cs (excerpt)

```
protected override void Update(GameTime gameTime)
{
    // Allows the game to exit
    if (GamePad.GetState(PlayerIndex.One).Buttons.Back == ButtonState.Pressed)
        this.Exit();
```

```
    // Set velocity from Flick gesture
    while (TouchPanel.IsGestureAvailable)
    {
        GestureSample gesture = TouchPanel.ReadGesture();

        if (gesture.GestureType == GestureType.Flick)
            velocity += gesture.Delta;
    }

    // Use velocity to adjust position and decelerate
    if (velocity != Vector2.Zero)
    {
        float elapsedSeconds = (float)gameTime.ElapsedGameTime.TotalSeconds;
        position += velocity * elapsedSeconds;
        float newMagnitude = velocity.Length() - DECELERATION * elapsedSeconds;
        velocity.Normalize();
        velocity *= Math.Max(0, newMagnitude);
    }

    // Display current position and velocity
    text.Remove(0, text.Length);
    text.AppendFormat("Position: {0} Velocity: {1}", position, velocity);

    base.Update(gameTime);
}
```

The *Draw* override draws both the *Texture2D* and the *StringBuilder*:

XNA Project: FlickInertia   File: Game1.cs (excerpt)

```
protected override void Draw(GameTime gameTime)
{
    GraphicsDevice.Clear(Color.CornflowerBlue);

    spriteBatch.Begin();
    spriteBatch.Draw(texture, position, Color.White);
    spriteBatch.DrawString(segoe14, text, Vector2.Zero, Color.White);
    spriteBatch.End();

    base.Draw(gameTime);
}
```

Yes, you can flick the image right off the screen. However, because the program responds to flicks anywhere on the screen, you can flick the screen again to bring it back into view.

The Mandelbrot Set

In 1980, Benoît Mandelbrot (1924–2010), a Polish-born French and American mathematician working for IBM, saw for the first time a graphic visualization of a recursive equation involving complex numbers that had been investigated earlier in the century. It looked something like this:

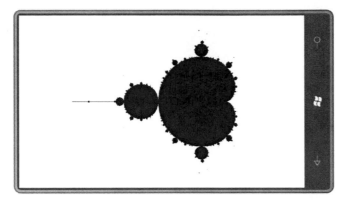

Since that time, the Mandelbrot Set (as it is called) has become a favorite plaything of computer programmers.

The Mandelbrot Set is graphed on the complex plane, where the horizontal axis represents real numbers (negative at the left and positive at the right) and the vertical axis represents imaginary numbers (negative at the bottom and positive at the top). Take any point in the plane and call it c, and set z equal to 0:

$z = 0$

Now perform the following recursive operation:

$z \leftarrow z^2 + c$

If the magnitude of z does not diverge to infinity, then c is said to belong to the Mandelbrot Set and is colored black in the above screen shot.

For some complex numbers (for example, the real number 0) it's very clear that the number belongs to the Mandelbrot Set. For others (for example, the real number 1) it's very clear that it does not. For many others, you just have to start cranking out the values. Fortunately, if the absolute value of z ever becomes greater than 2 after a finite number of iterations, you know that c does not belong to the Mandelbrot Set.

Each number c that does not belong to the Mandelbrot Set has an associated "iteration" factor, which is the number of iterations calculating z that occur before the absolute value becomes greater than 2. Many people who compute visualizations of the Mandelbrot Set use that iteration factor to select a color for that point so that areas not in the Mandelbrot Set become rather more interesting:

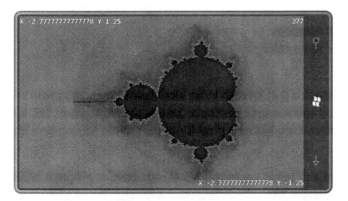

The text at the upper-left corner indicates the complex coordinate associated with that corner, and similarly for the lower-right corner. The number in the upper-right corner is a global iteration count.

One of the interesting characteristics of the Mandelbrot Set is that no matter how much you zoom in, the complexity of the image does not decrease:

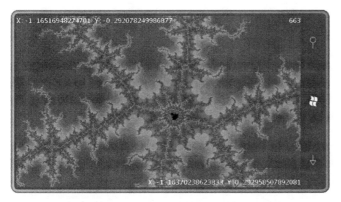

That qualifies the Mandelbrot Set as a fractal, a branch of mathematics that Benoît Mandelbrot pioneered. Considering the simplicity of the algorithm that produces this image, the results are truly astonishing.

Can you think of a better program to demonstrate multi-touch dragging and zooming as well as algorithmically generating pixels in a *Texture2D*?

Very often when programmers write Mandelbrot Set programs, they decide on a particular maximum iteration factor, for example, 100 or 1000. Then for each pixel, z is calculated up to that maximum number, and if it hasn't diverged by then, the pixel is set to black. In pseudocode, it's something like this:

```
For each pixel
{
        Perform up to MAX iterations
        Set pixel to black or some color
}
```

The problem with this approach is that it tends to be inadequate when you zoom in a great deal. Generally the more you zoom in on a particular area of the Mandelbrot Set, the more iterations are needed to determine whether a pixel is not part of the set and how it should be colored.

That problem implied to me a different approach: My MandelbrotSet program initially sets all the pixels to black and then performs the following in a second thread of execution:

```
Do forever
{
        For each pixel
        {
                Perform another iteration if necessary
                Possibly set pixel to some color
        }
}
```

This approach creates a screen that progressively gets more interesting the longer you wait. The downside is that about 17 megabytes of memory is required to support the data structure necessary for this job. That's too large to be saved during tombstoning. The overall performance also seems to be slower than more traditional approaches.

Here is the *PixelInfo* structure used to store information for each pixel. The program retains an array of these structures that parallels the normal *pixels* array used for writing data to the *Texture2D*:

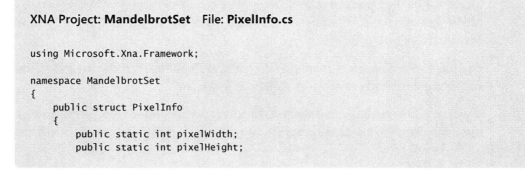

XNA Project: **MandelbrotSet**   File: **PixelInfo.cs**

```
using Microsoft.Xna.Framework;

namespace MandelbrotSet
{
    public struct PixelInfo
    {
        public static int pixelWidth;
        public static int pixelHeight;
```

```
            public static double xPixelCoordAtComplexOrigin;
            public static double yPixelCoordAtComplexOrigin;
            public static double unitsPerPixel;

            public static bool hasNewColors;
            public static int firstNewIndex;
            public static int lastNewIndex;

            public double cReal;
            public double cImag;
            public double zReal;
            public double zImag;
            public int iteration;
            public bool finished;
            public uint packedColor;

            public PixelInfo(int pixelIndex, uint[] pixels)
            {
                int x = pixelIndex % pixelWidth;
                int y = pixelIndex / pixelWidth;
                cReal = (x - xPixelCoordAtComplexOrigin) * unitsPerPixel;
                cImag = (yPixelCoordAtComplexOrigin - y) * unitsPerPixel;
                zReal = 0;
                zImag = 0;
                iteration = 0;
                finished = false;
                packedColor = pixels != null ? pixels[pixelIndex] : Color.Black.
PackedValue;
            }

            public bool Iterate()
            {
                double zImagSquared = zImag * zImag;
                zImag = 2 * zReal * zImag + cImag;
                zReal = zReal * zReal - zImagSquared + cReal;

                if (zReal * zReal + zImag * zImag >= 4.0)
                {
                    finished = true;
                    return true;
                }
                iteration++;
                return false;
            }
        }
    }
}
```

Skip down to the instance fields. I originally wrote a structure called *Complex* for encapsulating complex numbers and performing the operations on those numbers, but I discovered that working directly with the real and imaginary parts improved performance significantly. This *PixelInfo* structure retains the *c* and *z* values I described above, the current *iteration*, and a Boolean *finished* that's set to *true* when it's known that the magnitude of *z* diverges to infinity. At this point the *iteration* value can be used to determine a color value.

The constructor calculates *cReal* and *cImag* from a *pixelIndex* that ranges from 0 up to (but not including) the product of the pixel width and height of the display. The static *pixelWidth* and *pixelHeight* fields are based on the screen dimensions and fixed throughout the duration of the program.

The calculation of *cReal* and *cImag* is also based on three other static fields. The *xPixelCoordAtComplexOrigin* and *yPixelCoordAtComplexOrigin* fields indicate the horizontal and vertical pixel coordinates that correspond to the origin of the complex plane. Obviously the use of *double* for these fields indicates that they are capable of representing fractional pixels. These two fields change with translation operations. The *unitsPerPixel* field indicates the range of real numbers or imaginary numbers currently associated with a single pixel. This value changes with scaling operations.

This *PixelInfo* structure contains more *double* values than in all the other XNA programs in this book combined. I originally made these values all *float*, of course (and *pixelCoordAtComplexOrigin* was a *Vector2*) but I made the leap to *double* the first time I zoomed in beyond the precision of *float*. Interestingly, moving from *float* to *double* had very little impact on performance.

The second argument to the constructor is optional. If it's present, the constructor will copy the corresponding color from the *pixels* array into its own *packedColor* field. You'll see how this works shortly.

The other three static fields are used for inter-thread communication. Basically, the thread that performs the calculations sets these fields when a color value changes; the fields are reset when the array of *PixelInfo* structures is used to update the *pixels* array and the *Texture2D*.

Finally, the *Iterate* method performs the basic iterative calculation using multiplication rather than *Math.Pow* calls for performance reasons. *Iterate* returns true if *z* is known to diverge to infinity.

With those static fields of *PixelInfo*, I managed to keep the fields of the *Game* derivative down to a reasonable number. You'll see the normal *pixels* array here as well as the *PixelInfo* array. The *pixelInfosLock* object is used for thread synchronization.

XNA Project: MandelbrotSet   File: Game1.cs (excerpt showing fields)

```
public class Game1 : Microsoft.Xna.Framework.Game
{
    GraphicsDeviceManager graphics;
    SpriteBatch spriteBatch;

    Viewport viewport;
    Texture2D texture;
```

```
    uint[] pixels;
    PixelInfo[] pixelInfos;
    Matrix drawMatrix = Matrix.Identity;
    int globalIteration = 0;
    object pixelInfosLock = new object();

    SpriteFont segoe14;
    StringBuilder upperLeftCoordText = new StringBuilder();
    StringBuilder lowerRightCoordText = new StringBuilder();
    StringBuilder upperRightStatusText = new StringBuilder();
    Vector2 lowerRightCoordPosition, upperRightStatusPosition;

    public Game1()
    {
        graphics = new GraphicsDeviceManager(this);
        Content.RootDirectory = "Content";

        // Frame rate is 30 fps by default for Windows Phone.
        TargetElapsedTime = TimeSpan.FromTicks(333333);

        // Set full screen & enable gestures
        graphics.IsFullScreen = true;
        TouchPanel.EnabledGestures = GestureType.FreeDrag | GestureType.DragComplete |
                                     GestureType.Pinch | GestureType.PinchComplete;
    }
    ...
}
```

The fields also include a *Matrix* object that handles translation and scaling but only as the gesture operations are in process. Once the user's fingers lift from the screen—and you'll notice that the *DragComplete* and *PinchComplete* gestures are also enabled so the program can determine when that happens—the entire *pixels* and *PixelInfo* arrays are rearranged and the *Matrix* object is set back to its default value. This turns out to be one of the more complex parts of the program.

The *LoadContent* override is surprisingly sparse:

XNA Project: **MandelbrotSet**   File: **Game1.cs** (excerpt)

```
protected override void LoadContent()
{
    // Create a new SpriteBatch, which can be used to draw textures.
    spriteBatch = new SpriteBatch(GraphicsDevice);

    viewport = this.GraphicsDevice.Viewport;
    segoe14 = this.Content.Load<SpriteFont>("Segoe14");
}
```

But that's only because much of the other initialization is performed in conjunction with tombstoning. Of course, I wanted to save the whole array of *PixelInfo* objects, but considering that each of them is 44 bytes in size, and the full array approaches 17 megabytes, you can understand why the Windows Phone 7 operating system seemed so reluctant to comply with my desires.

Instead, the program tombstones four items necessary to restart the program reasonably: The static *xPixelCoordAtComplexOrigin*, *yPixelCoordAtComplexOrigin* and *unitsPerPixel* fields in *PixelInfo* allow the program to re-create the *PixelInfo* array. In addition, the program saves the entire screen image as a PNG file and restores that. When the program returns from tombstoning, it looks the same as when it left, but that's somewhat deceptive because it needs to start the calculations over with each pixel. Consequently, the screen may sit there for awhile before anything gets updated.

The code to save and restore *Texture2D* objects during tombstoning is standard and fairly simple, but I decided to make a couple methods to encapsulate the job. The static *Texture2DExtensions* class in the Petzold.Phone.Xna library contains the following two methods. The first is an extension method, so you can call it directly on a *Texture2D* object:

XNA Project: Petzold.Phone.Xna   File: Texture2DExtensions.cs (excerpt)

```
public static void SaveToPhoneServiceState(this Texture2D texture, string key)
{
    MemoryStream memoryStream = new MemoryStream();
    texture.SaveAsPng(memoryStream, texture.Width, texture.Height);
    PhoneApplicationService.Current.State[key] = memoryStream.GetBuffer();
}
```

The method creates a *MemoryStream* object and just passes that to the *SaveAsPng* method of the *Texture2D*. The *MemoryStream* itself can't be serialized but a *GetBuffer* method on the *MemoryStream* returns an array of bytes and that can be serialized.

The companion load method is not an extension method because it results in the creation of a new *Texture2D* object. A byte array is retrieved from storage and passed to a *MemoryStream* constructor, which is then used with the static *Texture2D.FromStream* method:

XNA Project: Petzold.Phone.Xna   File: Texture2DExtensions.cs (excerpt)

```
public static Texture2D LoadFromPhoneServiceState(GraphicsDevice graphicsDevice,
string key)
{
    Texture2D texture = null;
```

```
    if (PhoneApplicationService.Current.State.ContainsKey(key))
    {
        byte[] buffer = PhoneApplicationService.Current.State[key] as byte[];
        MemoryStream memoryStream = new MemoryStream(buffer);
        texture = Texture2D.FromStream(graphicsDevice, memoryStream);
        memoryStream.Close();
    }
    return texture;
}
```

Here are the *OnActivated* and *OnDeactivated* overrides in MandelbrotSet that makes use of those two methods, and a method named *InitializePixelInfo*:

XNA Project: MandelbrotSet   File: Game1.cs (excerpt)

```
protected override void OnActivated(object sender, EventArgs args)
{
    PhoneApplicationService appService = PhoneApplicationService.Current;

    if (appService.State.ContainsKey("xOrigin") &&
        appService.State.ContainsKey("yOrigin") &&
        appService.State.ContainsKey("resolution"))
    {
        PixelInfo.xPixelCoordAtComplexOrigin = (double)appService.State["xOrigin"];
        PixelInfo.yPixelCoordAtComplexOrigin = (double)appService.State["yOrigin"];
        PixelInfo.unitsPerPixel = (double)appService.State["resolution"];
    }
    else
    {
        // Program running from beginning
        PixelInfo.xPixelCoordAtComplexOrigin = 2 * viewport.Width / 3f;
        PixelInfo.yPixelCoordAtComplexOrigin = viewport.Height / 2;
        PixelInfo.unitsPerPixel = Math.Max(2.5 / viewport.Height,
                                           3.0 / viewport.Width);
    }

    UpdateCoordinateText();

    // Restore bitmap from tombstoning or recreate it
    texture = Texture2DExtensions.LoadFromPhoneServiceState(this.GraphicsDevice,
                                                        "mandelbrotBitmap");
    if (texture == null)
        texture = new Texture2D(this.GraphicsDevice, viewport.Width, viewport.Height);

    // Get texture information and pixels array
    PixelInfo.pixelWidth = texture.Width;
    PixelInfo.pixelHeight = texture.Height;
    int numPixels = PixelInfo.pixelWidth * PixelInfo.pixelHeight;
    pixels = new uint[numPixels];
    texture.GetData<uint>(pixels);
```

```
    // Create and initialize PixelInfo array
    pixelInfos = new PixelInfo[numPixels];
    InitializePixelInfo(pixels);

    // Start up the calculation thread
    Thread thread = new Thread(PixelSetterThread);
    thread.Start();

    base.OnActivated(sender, args);
}

protected override void OnDeactivated(object sender, EventArgs args)
{
    PhoneApplicationService.Current.State["xOrigin"] = PixelInfo
.xPixelCoordAtComplexOrigin;
    PhoneApplicationService.Current.State["yOrigin"] = PixelInfo
.yPixelCoordAtComplexOrigin;
    PhoneApplicationService.Current.State["resolution"] = PixelInfo.unitsPerPixel;

    texture.SaveToPhoneServiceState("mandelbrotBitmap");

    base.OnDeactivated(sender, args);
}

void InitializePixelInfo(uint[] pixels)
{
    for (int index = 0; index < pixelInfos.Length; index++)
    {
        pixelInfos[index] = new PixelInfo(index, pixels);
    }

    PixelInfo.hasNewColors = true;
    PixelInfo.firstNewIndex = 0;
    PixelInfo.lastNewIndex = pixelInfos.Length - 1;
}
```

As *OnActivated* completes, everything is initialized and ready, and so it starts up a second thread based on the *PixelSetterThread* method. This method spends the rest of eternity looping through all the members of the *PixelInfo* array indexed by *pixelIndex* and calling the *Iterate* method. If *Iterate* returns true, then a color is assigned to the pixel:

XNA Project: MandelbrotSet   File: Game1.cs (excerpt)

```
void PixelSetterThread()
{
    int pixelIndex = 0;

    while (true)
    {
        lock (pixelInfosLock)
```

```
            {
                if (!pixelInfos[pixelIndex].finished)
                {
                    if (pixelInfos[pixelIndex].Iterate())
                    {
                        int iteration = pixelInfos[pixelIndex].iteration;
                        pixelInfos[pixelIndex].packedColor =
                                        GetPixelColor(iteration).PackedValue;

                        PixelInfo.hasNewColors = true;
                        PixelInfo.firstNewIndex = Math.Min(PixelInfo.firstNewIndex,
pixelIndex);
                        PixelInfo.lastNewIndex = Math.Max(PixelInfo.lastNewIndex,
pixelIndex);
                    }
                    else
                    {
                        // Special case: On scale up, prevent blocks of color from
                        //          remaining inside the Mandelbrot Set
                        if (pixelInfos[pixelIndex].iteration == 500 &&
                            pixelInfos[pixelIndex].packedColor != Color.Black.PackedValue)
                        {
                            pixelInfos[pixelIndex].packedColor = Color.Black.PackedValue;

                            PixelInfo.hasNewColors = true;
                            PixelInfo.firstNewIndex =
                                        Math.Min(PixelInfo.firstNewIndex, pixelIndex);
                            PixelInfo.lastNewIndex =
                                        Math.Max(PixelInfo.lastNewIndex, pixelIndex);
                        }
                    }
                }

                if (++pixelIndex == pixelInfos.Length)
                {
                    pixelIndex = 0;
                    globalIteration++;
                }
            }
        }
    }
}

Color GetPixelColor(int iteration)
{
    float proportion = (iteration / 32f) % 1;

    if (proportion < 0.5)
        return new Color(1 - 2 * proportion, 0, 2 * proportion);

    proportion = 2 * (proportion - 0.5f);

    return new Color(0, proportion, 1 - proportion);
}
```

Although it's important for this thread to perform the calculations as quickly as possible, it also tries to relieve some work that must be performed in the *Update* override (coming up). By setting static fields in the *PixelInfo* structure, the thread indicates the minimum and maximum pixel indices that have been changed.

I mentioned earlier that most simple Mandelbrot programs I've seen set a maximum for the number of iterations. (A pseudocode algorithm in the Wikipedia entry on the Mandelbrot Set sets *max_iteration* to 1000.) The only place in my implementation where I had to use an iteration maximum is right in here. As you'll see shortly, when you use a pair of fingers to zoom in on the viewing area, the program needs to entirely start from scratch with a new array of *PixelInfo* structures. But for visualization purposes it expands the *Texture2D* to approximate the eventual image. This expansion often results in some pixels in the Mandelbrot Set being colored, and the algorithm I'm using here would never restore those pixels to black. So, if the *iteration* count on a particular pixel reaches 500, and if the pixel is not black, it's set to black. That pixel could very well later be set to some other color, but that's not known at this point.

Here's the first section of the *Update* override that transfers color information from the *PixelInfo* array calculated in the second thread into the *pixels* array, and then updates the *Texture2D* from that array:

XNA Project: **MandelbrotSet**   File: **Game1.cs (excerpt)**

```csharp
protected override void Update(GameTime gameTime)
{
    // Allows the game to exit
    if (GamePad.GetState(PlayerIndex.One).Buttons.Back == ButtonState.Pressed)
        this.Exit();

    // Update texture from pixels array from pixelInfos array
    if (PixelInfo.hasNewColors)
    {
        lock (pixelInfosLock)
        {
            // Transfer new colors to pixels array
            for (int pixelIndex = PixelInfo.firstNewIndex;
                     pixelIndex <= PixelInfo.lastNewIndex;
                     pixelIndex++)
            {
                pixels[pixelIndex] = pixelInfos[pixelIndex].packedColor;
            }

            // Transfer new pixels to texture
            int firstRow = PixelInfo.firstNewIndex / texture.Width;
            int numRows = PixelInfo.lastNewIndex / texture.Width - firstRow + 1;
            Rectangle rect = new Rectangle(0, firstRow, texture.Width, numRows);
            texture.SetData<uint>(0, rect, pixels, firstRow * texture.Width,
                                                  numRows * texture.Width);
```

```
            // Reset PixelInfo
            PixelInfo.hasNewColors = false;
            PixelInfo.firstNewIndex = Int32.MaxValue;
            PixelInfo.lastNewIndex = 0;
        }
    }

    // Update globalIteration display
    upperRightStatusText.Remove(0, upperRightStatusText.Length);
    upperRightStatusText.AppendFormat("{0}", globalIteration + 1);
    Vector2 textSize = segoe14.MeasureString(upperRightStatusText);
    upperRightStatusPosition = new Vector2(viewport.Width - textSize.X, 0);
    ...
}
```

Pan and Zoom

The remainder of the *Update* override is devoted to dealing with touch input. The idea here is simple: As you're touching the screen, moving it around, perhaps zooming in or zooming out, nothing irrevocable happens. The screen seems to be moving and zooming because a *Matrix* object named *drawMatrix* is being modified, and that's used in the *Begin* call of the *SpriteBatch*.

However, once your finger or fingers lift from the screen, then the program changes both the *PixelInfo* array and the *pixels* array for the new position and zoom level of the screen. There is no attempt to retain anything that is now off the screen.

Here's the handling of the *FreeDrag* and *DragComplete* gestures for translation operations:

XNA Project: **MandelbrotSet**   File: **Game1.cs (excerpt)**

```
protected override void Update(GameTime gameTime)
{
    ...
    // Read touch gestures
    while (TouchPanel.IsGestureAvailable)
    {
        GestureSample gesture = TouchPanel.ReadGesture();

        switch (gesture.GestureType)
        {
            case GestureType.FreeDrag:
                // Adjust drawMatrix for shifting
                drawMatrix.M41 += gesture.Delta.X;
                drawMatrix.M42 += gesture.Delta.Y;
                break;
```

```
          case GestureType.DragComplete:
              // Update texture from pixels from shifted pixelInfos
              lock (pixelInfosLock)
              {
                  pixelInfos = TranslatePixelInfo(pixelInfos, drawMatrix);

                  for (int pixelIndex = 0; pixelIndex < pixelInfos.Length;
pixelIndex++)
                      pixels[pixelIndex] = pixelInfos[pixelIndex].packedColor;

                  PixelInfo.hasNewColors = false;
                  PixelInfo.firstNewIndex = Int32.MaxValue;
                  PixelInfo.lastNewIndex = 0;
              }
              texture.SetData<uint>(pixels);

              drawMatrix = Matrix.Identity;
              globalIteration = 0;
              break;
          ...
      }
      UpdateCoordinateText();
  }
  base.Update(gameTime);
}
```

As the user is moving one finger around the screen, only the *drawMatrix* is affected, but when the finger lifts off the screen the *DragComplete* gesture processing makes a call to the *TranslatePixelInfo* method to move elements in the array of *PixelInfo* structures in accordance with the final selected position. Fortunately, pixels moved from one part of the screen to another can be preserved; new pixel locations start out as black. *Update* then transfers the pixel colors from the *PixelInfo* array to the *pixels* array and updates the *Texture2D* from that. When that's done, the *drawMatrix* can be set back to the identity matrix.

The *TranslatePixelInfo* method uses the final *drawMatrix* translation factors to set new values of the *PixelInfo.xPixelCoordAtComplexOrigin* and the *PixelInfo.yPixelCoordAtComplexOrigin* fields and shifts the *PixelInfo* members around:

XNA Project: **MandelbrotSet**   File: **Game1.cs (excerpt)**

```
PixelInfo[] TranslatePixelInfo(PixelInfo[] srcPixelInfos, Matrix drawMatrix)
{
    int x = (int)(drawMatrix.M41 + 0.5);
    int y = (int)(drawMatrix.M42 + 0.5);
    PixelInfo.xPixelCoordAtComplexOrigin += x;
    PixelInfo.yPixelCoordAtComplexOrigin += y;
    PixelInfo[] dstPixelInfos = new PixelInfo[srcPixelInfos.Length];
```

```
    for (int dstY = 0; dstY < PixelInfo.pixelHeight; dstY++)
    {
        int srcY = dstY - y;
        int srcRow = srcY * PixelInfo.pixelWidth;
        int dstRow = dstY * PixelInfo.pixelWidth;

        for (int dstX = 0; dstX < PixelInfo.pixelWidth; dstX++)
        {
            int srcX = dstX - x;
            int dstIndex = dstRow + dstX;

            if (srcX >= 0 && srcX < PixelInfo.pixelWidth &&
                srcY >= 0 && srcY < PixelInfo.pixelHeight)
            {
                int srcIndex = srcRow + srcX;
                dstPixelInfos[dstIndex] = pixelInfos[srcIndex];
            }
            else
            {
                dstPixelInfos[dstIndex] = new PixelInfo(dstIndex, null);
            }
        }
    }
    return dstPixelInfos;
}
```

With zooming, the opposite approach is taken. It is the very nature of the Mandelbrot Set that each point is unique and can't be approximated from its neighbors. For this reason, any zooming operation must result in the entire *PixelInfo* array being recreated and all calculations starting over from the beginning.

However, the visuals can be retained as a temporary approximation. For this reason, *Update* handles the *PinchComplete* gesture by applying the transform to the *pixels* array, and then using that to set colors in the *PixelInfo* array. When you zoom in you'll see something that might first look like this:

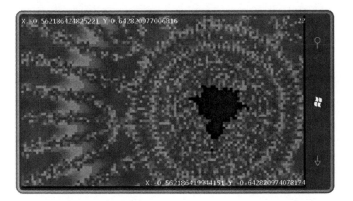

But wait a little while and it becomes this:

The *Pinch* code should look familiar except that it determines whether the horizontal or vertical delta dominates. This information is passed to the *ComputeScaleMatrix* method:

XNA Project: MandelbrotSet   File: Game1.cs (excerpt)

```
protected override void Update(GameTime gameTime)
{
    ...
    // Read touch gestures
    while (TouchPanel.IsGestureAvailable)
    {
        GestureSample gesture = TouchPanel.ReadGesture();

        switch (gesture.GestureType)
        {
            ...
            case GestureType.Pinch:
                bool xDominates = Math.Abs(gesture.Delta.X) + Math.Abs(gesture
.Delta2.X) >
                                  Math.Abs(gesture.Delta.Y) + Math.Abs(gesture
.Delta2.Y);

                Vector2 oldPoint1 = gesture.Position - gesture.Delta;
                Vector2 newPoint1 = gesture.Position;
                Vector2 oldPoint2 = gesture.Position2 - gesture.Delta2;
                Vector2 newPoint2 = gesture.Position2;

                drawMatrix *= ComputeScaleMatrix(oldPoint1, oldPoint2, newPoint2,
                                                 xDominates);
                drawMatrix *= ComputeScaleMatrix(newPoint2, oldPoint1, newPoint1,
                                                 xDominates);
                break;

            case GestureType.PinchComplete:
                // Set texture from zoomed pixels
                pixels = ZoomPixels(pixels, drawMatrix);
                texture.SetData<uint>(pixels);
```

```
                        // Set new PixelInfo parameters
                        PixelInfo.xPixelCoordAtComplexOrigin *= drawMatrix.M11;
                        PixelInfo.xPixelCoordAtComplexOrigin += drawMatrix.M41;
                        PixelInfo.yPixelCoordAtComplexOrigin *= drawMatrix.M22;
                        PixelInfo.yPixelCoordAtComplexOrigin += drawMatrix.M42;
                        PixelInfo.unitsPerPixel /= drawMatrix.M11;

                        // Reinitialize PpixelInfos
                        lock (pixelInfosLock)
                        {
                            InitializePixelInfo(pixels);
                        }

                        drawMatrix = Matrix.Identity;
                        globalIteration = 0;
                        break;
                }
            UpdateCoordinateText();
        }
        base.Update(gameTime);
}
```

The *ComputeScaleMatrix* method is very similar to the one in *DragAndPinch* except that it scales uniformly based on the Boolean argument to the method:

XNA Project: MandelbrotSet   File: Game1.cs (excerpt)

```
Matrix ComputeScaleMatrix(Vector2 refPoint, Vector2 oldPoint, Vector2 newPoint,
                          bool xDominates)
{
    float scale = 1;

    if (xDominates)
        scale = (newPoint.X - refPoint.X) / (oldPoint.X - refPoint.X);
    else
        scale = (newPoint.Y - refPoint.Y) / (oldPoint.Y - refPoint.Y);

    if (float.IsNaN(scale) || float.IsInfinity(scale) || scale < 0)
    {
        return Matrix.Identity;
    }

    scale = Math.Min(1.1f, Math.Max(0.9f, scale));

    Matrix matrix = Matrix.CreateTranslation(-refPoint.X, -refPoint.Y, 0);
    matrix *= Matrix.CreateScale(scale, scale, 1);
    matrix *= Matrix.CreateTranslation(refPoint.X, refPoint.Y, 0);

    return matrix;
}
```

The *ZoomPixels* method called for the *PinchComplete* gesture obtains the inverse of the *Matrix* for use in calculating source pixel coordinates from destination pixel coordinates. Fortunately, inverting the matrix is simply a matter of calling the static *Matrix.Invert* method. An earlier version of the program called *Matrix.CreateScale* (above) with zero as the third argument. This created an uninvertible matrix, and calling *Invert* created a matrix with NaN ("not a number") values in all the fields. That's no good.

XNA Project: **MandelbrotSet**   File: **Game1.cs** (excerpt)

```
uint[] ZoomPixels(uint[] srcPixels, Matrix matrix)
{
    Matrix invMatrix = Matrix.Invert(matrix);
    uint[] dstPixels = new uint[srcPixels.Length];

    for (int dstY = 0; dstY < PixelInfo.pixelHeight; dstY++)
    {
        int dstRow = dstY * PixelInfo.pixelWidth;

        for (int dstX = 0; dstX < PixelInfo.pixelWidth; dstX++)
        {
            int dstIndex = dstRow + dstX;
            Vector2 dst = new Vector2(dstX, dstY);
            Vector2 src = Vector2.Transform(dst, invMatrix);
            int srcX = (int)(src.X + 0.5f);
            int srcY = (int)(src.Y + 0.5f);

            if (srcX >= 0 && srcX < PixelInfo.pixelWidth &&
                srcY >= 0 && srcY < PixelInfo.pixelHeight)
            {
                int srcIndex = srcY * PixelInfo.pixelWidth + srcX;
                dstPixels[dstIndex] = srcPixels[srcIndex];
            }
            else
            {
                dstPixels[dstIndex] = Color.Black.PackedValue;
            }
        }
    }
    return dstPixels;
}
```

All the exciting work is now finished. But it is considered *essential* in Mandelbrot programs to have some kind of display indicating where you are in the complex plane. The *UpdateCoordinateText* method is responsible for calculating the upper-left and lower-right coordinates, formatting them in *StringBuilder* objects, and determining where they should be displayed:

XNA Project: **MandelbrotSet**   File: **Game1.cs** (excerpt)

```
void UpdateCoordinateText()
{
    double xAdjustedPixelCoord =
        PixelInfo.xPixelCoordAtComplexOrigin * drawMatrix.M11 + drawMatrix.M41;
    double yAdjustedPixelCoord =
        PixelInfo.yPixelCoordAtComplexOrigin * drawMatrix.M22 + drawMatrix.M42;
    double adjustedUnitsPerPixel = PixelInfo.unitsPerPixel / drawMatrix.M11;

    double xUpperLeft = -adjustedUnitsPerPixel * xAdjustedPixelCoord;
    double yUpperLeft = adjustedUnitsPerPixel * yAdjustedPixelCoord;

    upperLeftCoordText.Remove(0, upperLeftCoordText.Length);
    upperLeftCoordText.AppendFormat("X:{0} Y:{1}", xUpperLeft, yUpperLeft);

    double xLowerRight = xUpperLeft + PixelInfo.pixelWidth * adjustedUnitsPerPixel;
    double yLowerRight = -yUpperLeft + PixelInfo.pixelHeight * adjustedUnitsPerPixel;

    lowerRightCoordText.Remove(0, lowerRightCoordText.Length);
    lowerRightCoordText.AppendFormat("X:{0} Y:{1}", xLowerRight, yLowerRight);

    Vector2 textSize = segoe14.MeasureString(lowerRightCoordText);
    lowerRightCoordPosition = new Vector2(viewport.Width - textSize.X,
                                          viewport.Height - textSize.Y);
}
```

After all that, the *Draw* method is very straightforward. Notice there are two calls to the *Begin* and *End* methods of *SpriteBatch*. The first requires the *Matrix* object that moves and scales the *Texture2D* while it's being manipulated and the second is for the text items:

XNA Project: **MandelbrotSet**   File: **Game1.cs** (excerpt)

```
protected override void Draw(GameTime gameTime)
{
    GraphicsDevice.Clear(Color.Black);

    // Draw Mandelbrot Set image
    spriteBatch.Begin(SpriteSortMode.Immediate, null, null, null, null, null,
drawMatrix);
    spriteBatch.Draw(texture, Vector2.Zero, null, Color.White,
                     0, Vector2.Zero, 1, SpriteEffects.None, 0);
    spriteBatch.End();

    // Draw coordinate and status text
    spriteBatch.Begin();
    spriteBatch.DrawString(segoe14, upperLeftCoordText, Vector2.Zero, Color.White);
    spriteBatch.DrawString(segoe14, lowerRightCoordText,
                           lowerRightCoordPosition, Color.White);
```

```
        spriteBatch.DrawString(segoe14, upperRightStatusText,
                                        upperRightStatusPosition, Color.White);
        spriteBatch.End();

        base.Draw(gameTime);
    }
```

Game Components

To conclude this chapter, I have two programs that display that same old *Texture2D*
I used earlier in this chapter, except that you'll be able to define a transform on this image
interactively by dragging the texture's corners.

To give your fingers a target to touch and drag, the programs display translucent disks at
the *Texture2D* corners. It would be nice to code these draggable translucent disks so they're
usable by multiple programs. In a traditional graphics programming environment, we might
think of something like this as a *control* but in XNA it's called a *game component*.

Components help modularize your XNA programs. Components can derive from the
GameComponent class but often they derive from *DrawableGameComponent* so they can
display something on the screen in addition to (and on top of) what goes out in the *Draw*
method of your *Game* class.

To add a new component class to your project, right-click the project name, select Add and
then New Item, and then pick Game Component from the list. You'll need to change the
base class to *DrawableGameComponent* and override the *Draw* method if you want the
component to participate in drawing.

A game generally instantiates the components that it needs either in the game's constructor
or during the *Initialize* method. The components officially become part of the game when
they are added to the *Components* collection defined by the *Game* class.

As with *Game*, a *DrawableGameComponent* derivative generally overrides the *Initialize*,
LoadContent, *Update*, and *Draw* methods. When the *Initialize* override of the *Game* derivative
calls the *Initialize* method in the base class, the *Initialize* methods in all the components
are called. Likewise, when the *LoadComponent*, *Update*, and *Draw* overrides in the *Game*
derivative call the method in the base class, the *LoadComponent*, *Update*, and *Draw* methods
in all the components are called.

As you know, the *Update* override normally handles touch input. In my experience that
attempting to access touch input in a game component is somewhat problematic. It seems as
if the game itself and the components end up competing for input.

To fix this, I decided that my *Game* derivative would be solely responsible for calling *TouchPanel.GetState*, but the game would then give the components the opportunity to process this touch input. To accommodate this concept, I created this interface for *GameComponent* and *DrawableGameComponent* derivatives:

XNA Project: **Petzold.Phone.Xna**   File: **IProcessTouch.cs**

```
using Microsoft.Xna.Framework.Input.Touch;

namespace Petzold.Phone.Xna
{
    public interface IProcessTouch
    {
        bool ProcessTouch(TouchLocation touch);
    }
}
```

When a game component implements this interface, the game calls the game component's *ProcessTouch* method for every *TouchLocation* object. If the game component needs to use that *TouchLocation*, it returns *true* from *ProcessTouch*, and the game then probably ignores that *TouchLocation*.

The first component I'll show you is called Dragger, and it is part of the Petzold.Phone.Xna library. *Dragger* derives from *DrawableGameComponent* and implements the *IProcessTouch* interface:

XNA Project: **Petzold.Phone.Xna**   File: **Dragger.cs** (excerpt showing fields)

```
public class Dragger : DrawableGameComponent, IProcessTouch
{
    SpriteBatch spriteBatch;
    int? touchId;

    public event EventHandler PositionChanged;

    public Dragger(Game game)
        : base(game)
    {
    }

    public Texture2D Texture { set; get; }
    public Vector2 Origin { set; get; }
    public Vector2 Position { set; get; }

    ...

}
```

The constructor of a *GameComponent* derivative must be passed the parent *Game* so the component can share some properties with the *Game* (such as the *GraphicsDevice* object). A *DrawableGameComponent* derivative will usually create a *SpriteBatch* for its own use just as a *Game* derivative does.

Dragger also defines a *touchId* field for help in processing touch input, a public event named *PositionChanged*, and three public properties: *Texture* of type *Texture2D*, a *Vector2* called *Origin* (which is commonly set to the center of the *Texture2D*) and another *Vector2* for the *Position*.

A program making use of *Dragger* could define a custom *Texture2D* for the component and set it through this public *Texture* property, at which time it would probably also set the *Origin* property. However, *Dragger* defines a default *Texture* property for itself during its *LoadContent* method:

XNA Project: Petzold.Phone.Xna   File: Dragger.cs (excerpt)

```
protected override void  LoadContent()
{
    spriteBatch = new SpriteBatch(this.GraphicsDevice);

    // Create default texture
    int radius = 48;
    Texture2D texture = new Texture2D(this.GraphicsDevice, 2 * radius, 2 * radius);
    uint[] pixels = new uint[texture.Width * texture.Height];

    for (int y = 0; y < texture.Height; y++)
        for (int x = 0; x < texture.Width; x++)
        {
            Color clr = Color.Transparent;

            if ((x - radius) * (x - radius) +
                (y - radius) * (y - radius) <
                radius * radius)
            {
                clr = new Color(0, 128, 128, 128);
            }
            pixels[y * texture.Width + x] = clr.PackedValue;
        }
    texture.SetData<uint>(pixels);

    Texture = texture;
    Origin = new Vector2(radius, radius);

    base.LoadContent();
}
```

The *Dragger* class implements the *IProcessTouch* interface so it has a *ProcessTouch* method that is called from the *Game* derivative for each *TouchLocation* object. The *ProcessTouch* method is interested in finger presses that occur over the component itself. If that is the case, it retains the ID and basically owns that finger until it lifts from the screen. For every movement of that finger, *Dragger* fires a *PositionChanged* event.

XNA Project: Petzold.Phone.Xna   File: Dragger.cs (excerpt)

```
public bool ProcessTouch(TouchLocation touch)
{
    if (Texture == null)
        return false;

    bool touchHandled = false;

    switch (touch.State)
    {
        case TouchLocationState.Pressed:
            if ((touch.Position.X > Position.X - Origin.X) &&
                (touch.Position.X < Position.X - Origin.X + Texture.Width) &&
                (touch.Position.Y > Position.Y - Origin.Y) &&
                (touch.Position.Y < Position.Y - Origin.Y + Texture.Height))
            {
                touchId = touch.Id;
                touchHandled = true;
            }
            break;

        case TouchLocationState.Moved:
            if (touchId.HasValue && touchId.Value == touch.Id)
            {
                TouchLocation previousTouch;
                touch.TryGetPreviousLocation(out previousTouch);
                Position += touch.Position - previousTouch.Position;

                // Fire the event!
                if (PositionChanged != null)
                    PositionChanged(this, EventArgs.Empty);

                touchHandled = true;
            }
            break;

        case TouchLocationState.Released:
            if (touchId.HasValue && touchId.Value == touch.Id)
            {
                touchId = null;
                touchHandled = true;
            }
            break;
    }
    return touchHandled;
}
```

The *Draw* override just draws the *Texture2D* at the new position:

XNA Project: Petzold.Phone.Xna   File: **Dragger.cs** (excerpt)

```
public override void Draw(GameTime gameTime)
{
    if (Texture != null)
    {
        spriteBatch.Begin();
        spriteBatch.Draw(Texture, Position, null, Color.White,
                         0, Origin, 1, SpriteEffects.None, 0);
        spriteBatch.End();
    }
    base.Draw(gameTime);
}
```

Now let's put this *Dragger* component to use in exploring rather more advanced transform math.

Affine and Non-Affine Transforms

Sometimes it's convenient to derive a transform that maps a particular set of points to a particular destination. For example, here's a program that incorporates three instances of the *Dragger* component I just described, and lets you drag three corners of the *Texture2D* to arbitrary locations on the screen:

This program uses an affine transform, which means that rectangles are always mapped to parallelograms. The fourth corner isn't draggable because it's always determined by the other three:

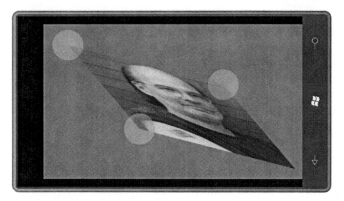

You can't choose just any three points. Everything goes kaflooey if you attempt to make an interior angle greater than 180°.

To nail down the mathematics, it will be easier to first assume that the original image we're trying to transform is 1 pixel wide and 1 pixel tall. We want a transform that produces the following mappings from the three corners of the image to three arbitrary points:

$(0,0) \rightarrow (x_0, y_0)$

$(1,0) \rightarrow (x_1, y_1)$

$(0,1) \rightarrow (x_2, y_2)$

These are, respectively, the upper-left, upper-right, and lower-left corners. Using the fields of the *Matrix* object defined in XNA, the transform formulas are:

$x' = \mathbf{M11} \cdot x + \mathbf{M21} \cdot y + \mathbf{M41}$

$y' = \mathbf{M12} \cdot x + \mathbf{M22} \cdot y + \mathbf{M42}$

It's easy to apply the transform to the points (0, 0), (1, 0), and (0, 1) and solve for the elements of the matrix:

$M11 = x_1 - x_0$

$M12 = y_1 - y_0$

$M21 = x_2 - x_0$

$M22 = y_2 - y_0$

$M41 = x_0$

$M42 = y_0$

A static class named *MatrixHelper* in the Petzold.Phone.Xna library has a method named *ComputeAffineTransform* that creates a *Matrix* object based on these formulas:

```
XNA Project: Petzold.Phone.Xna   File: MatrixHelper.cs (excerpt)

static Matrix ComputeAffineTransform(Vector2 ptUL, Vector2 ptUR, Vector2 ptLL)
{
    return new Matrix()
    {
        M11 = (ptUR.X - ptUL.X),
        M12 = (ptUR.Y - ptUL.Y),
        M21 = (ptLL.X - ptUL.X),
        M22 = (ptLL.Y - ptUL.Y),
        M33 = 1,
        M41 = ptUL.X,
        M42 = ptUL.Y,
        M44 = 1
    };
}
```

This method isn't public because it's not very useful by itself. It's not very useful because the formulas are based on transforming an image that is one-pixel wide and one-pixel tall. Notice, however, that the code sets *M33* and *M44* to 1. This doesn't happen automatically and it is essential for the matrix to work right.

To compute a *Matrix* for an affine transform that applies to an object of a particular size, this public method is much more useful:

```
XNA Project: Petzold.Phone.Xna   File: MatrixHelper.cs (excerpt)

public static Matrix ComputeMatrix(Vector2 size, Vector2 ptUL, Vector2 ptUR, Vector2 ptLL)
{
    // Scale transform
    Matrix S = Matrix.CreateScale(1 / size.X, 1 / size.Y, 1);

    // Affine transform
    Matrix A = ComputeAffineTransform(ptUL, ptUR, ptLL);

    // Product of two transforms
    return S * A;
}
```

The first transform scales the object down to a 1×1 size before applying the computed affine transform.

The AffineTransform project is responsible for the two screen shots shown above. It creates three instances of the *Dragger* component in its *Initialize* override, sets a handler for the *PositionChanged* event, and adds the component to the *Components* collection:

XNA Project: **AffineTransform**   File: **Game1.cs (excerpt)**

```
public class Game1 : Microsoft.Xna.Framework.Game
{
    GraphicsDeviceManager graphics;
    SpriteBatch spriteBatch;

    Texture2D texture;
    Matrix matrix = Matrix.Identity;
    Dragger draggerUL, draggerUR, draggerLL;

    . . .

    protected override void Initialize()
    {
        draggerUL = new Dragger(this);
        draggerUL.PositionChanged += OnDraggerPositionChanged;
        this.Components.Add(draggerUL);

        draggerUR = new Dragger(this);
        draggerUR.PositionChanged += OnDraggerPositionChanged;
        this.Components.Add(draggerUR);

        draggerLL = new Dragger(this);
        draggerLL.PositionChanged += OnDraggerPositionChanged;
        this.Components.Add(draggerLL);

        base.Initialize();
    }
    . . .
}
```

Don't forget to add the components to the *Components* collection of the *Game* class!

The *LoadContent* override is responsible for loading the image that will be transformed and initializing the *Position* properties of the three *Dragger* components at the three corners of the image:

XNA Project: **AffineTransform**   File: **Game1.cs (excerpt)**

```
protected override void LoadContent()
{
    // Create a new SpriteBatch, which can be used to draw textures.
    spriteBatch = new SpriteBatch(GraphicsDevice);
```

```
        Viewport viewport = this.GraphicsDevice.Viewport;
        texture = this.Content.Load<Texture2D>("PetzoldTattoo");

        draggerUL.Position = new Vector2((viewport.Width - texture.Width) / 2,
                                         (viewport.Height - texture.Height) / 2);

        draggerUR.Position = draggerUL.Position + new Vector2(texture.Width, 0);
        draggerLL.Position = draggerUL.Position + new Vector2(0, texture.Height);

        OnDraggerPositionChanged(null, EventArgs.Empty);
    }
```

Dragger only fires its *PositionChanged* event when the component is actually dragged by the user, so the *LoadContent* method concludes by simulating a *PositionChanged* event, which calculates an initial *Matrix* based on the size of the *Texture2D* and the initial positions of the *Dragger* components:

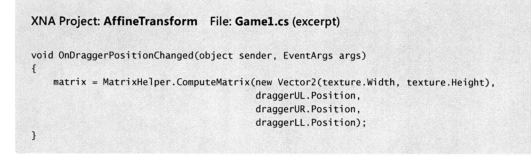

XNA Project: AffineTransform   File: Game1.cs (excerpt)

```
void OnDraggerPositionChanged(object sender, EventArgs args)
{
    matrix = MatrixHelper.ComputeMatrix(new Vector2(texture.Width, texture.Height),
                                        draggerUL.Position,
                                        draggerUR.Position,
                                        draggerLL.Position);
}
```

The program doesn't need to handle any touch input of its own, but *Dragger* implements the *IProcessTouch* interface, so the program funnels touch input to the *Dragger* components. These *Dragger* components respond by possibly moving themselves and setting new *Position* properties, which will cause *PositionChanged* events to be fired.

XNA Project: AffineTransform   File: Game1.cs (excerpt)

```
protected override void Update(GameTime gameTime)
{
    // Allows the game to exit
    if (GamePad.GetState(PlayerIndex.One).Buttons.Back == ButtonState.Pressed)
        this.Exit();

    TouchCollection touches = TouchPanel.GetState();

    foreach (TouchLocation touch in touches)
    {
        bool touchHandled = false;
```

```
            foreach (GameComponent component in this.Components)
            {
                if (component is IProcessTouch &&
                    (component as IProcessTouch).ProcessTouch(touch))
                {
                    touchHandled = true;
                    break;
                }
            }

            if (touchHandled == true)
                continue;
        }

        base.Update(gameTime);
    }
```

It is possible for the program to dispense with setting handlers for the *PositionChanged* event of the *Dragger* components and instead poll the *Position* properties during each *Update* call and recalculate a *Matrix* from those values. However, recalculating a *Matrix* only when one of the *Position* properties actually changes is much more efficient.

The *Draw* override uses that *Matrix* to display the texture:

XNA Project: **AffineTransform**   File: **Game1.cs** (excerpt)

```
protected override void Draw(GameTime gameTime)
{
    GraphicsDevice.Clear(Color.CornflowerBlue);

    spriteBatch.Begin(SpriteSortMode.Immediate, null, null, null, null, null, matrix);
    spriteBatch.Draw(texture, Vector2.Zero, Color.White);
    spriteBatch.End();

    base.Draw(gameTime);
}
```

As you experiment with AffineTransform, you'll want to avoid making the interior angles at any corner greater than 180°. (In other words, keep it convex.) Affine transforms can express familiar operations like translation, scaling, rotation, and skew, but they never transform a square into anything more exotic than a parallelogram.

Non-affine transforms are much more common in 3D than 2D. In 3D, non-affine transforms are necessary to implement perspective effects. A long straight desert highway in a 3D world must seem to get narrower as it recedes into the distance, just like in the real world. Although we know that the sides of the road remains parallel, visually they seem to converge at infinity. This tapering effect is characteristic of non-affine transforms.

The complete matrix transform for a three-dimensional coordinate point looks like this:

$$|x\ y\ z\ 1| \times \begin{vmatrix} M11 & M12 & M13 & M14 \\ M21 & M22 & M23 & M24 \\ M31 & M32 & M33 & M34 \\ M41 & M42 & M43 & M44 \end{vmatrix} = |x'\ y'\ z'\ w'|$$

Because x, y, and z are already the last three letters of the alphabet, the fourth dimension is represented with the letter w. The three-dimensional coordinate point is first expressed as a four-dimensional point for multiplying by the 4×4 matrix. The following formulas result from the matrix multiplication:

$x' = M11 \quad x + M21 \quad y + M31 \quad z + M41$

$y' = M12 \quad x + M22 \quad y + M32 \quad z + M42$

$z' = M13 \quad x + M23 \quad y + M33 \quad z + M43$

$w' = M14 \quad x + M24 \quad y + M34 \quad z + M44$

For an affine transform, $M14$, $M24$, and $M34$ are all zero, and $M44$ is 1, so w' is 1, and the entire transform occurs on a plane in 4D space. For non-affine transforms, w' is not 1, and to project 4D space back into 3D space, the three-dimensaional point must be constructed from the four-dimensional point (x', y', z', w') like so:

$$\left(\frac{x'}{w'}, \frac{y'}{w'}, \frac{z'}{w'} \right)$$

It's the division here that causes tapering. If $M14$ is a positive number, for example, then w'' will increase for increasing x, and the graphical object will get progressively smaller as x gets larger.

What happens if w' becomes zero? That's the *non-affine* part of this process: Coordinates can become infinite. Generally you'll want to keep infinite objects out of sight because they tend to hog the screen.

Although non-affine transforms are essential for 3D graphics programming, I wasn't even sure if *SpriteBatch* supported two-dimensional non-affine transforms until I tried them, and I was pleased to discover that XNA says "No problem!" What this means is that you can use non-affine transforms in 2D programming to simulate perspective effects.

A non-affine transform in 2D can transform a square into a simple convex quadrilateral—a four-sided figure where the sides meet only at the corners, and interior angles at any corner are less than 180°. Here's one example:

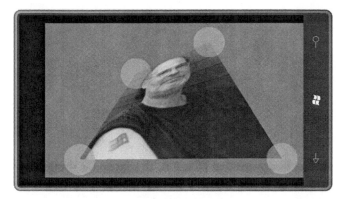

This one makes me look really smart:

This program is called NonAffineTransform and it's just like AffineTransform except it has a fourth *Dragger* component and it calls a somewhat more sophisticated method in the *MatrixHelper* class in Petzold.Phone.Xna. You can move the little disks around with a fair amount of freedom; as long as you're not trying to form a concave quadrilateral, you'll get an image stretched to fit.

Again, let's nail down the mathematics by assuming that the original image we're trying to transform is 1 pixel wide and 1 pixel tall. Now we want a transform that produces mappings from the four corners of a square to four arbitrary points:

$(0,0) \rightarrow (x_0, y_0)$

$(1,0) \rightarrow (x_1, y_1)$

$(0,1) \rightarrow (x_2, y_2)$

$(1,1) \rightarrow (x_3, y_3)$

The transform we desire will be much easier to derive if we break it down into two transforms:

$(0,0) \rightarrow (0,0) \rightarrow (x_0, y_0)$

$(1,0) \rightarrow (1,0) \rightarrow (x_1, y_1)$

$(0,1) \rightarrow (0,1) \rightarrow (x_2, y_2)$

$(1,1) \rightarrow (a,b) \rightarrow (x_3, y_3)$

The first transform is a non-affine transform that I'll call **B**. The second is something that I'll force to be an affine transform called **A** (for "affine"). The composite transform is **B** × **A**. The task here is to derive the two transforms plus the point (a, b).

I've already defined the affine transform. But I want this affine transform to map a point (a, b) to the point (x_3, y_3). What is the point (a, b)? If we apply the affine transform to (a, b) and solve for a and b, we get:

$$a = \frac{\dfrac{M22}{M11} \dfrac{x_3 - M21}{M22 - M12} \dfrac{y_3 + M21}{M21} \dfrac{M42 - M22}{} \quad M41}{}$$

$$b = \frac{\dfrac{M11}{M11} \dfrac{y_3 - M12}{M22 - M12} \dfrac{x_3 + M12}{M21} \dfrac{M41 - M11}{} \quad M42}{}$$

Now let's focus on the non-affine transform, which needs to produce the following mappings:

$(0,0) \rightarrow (0,0)$

$(1,0) \rightarrow (1,0)$

$(0,1) \rightarrow (0,1)$

$(1,1) \rightarrow (a,b)$

The generalized non-affine 2D transform formulas (using field names from the *Matrix* structure and incorporating the division by w') are:

$$x' = \frac{M11}{M14} \frac{x + M21}{x + M24} \frac{y + M41}{y + M44}$$

$$y' = \frac{M12}{M14} \frac{x + M22}{x + M24} \frac{y + M42}{y + M44}$$

The point $(0, 0)$ is mapped to $(0, 0)$, which tells us that *M41* and *M42* are zero, and *M44* is non-zero. Let's go out on a limb and say *M44* is 1.

The point $(1, 0)$ is mapped to $(1, 0)$, which tells us that *M12* is zero and *M14* = *M11* – 1.

The point $(0, 1)$ is mapped to $(0, 1)$, which tells us that *M21* is zero and *M24* = *M22* – 1.

The point (1, 1) is mapped to (*a*, *b*), which requires a bit of algebra to derive:

$$M11 = \frac{a}{a + b - 1}$$

$$M22 = \frac{b}{a + b - 1}$$

And *a* and *b* have already been calculated in connection with the affine transform.

This math has been incorporated into a second static *MatrixHelper.ComputeMatrix* method in the Petzold.Phone.Xna library:

XNA Project: Petzold.Phone.Xna   File: MatrixHelper.cs

```
public static Matrix ComputeMatrix(Vector2 size, Vector2 ptUL, Vector2 ptUR,
                                   Vector2 ptLL, Vector2 ptLR)
{
    // Scale transform
    Matrix S = Matrix.CreateScale(1 / size.X, 1 / size.Y, 1);

    // Affine transform
    Matrix A = ComputeAffineTransform(ptUL, ptUR, ptLL);

    // Non-Affine transform
    Matrix B = new Matrix();
    float den = A.M11 * A.M22 - A.M12 * A.M21;
    float a = (A.M22 * ptLR.X - A.M21 * ptLR.Y +
            A.M21 * A.M42 - A.M22 * A.M41) / den;

    float b = (A.M11 * ptLR.Y - A.M12 * ptLR.X +
            A.M12 * A.M41 - A.M11 * A.M42) / den;

    B.M11 = a / (a + b - 1);
    B.M22 = b / (a + b - 1);
    B.M33 = 1;
    B.M14 = B.M11 - 1;
    B.M24 = B.M22 - 1;
    B.M44 = 1;

    // Product of three transforms
    return S * B * A;
}
```

I won't show you the NonAffineTransform program here because it's pretty much the same as the AffineTransform program but with a fourth *Dragger* component whose *Position* property is passed to the second *ComputeMatrix* method.

The big difference with the new program is that non-affine transforms are much more fun!

Chapter 11
Touch and Play

Often when learning a new programming environment, a collection of techniques are acquired that don't necessary add up to the skills required to create a complete program. This chapter is intended to compensate for that problem by presenting two rather archetypal programs for the phone called PhingerPaint and PhreeCell. The first is a simple drawing program; the second is a version of the classic solitaire game. A third program called SpinPaint shares some code with PhingerPaint but provides a much different experience.

All these programs use components, process touch input in various degrees of sophistication, and dynamically manipulate *Texture2D* objects. While these programs are certainly not of commercial quality, I think they provide at least a little better sense of what a "real program" looks like.

More Game Components

When first exploring the subject of dynamic *Texture2D* objects, I described some simple finger-painting programs. PhingerPaint is slightly more sophisticated than those, as this screen shot suggests:

PhingerPaint has a total of 14 instances of two classes named *ColorBlock* and *Button* that derive from *DrawableGameComponent*. To select a drawing color, you touch one of the colored squares at top. You can also use the buttons on the bottom to clear the entire canvas or save the artwork to the phone's photo library in a special album reserved for applications called Saved Pictures. From there you can email the picture, or you can move it to your PC during the next time you synchronize your phone. (What you can't do is continue working on the picture during another session. Perhaps someday I'll add that feature.)

Button behaves very much like a traditional graphical button. It normally displays white text with a white border, but when you put your finger on the surface, the colors invert to display black text on a white background. If you slide your finger off, the colors flip back to normal, but the button is still keeping track of that finger. Slide your finger back and the colors reverse themselves again. Lifting your finger from the button causes it to fire a *Click* event.

Because I'll be using *Button* in more than one program, it's part of the Petzold.Phone .Xna library. Here's the beginning of the class with the private fields, the public event, the constructor, and public properties:

XNA Project: Petzold.Phone.Xna   File: Button.cs (excerpt)

```
public class Button : DrawableGameComponent, IProcessTouch
{
    SpriteBatch spriteBatch;
    Texture2D tinyTexture;
    Vector2 textPosition;
    bool isPressed;
    int? touchId = null;

    public event EventHandler Click;

    public Button(Game game, string text)
        : base(game)
    {
        Text = text;
    }

    public Rectangle Destination { set; get; }
    public SpriteFont SpriteFont { set; get; }
    public string Text { set; get; }
    . . .
}
```

Normally the game component constructor has an argument of type *Game*, which is the parent of the component, and from which the *GameComponent* base class extracts the *GraphicsDevice*. I added a constructor argument of type *string* for the button text, but that text can also be set later through the public *Text* property.

I decided that the parent *Game* derivative should be responsible for setting the font for the *Button* and the all-important *Destination* property, which is the location and size of the *Button* relative to the screen.

The *LoadContent* override in the game component performs a similar function as in the game class. The *Button* class creates a tiny 1 × 1 pixel white *Texture2D* for displaying the button border and the reverse-video background.

XNA Project: **Petzold.Phone.Xna**   File: **Button.cs (excerpt)**

```
protected override void LoadContent()
{
    spriteBatch = new SpriteBatch(this.GraphicsDevice);

    tinyTexture = new Texture2D(this.GraphicsDevice, 1, 1);
    tinyTexture.SetData<uint>(new uint[] { Color.White.PackedValue });

    base.LoadContent();
}
```

The public *SpriteFont* and *Destination* properties of *Button* might be set at any time after the *Button* class is created. For this reason it's the *Update* method that accesses this information to determine the text size and the position of the text:

XNA Project: **Petzold.Phone.Xna**   File: **Button.cs (excerpt)**

```
public override void Update(GameTime gameTime)
{
    if (SpriteFont != null && !String.IsNullOrEmpty(Text))
    {
        Vector2 textSize = SpriteFont.MeasureString(Text);
        textPosition =
            new Vector2((int)(Destination.Left + (Destination.Width - textSize.X) / 2),
                        (int)(Destination.Top + (Destination.Height - textSize.Y) / 2));
    }
    base.Update(gameTime);
}
```

The *Button* class implements the *IProcessTouch* interface that I discussed in the previous chapter, which means it has a *ProcessTouch* method that is called from the *Game1* class with each *TouchLocation* object. For an initial finger press, *ProcessTouch* checks if the position of the touch point is within the *Destination* rectangle. If so, then it saves the touch ID and essentially owns that ID until the finger is released.

XNA Project: **Petzold.Phone.Xna**   File: **Button.cs** (excerpt)

```
public bool ProcessTouch(TouchLocation touch)
{
    bool touchHandled = false;
    bool isInside = Destination.Contains((int)touch.Position.X,
                                         (int)touch.Position.Y);
    switch (touch.State)
    {
        case TouchLocationState.Pressed:
            if (isInside)
            {
                isPressed = true;
                touchId = touch.Id;
                touchHandled = true;
            }
            break;

        case TouchLocationState.Moved:
            if (touchId.HasValue && touchId.Value == touch.Id)
            {
                isPressed = isInside;
                touchHandled = true;
            }
            break;

        case TouchLocationState.Released:
            if (touchId.HasValue && touchId.Value == touch.Id)
            {
                if (isInside && Click != null)
                    Click(this, EventArgs.Empty);

                touchId = null;
                isPressed = false;
                touchHandled = true;
            }
            break;
    }
    return touchHandled;
}
```

If the finger is released when it is inside the *Destination* rectangle, then *Button* fires a *Click* event.

The *Draw* override draws the button, which is basically a border consisting of a white rectangle with a somewhat smaller black rectangle on top, with the text string:

XNA Project: **Petzold.Phone.Xna**   File: **Button.cs** (excerpt)

```
public override void Draw(GameTime gameTime)
{
    spriteBatch.Begin();

    if (isPressed)
    {
        // Draw reverse-video background
        spriteBatch.Draw(tinyTexture, Destination, Color.White);
    }
    else
    {
        // Draw button border and background
        Rectangle rect = Destination;

        spriteBatch.Draw(tinyTexture, rect, Color.White);
        rect.Inflate(-3, -3);
        spriteBatch.Draw(tinyTexture, rect, Color.Black);
    }

    // Draw button text
    if (SpriteFont != null && !String.IsNullOrEmpty(Text))
        spriteBatch.DrawString(SpriteFont, Text, textPosition,
                               isPressed ? Color.Black : Color.White);

    spriteBatch.End();

    base.Draw(gameTime);
}
```

ColorBlock, on the other hand, is part of the PhingerPaint program, and it does not implement the *IProcessTouch* interface. Here it is in its entirety:

XNA Project: **PhingerPaint**   File: **ColorBlock.cs** (complete)

```
using System;
using Microsoft.Xna.Framework;
using Microsoft.Xna.Framework.Graphics;
using Microsoft.Xna.Framework.Input.Touch;

namespace PhingerPaint
{
    public class ColorBlock : DrawableGameComponent
    {
        SpriteBatch spriteBatch;
        Texture2D block;
```

```
        public ColorBlock(Game game) : base(game)
        {
        }

        public Color Color { set; get; }
        public Rectangle Destination { set; get; }
        public bool IsSelected { set; get; }

        public override void Initialize()
        {
            base.Initialize();
        }

        protected override void LoadContent()
        {
            spriteBatch = new SpriteBatch(this.GraphicsDevice);
            block = new Texture2D(this.GraphicsDevice, 1, 1);
            block.SetData<uint>(new uint[] { Color.White.PackedValue });

            base.LoadContent();
        }

        public override void Update(GameTime gameTime)
        {
            base.Update(gameTime);
        }

        public override void Draw(GameTime gameTime)
        {
            Rectangle rect = Destination;

            spriteBatch.Begin();
            spriteBatch.Draw(block, rect, IsSelected ? Color.White : Color.DarkGray);
            rect.Inflate(-6, -6);
            spriteBatch.Draw(block, rect, Color);
            spriteBatch.End();

            base.Draw(gameTime);
        }
    }
}
```

ColorBlock relies on three public properties—*Color, Destination,* and *IsSelected*—to govern its appearance. Notice during the *LoadContent* method that it too creates a *Texture2D* that is exactly one pixel in size. This *block* object is drawn twice in the *Draw* method. First it's drawn to the entire dimensions of the *Destination* rectangle as either dark gray or white, depending on the value of *IsSelected*. Then it's contracted in size by six pixels on all sides and drawn again based on the *Color* property.

The PhingerPaint Canvas

The components created by PhingerPaint are stored as fields along with some of the other expected information:

XNA Project: PhingerPaint   File: Game1.cs (excerpt showing fields)

```
public class Game1 : Microsoft.Xna.Framework.Game
{
    GraphicsDeviceManager graphics;
    SpriteBatch spriteBatch;

    Texture2D canvas;
    Vector2 canvasSize;
    Vector2 canvasPosition;
    uint[] pixels;
    List<float> xCollection = new List<float>();

    Button clearButton, saveButton;
    string filename;

    List<ColorBlock> colorBlocks = new List<ColorBlock>();
    Color drawingColor = Color.Blue;
    int? touchIdToIgnore;
    ...
}
```

The *List* stores the 12 *ColorBlock* components and *drawingColor* is the currently selected color. The main canvas is, of course, the *Texture2D* object called *canvas* and the *pixels* array stores the texture's pixels. The *xCollection* object is repeatedly reused in calls to the *RoundCappedLine* class.

The constructor sets the back buffer for portrait mode, but it sets the height to 768 rather than 800. This leaves enough space for the status bar so the back buffer is allowed to display in its full size:

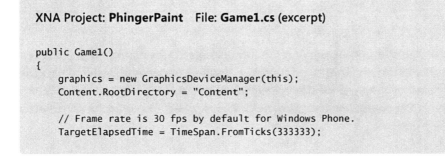

XNA Project: PhingerPaint   File: Game1.cs (excerpt)

```
public Game1()
{
    graphics = new GraphicsDeviceManager(this);
    Content.RootDirectory = "Content";

    // Frame rate is 30 fps by default for Windows Phone.
    TargetElapsedTime = TimeSpan.FromTicks(333333);
```

```
        // Set to portrait mode but leave room for status bar
        graphics.PreferredBackBufferWidth = 480;
        graphics.PreferredBackBufferHeight = 768;
    }
```

The *Initialize* override is responsible for creating the *Button* and *ColorBlack* components, partially initializing them, and adding them to the *Components* collection of the *Game* class. This ensures that they get their own calls to *Initialize*, *LoadContent*, *Update*, and *Draw*.

XNA Project: **PhingerPaint**   File: **Game1.cs** (excerpt)

```
protected override void Initialize()
{
    // Create Button components
    clearButton = new Button(this, "clear");
    clearButton.Click += OnClearButtonClick;
    this.Components.Add(clearButton);

    saveButton = new Button(this, "save");
    saveButton.Click += OnSaveButtonClick;
    this.Components.Add(saveButton);

    // Create ColorBlock components
    Color[] colors = { Color.Red, Color.Green, Color.Blue,
                    Color.Cyan, Color.Magenta, Color.Yellow,
                    Color.Black, new Color(0.2f, 0.2f, 0.2f),
                            new Color(0.4f, 0.4f, 0.4f),
                            new Color(0.6f, 0.6f, 0.6f),
                            new Color(0.8f, 0.8f, 0.8f), Color.White };

    foreach (Color clr in colors)
    {
        ColorBlock colorBlock = new ColorBlock(this);
        colorBlock.Color = clr;
        colorBlocks.Add(colorBlock);
        this.Components.Add(colorBlock);
    }
    base.Initialize();
}
```

The remainder of the initialization of the components occurs during the *LoadContent* override when the font can be loaded for the *Button* components. It seems a little odd to set a back buffer to an explicit size in the constructor, and yet calculate dimensions more abstractly in the *LoadContent* method, but it's usually best to keep code as generalized and as flexible as possible.

XNA Project: PhingerPaint   File: Game1.cs (excerpt)

```
protected override void LoadContent()
{
    spriteBatch = new SpriteBatch(GraphicsDevice);

    Rectangle clientBounds = this.GraphicsDevice.Viewport.Bounds;
    SpriteFont segoe14 = this.Content.Load<SpriteFont>("Segoe14");

    // Set up Button components
    clearButton.SpriteFont = segoe14;
    saveButton.SpriteFont = segoe14;

    Vector2 textSize = segoe14.MeasureString(clearButton.Text);
    int buttonWidth = (int)(2 * textSize.X);
    int buttonHeight = (int)(1.5 * textSize.Y);

    clearButton.Destination =
        new Rectangle(clientBounds.Left + 20,
                      clientBounds.Bottom - 2 - buttonHeight,
                      buttonWidth, buttonHeight);

    saveButton.Destination =
        new Rectangle(clientBounds.Right - 20 - buttonWidth,
                      clientBounds.Bottom - 2 - buttonHeight,
                      buttonWidth, buttonHeight);

    int colorBlockSize = clientBounds.Width / (colorBlocks.Count / 2) - 2;
    int xColorBlock = 2;
    int yColorBlock = 2;

    foreach (ColorBlock colorBlock in colorBlocks)
    {
        colorBlock.Destination = new Rectangle(xColorBlock, yColorBlock,
                                                colorBlockSize, colorBlockSize);
        xColorBlock += colorBlockSize + 2;

        if (xColorBlock + colorBlockSize > clientBounds.Width)
        {
            xColorBlock = 2;
            yColorBlock += colorBlockSize + 2;
        }
    }

    canvasPosition = new Vector2(0, 2 * colorBlockSize + 6);
    canvasSize = new Vector2(clientBounds.Width,
                             clientBounds.Height - canvasPosition.Y
                                                 - buttonHeight - 4);
}
```

The *LoadContent* method concludes by calculating a location and size for the *Texture2D* used as a canvas. But *LoadContent* doesn't take the final step in actually creating that *Texture2D* because the *LoadContent* method might soon be followed by a call to the *OnActivated* override which signals either that the program is starting up, or it's returning from a tombstoned state.

It is important for PhingerPaint to implement tombstoning because users tend to become enraged when their creative efforts disappear from the screen. For that reason the *OnDeactivated* override saves the image to the *PhoneApplicationService* in PNG format, and the *OnActivated* override gets it back out. I chose PNG for this process because it's a lossless compression format, and I felt that the image should be restored exactly to its original state.

To slightly ease the process of saving and loading *Texture2D* object, I used the methods in the *Texture2DExtensions* class in the Petzold.Phone.Xna library that I described in the previous chapter. The *OnActivated* method calls *LoadFromPhoneService* to obtain a saved *Texture2D*, and if that's not available, only then does it create a new one and clear it.

The use of the *PhoneApplicationService* class requires references to the System.Windows and Microsoft.Phone assemblies, and a *using* directive for *Microosft.Phone.Shell*.

XNA Project: **PhingerPaint**   File: **Game1.cs** (excerpt)

```
protected override void OnActivated(object sender, EventArgs args)
{
    // Recover from tombstoning
    bool newlyCreated = false;
    canvas = Texture2DExtensions.LoadFromPhoneServiceState(this.GraphicsDevice,
                                                           "canvas");
    if (canvas == null)
    {
        // Otherwise create new Texture2D
        canvas = new Texture2D(this.GraphicsDevice, (int)canvasSize.X,
                                                    (int)canvasSize.Y);
        newlyCreated = true;
    }

    // Create pixels array
    pixels = new uint[canvas.Width * canvas.Height];
    canvas.GetData<uint>(pixels);

    if (newlyCreated)
        ClearPixelArray();

    // Get drawing color from State, initialize selected ColorBlock
    if (PhoneApplicationService.Current.State.ContainsKey("color"))
        drawingColor = (Color)PhoneApplicationService.Current.State["color"];

    foreach (ColorBlock colorBlock in colorBlocks)
        colorBlock.IsSelected = colorBlock.Color == drawingColor;

    base.OnActivated(sender, args);
}
```

The *OnDeactivated* override stores the *Texture2D* using the *SaveToPhoneServiceState* extension method:

XNA Project: PhingerPaint   File: Game1.cs (excerpt)

```
protected override void OnDeactivated(object sender, EventArgs args)
{
    PhoneApplicationService.Current.State["color"] = drawingColor;
    canvas.SaveToPhoneServiceState("canvas");
    base.OnDeactivated(sender, args);
}
```

If the program is starting up, *OnActivated* calls a method named *ClearPixelArray*:

XNA Project: PhingerPaint   File: Game1.cs (excerpt)

```
void ClearPixelArray()
{
    for (int y = 0; y < canvas.Height; y++)
        for (int x = 0; x < canvas.Width; x++)
        {
            pixels[x + canvas.Width * y] = Color.GhostWhite.PackedValue;
        }

    canvas.SetData<uint>(pixels);
}

void OnClearButtonClick(object sender, EventArgs e)
{
    ClearPixelArray();
}
```

You'll also notice the *Click* event handler for the "clear" *Button* also calls this method. As you'll recall, the *Button* class fires the *Click* event based on touch input, and *Button* gets touch input when the parent *Game* class calls the *ProcessTouch* method from its own *Update* override. This means that this *OnClearButtonClick* method is actually called during a call to the *Update* override of this class.

When the user presses the Button labeled "save" the program must display some kind of dialog box to let the user type in a filename. An XNA program can get keyboard input in one of two ways: a low-level approach involving *Keyboard* and a high-level approach by calling the *Guide.BeginShowKeyboardInput* method in the *Microsoft.Xna.Framework. GamerServices* namespace. I chose the high-level option. *Guide.BeginShowKeyboardInput* wants some initialization information and a callback function, so the method fabricates a unique filename from the current date and time:

```
XNA Project: PhingerPaint   File: Game1.cs (excerpt)

void OnSaveButtonClick(object sender, EventArgs e)
{
    DateTime dt = DateTime.Now;
    filename =
        String.Format("PhingerPaint-{0:D2}-{1:D2}-{2:D2}-{3:D2}-{4:D2}-{5:D2}",
                        dt.Year % 100, dt.Month, dt.Day, dt.Hour, dt.Minute, dt.Second);

    Guide.BeginShowKeyboardInput(PlayerIndex.One, "phinger paint save file",
                        "enter filename:", filename, KeyboardCallback, null);
}
```

The *Guide.BeginShowKeyboardInput* call causes the program to receive a call to *OnDeactivated*, after which the following screen is displayed:

The only parts of this screen you can customize are the text strings in the headings and the initial text in the text-entry box. The screen looks much better in portrait mode than in landscape mode. In landscape mode, all the text headings, the text-entry box, and the on-screen keyboard are re-oriented but the two buttons are not, and the combination looks very peculiar. One look at it and you might never call *Guide.BeginShowKeyboardInput* from a landscape-mode program!

When either the "OK" or "Cancel" button is clicked, the program is re-activated and the callback function in *PhingerPaint* is called:

XNA Project: PhingerPaint   File: **Game1.cs** (excerpt)

```
void KeyboardCallback(IAsyncResult result)
{
    filename = Guide.EndShowKeyboardInput(result);
}
```

Your program should assume that this callback function is being called asynchronously (as the argument implies) so you shouldn't do a whole lot here except call *Guide .EndShowKeyboardInput* and save the return value in a field. If the user pressed the "OK" button, then the return value is the final text entered into the text-entry field. If the user pressed "Cancel" or the Back button, then *Guide.EndShowKeyboardInput* returns *null*.

A good place to do something with that return value is during the next call to the program's *Update* override:

XNA Project: PhingerPaint   File: **Game1.cs** (excerpt)

```
protected override void Update(GameTime gameTime)
{
    if (GamePad.GetState(PlayerIndex.One).Buttons.Back == ButtonState.Pressed)
        this.Exit();

    // If the Save File dialog box has returned, save the image
    if (!String.IsNullOrEmpty(filename))
    {
        canvas.SaveToPhotoLibrary(filename);
        filename = null;
    }
    ...
}
```

Notice that the logic checks if the *filename* field is non-*null* and non-empty but at the end it sets the filename field back to *null* to ensure that it's saved only once.

SaveToPhotoLibrary is not a real method of the *Texture2D* class! It's another extension method in the *Texture2DExtensions* class in the Petzold.Phone.Xna library.

XNA Project: Petzold.Phone.Xna   File: **Texture2DExtensions.cs** (excerpt)

```
public static void SaveToPhotoLibrary(this Texture2D texture, string filename)
{
    MemoryStream memoryStream = new MemoryStream();
    texture.SaveAsJpeg(memoryStream, texture.Width, texture.Height);
```

```
        memoryStream.Position = 0;
        MediaLibrary mediaLibrary = new MediaLibrary();
        mediaLibrary.SavePicture(filename, memoryStream);
        memoryStream.Close();
    }
```

This is the standard code for saving a *Texture2D* to the Saved Pictures album of the phone's photo library. Although PhingerPaint uses the PNG format when saving the image during tombstoning, pictures saved to the photo library must be JPEG. The *SaveAsJpeg* method saves the whole image to a *MemoryStream*, and then the *MemoryStream* position is reset and it's passed to the *SavePicture* method of *MediaLibrary* with a filename.

If you're deploying to an actual phone, and you're running the desktop Zune software so Visual Studio can communicate with the phone, this code will raise an exception. When Zune is running it wants exclusive access to the phone's media library. You'll need to terminate the Zune program and instead run the WPDTPTConnect tool, either WPDTPTConnect32.exe or WPDTPTConnect64.exe depending on whether you run 32-bit or 64-bit Windows.

Of course, most of the *Update* override is devoted to handling touch input. I chose to use the low-level touch input so you can draw with multiple fingers on the canvas. The *Button* basically handles its own touch input based on the *IProcessTouch* interface but *ColorBlock* is handled differently. The *Update* method in the game class itself handles the *ColorBlock* components as well as the *Texture2D* canvas.

The *ColorBlock* components are treated more simply than the *Button*. Just a touch on a *ColorBlock* selects that item and switches the program to that color. The touch ID is retained and not allowed to be used for anything else.

XNA Project: PhingerPaint   File: Game1.cs (excerpt)

```
protected override void Update(GameTime gameTime)
{
    ...
    TouchCollection touches = TouchPanel.GetState();

    foreach (TouchLocation touch in touches)
    {
        // Ignore further activity of ColorBlock push
        if (touchIdToIgnore.HasValue && touch.Id == touchIdToIgnore.Value)
            continue;

        // Let Button components have first dibs on touch
        bool touchHandled = false;
```

```
            foreach (GameComponent component in this.Components)
                if (component is IProcessTouch &&
                    (component as IProcessTouch).ProcessTouch(touch))
                {
                    touchHandled = true;
                    break;
                }

        if (touchHandled)
            continue;

        // Check for tap on ColorBlock
        if (touch.State == TouchLocationState.Pressed)
        {
            Vector2 position = touch.Position;
            ColorBlock newSelectedColorBlock = null;

            foreach (ColorBlock colorBlock in colorBlocks)
            {
                Rectangle rect = colorBlock.Destination;

                if (position.X >= rect.Left && position.X < rect.Right &&
                    position.Y >= rect.Top && position.Y < rect.Bottom)
                {
                    drawingColor = colorBlock.Color;
                    newSelectedColorBlock = colorBlock;
                }
            }

            if (newSelectedColorBlock != null)
            {
                foreach (ColorBlock colorBlock in colorBlocks)
                    colorBlock.IsSelected = colorBlock == newSelectedColorBlock;

                touchIdToIgnore = touch.Id;
            }
            else
            {
                touchIdToIgnore = null;
            }
        }
        ...
    }
    ...
}
```

The remainder of the touch processing is for actual drawing, and it's only interested in *State* values of *TouchLocationState.Moved*. That state allows a call to the *TryGetPreviousLocation* method, and the two points can then be passed to the constructor of the *RoundCappedLine* class in *Petzold.Phone.Xna*. That provides ranges of pixels to color for each little piece of a total brushstroke:

```
XNA Project: PhingerPaint   File: Game1.cs (excerpt)

protected override void Update(GameTime gameTime)
{
    ...
    // Process touch input
    bool canvasNeedsUpdate = false;
    TouchCollection touches = TouchPanel.GetState();

    foreach (TouchLocation touch in touches)
    {
        ...
        // Check for drawing movement
        else if (touch.State == TouchLocationState.Moved)
        {
            TouchLocation prevTouchLocation;
            touch.TryGetPreviousLocation(out prevTouchLocation);

            Vector2 point1 = prevTouchLocation.Position - canvasPosition;
            Vector2 point2 = touch.Position - canvasPosition;

            // Sure hope touchLocation.Pressure comes back!
            float radius = 12;
            RoundCappedLine line = new RoundCappedLine(point1, point2, radius);

            int yMin = (int)(Math.Min(point1.Y, point2.Y) - radius);
            int yMax = (int)(Math.Max(point1.Y, point2.Y) + radius);

            yMin = Math.Max(0, Math.Min(canvas.Height, yMin));
            yMax = Math.Max(0, Math.Min(canvas.Height, yMax));

            for (int y = yMin; y < yMax; y++)
            {
                xCollection.Clear();
                line.GetAllX(y, xCollection);

                if (xCollection.Count == 2)
                {
                    int xMin = (int)(Math.Min(xCollection[0], xCollection[1]) + 0.5f);
                    int xMax = (int)(Math.Max(xCollection[0], xCollection[1]) + 0.5f);

                    xMin = Math.Max(0, Math.Min(canvas.Width, xMin));
                    xMax = Math.Max(0, Math.Min(canvas.Width, xMax));

                    for (int x = xMin; x < xMax; x++)
                    {
                        pixels[y * canvas.Width + x] = drawingColor.PackedValue;
                    }
```

```
                    canvasNeedsUpdate = true;
                }
            }
        }
    }

    if (canvasNeedsUpdate)
        canvas.SetData<uint>(pixels);

    base.Update(gameTime);
}
```

It's always very satisfying when everything has prepared the *Draw* override for a very simple job. The *ColorBlock* and *Button* components draw themselves, so the *Draw* method here need only render the *canvas*:

XNA Project: **PhingerPaint**   File: **Game1.cs** (excerpt)

```
protected override void Draw(GameTime gameTime)
{
    this.GraphicsDevice.Clear(Color.Black);

    spriteBatch.Begin();
    spriteBatch.Draw(canvas, canvasPosition, Color.White);
    spriteBatch.End();

    base.Draw(gameTime);
}
```

A Little Tour Through SpinPaint

SpinPaint has an unusual genesis. I wrote the first version one morning while attending a two-day class on programming for Microsoft Surface—those coffee-table computers designed for public places. That version was written for the Windows Presentation Foundation and could be used by several people sitting around the machine.

I originally wanted to have a Silverlight version of SpinPaint in this book to demonstrate *WriteableBitmap*, but the performance was just terrible. I wrote the first XNA version for the Zune HD before I had an actual Windows Phone, and then I ported that version to the one I'll show you here.

SpinPaint comes up with a white disk that rotates 12 times per minute. You'll also notice that the title of the program cycles through a series of colors every 10 seconds:

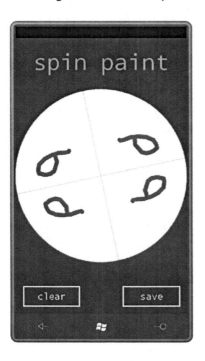

When you touch the disk, it paints with that title color as if your finger is a brush and the disk is moving below it, but the painted line is also flipped around the horizontal and vertical axes:

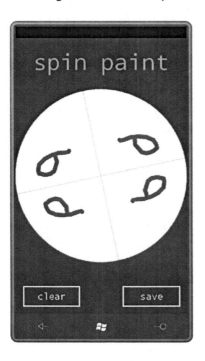

As you continue to paint, you can get some fancy designs:

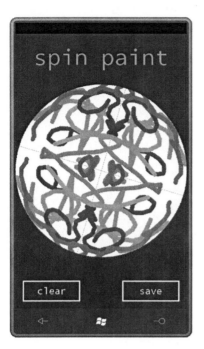

Obviously you'll want to press the "save" button to save the result to the phone's photo library, and later email it to your friends.

As with the PhingerPaint program, you can use up to four fingers for simultaneous drawing, and that's why both programs use the low-level touch input rather than the gesture interface.

The SpinPaint Code

SpinPaint needs to handle touch in a very special way. Not only can fingers move on the screen, but the disk rotates underneath the fingers, so even if a finger isn't moving it's still going to be drawing. Unlike PhingerPaint, this program needs to keep track of each finger. For that reason, it defines a *Dictionary* with an integer key (which is the touch ID) that maintains objects of type *TouchInfo*, a small class internal to *Game1* that stores two touch positions:

XNA Project: **SpinPaint**   File: **Game1.cs (excerpt showing fields)**

```
public class Game1 : Microsoft.Xna.Framework.Game
{
    GraphicsDeviceManager graphics;
    SpriteBatch spriteBatch;
```

```
        // Fields involved with spinning disk texture
        Texture2D diskTexture;
        uint[] pixels;
        Vector2 displayCenter;
        Vector2 textureCenter;
        int radius;
        Color currentColor;

        // Touch information and line-drawing fields
        class TouchInfo
        {
            public Vector2 PreviousPosition;
            public Vector2 CurrentPosition;
        }
        Dictionary<int, TouchInfo> touchDictionary = new Dictionary<int, TouchInfo>();
        float currentAngle;
        float previousAngle;
        List<float> xCollection = new List<float>();

        // Buttons and titles
        Button clearButton, saveButton;
        SpriteFont segoe14;
        SpriteFont segoe48;
        string titleText = "spin paint";
        Vector2 titlePosition;
        string filename;
        ...
    }
```

The constructor sets the back buffer for portrait mode, but like PhingerPaint it sets the height to 768 rather than 800 to make room for the status bar:

XNA Project: SpinPaint   File: Game1.cs (excerpt)

```
public Game1()
{
    graphics = new GraphicsDeviceManager(this);
    Content.RootDirectory = "Content";

    // Frame rate is 30 fps by default for Windows Phone.
    TargetElapsedTime = TimeSpan.FromTicks(333333);

    // Portrait, but allow room for status bar at top
    graphics.PreferredBackBufferWidth = 480;
    graphics.PreferredBackBufferHeight = 768;
}
```

Making room for the status bar means that you're seeing the full back buffer dimensions on the screen.

The two *Button* components are created during the *Initialize* method. They have their *Text* properties assigned and *Click* event handlers attached but nothing else quite yet:

XNA Project: SpinPaint   File: Game1.cs (excerpt)

```
protected override void Initialize()
{
    // Create button components
    clearButton = new Button(this, "clear");
    clearButton.Click += OnClearButtonClick;
    this.Components.Add(clearButton);

    saveButton = new Button(this, "save");
    saveButton.Click += OnSaveButtonClick;
    this.Components.Add(saveButton);

    base.Initialize();
}
```

Notice the all-important step of adding the components to the *Components* collection of the *Game* class. If you forget to do that, they won't show up at all and you'll probably find yourself very baffled. (I speak from experience.)

The program can't position the buttons until it knows how large they should be, and that information isn't available until fonts are loaded, and that doesn't happen until the *LoadContent* override. Here is where the buttons are assigned both a font and a destination:

XNA Project: SpinPaint   File: Game1.cs (excerpt)

```
protected override void LoadContent()
{
    spriteBatch = new SpriteBatch(GraphicsDevice);

    // Get display information
    Rectangle clientBounds = this.GraphicsDevice.Viewport.Bounds;
    displayCenter = new Vector2(clientBounds.Center.X, clientBounds.Center.Y);

    // Load fonts and calculate title position
    segoe14 = this.Content.Load<SpriteFont>("Segoe14");
    segoe48 = this.Content.Load<SpriteFont>("Segoe48");
    titlePosition = new Vector2((int)((clientBounds.Width -
                            segoe48.MeasureString(titleText).X) / 2), 20);

    // Set button fonts and destinations
    clearButton.SpriteFont = segoe14;
    saveButton.SpriteFont = segoe14;
    Vector2 textSize = segoe14.MeasureString(clearButton.Text);
```

```
    int buttonWidth = (int)(2 * textSize.X);
    int buttonHeight = (int)(1.5 * textSize.Y);

    clearButton.Destination =
        new Rectangle(clientBounds.Left + 20,
                        clientBounds.Bottom - 20 - buttonHeight,
                        buttonWidth, buttonHeight);
    saveButton.Destination =
        new Rectangle(clientBounds.Right - 20 - buttonWidth,
                        clientBounds.Bottom - 20 - buttonHeight,
                        buttonWidth, buttonHeight);
}
```

The *LoadContent* method doesn't create the *Texture2D* used for painting because that job
needs to be incorporated into the tombstoning logic.

As in PhingerPaint, the *OnDeactivated* override saves the image in PNG format, and the
OnActivated override gets it back out. Both methods call methods in the *TextureExtensions*
class in the Petzold.Phone.Xna library. If there's nothing to retrieve, then the program is
starting up fresh and a new *Texture2D* needs to be created.

XNA Project: SpinPaint   File: Game1.cs (excerpt)

```
protected override void OnActivated(object sender, EventArgs args)
{
    // Recover from tombstoning
    bool newlyCreated = false;
    diskTexture = Texture2DExtensions.LoadFromPhoneServiceState(this.GraphicsDevice,
                                                                "disk");
    // Or create the Texture2D
    if (diskTexture == null)
    {
        Rectangle clientBounds = this.GraphicsDevice.Viewport.Bounds;
        int textureDimension = Math.Min(clientBounds.Width, clientBounds.Height);
        diskTexture = new Texture2D(this.GraphicsDevice, textureDimension,
                                                         textureDimension);
        newlyCreated = true;
    }

    pixels = new uint[diskTexture.Width * diskTexture.Height];
    radius = diskTexture.Width / 2;
    textureCenter = new Vector2(radius, radius);

    if (newlyCreated)
    {
        ClearPixelArray();
    }
```

```
        else
        {
            diskTexture.GetData<uint>(pixels);
        }

        base.OnActivated(sender, args);
    }

    protected override void OnDeactivated(object sender, EventArgs args)
    {
        diskTexture.SaveToPhoneServiceState("disk");
        base.OnDeactivated(sender, args);
    }
```

If a new *Texture2D* is created, then it is initialized with a *pixels* array that contains a circular area set to white except for a couple light gray lines that help suggest to the user that the disk is really spinning.

XNA Project: SpinPaint   File: Game1.cs (excerpt)

```
void ClearPixelArray()
{
    for (int y = 0; y < diskTexture.Height; y++)
        for (int x = 0; x < diskTexture.Width; x++)
            if (IsWithinCircle(x, y))
            {
                Color clr = Color.White;

                // Lines that criss cross quadrants
                if (x == diskTexture.Width / 2 || y == diskTexture.Height / 2)
                    clr = Color.LightGray;

                pixels[y * diskTexture.Width + x] = clr.PackedValue;
            }
    diskTexture.SetData<uint>(pixels);
}

bool IsWithinCircle(int x, int y)
{
    x -= diskTexture.Width / 2;
    y -= diskTexture.Height / 2;

    return x * x + y * y < radius * radius;
}

void OnClearButtonClick(object sender, EventArgs args)
{
    ClearPixelArray();
}
```

The *ClearPixelArray* is also called when the user presses the "clear" button.

The logic for the "save" button is virtually identical to that in PhingerPaint:

XNA Project: SpinPaint   File: Game1.cs (excerpt)

```
void OnSaveButtonClick(object sender, EventArgs args)
{
    DateTime dt = DateTime.Now;
    string filename =
        String.Format("spinpaint-{0:D2}-{1:D2}-{2:D2}-{3:D2}-{4:D2}-{5:D2}",
                      dt.Year % 100, dt.Month, dt.Day, dt.Hour, dt.Minute, dt.Second);

    Guide.BeginShowKeyboardInput(PlayerIndex.One, "spin paint save file",
                                 "enter filename:", filename, KeyboardCallback, null);
}
void KeyboardCallback(IAsyncResult result)
{
    filename = Guide.EndShowKeyboardInput(result);
}
```

Also as in PhingerPaint, the file is saved to the photo library during the *Update* override:

XNA Project: SpinPaint   File: Game1.cs (excerpt)

```
protected override void Update(GameTime gameTime)
{
    // Allows the game to exit
    if (GamePad.GetState(PlayerIndex.One).Buttons.Back == ButtonState.Pressed)
        this.Exit();

    // If the Save File dialog has returned, save the image
    if (!String.IsNullOrEmpty(filename))
    {
        diskTexture.SaveToPhotoLibrary(filename);
        filename = null;
    }
    ...
}
```

The Actual Drawing

The remainder of the *Update* override does the really hard stuff: drawing on the disk based on touch input and the disk's revolution.

Update processing begins with the calculation of a current angle of the spinning disk and a current color to paint it:

```
protected override void Update(GameTime gameTime)
{
    ...
    // Disk rotates every 5 seconds
    double seconds = gameTime.TotalGameTime.TotalSeconds;
    currentAngle = (float)(2 * Math.PI * seconds / 5);

    // Colors cycle every 10 seconds
    float fraction = (float)(6 * (seconds % 10) / 10);

    if (fraction < 1)
        currentColor = new Color(1, fraction, 0);
    else if (fraction < 2)
        currentColor = new Color(2 - fraction, 1, 0);
    else if (fraction < 3)
        currentColor = new Color(0, 1, fraction - 2);
    else if (fraction < 4)
        currentColor = new Color(0, 4 - fraction, 1);
    else if (fraction < 5)
        currentColor = new Color(fraction - 4, 0, 1);
    else
        currentColor = new Color(1, 0, 6 - fraction);

    // First assume no finger movement
    foreach (TouchInfo touchInfo in touchDictionary.Values)
        touchInfo.CurrentPosition = touchInfo.PreviousPosition;
    ...
}
```

While any finger is currently touching the screen, the program maintains a *TouchInfo* object with *CurrentPosition* and *PreviousPosition*. These positions are always relative to the *Texture2D* canvas not taking account of spinning. For that reason, this section of the *Update* override concludes with the *CurrentPosition* field being set from the *PreviousPosition* field under the assumption that no fingers have moved.

At this point, *Update* is now ready to look at touch input, first calling the *ProcessTouch* method in each button and then finding new positions of existing fingers or new touches. Translating touch input relative to the screen to touch input relative to the *Texture2D* is the responsibility of the little *TranslateToTexture* method that follows *Update* here.

```
protected override void Update(GameTime gameTime)
{
    ...
```

```csharp
        // Get all touches
        TouchCollection touches = TouchPanel.GetState();

        foreach (TouchLocation touch in touches)
        {
            // Let Button components have first dibs on touch
            bool touchHandled = false;

            foreach (GameComponent component in this.Components)
            {
                if (component is IProcessTouch &&
                    (component as IProcessTouch).ProcessTouch(touch))
                {
                    touchHandled = true;
                    break;
                }
            }

            if (touchHandled)
                continue;

            // Set TouchInfo items from touch information
            int id = touch.Id;

            switch (touch.State)
            {
                case TouchLocationState.Pressed:
                    if (!touchDictionary.ContainsKey(id))
                        touchDictionary.Add(id, new TouchInfo());

                    touchDictionary[id].PreviousPosition = TranslateToTexture(touch
.Position);
                    touchDictionary[id].CurrentPosition = TranslateToTexture(touch
.Position);
                    break;

                case TouchLocationState.Moved:
                    if (touchDictionary.ContainsKey(id))
                        touchDictionary[id].CurrentPosition =
                                    TranslateToTexture(touch.Position);
                    break;

                case TouchLocationState.Released:
                    if (touchDictionary.ContainsKey(id))
                        touchDictionary.Remove(id);
                    break;
            }
        }
        ...
}

Vector2 TranslateToTexture(Vector2 point)
{
    return point - displayCenter + textureCenter;
}
```

To take account of the spinning of the disk, the fields include *previousAngle* and *currentAngle*. *Update* now calculates two matrices called *previousRotation* and *currentRotation* based on these two fields. Notice that these matrices are obtained from calls to *Matrix.CreateRotationZ* but they are bracketed with multiplications by translation transforms that adjust the rotation so it is relative to the center of the *Texture2D*:

XNA Project: **SpinPaint**   File: **Game1.cs** (excerpt)

```
protected override void Update(GameTime gameTime)
{
    . . .
    // Calculate transforms for rotation
    Matrix translate1 = Matrix.CreateTranslation(-textureCenter.X, -textureCenter.Y,
0);
    Matrix translate2 = Matrix.CreateTranslation(textureCenter.X, textureCenter.Y, 0);

    Matrix previousRotation = translate1 *
                                    Matrix.CreateRotationZ(-previousAngle) *
                                            translate2;
    Matrix currentRotation = translate1 *
                                    Matrix.CreateRotationZ(-currentAngle) *
                                            translate2;
    . . .
}
```

Once those transforms are determined, then they can be applied to the *PreviousPosition* and *CurrentPosition* fields of the *TouchInfo* object using the state *Vector2.Transform* method, and then passed to *RoundCappedLine* to obtain the information necessary to draw a line on the *Texture2D*:

XNA Project: **SpinPaint**   File: **Game1.cs** (excerpt)

```
protected override void Update(GameTime gameTime)
{
    . . .
    bool textureNeedsUpdate = false;

    foreach (TouchInfo touchInfo in touchDictionary.Values)
    {
        // Now draw from previous to current points
        Vector2 point1 = Vector2.Transform(touchInfo.PreviousPosition,
previousRotation);
        Vector2 point2 = Vector2.Transform(touchInfo.CurrentPosition, currentRotation);
        float radius = 6;

        RoundCappedLine line = new RoundCappedLine(point1, point2, radius);

        int yMin = (int)(Math.Min(point1.Y, point2.Y) - radius);
```

```
                int yMax = (int)(Math.Max(point1.Y, point2.Y) + radius);

            yMin = Math.Max(0, Math.Min(diskTexture.Height, yMin));
            yMax = Math.Max(0, Math.Min(diskTexture.Height, yMax));

            for (int y = yMin; y < yMax; y++)
            {
                xCollection.Clear();
                line.GetAllX(y, xCollection);

                if (xCollection.Count == 2)
                {
                    int xMin = (int)(Math.Min(xCollection[0], xCollection[1]) + 0.5f);
                    int xMax = (int)(Math.Max(xCollection[0], xCollection[1]) + 0.5f);

                    xMin = Math.Max(0, Math.Min(diskTexture.Width, xMin));
                    xMax = Math.Max(0, Math.Min(diskTexture.Width, xMax));

                    for (int x = xMin; x < xMax; x++)
                    {
                        if (IsWithinCircle(x, y))
                        {
                            // Draw pixel in four quadrants
                            int xFlip = diskTexture.Width - x;
                            int yFlip = diskTexture.Height - y;

                            pixels[y * diskTexture.Width + x] = currentColor.PackedValue;
                            pixels[y * diskTexture.Width + xFlip] = currentColor
.PackedValue;
                            pixels[yFlip * diskTexture.Width + x] = currentColor
.PackedValue;
                            pixels[yFlip * diskTexture.Width + xFlip] =
                                                        currentColor.PackedValue;
                        }
                    }
                    textureNeedsUpdate = true;
                }
            }
        }

        if (textureNeedsUpdate)
        {
            // Update the texture from the pixels array
            this.GraphicsDevice.Textures[0] = null;
            diskTexture.SetData<uint>(pixels);
        }

        // Prepare for next time through
        foreach (TouchInfo touchInfo in touchDictionary.Values)
            touchInfo.PreviousPosition = touchInfo.CurrentPosition;

        previousAngle = currentAngle;

        base.Update(gameTime);
    }
```

The actual *Draw* override is amazingly tiny. All it renders is the rotating *diskTexture* and the application name with its changing color that appears at the top of the screen:

XNA Project: **SpinPaint**   File: **Game1.cs** (excerpt)

```
protected override void Draw(GameTime gameTime)
{
    GraphicsDevice.Clear(Color.Navy);

    spriteBatch.Begin();
    spriteBatch.Draw(diskTexture, displayCenter, null, Color.White,
                     currentAngle, textureCenter, 1, SpriteEffects.None, 0);
    spriteBatch.DrawString(segoe48, titleText, titlePosition, currentColor);
    spriteBatch.End();

    base.Draw(gameTime);
}
```

PhreeCell and a Deck of Cards

I originally thought that my PhreeCell solitaire game would have no features beyond what was strictly necessary to play the game. My wife—who has played FreeCell under Windows and who only rarely can't complete a deal—made it clear that PhreeCell would need two features that I hadn't planned on implementing: First and most importantly, there had to be some kind of positive feedback from the program acknowledging that the player has won. I implemented this as a *DrawableGameComponent* derivative called *CongratulationsComponent*.

The second essential feature was something I called "auto move." If a card can be legally moved to the suit piles at the upper right of the board, and there was no reason to do otherwise, then the card is automatically moved. Other than that, PhreeCell has no amenities. There is no animated "deal" at the beginning of play, you cannot simply "click" to indicate a destination spot, and there is no way to move multiple cards in one shot. There is no undo and no hints.

My coding for PhreeCell began not with an XNA program but with a Windows Presentation Foundation program to generate a single 1040 × 448 bitmap containing all 52 playing cards, each of which is 96 pixels wide and 112 pixels tall. This program uses mostly *TextBlock* objects to adorn a *Canvas* with numbers, letters, and suit symbols. It then passes the *Canvas* to a *RenderTargetBitmap* and saves the result out to a file named cards.png. In the XNA PhreeCell project, I added this file to the program's content.

Within the PhreeCell project, each card is an object of type *CardInfo*:

XNA Project: **PhreeCell**   File: **CardInfo.cs**

```
using System;
using Microsoft.Xna.Framework;

namespace PhreeCell
{
    class CardInfo
    {
        static string[] ranks = { "Ace", "Deuce", "Three", "Four",
                                  "Five", "Six", "Seven", "Eight",
                                  "Nine", "Ten", "Jack", "Queen", "King" };
        static string[] suits = { "Spades", "Clubs", "Hearts", "Diamonds" };

        public int Suit { protected set; get; }
        public int Rank { protected set; get; }

        public Vector2 AutoMoveOffset { set; get; }
        public TimeSpan AutoMoveTime { set; get; }
        public float AutoMoveInterpolation { set; get; }

        public CardInfo(int suit, int rank)
        {
            Suit = suit;
            Rank = rank;
        }

        // used for debugging purposes
        public override string ToString()
        {
            return ranks[Rank] + " of " + suits[Suit];
        }
    }
}
```

At first, this class simply had *Suit* and *Rank* properties. I added the static *string* arrays and *ToString* for display purposes while debugging, and I added the three *AutoMove* fields when I implemented that feature. *CardInfo* itself has no information about where the card is actually located during play. That's retained elsewhere.

The Playing Field

Here's the opening PhreeCell screen:

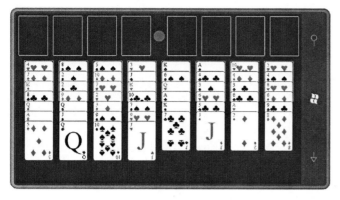

I'll assume you're familiar with the rules. All 52 cards are dealt face up in 8 columns that I refer to in the program as "piles." At the upper left are four spots for holding individual cards. I refer to these four areas as "holds." At the upper-right are four spots for stacking ascending cards of the same suit; these are called "finals." The red dot in the middle is the replay button.

For convenience, I split the *Game1* class into two files. The first is the normal Game1.cs file; the second is named Game1.Helpers.cs. The Game1.cs file contains only those methods typically found in a small game that also implements tombstoning logic. Game1.Helpers.cs has everything else. I created the file by adding a new class to the project. In both files, the *Game1* class derives from *Game*, and in both files the *partial* keyword indicates that the class is split between multiple files. The Helpers file has no instance fields—just *const* and *static readonly*. The Game1.cs file has one *static* field and all the instance fields:

XNA Project: PhreeCell   File: Game1.cs (excerpt showing fields)

```
public partial class Game1 : Microsoft.Xna.Framework.Game
{
    static readonly TimeSpan AutoMoveDuration = TimeSpan.FromSeconds(0.25);

    GraphicsDeviceManager graphics;
    SpriteBatch spriteBatch;
    CongratulationsComponent congratsComponent;

    Texture2D cards;
    Texture2D surface;
    Rectangle[] cardSpots = new Rectangle[16];

    Matrix displayMatrix;
    Matrix inverseMatrix;

    CardInfo[] deck = new CardInfo[52];
    List<CardInfo>[] piles = new List<CardInfo>[8];
    CardInfo[] holds = new CardInfo[4];
    List<CardInfo>[] finals = new List<CardInfo>[4];
```

```
        bool firstDragInGesture = true;
        CardInfo touchedCard;
        Vector2 touchedCardPosition;
        object touchedCardOrigin;
        int touchedCardOriginIndex;
        ...
    }
```

The program uses only two *Texture2D* objects: The *cards* object is the bitmap containing all 52 cards; individual cards are displayed by defining rectangular subsets of this bitmap. The *surface* is the dark blue area you see in the screen shot that also includes the white rectangles and the red button. The coordinates of those 16 white rectangles—there are eight more under the top card in each pile—are stored in the *cardSpots* array.

The *displayMatrix* field is normally the identity matrix. However, if you're a Free Cell player you know that sometimes the piles of cards can grow long. In this case, the *displayMatrix* performs vertical scaling to compress the entire playing area. The *inverseMatrix* is the inverse of that matrix and is necessary to convert screen-relative touch input to points on the compressed bitmap.

The next block of fields are the basic data structures used by the program. The *deck* array contains all 52 *CardInfo* objects created early in the program and re-used until the program is terminated. During play, copies of those cards are also in *piles*, *holds*, and *finals*. I originally thought *finals* would be an array like *holds* because only the top card need be displayed, but I discovered that the auto-move feature potentially required more cards to be visible.

The other fields are connected with touching and moving cards with the fingers. The *touchedCardPosition* field is the current position of the moving card. The *touchedCardOrigin* field stores the object where the moving card came from and is either the *holds* or *piles* array, while *touchedCardOriginIndex* is the array index. These are used to return the card to its original spot if the user tries to move the card illegally.

The *Game1* constructor indicates that the game wants a playing area of 800 pixels wide and 480 pixels high without the status bar. Three types of gestures are also enabled:

XNA Project: PhreeCell   File: Game1.cs (excerpt)

```
public Game1()
{
    graphics = new GraphicsDeviceManager(this);
    graphics.IsFullScreen = true;
    Content.RootDirectory = "Content";
```

```
    // Frame rate is 30 fps by default for Windows Phone.
    TargetElapsedTime = TimeSpan.FromTicks(333333);


    graphics.IsFullScreen = true;
    graphics.PreferredBackBufferWidth = 800;
    graphics.PreferredBackBufferHeight = 480;

    // Enable gestures
    TouchPanel.EnabledGestures = GestureType.Tap |
                                 GestureType.FreeDrag |
                                 GestureType.DragComplete;
}
```

The *Initialize* method creates the *CardInfo* objects for the *decks* array, and initializes the *piles* and *finals* arrays with *List* objects. It also creates the *CongratulationsComponent* and adds it to the *Components* collection:

XNA Project: PhreeCell   File: Game1.cs (excerpt)

```
protected override void Initialize()
{
    // Initialize deck
    for (int suit = 0; suit < 4; suit++)
        for (int rank = 0; rank < 13; rank++)
        {
            CardInfo cardInfo = new CardInfo(suit, rank);
            deck[suit * 13 + rank] = cardInfo;
        }

    // Create the List objects for the 8 piles
    for (int pile = 0; pile < 8; pile++)
        piles[pile] = new List<CardInfo>();

    // Create the List objects for the 4 finals
    for (int final = 0; final < 4; final++)
        finals[final] = new List<CardInfo>();

    // Create congratulations component
    congratsComponent = new CongratulationsComponent(this);
    congratsComponent.Enabled = false;
    this.Components.Add(congratsComponent);
    base.Initialize();
}
```

The *LoadContent* method loads the bitmap containing the card images, and also calls two methods in the portion of the *Game1* class implemented in Game1.Helpers.cs:

XNA Project: **PhreeCell**   File: **Game1.cs** (excerpt)

```
protected override void LoadContent()
{
    spriteBatch = new SpriteBatch(GraphicsDevice);

    // Load large bitmap containing cards
    cards = this.Content.Load<Texture2D>("cards");

    // Create the 16 rectangular areas for the cards and the bitmap surface
    CreateCardSpots(cardSpots);
    surface = CreateSurface(this.GraphicsDevice, cardSpots);
}
```

In a commercial program, I would definitely design a second set of cards specifically for the small display; these would certainly be more attractive than cards that are scaled to 60% of their designed size.

The Game1.Helpers.cs file begins with a bunch of constant fields that define all the pixel dimensions of the playing field:

XNA Project: **PhreeCell**   File: **Game1.Helper.cs** (excerpt showing fields)

```
public partial class Game1 : Microsoft.Xna.Framework.Game
{
    const int wCard = 80;        // width of card
    const int hCard = 112;       // height of card

    // Horizontal measurements
    const int wSurface = 800;    // width of surface
    const int xGap = 16;         // space between piles
    const int xMargin = 8;       // margin on left and right

    // gap between "holds" and "finals"
    const int xMidGap = wSurface - (2 * xMargin + 8 * wCard + 6 * xGap);

    // additional margin on second row
    const int xIndent = (wSurface - (2 * xMargin + 8 * wCard + 7 * xGap)) / 2;

    // Vertical measurements
    const int yMargin = 8;       // vertical margin on top row
    const int yGap = 16;         // vertical margin between rows
    const int yOverlay = 28;     // visible top of cards in piles
    const int hSurface = 2 * yMargin + yGap + 2 * hCard + 19 * yOverlay;
```

```
    // Replay button
    const int radiusReplay = xMidGap / 2 - 8;
    static readonly Vector2 centerReplay =
                        new Vector2(wSurface / 2, xMargin + hCard / 2);
    ...
}
```

Notice that *wSurface*—the width of the playing field—is defined to be 800 pixels because that's the width of the large phone display. However, the vertical dimension might need to be greater than 480. It is possible for there to be 20 overlapping cards in the *piles* area. To accommodate that possibility, *hSurface* is calculated as a maximum possible height based on these 20 overlapping cards.

The *CreateCardSpots* method uses those constants to calculate 16 *Rectangle* objects indicating where the cards are positioned on the playing fields. The top row has the *holds* and *finals*, and the bottom row is for the *piles*:

XNA Project: PhreeCell   File: Game1.Helper.cs (excerpt)

```
static void CreateCardSpots(Rectangle[] cardSpots)
{
    // Top row
    int x = xMargin;
    int y = yMargin;

    for (int i = 0; i < 8; i++)
    {
        cardSpots[i] = new Rectangle(x, y, wCard, hCard);
        x += wCard + (i == 3 ? xMidGap : xGap);
    }

    // Bottom row
    x = xMargin + xIndent;
    y += hCard + yGap;

    for (int i = 8; i < 16; i++)
    {
        cardSpots[i] = new Rectangle(x, y, wCard, hCard);
        x += wCard + xGap;
    }
}
```

The *CreateSurface* method creates the bitmap used for the playing field. The size of the bitmap is based on *hSurface* (set as a constant 800) and *wSurface*, which is much more than

480. To draw the white rectangles and red replay button, it directly manipulates pixels and sets those to the bitmap:

XNA Project: PhreeCell   **File: Game1.Helper.cs (excerpt)**

```
static Texture2D CreateSurface(GraphicsDevice graphicsDevice, Rectangle[] cardSpots)
{
    uint backgroundColor = new Color(0, 0, 0x60).PackedValue;
    uint outlineColor = Color.White.PackedValue;
    uint replayColor = Color.Red.PackedValue;
    Texture2D surface = new Texture2D(graphicsDevice, wSurface, hSurface);
    uint[] pixels = new uint[wSurface * hSurface];

    for (int i = 0; i < pixels.Length; i++)
    {
        if ((new Vector2(i % wSurface, i / wSurface) - centerReplay).LengthSquared() <
                            radiusReplay * radiusReplay)
            pixels[i] = replayColor;
        else
            pixels[i] = backgroundColor;
    }

    foreach (Rectangle rect in cardSpots)
    {
        // tops of rectangles
        for (int x = 0; x < wCard; x++)
        {
            pixels[(rect.Top - 1) * wSurface + rect.Left + x] = outlineColor;
            pixels[rect.Bottom * wSurface + rect.Left + x] = outlineColor;
        }
        // sides of rectangles
        for (int y = 0; y < hCard; y++)
        {
            pixels[(rect.Top + y) * wSurface + rect.Left - 1] = outlineColor;
            pixels[(rect.Top + y) * wSurface + rect.Right] = outlineColor;
        }
    }

    surface.SetData<uint>(pixels);
    return surface;
}
```

The other static methods in the *Game1* class are fairly self-explanatory.

```
XNA Project: PhreeCell    File: Game1.Helper.cs (excerpt)

static void ShuffleDeck(CardInfo[] deck)
{
    Random rand = new Random();

    for (int card = 0; card < 52; card++)
    {
        int random = rand.Next(52);
        CardInfo swap = deck[card];
        deck[card] = deck[random];
        deck[random] = swap;
    }
}

static bool IsWithinRectangle(Vector2 point, Rectangle rect)
{
    return point.X >= rect.Left &&
           point.X <= rect.Right &&
           point.Y >= rect.Top &&
           point.Y <= rect.Bottom;
}

static Rectangle GetCardTextureSource(CardInfo cardInfo)
{
    return new Rectangle(wCard * cardInfo.Rank,
                         hCard * cardInfo.Suit, wCard, hCard);
}

static CardInfo TopCard(List<CardInfo> cardInfos)
{
    if (cardInfos.Count > 0)
        return cardInfos[cardInfos.Count - 1];

    return null;
}
```

GetCardTextureSource is used in conjunction with the large *cards* bitmap. It simply returns a *Rectangle* object corresponding to a particular card. *TopCard* returns the last item in a *List<CardInfo>* collection, which is useful for obtaining the topmost card in one of the *piles* or *finals* collections.

At the conclusion of the *LoadContent* override, the game is almost ready to call the *Replay* method, which shuffles the deck and "deals" cards into the *piles* collections. However, there is tombstoning to deal with. This program was originally built around the *piles*, *holds*, and *finals* arrays and collections before tombstoning was implemented. I was pleased when I realized that these three items were the only part of the program that needed to be saved and retrieved during tombstoning. However, it bothered me that these three objects contained references to the 52 instances of *CardInfo* stored in *deck*, and I wanted to maintain that relationship, so I ended up saving and retrieving not instances of *CardInfo*, but an integer index 0 through 52. This required a bit of rather boring code:

XNA Project: PhreeCell   File: Game1.cs (excerpt)

```
protected override void OnDeactivated(object sender, EventArgs args)
{
    PhoneApplicationService appService = PhoneApplicationService.Current;

    // Save piles integers
    List<int>[] piles = new List<int>[8];

    for (int i = 0; i < piles.Length; i++)
    {
        piles[i] = new List<int>();

        foreach (CardInfo cardInfo in this.piles[i])
            piles[i].Add(13 * cardInfo.Suit + cardInfo.Rank);
    }
    appService.State["piles"] = piles;

    // Save finals integers
    List<int>[] finals = new List<int>[4];

    for (int i = 0; i < finals.Length; i++)
    {
        finals[i] = new List<int>();

        foreach (CardInfo cardInfo in this.finals[i])
            finals[i].Add(13 * cardInfo.Suit + cardInfo.Rank);
    }
    appService.State["finals"] = finals;

    // Save holds integers
    int[] holds = new int[4];

    for (int i = 0; i < holds.Length; i++)
    {
        if (this.holds[i] == null)
            holds[i] = -1;
        else
            holds[i] = 13 * this.holds[i].Suit + this.holds[i].Rank;
    }
    appService.State["holds"] = holds;

    base.OnDeactivated(sender, args);
}

protected override void OnActivated(object sender, EventArgs args)
{
    PhoneApplicationService appService = PhoneApplicationService.Current;
```

```
        if (appService.State.ContainsKey("piles"))
        {
            // Retrieve piles integers
            List<int>[] piles = appService.State["piles"] as List<int>[];

            for (int i = 0; i < piles.Length; i++)
            {
                foreach (int cardindex in piles[i])
                    this.piles[i].Add(deck[cardindex]);
            }

            // Retrieve finals integers
            List<int>[] finals = appService.State["finals"] as List<int>[];

            for (int i = 0; i < finals.Length; i++)
            {
                foreach (int cardindex in finals[i])
                    this.finals[i].Add(deck[cardindex]);
            }

            // Retrieve holds integers
            int[] holds = appService.State["holds"] as int[];

            for (int i = 0; i < holds.Length; i++)
            {
                if (holds[i] != -1)
                    this.holds[i] = deck[holds[i]];
            }
            CalculateDisplayMatrix();
        }
        else
        {
            Replay();
        }
        base.OnActivated(sender, args);
}
```

The great news is that at the very end of the *OnActivated* override, the *Replay* method is called to actually start the game.

Play and Replay

Replay is in the Game1.Helper.cs class:

XNA Project: **PhreeCell**   File: **Game1.Helper.cs** (excerpt)

```
void Replay()
{
    for (int i = 0; i < 4; i++)
```

```
        holds[i] = null;

    foreach (List<CardInfo> final in finals)
        final.Clear();

    foreach (List<CardInfo> pile in piles)
        pile.Clear();

    ShuffleDeck(deck);

    // Apportion cards to piles
    for (int card = 0; card < 52; card++)
    {
        piles[card % 8].Add(deck[card]);
    }
    CalculateDisplayMatrix();
}
```

The method clears out the *holds* array, and the *finals* and *piles* collections, randomizes the deck of cards, and apportions them into the eight collections in *piles*. The method is concluded with a call to *CalculateDisplayMatrix*. This is not the only time this method is called. It's also called from *OnActivated* when the program is recovering from tombstoning. Thereafter, any time a card is moved from, or added to, one of the *piles* collections, the display matrix is re-calculated just in case.

This matrix is responsible for the height of the playing area if more space is required for viewing all the cards in the *piles* area. The program doesn't handle this issue very elegantly. It simply makes the entire playing field a little shorter, including all the cards and even the replay button:

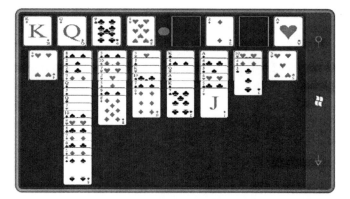

I'm not entirely happy with this solution, but here's the *CalculateDisplayMatrix* method that does it:

XNA Project: **PhreeCell**   File: **Game1.Helper.cs** (excerpt)

```
void CalculateDisplayMatrix()
{
    // This will be 480 based on preferred back buffer settings
    int viewportHeight = this.GraphicsDevice.Viewport.Height;

    // Figure out the total required height and scale vertically
    int maxCardsInPiles = 0;

    foreach (List<CardInfo> pile in piles)
        maxCardsInPiles = Math.Max(maxCardsInPiles, pile.Count);

    int requiredHeight = 2 * yMargin + yGap + 2 * hCard +
                                 yOverlay * (maxCardsInPiles - 1);

    // Set the matrix for compressed Y if needed to show all cards
    if (requiredHeight > viewportHeight)
        displayMatrix = Matrix.CreateScale(1, (float)viewportHeight / requiredHeight,
1);
    else
        displayMatrix = Matrix.Identity;

    // Find the inverse matrix for hit-testing
    inverseMatrix = Matrix.Invert(displayMatrix);
}
```

The *displayMatrix* is used in the *Begin* call of *SpriteBatch* so it's applied to everything in one grand swoop. Although just a little bit out of my customary sequence, you are now ready to look at the *Draw* method in the *Game1* class.

XNA Project: **PhreeCell**   File: **Game1.cs** (excerpt)

```
protected override void Draw(GameTime gameTime)
{
    spriteBatch.Begin(SpriteSortMode.Immediate, null, null, null, null, null,
                    displayMatrix);
    spriteBatch.Draw(surface, Vector2.Zero, Color.White);

    // Draw holds
    for (int hold = 0; hold < 4; hold++)
    {
        CardInfo cardInfo = holds[hold];

        if (cardInfo != null)
        {
            Rectangle source = GetCardTextureSource(cardInfo);
            Vector2 destination = new Vector2(cardSpots[hold].X, cardSpots[hold].Y);
```

```
                    spriteBatch.Draw(cards, destination, source, Color.White);
            }
        }

        // Draw piles
        for (int pile = 0; pile < 8; pile++)
        {
            Rectangle cardSpot = cardSpots[pile + 8];

            for (int card = 0; card < piles[pile].Count; card++)
            {
                CardInfo cardInfo = piles[pile][card];
                Rectangle source = GetCardTextureSource(cardInfo);
                Vector2 destination = new Vector2(cardSpot.X, cardSpot.Y + card *
yOverlay);
                spriteBatch.Draw(cards, destination, source, Color.White);
            }
        }

        // Draw finals including all previous cards (for auto-move)
        for (int pass = 0; pass < 2; pass++)
        {
            for (int final = 0; final < 4; final++)
            {
                for (int card = 0; card < finals[final].Count; card++)
                {
                    CardInfo cardInfo = finals[final][card];

                    if (pass == 0 && cardInfo.AutoMoveInterpolation == 0 ||
                        pass == 1 && cardInfo.AutoMoveInterpolation != 0)
                    {
                        Rectangle source = GetCardTextureSource(cardInfo);
                        Vector2 destination =
                                new Vector2(cardSpots[final + 4].X,
                                            cardSpots[final + 4].Y) +
                                    cardInfo.AutoMoveInterpolation * cardInfo.
AutoMoveOffset;
                        spriteBatch.Draw(cards, destination, source, Color.White);
                    }
                }
            }
        }

        // Draw touched card
        if (touchedCard != null)
        {
            Rectangle source = GetCardTextureSource(touchedCard);
            spriteBatch.Draw(cards, touchedCardPosition, source, Color.White);
        }

        spriteBatch.End();

        base.Draw(gameTime);
}
```

After calling *Begin* on the *SpriteBatch* object and displaying the *surface* bitmap for the playing field, the method is ready for drawing cards. It begins with the easy one—the four possible cards in the *holds* array. The little *GetCardTextureSource* method returns a *Rectangle* for the position of the card within the cards bitmap, and the *cardSpot* array provides the point where each card is to appear.

The next section is a little more complicated. When displaying the cards in the *piles* area, the *cardSpot* location must be offset to accommodate the overlapping cards. The really problematic area is the *finals*, and it's problematic because of the auto-move feature. As you'll see, when a card is eligible for auto-move, it is removed from its previous *holds* array or *piles* collection and put into a *finals* collection. However, the location of the card must be animated from its previous position to its new position. This is the purpose of the *AutoMoveOffset* and *AutoMoveInterpolation* properties that are part of *CardInfo*.

However, the *Draw* method wants to display each of the four *finals* collections sequentially from left to right, and then within each collection from the beginning (which is always an ace) to the end, which is the topmost card. I discovered this didn't always work, and an animated card sometimes seemed briefly to slide under a card in one of the other *finals* stacks. That's why the loop to display the *finals* collections has two passes—one for the non-animated cards and another for any animated auto-move cards. (Although the program only animates one card at a time, an earlier version animated multiple cards.)

Draw finishes with the card that the user might be currently dragging.

The *Update* method is concerned almost exclusively with implementing the animation for the auto-move feature and processing touch. The larger section with the nested *foreach* loops moves cards that have already been tagged for auto-move and hence have already been moved into the *finals* collections.

XNA Project: PhreeCell   File: Game1.cs (excerpt)

```
protected override void Update(GameTime gameTime)
{
    if (GamePad.GetState(PlayerIndex.One).Buttons.Back == ButtonState.Pressed)
        this.Exit();

    // Process auto-move card and perhaps initiate next auto-move
    bool checkForNextAutoMove = false;

    foreach (List<CardInfo> final in finals)
        foreach (CardInfo cardInfo in final)
        {
            if (cardInfo.AutoMoveTime > TimeSpan.Zero)
            {
                cardInfo.AutoMoveTime -= gameTime.ElapsedGameTime;
```

```
                if (cardInfo.AutoMoveTime <= TimeSpan.Zero)
                {
                    cardInfo.AutoMoveTime = TimeSpan.Zero;
                    checkForNextAutoMove = true;
                }
                cardInfo.AutoMoveInterpolation = (float)cardInfo.AutoMoveTime.Ticks /
                                                           AutoMoveDuration.Ticks;
            }
        }

    if (checkForNextAutoMove && !AnalyzeForAutoMove() && HasWon())
    {
        congratsComponent.Enabled = true;
    }
    ...
}
```

Cards are actually tagged for auto-move in the final section of that code with a call to the *AnalyzeforAutoMove* method in the Game1.Helpers.cs file. (*AnalyzeForAutoMove* is also called later in the *Update* override after a card has been moved manually.) This method loops through the *holds* and the *piles* and calls *CheckForAutoMove* for each topmost card. If *CheckForAutoMove* returns *true*, then that method has already transferred the card to the appropriate *finals* collection and it must be removed from where it was. Three properties of *CardInfo* are then initialized for the actual movement shown above in *Update*:

XNA Project: PhreeCell   File: Game1.Helpers.cs (excerpt)

```
bool AnalyzeForAutoMove()
{
    for (int hold = 0; hold < 4; hold++)
    {
        CardInfo cardInfo = holds[hold];

        if (cardInfo != null && CheckForAutoMove(cardInfo))
        {
            holds[hold] = null;
            cardInfo.AutoMoveOffset += new Vector2(cardSpots[hold].X,
cardSpots[hold].Y);
            cardInfo.AutoMoveInterpolation = 1;
            cardInfo.AutoMoveTime = AutoMoveDuration;
            return true;
        }
    }

    for (int pile = 0; pile < 8; pile++)
    {
        CardInfo cardInfo = TopCard(piles[pile]);
```

```
            if (cardInfo != null && CheckForAutoMove(cardInfo))
            {
                piles[pile].Remove(cardInfo);
                cardInfo.AutoMoveOffset += new Vector2(cardSpots[pile + 8].X,
                                    cardSpots[pile + 8].Y + piles[pile].Count * yOverlay);
                cardInfo.AutoMoveInterpolation = 1;
                cardInfo.AutoMoveTime = AutoMoveDuration;
                return true;
            }
        }
    }
    return false;
}
```

The logic to determine what cards (if any) should be auto-moved turned out to be one of the
lengthier parts of the program. The complication is that no card should be moved to the *finals*
collection if it can still be used strategically. For example, a 4 of hearts shouldn't be moved to a
finals collection if a 3 of spades or 3 of clubs is still somewhere in the *piles* or *holds* collections.

XNA Project: PhreeCell   File: Game1.Helpers.cs (excerpt)

```
bool CheckForAutoMove(CardInfo cardInfo)
{
    if (cardInfo.Rank == 0)      // ie, ace
    {
        for (int final = 0; final < 4; final++)
            if (finals[final].Count == 0)
            {
                finals[final].Add(cardInfo);
                cardInfo.AutoMoveOffset = -new Vector2(cardSpots[final + 4].X,
                                                    cardSpots[final + 4].Y);
                return true;
            }
    }
    else if (cardInfo.Rank == 1)    // ie, deuce
    {
        for (int final = 0; final < 4; final++)
        {
            CardInfo topCardInfo = TopCard(finals[final]);

            if (topCardInfo != null &&
                topCardInfo.Suit == cardInfo.Suit &&
                topCardInfo.Rank == 0)
            {
                finals[final].Add(cardInfo);
                cardInfo.AutoMoveOffset = -new Vector2(cardSpots[final + 4].X,
                                                    cardSpots[final + 4].Y);
                return true;
            }
        }
    }
```

```
    else
    {
        int slot = -1;
        int count = 0;

        for (int final = 0; final < 4; final++)
        {
            CardInfo topCardInfo = TopCard(finals[final]);

            if (topCardInfo != null)
            {
                if (topCardInfo.Suit == cardInfo.Suit &&
                    topCardInfo.Rank == cardInfo.Rank - 1)
                {
                    slot = final;
                }
                else if (topCardInfo.Suit < 2 != cardInfo.Suit < 2 &&
                        topCardInfo.Rank >= cardInfo.Rank - 1)
                {
                    count++;
                }
            }
        }
        if (slot >= 0 && count == 2)
        {
            cardInfo.AutoMoveOffset = -new Vector2(cardSpots[slot + 4].X,
                                                    cardSpots[slot + 4].Y);
            finals[slot].Add(cardInfo);
            return true;
        }
    }
    return false;
}
```

Back in the *Update* override, following the animation for auto-move cards, *Update* checks if the user is trying to "pick up" a card by touching it. Picking up that particular card might be legal or not. If a card is already being moved and the user is trying to "set down" the card, then that too might be illegal. The legality is established by calls to *TryPickUpCard* and *TryPutDownCard*. Notice that the finger position is adjusted by *inverseMatrix* so it agrees with the actual locations of the cards.

XNA Project: PhreeCell   File: Game1.cs (excerpt)

```
protected override void Update(GameTime gameTime)
{
    ...
    while (TouchPanel.IsGestureAvailable)
    {
        GestureSample gesture = TouchPanel.ReadGesture();
```

```
            // Adjust position and delta for compressed image
            Vector2 position = Vector2.Transform(gesture.Position, inverseMatrix);
            Vector2 delta = position - Vector2.Transform(gesture.Position - gesture.Delta,
                                                         inverseMatrix);
        switch (gesture.GestureType)
        {
            case GestureType.Tap:
                // Check if Replay is pressed
                if ((gesture.Position - centerReplay).Length() < radiusReplay)
                {
                    congratsComponent.Enabled = false;
                    Replay();
                }
                break;

            case GestureType.FreeDrag:
                // Continue to move a dragged card
                if (touchedCard != null)
                {
                    touchedCardPosition += delta;
                }
                // Try to pick up a card
                else if (firstDragInGesture)
                {
                    TryPickUpCard(position);
                }
                firstDragInGesture = false;
                break;

            case GestureType.DragComplete:
                if (touchedCard != null && TryPutDownCard(touchedCard))
                {
                    CalculateDisplayMatrix();

                    if (!AnalyzeForAutoMove() && HasWon())
                    {
                        congratsComponent.Enabled = true;
                    }
                }
                firstDragInGesture = true;
                touchedCard = null;
                break;
        }
    }
    base.Update(gameTime);
}
```

Those two methods *TryPickUpCard* and *TryPutDownCard* are both implemented in the Game1.Helpers.cs file and really establish the rules of the game.

TryPickUpCard is the simpler of the two methods. It only gets passed a touch position somewhere on the screen and must determine which card is being touched. Only a card in one of the *holds* collections or on top of one of the *piles* collection is eligible to be picked up, but otherwise the method doesn't bother with determining if the user can actually do something useful with that card:

XNA Project: PhreeCell   File: Game1.Helpers.cs (excerpt)

```
bool TryPickUpCard(Vector2 position)
{
    for (int hold = 0; hold < 4; hold++)
    {
        if (holds[hold] != null && IsWithinRectangle(position, cardSpots[hold]))
        {
            Point pt = cardSpots[hold].Location;

            touchedCard = holds[hold];
            touchedCardOrigin = holds;
            touchedCardOriginIndex = hold;
            touchedCardPosition = new Vector2(pt.X, pt.Y);
            holds[hold] = null;
            return true;
        }
    }

    for (int pile = 0; pile < 8; pile++)
    {
        if (piles[pile].Count > 0)
        {
            Rectangle pileSpot = cardSpots[pile + 8];
            pileSpot.Offset(0, yOverlay * (piles[pile].Count - 1));

            if (IsWithinRectangle(position, pileSpot))
            {
                Point pt = pileSpot.Location;
                int pileIndex = piles[pile].Count - 1;

                touchedCard = piles[pile][pileIndex];
                touchedCardOrigin = piles;
                touchedCardOriginIndex = pile;
                touchedCardPosition = new Vector2(pt.X, pt.Y);
                piles[pile].RemoveAt(pileIndex);
                return true;
            }
        }
    }
    return false;
}
```

Once a card has been picked up, *TryPickUpCard* has already set the fields involving the touched card that are then used in the *Update* method for subsequently dragging that card around the screen.

The *TryPutDownCard* allows cards to be deposited in a *piles* collection or the *holds* array or a *finals* collection but must enforce the rules. If the drop is not legal, then the card is simply restored to its original spot directly without any animation:

XNA Project: **PhreeCell**   File: **Game1.Helpers.cs (excerpt)**

```
bool TryPutDownCard(CardInfo touchedCard)
{
    Vector2 cardCenter = new Vector2(touchedCardPosition.X + wCard / 2,
                                     touchedCardPosition.Y + hCard / 2);

    for (int cardSpot = 0; cardSpot < 16; cardSpot++)
    {
        Rectangle rect = cardSpots[cardSpot];

        // Greatly expand the card-spot rectangle for the piles
        if (cardSpot >= 8)
            rect.Inflate(0, hSurface - rect.Bottom);

        if (IsWithinRectangle(cardCenter, rect))
        {
            // Check if the hold is empty
            if (cardSpot < 4)
            {
                int hold = cardSpot;

                if (holds[hold] == null)
                {
                    holds[hold] = touchedCard;
                    return true;
                }
            }

            else if (cardSpot < 8)
            {
                int final = cardSpot - 4;

                if (TopCard(finals[final]) == null)
                {
                    if (touchedCard.Rank == 0)  // ie, an ace
                    {
                        finals[final].Add(touchedCard);
                        return true;
                    }
                }
                else if (touchedCard.Suit == TopCard(finals[final]).Suit &&
                         touchedCard.Rank == TopCard(finals[final]).Rank + 1)
                {
                    finals[final].Add(touchedCard);
                    return true;
                }
            }
```

```
            else
            {
                int pile = cardSpot - 8;

                if (piles[pile].Count == 0)
                {
                    piles[pile].Add(touchedCard);
                    return true;
                }
                else
                {
                    CardInfo topCard = TopCard(piles[pile]);

                    if (touchedCard.Suit < 2 != topCard.Suit < 2 &&
                        touchedCard.Rank == topCard.Rank - 1)
                    {
                        piles[pile].Add(touchedCard);
                        return true;
                    }
                }
            }

            // The card was in a card-spot rectangle but wasn't a legal drop
            break;
        }
    }

    // Restore the card to its original place
    if (touchedCardOrigin is CardInfo[])
    {
        (touchedCardOrigin as CardInfo[])[touchedCardOriginIndex] = touchedCard;
    }
    else
    {
        ((touchedCardOrigin as List<CardInfo>[])[touchedCardOriginIndex]).
Add(touchedCard);
    }
    return false;
}
```

But all that work is justified by a return value of *true* from the following method that simply determines if the top card in each of the *finals* collections is a king:

XNA Project: PhreeCell   File: Game1.Helpers.cs (excerpt)

```
bool HasWon()
{
    bool hasWon = true;

    foreach (List<CardInfo> cardInfos in finals)
```

```
                hasWon &= cardInfos.Count > 0 && TopCard(cardInfos).Rank == 12;

        return hasWon;
    }
```

The *Update* method uses that to enable the *CongratulationsComponent*, shown here in its
entirety:

XNA Project: PhreeCell   File: CongratulationsComponent.cs

```
using System;
using Microsoft.Xna.Framework;
using Microsoft.Xna.Framework.Graphics;

namespace PhreeCell
{
    public class CongratulationsComponent : DrawableGameComponent
    {
        const float SCALE_SPEED = 0.5f;                    // half-size per second
        const float ROTATE_SPEED = 3 * MathHelper.TwoPi;   // 3 revolutions per
second

        SpriteBatch spriteBatch;
        SpriteFont pericles108;
        string congratulationsText = "You Won!";
        float textScale;
        float textAngle;
        Vector2 textPosition;
        Vector2 textOrigin;

        public CongratulationsComponent(Game game) : base(game)
        {
        }

        protected override void LoadContent()
        {
            spriteBatch = new SpriteBatch(this.GraphicsDevice);
            pericles108 = this.Game.Content.Load<SpriteFont>("Pericles108");
            textOrigin = pericles108.MeasureString(congratulationsText) / 2;
            Viewport viewport = this.GraphicsDevice.Viewport;
            textPosition = new Vector2(Math.Max(viewport.Width, viewport.Height) / 2,
                                Math.Min(viewport.Width, viewport.Height) / 2);
            base.LoadContent();
        }

        protected override void OnEnabledChanged(object sender, EventArgs args)
        {
            Visible = Enabled;

            if (Enabled)
```

```
            {
                textScale = 0;
                textAngle = 0;
            }
        }

        public override void Update(GameTime gameTime)
        {
            if (textScale < 1)
            {
                textScale +=
                    SCALE_SPEED * (float)gameTime.ElapsedGameTime.TotalSeconds;
                textAngle +=
                    ROTATE_SPEED * (float)gameTime.ElapsedGameTime.TotalSeconds;
            }
            else if (textAngle != 0)
            {
                textScale = 1;
                textAngle = 0;
            }

            base.Update(gameTime);
        }

        public override void Draw(GameTime gameTime)
        {
            spriteBatch.Begin();
            spriteBatch.DrawString(pericles108, congratulationsText, textPosition,
                                Color.White, textAngle, textOrigin, textScale,
                                SpriteEffects.None, 0);
            spriteBatch.End();
            base.Draw(gameTime);
        }
    }
}
```

It's not much: It just expands some spinning text and then deposits it in the center of the screen:

At this point, you can press the red button to play again. Good luck!

Chapter 12
Tilt and Play

If the primary means of user interface in a Windows Phone 7 is touch, then what is the second most important? It depends on the application, of course, but in many Silverlight applications, I suspect the keyboard will still play a big role. In many XNA programs, however, the second most important means of user-interface is probably the accelerometer— particularly in arcade-type games where moving the phone itself can take the place of traditional hand controllers. For example, a game that drives a car around a race track or through a town can respond to left and right tilts of the phone by turning the car, and perhaps front to back tilts can control the gas pedal.

3D Vectors

As you saw in Chapter 5, the data from the phone's accelerometer is essentially a 3D vector (*x, y, z*) in a coordinate system that is fixed relative to the phone. The accelerometer coordinate system remains fixed regardless whether you hold the phone in portrait mode:

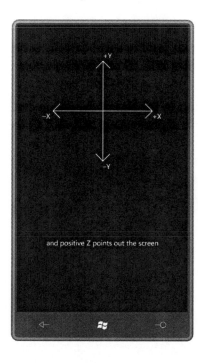

Or left landscape:

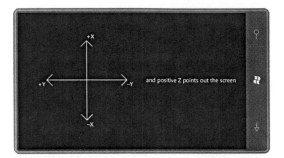

Or right landscape:

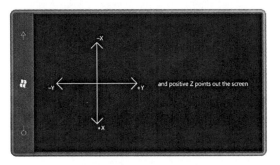

Notice that Y coordinates increase going up the phone, just like a real Cartesian coordinate system and the XNA 3D coordinate system, but not like XNA 2D coordinates where values of Y increase going down.

If the phone is held still, the acceleration vector points to the part of the phone that is closest to the earth. For example, if the acceleration vector is approximately **(0.7,–0.7, 0)** then the phone is being held like this:

The value of 0.7 in the example is, of course, the approximate square root of ½. If you calculate the magnitude of the acceleration vector using the Pythagorean Theorem

$$\sqrt{x^2 + y^2 + z^2}$$

the result should be about 1 if the phone is held still. A phone lying on a level surface has an acceleration vector of approximately **(0, 0, –1)**, which is the same value displayed by the phone emulator.

I say "approximately" because the phone's accelerometer is not a very precise piece of hardware. The magnitude of the vector is supposed to be in units of the gravity on the surface of the earth, traditionally denoted as *g*, and approximately 32 feet per second squared. However, you'll often see as much as a 5% error in the figure.

You'll also notice that the X, Y, and Z components of the accelerometer reading for a phone lying on a level surface might also be several percentage points in error. If you're writing a program that uses the accelerometer for a carpenter's level, you'll want to include an option to "calibrate" the accelerometer, which really means to adjust all future readings based on the reading when the user presses the "calibrate" button.

The data from the accelerometer is also often very jittery, as you undoubtedly discovered when running the two accelerometer programs shown in Chapter 5. Data smoothing is also a big part of accelerometer usage.

In this chapter I'll be using a very simple low-pass filtering technique for smoothing the data and I won't get into calibration issues. A library that can help you out with both of these issues can be found in Dave Edson's blog entry "Using the Accelerometer on Windows Phone 7" at http://windowsteamblog.com/windows_phone/b/wpdev/archive/2010/09/08/using-the-accelerometer-on-windows-phone-7.aspx.

All the programs in this chapter require references to the Microsoft.Devices.Sensors assembly and *using* directives for the *Microsoft.Devices.Sensors* namespace.

A Better Bubble Visualization

The AccelerometerVisualization program is a modest step up from the XnaAccelerometer program in Chapter 5. That earlier program just showed a floating "bubble" without any kind of scale or numeric values. This one adds a scale (consisting of concentric circles) and some textual information:

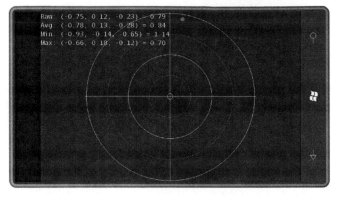

AccelerometerVisualization also implements perhaps the most basic type of smoothing: a low-pass filter that averages the current value with a previously smoothed value. The raw accelerometer reading is indicated by the label "Raw" while the smoothed value is "Avg" ("average"). Minimum and maximum values are also displayed. These are calculated using the static *Vector3.Min* and *Vector3.Max* methods that find the minimum and maximum values of the X, Y, and Z components separately. The red ball is scaled to the magnitude of the vector and turns green when the accelerometer vector Z component is positive.

Here are the program's fields:

XNA Project: **AccelerometerVisualization**   File: **Game1.cs** (excerpt showing fields)

```
public class Game1 : Microsoft.Xna.Framework.Game
{
    const int BALL_RADIUS = 8;

    GraphicsDeviceManager graphics;
    SpriteBatch spriteBatch;

    Viewport viewport;
    SpriteFont segoe14;
    StringBuilder stringBuilder = new StringBuilder();

    int unitRadius;
    Vector2 screenCenter;
    Texture2D backgroundTexture;
    Vector2 backgroundTextureCenter;
    Texture2D ballTexture;
    Vector2 ballTextureCenter;
    Vector2 ballPosition;
    float ballScale;
    bool isZNegative;

    Vector3 accelerometerVector;
    object accerlerometerVectorLock = new object();
```

```
        Vector3 oldAcceleration;
        Vector3 minAcceleration = Vector3.One;
        Vector3 maxAcceleration = -Vector3.One;
        ...
    }
```

Although the program displays something akin to a "bubble" that moves in the opposite direction as gravity and the acceleration vector, it's referred to in this program as a "ball". The field named *oldAcceleration* is used for smoothing the values; whenever the display is updated, *oldAcceleration* is the previously smoothed ("Avg") value.

By default, XNA programs adjust themselves to both left-landscape and right-landscape orientations. This default behavior is something that application programs almost never need to worry about—*except* when dealing with the accelerometer. In left-landscape mode, the accelerometer X axis increases going up the screen, and the accelerometer Y axis increases going left across the screen. In right-landscape mode, the accelerometer X axis increases going down the screen, and the accelerometer Y axis increases going right across the screen.

If you want to limit the confusion, the constructor of the *Game1* class is the place to set the *SupportedOrientations* property of the *GraphicsDeviceManager* object (referenced by the *graphics* field) to *DisplayOrientation.LandscapeLeft*. My program doesn't do that, and the display accomodates *LandscapeRight* orientations. However, it does use the constructor to set the back buffer size to allow room for the phone status bar:

XNA Project: **AccelerometerVisualization**   File: **Game1.cs** (excerpt)

```
public Game1()
{
    graphics = new GraphicsDeviceManager(this);
    Content.RootDirectory = "Content";

    // Frame rate is 30 fps by default for Windows Phone.
    TargetElapsedTime = TimeSpan.FromTicks(333333);

    // Landscape but leave room for the status bar
    graphics.PreferredBackBufferWidth = 728;
    graphics.PreferredBackBufferHeight = 480;
}
```

The *Initialize* override creates the *Accelerometer* object, sets an event handler, and starts it up:

XNA Project: **AccelerometerVisualization**   File: **Game1.cs** (excerpt)

```
protected override void Initialize()
```

```
    {
        Accelerometer accelerometer = new Accelerometer();
        accelerometer.ReadingChanged += OnAccelerometerReadingChanged;

        try
        {
            accelerometer.Start();
        }
        catch
        {
        }

        base.Initialize();
    }
```

The *ReadingChanged* handler is called asynchronously, so the proper behavior is simply to save the value in code protected by a *lock* block:

XNA Project: AccelerometerVisualization   File: Game1.cs (excerpt)

```
void OnAccelerometerReadingChanged(object sender, AccelerometerReadingEventArgs args)
{
    lock (accerlerometerVectorLock)
    {
        accelerometerVector = new Vector3((float)args.X, (float)args.Y, (float)
args.Z);
    }
}
```

If you perform some experiments with this *ReadingChanged* handler, you'll discover that it's called close to 50 times per second, rather more frequently than the video refresh rate, so you might want to implement smoothing right in this handler. (I do just that in some later programs in this chapter.)

The *LoadContent* override in this program is primarily responsible for preparing the two textures—the large *backgroundTexture* field that covers the entire surface with the concentric circles, and the *ballTexture* that floats around. The code that draws lines and circles on *backgroundTexture* is rather *ad hoc*, involving simple loops and a couple methods to set pixel colors.

XNA Project: AccelerometerVisualization   File: Game1.cs (excerpt)

```
protected override void LoadContent()
{
    // Create a new SpriteBatch, which can be used to draw textures.
    spriteBatch = new SpriteBatch(this.GraphicsDevice);
```

```csharp
    // Get screen and font information
    viewport = this.GraphicsDevice.Viewport;
    screenCenter = new Vector2(viewport.Width / 2, viewport.Height / 2);
    segoe14 = this.Content.Load<SpriteFont>("Segoe14");

    // This is the pixel equivalent of a vector magnitude of 1
    unitRadius = (viewport.Height - BALL_RADIUS) / 2;

    // Create and draw background texture
    backgroundTexture =
        new Texture2D(this.GraphicsDevice, viewport.Height, viewport.Height);
    backgroundTextureCenter =
        new Vector2(viewport.Height / 2, viewport.Height / 2);

    Color[] pixels = new Color[backgroundTexture.Width * backgroundTexture.Height];

    // Draw horizontal line
    for (int x = 0; x < backgroundTexture.Width; x++)
        SetPixel(backgroundTexture, pixels,
                    x, backgroundTexture.Height / 2, Color.White);

    // Draw vertical line
    for (int y = 0; y < backgroundTexture.Height; y++)
        SetPixel(backgroundTexture, pixels,
                    backgroundTexture.Width / 2, y, Color.White);

    // Draw circles
    DrawCenteredCircle(backgroundTexture, pixels, unitRadius, Color.White);
    DrawCenteredCircle(backgroundTexture, pixels, 3 * unitRadius / 4, Color.Gray);
    DrawCenteredCircle(backgroundTexture, pixels, unitRadius / 2, Color.White);
    DrawCenteredCircle(backgroundTexture, pixels, unitRadius / 4, Color.Gray);
    DrawCenteredCircle(backgroundTexture, pixels, BALL_RADIUS, Color.White);

    // Set the pixels to the background texture
    backgroundTexture.SetData<Color>(pixels);

    // Create and draw ball texture
    ballTexture = new Texture2D(this.GraphicsDevice,
                                2 * BALL_RADIUS, 2 * BALL_RADIUS);
    ballTextureCenter = new Vector2(BALL_RADIUS, BALL_RADIUS);
    pixels = new Color[ballTexture.Width * ballTexture.Height];
    DrawFilledCenteredCircle(ballTexture, pixels, BALL_RADIUS);
    ballTexture.SetData<Color>(pixels);
}

void DrawCenteredCircle(Texture2D texture, Color[] pixels, int radius, Color clr)
{
    Point center = new Point(texture.Width / 2, texture.Height / 2);
    int halfPoint = (int)(0.707 * radius + 0.5);

    for (int y = -halfPoint; y <= halfPoint; y++)
    {
        int x1 = (int)Math.Round(Math.Sqrt(radius * radius - Math.Pow(y, 2)));
        int x2 = -x1;
```

```
            SetPixel(texture, pixels, x1 + center.X, y + center.Y, clr);
            SetPixel(texture, pixels, x2 + center.X, y + center.Y, clr);

            // Since symmetric, just swap coordinates for other piece
            SetPixel(texture, pixels, y + center.X, x1 + center.Y, clr);
            SetPixel(texture, pixels, y + center.X, x2 + center.Y, clr);
        }
    }

    void DrawFilledCenteredCircle(Texture2D texture, Color[] pixels, int radius)
    {
        Point center = new Point(texture.Width / 2, texture.Height / 2);

        for (int y = -radius; y < radius; y++)
        {
            int x1 = (int)Math.Round(Math.Sqrt(radius * radius - Math.Pow(y, 2)));

            for (int x = -x1; x < x1; x++)
                SetPixel(texture, pixels, x + center.X, y + center.Y, Color.White);
        }
    }

    void SetPixel(Texture2D texture, Color[] pixels, int x, int y, Color clr)
    {
        pixels[y * texture.Width + x] = clr;
    }
```

It was this logic that prompted me to explicitly set the back buffer width to 728. When set at the default 800 pixels, the actual display is compressed by about 10% to make room for the status bar. Because the lines and circles I'm drawing are only one-pixel wide and obviously don't implement anti-aliasing, they lost a bit of sharpness when the display was compressed.

Several interesting things happen in the *Update* override. The method is basically responsible for grabbing the accelerometer vector and displaying it in both graphical and visual forms. In this method, the raw value is named *newAcceleration*, while the smoothed value is *avgAcceleration*:

XNA Project: AccelerometerVisualization   File: **Game1.cs (excerpt)**

```
protected override void Update(GameTime gameTime)
{
    if (GamePad.GetState(PlayerIndex.One).Buttons.Back == ButtonState.Pressed)
        this.Exit();

    Vector3 newAcceleration = Vector3.Zero;

    lock (accerlerometerVectorLock)
    {
        newAcceleration = accelerometerVector;
    }
```

```
        maxAcceleration = Vector3.Max(maxAcceleration, newAcceleration);
        minAcceleration = Vector3.Min(minAcceleration, newAcceleration);

        // Low-pass filter smoothing
        Vector3 avgAcceleration = 0.5f * oldAcceleration + 0.5f * newAcceleration;

        stringBuilder.Remove(0, stringBuilder.Length);
        stringBuilder.AppendFormat("Raw: ({0:F2}, {1:F2}, {2:F2}) = {3:F2}\n",
                            newAcceleration.X, newAcceleration.Y,
                            newAcceleration.Z, newAcceleration.Length());
        stringBuilder.AppendFormat("Avg: ({0:F2}, {1:F2}, {2:F2}) = {3:F2}\n",
                            avgAcceleration.X, avgAcceleration.Y,
                            avgAcceleration.Z, avgAcceleration.Length());
        stringBuilder.AppendFormat("Min: ({0:F2}, {1:F2}, {2:F2}) = {3:F2}\n",
                            minAcceleration.X, minAcceleration.Y,
                            minAcceleration.Z, minAcceleration.Length());
        stringBuilder.AppendFormat("Max: ({0:F2}, {1:F2}, {2:F2}) = {3:F2}",
                            maxAcceleration.X, maxAcceleration.Y,
                            maxAcceleration.Z, maxAcceleration.Length());

        ballScale = avgAcceleration.Length();
        int sign = this.Window.CurrentOrientation ==
                                    DisplayOrientation.LandscapeLeft ? 1 : -1;
        ballPosition =
            new Vector2(screenCenter.X + sign * unitRadius * avgAcceleration.Y /
    ballScale,
                        screenCenter.Y + sign * unitRadius * avgAcceleration.X /
    ballScale);
        isZNegative = avgAcceleration.Z < 0;

        oldAcceleration = avgAcceleration;

        base.Update(gameTime);
    }
```

The *accelerometerVector* field is saved by the *ReadingChanged* handler in a second thread using a *lock* block so accessing it from the program's main thread requires another *lock* block using the same object:

```
lock (accerlerometerVectorLock)
{
    newAcceleration = accelerometerVector;
}
```

The smoothed value is then calculated from this raw value and *oldAcceleration*:

```
Vector3 avgAcceleration = 0.5f * oldAcceleration + 0.5f * newAcceleration;
```

After *Update* uses this *avgAcceleration* for display purposes, it replaces the *oldAcceleration* field:

```
oldAcceleration = avgAcceleration;
```

This is a type of smoothing known as a *low-pass filter*. High-frequency jitter is eliminated by averaging the value with earlier values. If v_0 is the current raw vector reading (*newAcceleration*), and v_{-1} is the previous raw reading, and v_{-2} is the raw reading before that, then the smoothed value is:

$$v = \frac{v_0}{2} + \frac{v_{-1}}{4} + \frac{v_{-2}}{8} + \frac{v_{-3}}{16} + \cdots$$

But all these old values don't need to be saved because they've already contributed to the calculation of *oldAcceleration*.

The influence of each reading is iteratively halved as it recedes further into the past. In theory, no reading ever stops affecting the smoothed value, but one second after a particular reading (or 30 calls to the *Update* override) the denominator on that reading is approximately one million, so the influence is very small.

You can adjust the weights between the old and the new but they must sum to 1. For example, this provides less smoothing by placing less weight on the earlier values:

```
Vector3 avgAcceleration = 0.25f * oldAcceleration + 0.75f * newAcceleration;
```

This one provides more smoothing:

```
Vector3 avgAcceleration = 0.75f * oldAcceleration + 0.25f * newAcceleration;
```

In the blog entry I mentioned earlier, Dave Edson expresses the low-pass filter slightly differently. Using my variable names, his formula is

```
Vector3 avgAcceleration = oldAcceleration + alpha * (newAcceleration - oldAcceleration);
```

where *alpha* ranges from 0 (smoothed to oblivion) to 1 (no smoothing at all). That blog entry also discusses alternatives to low-pass filtering when a program might be interested in sudden changes or jerks.

The other interesting activity of *Update* involves compensating for the two different landscape orientations, which of course are ultimately based on the accelerometer vector. Suppose the phone is in *LandscapeLeft* mode:

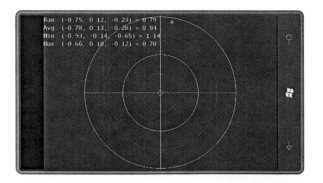

Increasing Y values of the accelerometer correspond with decreasing X values of the graphical display, and increasing X values of the accelerometer correspond with decreasing Y values of the graphical display. However, the intent here is to show a bubble that rises against gravity, so

Increase in accelerometer Y → increase in graphical X

Increase in accelerometer X → increase in graphical Y

Now turn the phone over so it goes into LandscapeRight mode:

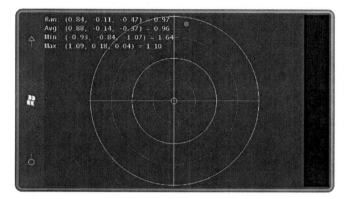

Now,

Increase in accelerometer Y → decrease in graphical X

Increase in accelerometer X → decrease in graphical Y

In the *Update* override a *sign* value is first calculated that is 1 for *LandscapeLeft* mode and –1 for *LandscapeRight*:

```
int sign = this.Window.CurrentOrientation == DisplayOrientation.LandscapeLeft ? 1 : -1;
```

If the X and Y components of the smoothed acceleration vector are both zero the ball should be positioned at the point (*screenCenter.X, screenCenter.Y*). Easy enough. The offsets from that center should be based on the *sign* value and the distance from the center to the outside radius:

```
ballPosition =
    new Vector2(screenCenter.X + sign * unitRadius * avgAcceleration.Y,
                screenCenter.Y + sign * unitRadius * avgAcceleration.X);
```

I was dissatisfied with this calculation, however. Because of the slight inaccuracies of the accelerometer values, sometimes the ball went completely outside the outer circle and off the screen. I decided to compensate for that by dividing by the length of the smoothed vector. This was already being used for scaling the ball:

```
ballScale = avgAcceleration.Length();
```

So I incorporated that into the position calculation:

```
ballPosition =
    new Vector2(screenCenter.X + sign * unitRadius * avgAcceleration.Y / ballScale,
                screenCenter.Y + sign * unitRadius * avgAcceleration.X / ballScale);
```

The *Draw* override draws the background, the ball, and the four lines of text:

XNA Project: AccelerometerVisualization   File: Game1.cs (excerpt)

```
protected override void Draw(GameTime gameTime)
{
    GraphicsDevice.Clear(Color.Navy);

    spriteBatch.Begin();
    spriteBatch.Draw(backgroundTexture, screenCenter, null, Color.White, 0,
                     backgroundTextureCenter, 1, SpriteEffects.None, 0);
    spriteBatch.Draw(ballTexture, ballPosition, null,
                     isZNegative ? Color.Red : Color.Lime, 0,
                     ballTextureCenter, ballScale, SpriteEffects.None, 0);
    spriteBatch.DrawString(segoe14, stringBuilder, Vector2.Zero, Color.White);
    spriteBatch.End();

    base.Draw(gameTime);
}
```

If you shake the phone, it's hard to see how the ball moves but you can see the influence in the minimum and maximum values. If your phone hardware is like my phone hardware, you'll never get the X, Y, and Z components of the raw acceleration vector outside the range of –2 and 2, with a total magnitude of 3.46. This seems to be a hardware limitation.

The Graphical Rendition

The programs in this chapter use smoothed accelerometer readings for moving and orienting objects. It's also possible to use sudden *changes* in the accelerometer readings, for example, to "throw" a pair of dice. The first step is to understand how the accelerometer readings change when you make sudden movements to the phone, and for that a historical graph might be helpful.

This is provided in the AccelerometerGraph program. Here's a typical display:

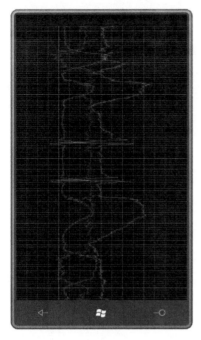

Because the intention of this program is to show you what's really coming through, it doesn't perform any smoothing. Red is X, green is Y, and blue is Z. (The mnemonic is RGB == XYZ.) From the perspective in portrait mode, the graph moves up the screen and new values are added at the bottom. Vertically, each pixel represents a video display refresh "tick"—1/30th second. The heavier horizontal lines represent seconds. The lighter horizontal lines are fifths of a second (six pixels). The vertical line in the center represents an acceleration component value of 0. The two other heavier vertical lines represent values of 1 (at the right) and –1 at the left. The left edge is –2 and the right edge is 2. From what you saw in the previous program, this should be adequate for displaying the complete range of possible values.

As you let the program run, the old data seems to crawl up the screen, and perhaps one's immediate instinct is to code it like that: Create a *Texture2D* the size of the screen and during every *Update* call just shift all the pixels by the width of the *Texture2D* so the top row disappears and the new row can be added at the end. But that's a lot of pixel shifting 30 times a second.

It makes more sense to insert the new data at a variable row number that is incremented with every *Update* call. (Let's call this the *insert row*.) In the *Draw* method, you can then draw the *Texture2D* twice divided into two parts. The first part is displayed at the top of the screen and begins with the row following the insert row and goes to the end of the *Texture2D*. The second part is drawn underneath the first part, and begins at the top of the *Texture2D* and ends with the insert row.

Because old data must be erased at the insert row to make way for new data, it makes sense to handle the fixed lines of the graph separately. That portion repeats itself vertically every 30 pixels so it can be a smaller bitmap that is displayed a bunch of times. In the fields of AccelerometerGraph, *backgroundTexture* has a height of 30 and *graphTexture* (which shows the red, green, and blue lines) has a height the size of the screen.

XNA Project: AccelerometerGraph   File: Game1.cs (excerpt showing fields)

```
public class Game1 : Microsoft.Xna.Framework.Game
{
    GraphicsDeviceManager graphics;
    SpriteBatch spriteBatch;

    int displayWidth, displayHeight;
    Texture2D backgroundTexture;
    Texture2D graphTexture;
    uint[] pixels;
    int totalTicks;
    int oldInsertRow;
    Vector3 oldAcceleration;

    Vector3 accelerometerVector;
    object accelerometerVectorLock = new object();

    public Game1()
    {
        graphics = new GraphicsDeviceManager(this);
        Content.RootDirectory = "Content";

        // Frame rate is 30 fps by default for Windows Phone.
        TargetElapsedTime = TimeSpan.FromTicks(333333);

        graphics.SupportedOrientations = DisplayOrientation.Portrait;
        graphics.PreferredBackBufferWidth = 480;
        graphics.PreferredBackBufferHeight = 768;
    }
    ...
}
```

The constructor ends by setting the orientation to portrait and defining a back-buffer height that allows the status bar to be displayed.

As usual, the *Initialize* method starts up the accelerometer:

XNA Project: AccelerometerGraph   File: Game1.cs (excerpt)

```
protected override void Initialize()
{
    Accelerometer accelerometer = new Accelerometer();
    accelerometer.ReadingChanged += OnAccelerometerReadingChanged;
```

```
    try
    {
        accelerometer.Start();
    }
    catch
    {
    }
    base.Initialize();
}

void OnAccelerometerReadingChanged(object sender, AccelerometerReadingEventArgs args)
{
    lock (accelerometerVectorLock)
    {
        accelerometerVector = new Vector3((float)args.X, (float)args.Y, (float)
args.Z);
    }
}
```

The *LoadContent* method is mostly dedicated to creating and initializing the
backgroundTexture that contains the horizontal and vertical lines. Although the code here
is fairly generalized, the height of *backgroundTexture* will be calculated as 30 pixels and
horizontal lines are drawn every 6 pixels.

XNA Project: **AccelerometerGraph**   File: **Game1.cs (excerpt)**

```
protected override void LoadContent()
{
    // Create a new SpriteBatch, which can be used to draw textures.
    spriteBatch = new SpriteBatch(GraphicsDevice);

    displayWidth = this.GraphicsDevice.Viewport.Width;
    displayHeight = this.GraphicsDevice.Viewport.Height;

    // Create background texture and initialize it
    int ticksPerSecond = 1000 / this.TargetElapsedTime.Milliseconds;
    int ticksPerFifth = ticksPerSecond / 5;
    backgroundTexture = new Texture2D(this.GraphicsDevice, displayWidth,
ticksPerSecond);
    pixels = new uint[backgroundTexture.Width * backgroundTexture.Height];

    for (int y = 0; y < backgroundTexture.Height; y++)
        for (int x = 0; x < backgroundTexture.Width; x++)
        {
            Color clr = Color.Black;

            if (y == 0 || x == backgroundTexture.Width / 2 ||
                        x == backgroundTexture.Width / 4 ||
```

```
                        x == 3 * backgroundTexture.Width / 4)
            {
                clr = new Color(128, 128, 128);
            }
            else if (y % ticksPerFifth == 0 ||
                    ((x - backgroundTexture.Width / 2) %
                                        (backgroundTexture.Width / 16) == 0))
            {
                clr = new Color(64, 64, 64);
            }

            pixels[y * backgroundTexture.Width + x] = clr.PackedValue;
        }
    backgroundTexture.SetData<uint>(pixels);

    // Create graph texture
    graphTexture = new Texture2D(this.GraphicsDevice, displayWidth, displayHeight);
    pixels = new uint[graphTexture.Width * graphTexture.Height];

    // Initialize
    oldInsertRow = graphTexture.Height - 2;
}
```

At the end, *LoadContent* creates the large *graphTexture* the size of the screen and re-creates the *pixels* array field specifically for this bitmap.

LoadContent concludes by setting *oldInsertRow* to the penultimate row of the *Texture2D*. As you'll see, the first calculation of *insertRow* performed in *Update* will set *insertRow* to the last row of the bitmap.

Each call to *Update* results in three straight lines being drawn on *graphTexture*, one red, one green, and one blue. If you think of each line being drawn from coordinates (x_1, y_1) to (x_2, y_2), then unless something happens that causes *Update* to lose ticks, y_2 should equal y_1 + 1. The X values of each colored line are based on the X, Y, and Z components of the old and new acceleration vectors.

The problem is that y_1 might be at the bottom of the Texture2D and y_2 might be at the top. In the following code, I found it easier to work with three Y values: *oldInsertRow* is what I refer to above as y_1, but both *newInsertRow* and *insertRow* represent y_2. The difference is that *insertRow* is always within the range of the *Texture2D* (that is, it's less than the height of the bitmap) but *newInsertRow* could be outside the range. The advantage of *newInsertRow* is that it's always guaranteed to be greater than *oldInsertRow*, and this makes the line-drawing algorithms a little easier rather than dealing with a line that begins at the bottom of the bitmap and ends at the top.

The primary objective of *Update* is the call to *DrawLines* with *oldInsertRow*, *newInsertRow*, and the old and new acceleration vectors:

XNA Project: AccelerometerGraph   File: Game1.cs (excerpt)

```
protected override void Update(GameTime gameTime)
{
    // Allows the game to exit
    if (GamePad.GetState(PlayerIndex.One).Buttons.Back == ButtonState.Pressed)
        this.Exit();

    Vector3 acceleration;

    lock (accelerometerVectorLock)
    {
        acceleration = accelerometerVector;
    }

    totalTicks = (int)Math.Round(gameTime.TotalGameTime.TotalSeconds /
                                     this.TargetElapsedTime.TotalSeconds);
    int insertRow = (totalTicks + graphTexture.Height - 1) % graphTexture.Height;

    // newInsertRow is always guaranteed to be greater than oldInsertRow,
    //  but might also be greater than the graphTexture height!
    int newInsertRow = insertRow < oldInsertRow ? insertRow + graphTexture.Height :
                                     insertRow;
    // Zero out pixels first
    for (int y = oldInsertRow + 1; y <= newInsertRow; y++)
        for (int x = 0; x < graphTexture.Width; x++)
            pixels[(y % graphTexture.Height) * graphTexture.Width + x] = 0;

    // Draw three lines based on old and new acceleration values
    DrawLines(graphTexture, pixels, oldInsertRow, newInsertRow,
            oldAcceleration, acceleration);

    this.GraphicsDevice.Textures[0] = null;

    if (newInsertRow >= graphTexture.Height)
    {
        graphTexture.SetData<uint>(pixels);
    }
    else
    {
        Rectangle rect = new Rectangle(0, oldInsertRow,
                                graphTexture.Width, newInsertRow - oldInsertRow +
1);
        graphTexture.SetData<uint>(0, rect,
                                pixels, rect.Y * rect.Width, rect.Height * rect.
Width);
    }

    oldInsertRow = insertRow;
    oldAcceleration = acceleration;

    base.Update(gameTime);
}
```

Towards the end of the *Update* override, the *graphTexture* is updated from the *pixels* array. If *newInsertRow* is not outside the range of the bitmap, then only two rows (or so) need to be updated; otherwise, the simpler brute-force form of the *SetData* call is used.

The actual line-drawing consists of a couple methods. The *DrawLines* method simply breaks the acceleration vectors into three components and makes three calls to a *DrawLine* method that calculates X values from the acceleration vector components:

XNA Project: AccelerometerGraph   File: Game1.cs (excerpt)

```
void DrawLines(Texture2D texture, uint[] pixels, int oldRow, int newRow,
            Vector3 oldAcc, Vector3 newAcc)
{
    DrawLine(texture, pixels, oldRow, newRow, oldAcc.X, newAcc.X, Color.Red);
    DrawLine(texture, pixels, oldRow, newRow, oldAcc.Y, newAcc.Y, Color.Green);
    DrawLine(texture, pixels, oldRow, newRow, oldAcc.Z, newAcc.Z, Color.Blue);
}

void DrawLine(Texture2D texture, uint[] pixels, int oldRow, int newRow,
            float oldAcc, float newAcc, Color clr)
{
    DrawLine(texture, pixels,
            texture.Width / 2 + (int)(oldAcc * texture.Width / 4), oldRow,
            texture.Width / 2 + (int)(newAcc * texture.Width / 4), newRow, clr);
}
```

The other *DrawLine* method implements a simple line-drawing algorithm by looping through the pixels based on the greater of the X differential or the Y differential. I experimented with implementing anti-aliasing here, but I never got it to look quite right.

XNA Project: AccelerometerGraph   File: Game1.cs (excerpt)

```
void DrawLine(Texture2D texture, uint[] pixels,
            int x1, int y1, int x2, int y2, Color clr)
{
    if (x1 == x2 && y1 == y2)
    {
        return;
    }
    else if (Math.Abs(y2 - y1) > Math.Abs(x2 - x1))
    {
        int sign = Math.Sign(y2 - y1);

        for (int y = y1; y != y2; y += sign)
        {
            float t = (float)(y - y1) / (y2 - y1);
            int x = (int)(x1 + t * (x2 - x1) + 0.5f);
```

```
                SetPixel(texture, pixels, x, y, clr);
            }
        }
        else
        {
            int sign = Math.Sign(x2 - x1);

            for (int x = x1; x != x2; x += sign)
            {
                float t = (float)(x - x1) / (x2 - x1);
                int y = (int)(y1 + t * (y2 - y1) + 0.5f);
                SetPixel(texture, pixels, x, y, clr);
            }
        }
    }

    // Note adjustment of Y and use of bitwise OR!
    void SetPixel(Texture2D texture, uint[] pixels, int x, int y, Color clr)
    {
        pixels[(y % texture.Height) * texture.Width + x] |= clr.PackedValue;
    }
```

The *SetPixel* method makes the adjustment for Y coordinates that might be beyond the actual rows of the bitmap. Also notice the use of the OR operation. If a blue line and a red line partially overlap, for example, then the overlapping part of the line will be rendered as magenta.

Finally, the *Draw* method draws both *Texture2D* objects using similar logic that repeatedly draws the texture until the screen is full:

XNA Project: AccelerometerGraph   File: Game1.cs (excerpt)

```
protected override void Draw(GameTime gameTime)
{
    spriteBatch.Begin();

    // Draw background texture
    int displayRow = -totalTicks % backgroundTexture.Height;

    while (displayRow < displayHeight)
    {
        spriteBatch.Draw(backgroundTexture, new Vector2(0, displayRow), Color.White);
        displayRow += backgroundTexture.Height;
    }

    // Draw graph texture
    displayRow = -totalTicks % graphTexture.Height;

    while (displayRow < displayHeight)
    {
        spriteBatch.Draw(graphTexture, new Vector2(0, displayRow), Color.White);
```

```
        displayRow += graphTexture.Height;
    }
    spriteBatch.End();

    base.Draw(gameTime);
}
```

Follow the Rolling Ball

The final four programs in this chapter treat the surface of the phone as a plane on which a ball is free to roll.

The creation of the ball itself is performed in a static method in the Petzold.Phone.Xna library called *Texture2DExtensions.CreateBall*:

XNA Project: Petzold.Phone.Xna   File: Texture2DExtensions.cs (excerpt)

```
public static Texture2D CreateBall(GraphicsDevice graphicsDevice, int radius)
{
    Texture2D ball = new Texture2D(graphicsDevice, 2 * radius, 2 * radius);
    Color[] pixels = new Color[ball.Width * ball.Height];
    int radiusSquared = radius * radius;

    for (int y = -radius; y < radius; y++)
    {
        int x2 = (int)Math.Round(Math.Sqrt(Math.Pow(radius, 2) - y * y));
        int x1 = -x2;

        for (int x = x1; x < x2; x++)
            pixels[(int)(ball.Width * (y + radius) + x + radius)] = Color.White;
    }
    ball.SetData<Color>(pixels);
    return ball;
}
```

But that's the easy part. The harder part is nailing down the physics of a ball rolling on an inclined plane. It will help first to examine the relationship between the accelerometer vector and the angles that describe how the phone is tilted.

Suppose your phone is sitting flat on a level surface such as a desk. Here's a view of the bottom of the phone:

Now pick up the left side of the phone:

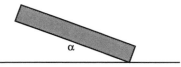

The phone makes an angle α with the level surface. Can the value of α be calculated from the accelerometer vector?

When the phone is lying flat on the table, the acceleration vector is (0, 0, −1). When you tip the phone as shown, perhaps the acceleration vector becomes (0.34, 0, −0.94). (Just offhand, it hardly seems likely that the squares of those numbers add up to 1, but they do.)

The accelerometer vector always points towards the earth, that is, at right angles to the level surface:

You can construct a right triangle where the accelerometer vector is the hypotenuse and the two other sides are parallel to the X and Z axes of the phone:

Those two sides have lengths that are equal to the X and Z components of the acceleration vector:

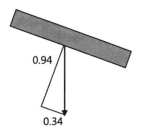

It can also be shown through the use of similar triangles that the angle opposite the shorter leg of this triangle is the same angle α that the phone makes with the level surface:

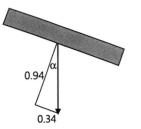

This means that the sine of α is 0.34 and the cosine of α is 0.94, and α is 20°.

In summary, the left-right tilt of the phone is equal to the inverse sine of the X component of the acceleration vector; similarly, the top-bottom tilt is equal to the inverse sine of the Y component.

Now let's roll a ball down that phone. A ball rolling down an inclined plane obviously experiences less acceleration than a ball in free fall:

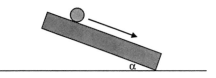

Galileo used balls rolling down long inclined planes to slow down the process of acceleration and study it in more detail.

The calculation of the acceleration of the rolling ball is a bit messy (see, for example, A. P. French, *Newtonian Mechanics*, W. W. Norton, 1971, pages 652-653) but in the absence of friction it turns out to be simply:

$$acceleration = \frac{2}{3} \cdot g - \sin(\alpha)$$

where *g* is the normal acceleration of 32 feet per second squared due to gravity. But even this is an excessive amount of detail for implementing a rolling ball in a simple Windows Phone 7 application. All that is really necessary to know is that the acceleration is proportional to the sine of α. And that is extremely fortuitous because it means that acceleration of a rolling ball across the width of the phone (in portrait mode) is proportional to the X component of the accelerometer vector! For a ball that rolls along a plane, then the acceleration is a two-dimensional vector that can be calculated directly from the X and Y components of the accelerometer vector.

The TiltAndRoll program seems to roll a ball around the surface of the screen based on the tilting of the screen. When the ball strikes one of the edges, it does not bounce but instead loses all its velocity in the direction perpendicular to the edge. The ball continues to roll along the edge if the tilt of the phone justifies it.

The TiltAndRoll program calculates a two-dimensional acceleration vector from the three-dimensional accelerometer vector and multiplies it by a constant named GRAVITY that is in units of pixels per second squared. You can determine what GRAVITY should theoretically equal by multiplying 32 feet per second squared by 12 inches per foot and then by 264 pixels per inch and 2/3 and you'll get something like 68,000, but in practical use that causes the ball to accelerate much too quickly. I've chosen something quite a bit lower, so as to make the effect almost as if the ball is moving through a thick liquid:

XNA Project: **TiltAndRoll**   File: **Game1.cs** (excerpt showing fields)

```csharp
public class Game1 : Microsoft.Xna.Framework.Game
{
    const float GRAVITY = 1000;      // pixels per second squared
    const int BALL_RADIUS = 16;
    const int BALL_SCALE = 16;

    GraphicsDeviceManager graphics;
    SpriteBatch spriteBatch;

    Viewport viewport;
    Texture2D ball;
    Vector2 ballCenter;
    Vector2 ballPosition;
    Vector2 ballVelocity = Vector2.Zero;
    Vector3 oldAcceleration, acceleration;
    object accelerationLock = new object();

    public Game1()
    {
        graphics = new GraphicsDeviceManager(this);
        Content.RootDirectory = "Content";

        // Frame rate is 30 fps by default for Windows Phone.
        TargetElapsedTime = TimeSpan.FromTicks(333333);

        // Restrict orientation to portrait
        graphics.SupportedOrientations = DisplayOrientation.Portrait;
        graphics.PreferredBackBufferWidth = 480;
        graphics.PreferredBackBufferHeight = 768;
    }
    ...
}
```

Of coure, you can increase the value of GRAVITY if you'd like.

To simplify the calculations, the constructor fixes a portrait orientation. The X and Y components of the accelerometer vector will match the coordinates of the display except that the accelerometer Y and the display Y increase in opposite directions.

The *Initialize* method starts up the accelerometer, and the *ReadingChanged* event handler itself handles the smoothing of the values:

XNA Project: **TiltAndRoll** File: **Game1.cs** (excerpt)

```
protected override void Initialize()
{
    Accelerometer accelerometer = new Accelerometer();
    accelerometer.ReadingChanged += OnAccelerometerReadingChanged;

    try { accelerometer.Start(); }
    catch {}

    base.Initialize();
}

void OnAccelerometerReadingChanged(object sender, AccelerometerReadingEventArgs args)
{
    lock (accelerationLock)
    {
        acceleration = 0.5f * oldAcceleration +
                        0.5f * new Vector3((float)args.X, (float)args.Y, (float)
args.Z);
        oldAcceleration = acceleration;
    }
}
```

You'll notice the constants above define both a BALL_RADIUS and a BALL_SCALE. Because the *Texture2DExtensions.CreateBall* method does not attempt to implement anti-aliasing, a smoother image results if the ball is made larger than the displayed size and XNA performs some smoothing when rendering it. Although the ball is created with a total radius of the product of BALL_RADIUS and BALL_SCALE, it is later displayed with a scaling factor of 1 / BALL_SCALE.

XNA Project: **TiltAndRoll** File: **Game1.cs** (excerpt)

```
protected override void LoadContent()
{
    // Create a new SpriteBatch, which can be used to draw textures.
    spriteBatch = new SpriteBatch(GraphicsDevice);

    viewport = this.GraphicsDevice.Viewport;
    ball = Texture2DExtensions.CreateBall(this.GraphicsDevice,
                                    BALL_RADIUS * BALL_SCALE);

    ballCenter = new Vector2(ball.Width / 2, ball.Height / 2);
    ballPosition = new Vector2(viewport.Width / 2, viewport.Height / 2);
}
```

The *ballPosition* initialized in *LoadContent* is a point stored as a *Vector2* object. Velocity is also stored as a *Vector2* object but this is a real vector in units of pixels per second. The velocity will tend to remain constant through the effect of inertia unless the ball hits one of the edges or the phone is tilted. All these calculations occur in the *Update* override:

XNA Project: TiltAndRoll   File: Game1.cs (excerpt)

```
protected override void Update(GameTime gameTime)
{
    // Allows the game to exit
    if (GamePad.GetState(PlayerIndex.One).Buttons.Back == ButtonState.Pressed)
        this.Exit();

    // Calculate new velocity and position
    Vector2 acceleration2D = Vector2.Zero;

    lock (accelerationLock)
    {
        acceleration2D = new Vector2(acceleration.X, -acceleration.Y);
    }
    float elapsedSeconds = (float)gameTime.ElapsedGameTime.TotalSeconds;
    ballVelocity += GRAVITY * acceleration2D * elapsedSeconds;
    ballPosition += ballVelocity * elapsedSeconds;

    // Check for hitting edge
    if (ballPosition.X - BALL_RADIUS < 0)
    {
        ballPosition.X = BALL_RADIUS;
        ballVelocity.X = 0;
    }
    if (ballPosition.X + BALL_RADIUS > viewport.Width)
    {
        ballPosition.X = viewport.Width - BALL_RADIUS;
        ballVelocity.X = 0;
    }
    if (ballPosition.Y - BALL_RADIUS < 0)
    {
        ballPosition.Y = BALL_RADIUS;
        ballVelocity.Y = 0;
    }
    if (ballPosition.Y + BALL_RADIUS > viewport.Height)
    {
        ballPosition.Y = viewport.Height - BALL_RADIUS;
        ballVelocity.Y = 0;
    }
    base.Update(gameTime);
}
```

The two crucial calculations are these:

```
ballVelocity += GRAVITY * acceleration2D * elapsedSeconds;
ballPosition += ballVelocity * elapsedSeconds;
```

The *acceleration2D* vector is simply the accelerometer vector with the Z coordinate ignored and the Y coordinate negated. The velocity vector is adjusted by the acceleration vector times the elapsed time in seconds. The ball position is then adjusted by the resultant ball velocity vector, also times the elapsed time in seconds.

It is the beauty of vectors that we really don't have to know whether the phone is tilted in the same direction as the velocity (and hence will tend to increase that velocity) or tilted in the opposite direction (in which case it tends to dampen the velocity), or tilted at some other angle that has no relation to the velocity vector.

The *if* statements that conclude *Update* processing check if the ball has gone beyond one of the edges, in which case it is brought back into view and that component of the velocity is set to zero. These are not *if* and *else* statements because the ball might simultaneously go outside the bounds of two edges and this case needs to be handled; if so, the ball will then come to rest in the corner.

The *Draw* method just draws the ball with the scaling factor:

XNA Project: **TiltAndRoll**   File: **Game1.cs** (excerpt)

```
protected override void Draw(GameTime gameTime)
{
    GraphicsDevice.Clear(Color.Navy);

    spriteBatch.Begin();
    spriteBatch.Draw(ball, ballPosition, null, Color.Pink, 0,
                    ballCenter, 1f / BALL_SCALE, SpriteEffects.None, 0);
    spriteBatch.End();

    base.Draw(gameTime);
}
```

The TiltAndBounce program is very much like TiltAndRoll except that the ball bounces off the edges, which means that when a ball hits one of the edges of the screen, one of the components of its velocity is negated. In a simple scheme, if the velocity is *(x, y)* when the ball hits the right or left edge of the screen (for example) then the velocity becomes *(–x, y)* as it bounces off. But that's unrealistic. You probably want the ball to lose some of its velocity in the bounce. For that reason, the fields in the TiltAndBounce program include a bounce attenuation factor of 2/3:

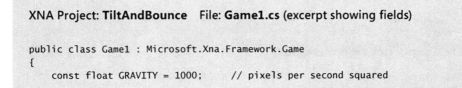

XNA Project: **TiltAndBounce**   File: **Game1.cs** (excerpt showing fields)

```
public class Game1 : Microsoft.Xna.Framework.Game
{
    const float GRAVITY = 1000;      // pixels per second squared
```

```
        const float BOUNCE = 2f / 3;      // fraction of velocity
        const int BALL_RADIUS = 16;
        const int BALL_SCALE = 16;

        GraphicsDeviceManager graphics;
        SpriteBatch spriteBatch;

        Viewport viewport;
        Texture2D ball;
        Vector2 ballCenter;
        Vector2 ballPosition;
        Vector2 ballVelocity = Vector2.Zero;
        Vector3 oldAcceleration, acceleration;
        object accelerationLock = new object();
        ...
    }
```

A ball with velocity **(x, y)** bouncing off the right or left edge of the screen has a post-bounce velocity of **(–BOUNCE·x, y)**.

The constructor is the same as TiltAndRoll as is the *Initialize* override, the *ReadingChanged* method, *LoadContent*, and *Draw*. The only difference is the *Update* method where the logic for hitting the edge now implements bouncing:

XNA Project: **TiltAndBounce**   File: **Game1.cs (excerpt)**

```
protected override void Update(GameTime gameTime)
{
    // Allows the game to exit
    if (GamePad.GetState(PlayerIndex.One).Buttons.Back == ButtonState.Pressed)
        this.Exit();

    // Calculate new velocity and position
    Vector2 acceleration2D = Vector2.Zero;

    lock (accelerationLock)
    {
        acceleration2D = new Vector2(acceleration.X, -acceleration.Y);
    }
    float elapsedSeconds = (float)gameTime.ElapsedGameTime.TotalSeconds;
    ballVelocity += GRAVITY * acceleration2D * elapsedSeconds;
    ballPosition += ballVelocity * elapsedSeconds;

    // Check for bouncing off edge
    bool needAnotherLoop = false;

    do
    {
        needAnotherLoop = false;
```

```
            if (ballPosition.X - BALL_RADIUS < 0)
            {
                ballPosition.X = -ballPosition.X + 2 * BALL_RADIUS;
                ballVelocity.X *= -BOUNCE;
                needAnotherLoop = true;
            }
            else if (ballPosition.X + BALL_RADIUS > viewport.Width)
            {
                ballPosition.X = -ballPosition.X - 2 * (BALL_RADIUS - viewport.Width);
                ballVelocity.X *= -BOUNCE;
                needAnotherLoop = true;
            }
            else if (ballPosition.Y - BALL_RADIUS < 0)
            {
                ballPosition.Y = -ballPosition.Y + 2 * BALL_RADIUS;
                ballVelocity.Y *= -BOUNCE;
                needAnotherLoop = true;
            }
            else if (ballPosition.Y + BALL_RADIUS > viewport.Height)
            {
                ballPosition.Y = -ballPosition.Y - 2 * (BALL_RADIUS - viewport.Height);
                ballVelocity.Y *= -BOUNCE;
                needAnotherLoop = true;
            }
        }
        while (needAnotherLoop);

        base.Update(gameTime);
    }
```

In the previous program, it was possible for the ball to go beyond two edges simultaneously, but those could be handled with a series of *if* statements. However, the bounce logic actually changes the position of the ball, which could cause the ball to go beyond another edge. For this reason, this logic needs to test the position of the ball repeatedly until there are no more adjustments to be made.

It's even possible to extend this bouncing logic into a simple game. The EdgeSlam program is very similar to TiltAndBounce except that one of the four sides is highlighted with a white bar. The objective is to maneuver the ball against that side. As soon as the ball strikes that side, another side is randomly highlighted. You get 1 point for every correct side you hit, and 5 points penalty for hitting a wrong side. The score is displayed in the center of the screen.

It turns out that the game is fairly easy to play until you make a mistake, at which point compensating for that mistake usually makes things worse. (It's much like life in that respect.)

The fields include the same constants you saw earlier with two more for the scoring:

XNA Project: EdgeSlam   File: Game1.cs (excerpt showing fields)

```
public class Game1 : Microsoft.Xna.Framework.Game
{
    const float GRAVITY = 1000;        // pixels per second squared
    const float BOUNCE = 2f / 3;       // fraction of velocity
    const int BALL_RADIUS = 16;
    const int BALL_SCALE = 16;
    const int HIT = 1;
    const int PENALTY = -5;

    GraphicsDeviceManager graphics;
    SpriteBatch spriteBatch;

    Viewport viewport;
    Vector2 screenCenter;

    SpriteFont segoe96;
    int score;
    StringBuilder scoreText = new StringBuilder();
    Vector2 scoreCenter;

    Texture2D tinyTexture;
    int highlightedSide;
    Random rand = new Random();

    Texture2D ball;
    Vector2 ballCenter;
    Vector2 ballPosition;
    Vector2 ballVelocity = Vector2.Zero;
    Vector3 oldAcceleration, acceleration;
    object accelerationLock = new object();

    public Game1()
    {
        graphics = new GraphicsDeviceManager(this);
        Content.RootDirectory = "Content";

        // Frame rate is 30 fps by default for Windows Phone.
        TargetElapsedTime = TimeSpan.FromTicks(333333);

        // Restrict orientation to portrait
        graphics.SupportedOrientations = DisplayOrientation.Portrait;
        graphics.PreferredBackBufferWidth = 480;
        graphics.PreferredBackBufferHeight = 768;
    }
    ...
}
```

The *SpriteFont* is used to display the score in big numbers in the center of the screen. The *tinyTexture* is used to highlight a random side, indicated by the value of *highlightedSide*.

The *Initialize* override and accelerometer *ReadingChanged* methods are the same as the ones you've seen already. *LoadContent* creates *tinyTexture* and loads a font as well as creating the ball:

XNA Project: EdgeSlam File: **Game1.cs (excerpt)**

```
protected override void LoadContent()
{
    // Create a new SpriteBatch, which can be used to draw textures.
    spriteBatch = new SpriteBatch(GraphicsDevice);

    viewport = this.GraphicsDevice.Viewport;
    screenCenter = new Vector2(viewport.Width / 2, viewport.Height / 2);

    ball = Texture2DExtensions.CreateBall(this.GraphicsDevice,
                                          BALL_RADIUS * BALL_SCALE);

    ballCenter = new Vector2(ball.Width / 2, ball.Height / 2);
    ballPosition = screenCenter;

    tinyTexture = new Texture2D(this.GraphicsDevice, 1, 1);
    tinyTexture.SetData<Color>(new Color[] { Color.White });

    segoe96 = this.Content.Load<SpriteFont>("Segoe96");
}
```

The *Update* method starts off just like the one in TiltAndBounce but the big *do* loop is a little more complex. When the ball strikes one of the edges the score needs to be adjusted depending on whether the particular side was highlighted or not:

XNA Project: EdgeSlam File: **Game1.cs (excerpt)**

```
protected override void Update(GameTime gameTime)
{
    // Allows the game to exit
    if (GamePad.GetState(PlayerIndex.One).Buttons.Back == ButtonState.Pressed)
        this.Exit();

    // Calculate new velocity and position
    Vector2 acceleration2D = Vector2.Zero;

    lock (accelerationLock)
    {
        acceleration2D = new Vector2(acceleration.X, -acceleration.Y);
    }
    float elapsedSeconds = (float)gameTime.ElapsedGameTime.TotalSeconds;
    ballVelocity += GRAVITY * acceleration2D * elapsedSeconds;
    ballPosition += ballVelocity * elapsedSeconds;
```

```
    // Check for bouncing off edge
    bool needAnotherLoop = false;
    bool needAnotherSide = false;

    do
    {
        needAnotherLoop = false;

        if (ballPosition.X - BALL_RADIUS < 0)
        {
            score += highlightedSide == 0 ? HIT : PENALTY;
            ballPosition.X = -ballPosition.X + 2 * BALL_RADIUS;
            ballVelocity.X *= -BOUNCE;
            needAnotherLoop = true;
        }
        else if (ballPosition.X + BALL_RADIUS > viewport.Width)
        {
            score += highlightedSide == 2 ? HIT : PENALTY;
            ballPosition.X = -ballPosition.X - 2 * (BALL_RADIUS - viewport.Width);
            ballVelocity.X *= -BOUNCE;
            needAnotherLoop = true;
        }
        else if (ballPosition.Y - BALL_RADIUS < 0)
        {
            score += highlightedSide == 1 ? HIT : PENALTY;
            ballPosition.Y = -ballPosition.Y + 2 * BALL_RADIUS;
            ballVelocity.Y *= -BOUNCE;
            needAnotherLoop = true;
        }
        else if (ballPosition.Y + BALL_RADIUS > viewport.Height)
        {
            score += highlightedSide == 3 ? HIT : PENALTY;
            ballPosition.Y = -ballPosition.Y - 2 * (BALL_RADIUS - viewport.Height);
            ballVelocity.Y *= -BOUNCE;
            needAnotherLoop = true;
        }
        needAnotherSide |= needAnotherLoop;
    }
    while (needAnotherLoop);

    if (needAnotherSide)
    {
        scoreText.Remove(0, scoreText.Length);
        scoreText.Append(score);
        scoreCenter = segoe96.MeasureString(scoreText) / 2;
        highlightedSide = rand.Next(4);
    }

    base.Update(gameTime);
}
```

If in the course of the bounce processing the *needAnotherSide* variable is set to *true*, then the *Update* override concludes by updating the *StringBuilder* named *scoreText* for the score and choosing another random side to highlight. The *scoreText* field is not set until the first score; I originally had logic to initialize it to zero, but the game starts off with the ball in the center of the screen, and the ball inside the circle of the zero looked very odd!

The *Draw* override determines where to position the *tinyTexture* based on *highlightedSide* and is also responsible for displaying the score:

XNA Project: EdgeSlam   File: Game1.cs (excerpt)

```
protected override void Draw(GameTime gameTime)
{
    GraphicsDevice.Clear(Color.Navy);

    spriteBatch.Begin();

    Rectangle rect = new Rectangle();

    switch (highlightedSide)
    {
        case 0: rect = new Rectangle(0, 0, 3, viewport.Height); break;
        case 1: rect = new Rectangle(0, 0, viewport.Width, 3); break;
        case 2: rect = new Rectangle(viewport.Width - 3, 0, 3, viewport.Height);
break;
        case 3: rect = new Rectangle(3, viewport.Height - 3, viewport.Width, 3);
break;
    }

    spriteBatch.Draw(tinyTexture, rect, Color.White);

    spriteBatch.DrawString(segoe96, scoreText, screenCenter,
                    Color.LightBlue, 0,
                    scoreCenter, 1, SpriteEffects.None, 0);

    spriteBatch.Draw(ball, ballPosition, null, Color.Pink, 0,
                    ballCenter, 1f / BALL_SCALE, SpriteEffects.None, 0);
    spriteBatch.End();

    base.Draw(gameTime);
}
```

Navigating a Maze

One natural for a rolling ball is a maze game, and of course this involves several problems, including creating a random maze and writing logic that keeps the ball within the confines of the maze.

After researching maze-generation algorithms a bit, I settled on perhaps the simplest, called "recursive division," which creates a maze that tends to look something like this:

As you can see, this is not a very interesting maze, but its most advantageous feature is that any area within the maze is accessible from any other area.

Conceptually, the area is divided into a grid of cells. In this example, there are five cells horizontally and eight cells vertically, for a total of 40. Each of these cells can have a "wall" on up to three of its four sides. Here's the simple public structure in the Petzold.Phone.Xna library that encapsulates the cell:

Project: Petzold.Phone.Xna   File: MazeCell.cs

```
namespace Petzold.Phone.Xna
{
    public struct MazeCell
    {
        public bool HasLeft { internal set; get; }
        public bool HasTop { internal set; get; }
        public bool HasRight { internal set; get; }
        public bool HasBottom { internal set; get; }

        public MazeCell(bool left, bool top, bool right, bool bottom) : this()
        {
            HasLeft = left;
            HasTop = top;
            HasRight = right;
            HasBottom = bottom;
        }
    }
}
```

All the cells along the top edge have their *HasTop* properties set to *true*, all the cells along the left edge have their *HasLeft* properties set to *true* and similarly for the right and bottom.

The array of *MazeCell* objects that comprise a maze is created and maintained by *MazeGrid*, which has a single constructor that accepts a width and height in number of cells (for example, 5 and 8 in the above example). Here's the *MazeGrid* constructor, three public properties, as well as the *Random* object:

Project: Petzold.Phone.Xna   File: MazeGrid.cs (excerpt)

```
public class MazeGrid
{
    Random rand = new Random();

    public MazeGrid(int width, int height)
    {
        Width = width;
        Height = height;
        Cells = new MazeCell[Width, Height];

        for (int y = 0; y < Height; y++)
            for (int x = 0; x < Width; x++)
            {
                Cells[x, y].HasLeft = x == 0;
                Cells[x, y].HasTop = y == 0;
                Cells[x, y].HasRight = x == Width - 1;
                Cells[x, y].HasBottom = y == Height - 1;
            }

        MazeChamber rootChamber = new MazeChamber(0, 0, Width, Height);
        DivideChamber(rootChamber);
    }

    public int Width { protected set; get; }
    public int Height { protected set; get; }
    public MazeCell[,] Cells { protected set; get; }
    ...
}
```

The constructor concludes by creating an object of type *MazeChamber* the same size as itself and calling *DivideChamber*, which is a recursive method I'll show you shortly. In this maze-generation algorithm, a chamber is a rectangular grid of cells with an interior that is devoid of walls. Each chamber is then divided in two with a wall placed randomly within the chamber (but generally going across the shortest dimension) with a single randomly selected gap. This process creates two chambers accessible to each other through that gap, and the sub-division continues until the chambers become the size of the cell.

MazeChamber is internal to the Petzold.Phone.Xna library. Here's the entire class with its own *Random* field:

```
Project: Petzold.Phone.Xna   File: MazeChamber.cs

using System;

namespace Petzold.Phone.Xna
{
    internal class MazeChamber
    {
        static Random rand = new Random();

        public MazeChamber(int x, int y, int width, int height)
            : base()
        {
            X = x;
            Y = y;
            Width = width;
            Height = height;
        }

        public int X { protected set; get; }
        public int Y { protected set; get; }
        public int Width { protected set; get; }
        public int Height { protected set; get; }

        public MazeChamber Chamber1 { protected set; get; }
        public MazeChamber Chamber2 { protected set; get; }

        public int Divide(bool divideWidth)
        {
            if (divideWidth)
            {
                int col = rand.Next(X + 1, X + Width - 1);
                Chamber1 = new MazeChamber(X, Y, col - X, Height);
                Chamber2 = new MazeChamber(col, Y, X + Width - col, Height);
                return col;
            }
            else
            {
                int row = rand.Next(Y + 1, Y + Height - 1);
                Chamber1 = new MazeChamber(X, Y, Width, row - Y);
                Chamber2 = new MazeChamber(X, row, Width, Y + Height - row);
                return row;
            }
        }
    }
}
```

The *Divide* method performs the actual separation of one chamber into two based on a randomly selected row or column and creates the two new *MazeChamber* objects. The recursive *DivideChamber* method in *MazeGrid* is responsible for calling that *Divide* method and defining the walls of the resultant cells except for the single gap:

Project: Petzold.Phone.Xna   File: MazeGrid.cs (excerpt)

```
void DivideChamber(MazeChamber chamber)
{
    if (chamber.Width == 1 && chamber.Height == 1)
    {
        return;
    }

    bool divideWidth = chamber.Width > chamber.Height;

    if (chamber.Width == 1 || chamber.Height >= 2 * chamber.Width)
    {
        divideWidth = false;
    }
    else if (chamber.Height == 1 || chamber.Width >= 2 * chamber.Height)
    {
        divideWidth = true;
    }
    else
    {
        divideWidth = Convert.ToBoolean(rand.Next(2));
    }

    int rowCol = chamber.Divide(divideWidth);

    if (divideWidth)
    {
        int col = rowCol;
        int gap = rand.Next(chamber.Y, chamber.Y + chamber.Height);

        for (int y = chamber.Y; y < chamber.Y + chamber.Height; y++)
        {
            Cells[col - 1, y].HasRight = y != gap;
            Cells[col, y].HasLeft = y != gap;
        }
    }
    else
    {
        int row = rowCol;
        int gap = rand.Next(chamber.X, chamber.X + chamber.Width);

        for (int x = chamber.X; x < chamber.X + chamber.Width; x++)
        {
            Cells[x, row - 1].HasBottom = x != gap;
            Cells[x, row].HasTop = x != gap;
        }
    }
}
```

```
        DivideChamber(chamber.Chamber1);
        DivideChamber(chamber.Chamber2);
}
```

I also realized that I needed to generalize the bouncing logic, and for that I needed a good
way to represent a geometric line segment that would allow calculating intersections and
performing other useful operations. This is a structure I called *Line2D*. The line segment is
defined with two points that also define a *Vector* property and a *Normal* property, which is
perpendicular to the *Vector*, so that conceptually the line has a direction and can also have an
"inside" and an "outside."

Project: Petzold.Phone.Xna   File: Line2D.cs

```csharp
using System;
using Microsoft.Xna.Framework;

namespace Petzold.Phone.Xna
{
    // represents line as pt1 + t(pt2 - pt1)
    public struct Line2D
    {
        public Line2D(Vector2 pt1, Vector2 pt2) : this()
        {
            Point1 = pt1;
            Point2 = pt2;

            Vector = Point2 - Point1;
            Normal = Vector2.Normalize(new Vector2(-Vector.Y, Vector.X));
        }

        public Vector2 Point1 { private set; get; }
        public Vector2 Point2 { private set; get; }
        public Vector2 Vector { private set; get; }
        public Vector2 Normal { private set; get; }
        public float Angle
        {
            get
            {
                return (float)Math.Atan2(this.Point2.Y - this.Point1.Y,
                                         this.Point2.X - this.Point1.X);
            }
        }

        public Line2D Shift(Vector2 shift)
        {
            return new Line2D(this.Point1 + shift, this.Point2 + shift);
        }
```

```
        public Line2D ShiftOut(Vector2 shift)
        {
            Line2D shifted = Shift(shift);
            Vector2 normalizedVector = Vector2.Normalize(Vector);
            float length = shift.Length();

            return new Line2D(shifted.Point1 - length * normalizedVector,
                              shifted.Point2 + length * normalizedVector);
        }

        public Vector2 Intersection(Line2D line)
        {
            float tThis, tThat;

            IntersectTees(line, out tThis, out tThat);

            return Point1 + tThis * (Point2 - Point1);
        }

        public Vector2 SegmentIntersection(Line2D line)
        {
            float tThis, tThat;

            IntersectTees(line, out tThis, out tThat);

            if (tThis < 0 || tThis > 1 || tThat < 0 || tThat > 1)
                return new Vector2(float.NaN, float.NaN);

            return Point1 + tThis * (Point2 - Point1);
        }

        void IntersectTees(Line2D line, out float tThis, out float tThat)
        {
            float den = line.Vector.Y * this.Vector.X - line.Vector.X * this.Vector.Y;

            tThis = (line.Vector.X * (this.Point1.Y - line.Point1.Y) -
                     line.Vector.Y * (this.Point1.X - line.Point1.X)) / den;

            tThat = (this.Vector.X * (this.Point1.Y - line.Point1.Y) -
                     this.Vector.Y * (this.Point1.X - line.Point1.X)) / den;
        }

        public override string ToString()
        {
            return String.Format("{0} --> {1}", this.Point1, this.Point2);
        }

        public static bool IsValid(Vector2 vector)
        {
            return !Single.IsNaN(vector.X) && !Single.IsInfinity(vector.X) &&
                   !Single.IsNaN(vector.Y) && !Single.IsInfinity(vector.Y);
        }
    }
}
```

Because the line is internally defined with parametric formulas, it is fairly easy to find intersections by equating the implicit *t* values associated with a point on the line.

All these preliminaries are in preparation for the TiltMaze project. Here are the fields that include a *tinyTexture* used to display the walls of the grid. The *List* collection of *Line2D* objects named *borders* is an extremely important part of this program. The *Line2D* objects in the *borders* collection define the outlines of the walls that separate cells. Each wall has a width defined by the WALL_WIDTH constant:

XNA Project: TiltMaze   File: Game1.cs (excerpt showing fields)

```
public class Game1 : Microsoft.Xna.Framework.Game
{
    const float GRAVITY = 1000;        // pixels per second squared
    const float BOUNCE = 2f / 3;       // fraction of velocity
    const int BALL_RADIUS = 16;
    const int BALL_SCALE = 16;
    const int WALL_WIDTH = 32;

    GraphicsDeviceManager graphics;
    SpriteBatch spriteBatch;

    Viewport viewport;
    Texture2D tinyTexture;

    MazeGrid mazeGrid = new MazeGrid(5, 8);
    List<Line2D> borders = new List<Line2D>();

    Texture2D ball;
    Vector2 ballCenter;
    Vector2 ballPosition;
    Vector2 ballVelocity = Vector2.Zero;
    Vector3 oldAcceleration, acceleration;
    object accelerationLock = new object();

    public Game1()
    {
        graphics = new GraphicsDeviceManager(this);
        Content.RootDirectory = "Content";

        // Frame rate is 30 fps by default for Windows Phone.
        TargetElapsedTime = TimeSpan.FromTicks(333333);

        // Restrict to portrait mode
        graphics.SupportedOrientations = DisplayOrientation.Portrait;
        graphics.PreferredBackBufferWidth = 480;
        graphics.PreferredBackBufferHeight = 768;
    }
    ...
}
```

As usual, the *Initialize* override defines the *Accelerometer* object and the *ReadingChanged* handler saves the smoothed value.

XNA Project: TiltMaze File: **Game1.cs** (excerpt)

```
protected override void Initialize()
{
    Accelerometer accelerometer = new Accelerometer();
    accelerometer.ReadingChanged += OnAccelerometerReadingChanged;

    try { accelerometer.Start(); }
    catch { }

    base.Initialize();
}

void OnAccelerometerReadingChanged(object sender, AccelerometerReadingEventArgs args)
{
    lock (accelerationLock)
    {
        acceleration = 0.5f * oldAcceleration +
                       0.5f * new Vector3((float)args.X, (float)args.Y, (float)
args.Z);
        oldAcceleration = acceleration;
    }
}
```

Much of the *LoadContent* method is devoted to building the *borders* collection, and I am exceptionally unhappy about this code. (It's very high on my list of revisions as soon as I find the time.) The code looks at each cell separately and then each side of that cell separately. If a particular side of a cell has a wall, then the border interior to that cell is defined by three *Line2D* objects:

XNA Project: TiltMaze File: **Game1.cs** (excerpt)

```
protected override void LoadContent()
{
    // Create a new SpriteBatch, which can be used to draw textures.
    spriteBatch = new SpriteBatch(GraphicsDevice);

    viewport = this.GraphicsDevice.Viewport;

    // Create texture for the walls of the maze
    tinyTexture = new Texture2D(this.GraphicsDevice, 1, 1);
    tinyTexture.SetData<Color>(new Color[] { Color.White });

    // Create ball
    ball = Texture2DExtensions.CreateBall(this.GraphicsDevice,
                                          BALL_RADIUS * BALL_SCALE);
```

```
ballCenter = new Vector2(ball.Width / 2, ball.Height / 2);
ballPosition = new Vector2((viewport.Width / mazeGrid.Width) / 2,
                           (viewport.Height / mazeGrid.Height) / 2);

// Initialize borders collection
borders.Clear();

// Create Line2D objects for walls of the maze
int cellWidth = viewport.Width / mazeGrid.Width;
int cellHeight = viewport.Height / mazeGrid.Height;
int halfWallWidth = WALL_WIDTH / 2;

for (int x = 0; x < mazeGrid.Width; x++)
    for (int y = 0; y < mazeGrid.Height; y++)
    {
        MazeCell mazeCell = mazeGrid.Cells[x, y];
        Vector2 ll = new Vector2(x * cellWidth, (y + 1) * cellHeight);
        Vector2 ul = new Vector2(x * cellWidth, y * cellHeight);
        Vector2 ur = new Vector2((x + 1) * cellWidth, y * cellHeight);
        Vector2 lr = new Vector2((x + 1) * cellWidth, (y + 1) * cellHeight);
        Vector2 right = halfWallWidth * Vector2.UnitX;
        Vector2 left = -right;
        Vector2 down = halfWallWidth * Vector2.UnitY;
        Vector2 up = -down;

        if (mazeCell.HasLeft)
        {
            borders.Add(new Line2D(ll + down, ll + down + right));
            borders.Add(new Line2D(ll + down + right, ul + up + right));
            borders.Add(new Line2D(ul + up + right, ul + up));
        }
        if (mazeCell.HasTop)
        {
            borders.Add(new Line2D(ul + left, ul + left + down));
            borders.Add(new Line2D(ul + left + down, ur + right + down));
            borders.Add(new Line2D(ur + right + down, ur + right));
        }
        if (mazeCell.HasRight)
        {
            borders.Add(new Line2D(ur + up, ur + up + left));
            borders.Add(new Line2D(ur + up + left, lr + down + left));
            borders.Add(new Line2D(lr + down + left, lr + down));
        }
        if (mazeCell.HasBottom)
        {
            borders.Add(new Line2D(lr + right, lr + right + up));
            borders.Add(new Line2D(lr + right + up, ll + left + up));
            borders.Add(new Line2D(ll + left + up, ll + left));
        }
    }
}
```

The problem is that too many *Line2D* objects enter the *borders* collection. When walls combine from the same cell or adjoining cell, many of these *Line2D* objects become superfluous because they are actually inside a composite wall.

That's not a really big problem in itself, but these superfluous *Line2D* objects seem to affect the functionality of the program. This is evident when a ball rolls down a long wall. At various points it seems to snag a bit as if it's encountering one of these phantom borders and bouncing off.

The problem evidently also involves some of the logic in the *Update* method. As I indicated earlier, I needed to find a method to bounce off walls that was more generalized, and this represents one approach. But again, I'm not happy about it. It relies upon the *borders* collection and introduces its own little errors:

XNA Project: TiltMaze   File: Game1.cs (excerpt)

```
protected override void Update(GameTime gameTime)
{
    // Allows the game to exit
    if (GamePad.GetState(PlayerIndex.One).Buttons.Back == ButtonState.Pressed)
        this.Exit();

    // Calculate new velocity and position
    Vector2 acceleration2D = Vector2.Zero;

    lock (accelerationLock)
    {
        acceleration2D = new Vector2(acceleration.X, -acceleration.Y);
    }
    float elapsedSeconds = (float)gameTime.ElapsedGameTime.TotalSeconds;
    ballVelocity += GRAVITY * acceleration2D * elapsedSeconds;
    Vector2 oldPosition = ballPosition;
    ballPosition += ballVelocity * elapsedSeconds;

    bool needAnotherLoop = false;

    do
    {
        needAnotherLoop = false;

        foreach (Line2D line in borders)
        {
            Line2D shiftedLine = line.ShiftOut(BALL_RADIUS * line.Normal);
            Line2D ballTrajectory = new Line2D(oldPosition, ballPosition);
            Vector2 intersection = shiftedLine.SegmentIntersection(ballTrajectory);
            float angleDiff = MathHelper.WrapAngle(line.Angle - ballTrajectory.Angle);

            if (Line2D.IsValid(intersection) && angleDiff > 0 &&
                Line2D.IsValid(Vector2.Normalize(ballVelocity)))
            {
```

```
                float beyond = (ballPosition - intersection).Length();
                ballVelocity = BOUNCE * Vector2.Reflect(ballVelocity, line.Normal);
                ballPosition = intersection + beyond * Vector2.Normalize(ballVelocity);
                needAnotherLoop = true;
                break;
            }
        }
    }
    while (needAnotherLoop);

    base.Update(gameTime);
}
```

For each *Line2D* object in the *borders* collection, the code calls a *ShiftOut* method in the structure that creates another line on the outside of the wall that is BALL_RADIUS from the border line and extends BALL_RADIUS on either side. I use this new *Line2D* object as a boundary line through which the center of the ball cannot pass and which provides a surface from which the center of the ball can bounce.

There are actually two problems with this approach: First, it doesn't work for the corners. If I really want to prevent the center of the ball from passing a boundary, that boundary should be a quarter arc at the corners of the walls. Secondly, for *Line2D* objects embedded in the walls, this new *Line2D* sticks out from the wall and causes the snagging effect I mentioned earlier.

The *Draw* override doesn't use the *borders* collection at all but performs a similar type of logic that draws sometimes overlapping rectangular textures:

XNA Project: **TiltMaze**   File: **Game1.cs (excerpt)**

```
protected override void Draw(GameTime gameTime)
{
    GraphicsDevice.Clear(Color.Navy);

    spriteBatch.Begin();

    // Draw the walls of the maze
    int cellWidth = viewport.Width / mazeGrid.Width;
    int cellHeight = viewport.Height / mazeGrid.Height;
    int halfWallWidth = WALL_WIDTH / 2;

    for (int x = 0; x < mazeGrid.Width; x++)
        for (int y = 0; y < mazeGrid.Height; y++)
        {
            MazeCell mazeCell = mazeGrid.Cells[x, y];
```

```
                    if (mazeCell.HasLeft)
                    {
                        Rectangle rect = new Rectangle(x * cellWidth,
                                                y * cellHeight - halfWallWidth,
                                                halfWallWidth, cellHeight + WALL_
WIDTH);
                        spriteBatch.Draw(tinyTexture, rect, Color.Green);
                    }

                    if (mazeCell.HasRight)
                    {
                        Rectangle rect = new Rectangle((x + 1) * cellWidth - halfWallWidth,
                                                y * cellHeight - halfWallWidth,
                                                halfWallWidth, cellHeight + WALL_
WIDTH);
                        spriteBatch.Draw(tinyTexture, rect, Color.Green);
                    }

                    if (mazeCell.HasTop)
                    {
                        Rectangle rect = new Rectangle(x * cellWidth - halfWallWidth,
                                                y * cellHeight,
                                                cellWidth + WALL_WIDTH, halfWallWidth);
                        spriteBatch.Draw(tinyTexture, rect, Color.Green);
                    }

                    if (mazeCell.HasBottom)
                    {
                        Rectangle rect = new Rectangle(x * cellWidth - halfWallWidth,
                                                (y + 1) * cellHeight - halfWallWidth,
                                                cellWidth + WALL_WIDTH, halfWallWidth);
                        spriteBatch.Draw(tinyTexture, rect, Color.Green);
                    }
                }
            }

    // Draw the ball
    spriteBatch.Draw(ball, ballPosition, null, Color.Pink, 0,
                ballCenter, 1f / BALL_SCALE, SpriteEffects.None, 0);

    spriteBatch.End();

    base.Draw(gameTime);
}
```

Of course, I know what I need to do: I need to go more global in constructing these walls. I need to know at every intersection how many walls meet at that point and define only the true outlines of these walls.

Just as many programming projects are never definitively finished, I suspect this book is not yet finished either.

Index

Symbols and Numbers

"d" namespace declarations, 14
"hello world" project in Silverlight, 8
"hello, phone" program in XNA, 21–29
"mc" namespace declarations, 14
{bin}\bin\Debug directory
    XAP files in, 21
{sixteen bit}16-bit color, 194

A

acceleration
    calculating, 366
    rotation and, 162
ACCELERATION constant, 163
acceleration vectors, 83, 346–47
    calculating, 367
    direction of, 84–85
    displaying, 85–89, 352
    offsets, 355
    phone tilt angles, relationship of, 364–66
    velocity of, 85
    zero X and Y components, 355
acceleration2D vector, 370
accelerometer, 8, 83–89, 345
    acceleration vectors, 346–47
    coordinate system, 84, 345–46
    data smoothing, 347
    graphical display of, 356–63
    hardware limitations, 356
    LandscapeLeft mode, 354–55
    LandscapeRight mode, 355
    left- and right-landscape orientations and, 349
    precision of, 295–347
    rolling ball programs, 364–88
    starting, 368
    sudden changes, 356
    visualizing functionality of, 347–56
    X, Y, and Z components, errors in, 347
    XnaAccelerometer project, 90–94
    Y coordinates, 346
Accelerometer class, 85
    Dispose method, 86
    Start method, 85–86
    State property, 86
    Stop method, 86
Accelerometer objects, creating, 349
accelerometer vectors, X and Y components, 367
AccelerometerGraph program, 356–63
AccelerometerReadingEventArgs arguments, 86
accelerometerVector field, 91, 353

accelerometerVectorLock variable, 91
AccelerometerVisualization project, 347–56
Action property, 55
Activated events, 130
activating programs, 126
ActualHeight property, 35
ActualWidth property, 35
Add New Item dialog box, 109
Add Reference dialog box, 207
affine transforms, 282–88. *See also* transforms
    constants in, 246
    defined, 245
    for rotation, 246
    for scaling, 246
    for translation, 246
    interior angles, 287
    mapping points in, 290
    mathematics for, 283–84
    matrix transform for, 288
    multiplicative constants in, 246
AffineTransform project, 285–88
AllowReadStreamBuffering property, 72
alpha channel, 205, 213
AnalyzeforAutoMove method, 336
angle variable
    calculating, 166–67, 182
    increasing, 163
animations
    initiating, 173
    maintaining, 174
animationStartTime, 175
anonymous methods, 88–89
App class, 11, 107
    PhoneApplicationFrame object creation, 13
    storing page data in, 116–18
App tag, 9
App.g.cs files, 12
    InitializeComponent method, 12
    problems with, 15
App.xaml files, 11
    namespace declarations, 12
    PhoneApplicationService class in, 122
    root element, 12
    structure, 11–12
App.xaml.cs files, 11
    event handlers in, 131
    structure, 11
Application class, 11–12
application settings, 130
    loading, 130
    saving, 130
    saving in event handlers, 137, 139

application settings, *continued*
  saving in isolated storage, 121
  storing, 130–33
application stack. *See* stack
Application.Current property, 37, 132
ApplicationIcon.png files, 9
applications. *See also* Silverlight programs; also XNA
    programs
  touch input, accommodating, 233
  writing, 4
ArcSegment structure, 221–22
AreaBoundingBox objects, 102–4
args argument, 36
args.Handled statement, 63
args.ManipulationContainer property, 59
args.OriginalSource property, 59
Ascender Corporation, 22
aspect ratio, 0–7
  bitmaps and, 69
  loss of, 240
  performance and battery consumption and, 41
  preserving, 240–42
assets, adding to XAP files, 21
Assisted GPS (A-GPS), 94–98
asynchronous reads, 72
attached properties, 38
attributes, 16
auto move feature, 321
  analyzing for, 336
  implementation, 335
  logic of, 337–38
AutoMoveInterpolation property, 335
AutoMoveOffset property, 335
avgAcceleration value, 352–53

B

back buffer, 40–41, 194
  default setting, 41
  portrait mode, 299, 312
  RenderTarget2D same size as, 203–6
  replacing with RenderTarget2D, 195
  width settings, 352
Back button, 5
  for terminating programs, 78
  navigating with, 113, 124–25
BackBufferFormat property, 194, 204
BackBufferHeight property, 194
BackBufferWidth property, 194
background colors
  as gradients, 215–17
  coloring, 203
  CornflowerBlue color, 27
background objects, creating, 216
Background.png files, 9
backgroundTexture field, 350
  creating and initializing, 359
BALL_RADIUS constant, 368, 387

BALL_SCALE constant, 368
ballTexture, 350
battery consumption, aspect ratio and, 41
Begin call
  for transforms, 247–48, 252–53
BeginInvoke method, 87
  calling, 88–89
  overloads, 88
BetterFingerPaint project, 223–28
binary objects, dowloading from Web, 70
Bing, 4
Bing Maps, 98
bit flags, 53
bitmap fonts, 161
bitmap transparency, 177
BitmapImage class, 73–74
BitmapImage objects, 78
bitmaps, 65–82. *See also* images
  adding as links, 68
  adding to content projects, 66
  as program content, 198
  aspect ratio and, 69
  back buffer, 194
  Build Action of Content vs.
      Resource, 75–76
  code, loading from, 74–76
  coloring, 176
  compression algorithms, 65
  dragging, 234–37
  Draw method and variants for, 169
  drawing on, 193
  embedding vs. downloading, 70
  file formats, 65
  filling, 218–20
  flipping, 170
  lines, rendering in, 217–19
  manipulating at pixel level, 66
  modifying, 229–32
  origin of, 206
  pixels, algorithmically manipulating, 193
  pixels, calculating, 193
  pixels, obtaining, 214
  positioning, 66–67
  rendering, 67–68
  saving, 82
  scaling, 93, 206–7, 213
  Stream objects, referencing with, 193
  stretching, 217
  tiling, 102–4
BitmapSource class, 73
block objects, drawing, 298
borders collection, 383
  building, 384
  unnecessary objects in, 386
bouncing ball logic, 371–72, 386–87
  generalizing, 381
bubble level, 89–94
  bubble position, calculating, 92

bubble size, calculating, 93
enhanced program, 347–56
Build Action
Content, 75
Content vs. Resource, 75–76
Resource, 74
Button class
constructor, 294
Destination property, 295
IProcessTouch interface, 295
of DrawableGameComponent, 294
private fields, 294
public event in, 294
public properties of, 294
SpriteFont property, 295
touch input, 303, 306
Button components
Click event handlers, attaching, 313
creating, 313
creating, initializing, and adding to a collection, 300
destination, assigning, 313
font for, loading, 300
fonts, assigning, 313
Text properties, assigning, 313

C

C#, popularity of, 5
CalculateDisplayMatrix method, 332
callback functions, asynchronous, 304–5
camera applications, debugging, 77
camera, capturing images with, 76–79
CameraCaptureTask objects, 76, 78
cameras, 7
capacitance-touch technology, 7
car.png, 177
carCenter field, 185
CardInfo class, 322
AutoMove fields, 322
AutoMoveOffset and
AutoMoveInterpolation properties, 335
Rank property, 322
string arrays, 322
Suit property, 322
ToString, 322
CardInfo objects, creating, 325
cards object, 324
cardSpot locations, calculating, 335
cardSpots array, 324
CarOnInfinityCourse project, 189–92
CarOnOvalCourse project, 186–88
CarOnPolylineCourse project, 180–85
CarOnRectangularCourse
project, 177–80
centering, 34
CharacterRegions tags, 23
CheckForAutoMove method, 336
ChooserBase class, 76

choosers, 76
tombstoning and, 78–79
circles
points on, 185
points on, calculating, 189
Clear method, 194, 197
ClearPixelArray method, 303, 316
ClientBounds property, 43
clock programs, 43–48
Closing event, 130
closing programs, 126
cloud services, 4–5
code paths, size-dependent, 6
code, loading bitmaps from, 74–76
code-behind files, 4, 11
Color argument, 169–70
color channel modulation, 169
color formats
for Texture2D objects, 215
of RenderTarget2D objects, 202–3
performance and, 203
color gradients, 194
Color objects, converting to uint, 214
Color property, 298
color representation in pixels, 194
Color structure
in Silverlight, 58
Lerp method, 176
PackedValue property, 214
color themes, 7, 18–19
Color.Black, 170
Color.Blue, 170
Color.Green, 170
Color.Lerp method, gradient interpolation, 215
Color.Red, 170
ColorBlock class, 294, 297–98
Color property, 298
Destination property, 298
IsSelected property, 298
ColorBlock components
creating, initializing, and adding to a collection, 300
handling, 306
storing, 299
compiling, 15
Complete method, calling, 60
Completed event handlers, 78, 80
completion events, 100
Components collection, 278
adding components to, 285, 300, 313
ComputeAffineTransform method, 284
ComputeMatrix method, 284
ComputeRotateAndTranslateMatrix method, 254
ComputeScaleAndRotateMatrix method, 255
ComputeScaleMatrix method, 251, 255, 274–75
ComputeTangents, 190
CongratulationsComponent, 321
creating, 325
enabling, 343–44

content area, 17
Content directory
    adding content, 171
    adding existing items, 171
content grid, 16–17
    elements, placing in, 32–33
content projects, adding bitmaps, 66
Content projects, XNA, 22
Content property, 118
ContentManager type, 24–25
ContentPanel field, 36
Control class, 15
controls, 15
coordinate systems, right-hand, 84
coordinates, infinite, 288
CornflowerBlue color, 27
CreateCardSpots method, 327
CreateRotationZ method, 248
CreateScale method, 248
CreateTranslation method, 248
    calling, 255
Cruise, Tom, 257
cspline, 190
cubic Hermite spline interpolation, 190
current thread, object access from, 87
CurrentOrientation property, 42
CurrentPosition field, 317
    transforms, applying to, 319
Curve class, 188
    cubic Hermite spline interpolation, 190
    Evaluate method, 191
    Keys property, 188
Curve instances, 188
Curve objects, X and Y coordinates in, 189
CurveKey class, 188
    Position property, 188
    Value property, 188
CurveKey objects, 188
CurveKeyCollection collection, 188
curves
    drawing with fingers, 210–13
    sprite movement along, 188–92
    tangents to, 190, 192
CurveTangent.Smooth, 190

D

data
    fields, saving as, 121
    passing to pages, 114–16
    retaining across instances, 121–23
    sharing among pages, 116–21
    transient data, 122
data smoothing, 347–49
    in ReadingChanged event handler, 368
    low-pass filter, 354
DateTime values, calculating, 46
Deactivated event, 130

deactivating programs, 126
Debug menu Stop Debugging option, 10
debugging camera applications, 77
DECELERATION constant, 258
deck array, 324
    initializing, 325
Decompose method, 253
delegate keyword, 88
delegates, 87
Delta property, 54, 211, 234
    in Update override, 238–39
Delta2 property, 234
DependencyObject class, 15, 87
DesignerHeight attributes, 15
DesignerWidth attributes, 15
destination argument, 171
destination pages, 113
    as dialog boxes, 114, 119–21
    calling methods in, 119
    initialization of, 121
    passing data to, 114–16
    setting properties in, 119
Destination property, 295, 298
    setting, 295
devices
    display sizes, 6
    hardware features, 7–8
    screen sizes, 5
dialog boxes, secondary pages as, 114, 119–21
dictionary
    for transient data, 122–23
    preservation of, 127–30
    storing data in, 122–23
Dictionary objects for touch information, 50
DirectlyOver property, 55–56
    mouse promotion, suspending, 56
Dispatcher class, 86–87
DispatcherTimer class, 43–44
display sizes, 6
    emulator, 10
    obtaining, 43
    pixel density and, 10
    width, 327
displayed time, updating, 46
displayMatrix field, vertical scaling in, 324
DisplayOrientation.LandscapeLeft, 349
DisplayOrientation.LandscapeRight, 349
displays
    aspect ratios, 0–7
    portrait vs. landscape mode, 6–7
    power consumption, 7
    resolution, 20
Distance method, 149
DistanceSquared method, 149
Divide method, 379
DivideChamber method, 378–79
double type, 35
DoubleTap gestures, 233

downloading items from Web, 70
DownloadProgress events, 74
Drag gestures, 200–1
  Delta property for, 234
  velocity, calculating, 257
DragAndDraw program, 198–202
DragAndPinch program, 249–53
DragComplete gestures, 199–200, 233, 265
  handling, 271–72
Dragger component, 279–82
  default Texture property, 280
  IProcessTouch interface, 286
  Position property, setting, 285
  PositionChanged event, 286
dragging
  delta vector for, 243
  scaling with, 240
DragPinchRotate project, 253–56
Draw class origin argument, 237
Draw method, 26–27, 43, 93
  bitmaps, rendering, 67–68
  block objects, drawing, 298
  calling, 194
  canvas, rendering in, 309
  Color argument, 169–70
  default code, 27–28
  drawing ball with scaling, 370
  override, 176
  SpriteInfo objects, looping
    through, 175
  with text color variable, 52
Draw method (SpriteBatch)
  Color argument, 169–70
  nullable Rectangle objects, 170
  position argument, 169
  Rectangle, 170
  rotation angle, 170
  SpriteBatch objects, 171
  Texture2D argument, 169
  variants of, 169–71
Draw override, 146, 194
  arguments in, 201
  buttons, drawing in, 296
  DrawLine calls, 207
  loops in, 195
  matrix field in, 250
  object rendering in, 209
  Rectangle argument, 201
  RenderTarget2D and Texture2D objects in, 193
  RenderTarget2D series and, 198
  rotation angle in, 244
  scaling factor in, 239
  Texture2D, drawing in, 236
DrawableGameComponent class, 278
  Button class, 294
  ColorBlock class, 294
DrawableGameComponent derivatives, 278
  SpriteBatch use, 280

drawing surface, letterboxing, 40
drawingColor, 299
DrawLine method, 207
DrawLines method, 362
drawMatrix
  changes to, 272
  translation factors, 272
DrawString method, 28
  calling, 194
  positions in, 143
  versions of, 157–58
  zero scaling, 158
dstIndex, 231
dstTexture, 230, 232
dxdt and dydt variables, 187
dynamic layout, 18, 31
  HorizontalAlignment property, 32
  VerticalAlignment property, 32
dynamic textures
  drawing over content, 204
  RenderTarget2D instances, 193–206
  transparency, 205–6

E

EdgeSlam program, 372–76
Edson, Dave, 347, 354
ElapsedGameTime property, 145
elements, 16
  dynamic layout, 18
  height and width of, 35
  in visual composition layer, 45
  names, assigning, 36
  organizing, 32
  placing, 32–33
  Silverlight, 15
  size information, 35
ellipseAngle, 187
ellipses
  parametric form of, 185–86
  points on, 185
  sprite movement around, 185–88
emulator
  accelerometer and, 89
  Back button, 10
  deploying programs to, 9
  display size, 10
  exiting, 10
  floating menu, 10
  multi-touch, testing, 49
  running continually, 10
  startup time, 9
EnabledGestures property, 233
event handlers, 36
  application settings,
    saving in, 137, 139
  attaching to events in code, 43–48
  creating, 35

events
  orientation changes, detecting, 6
  thread safety, 44
execution, terminating, 10
Extensible Application Markup Language (XAML), 4
extension methods, 266

F

fields
  objects, defining as, 78
  saving data as, 121
files, saving, 305
filling shapes, 218–20
finals array, 324
  initializing, 325
finals collections, displaying, 335
finger paint programs, 210
finger position
  finding, 50
  updating, 243
finger presses
  initial, 295
  release of, 296
finger tapping, 50
finger touching, tracking, 50, 233
fingers. *See also* touch
  distance of movement, tracking, 234, 238–39
  drawing lines and curves with, 210–13
  finger presses, tracking, 280
  lifting off screen, 272
  locating, 211
  movement of, 234
  multiple, handling, 228–29
  position of, 200–1, 234, 249
  previous position, determining, 238
  scaling operations for, 251
  touching object or outside object, 237
  tracking, 50, 233
FlawedFingerPaint project, 210–13
Flick gestures, 233, 257–59
  Delta property for, 234
  enabling, 258
  position information, 257
FlickInertia project, 257–59
FlipHorizontally, 158
flipping, 158, 170
FlipVertically, 158
FlyAwayHello program, 171–76
  bitmaps, loading, 198
FM radio, 8
font colors, changing, 19
font sizes, points and pixels, 19–21
FontFamily settings, 15
FontName tags, 23
fonts
  bitmap fonts, 161
  CharacterRegions tags, 23

  embedded, 22
  FontName tags, 23
  in XNA applications, 22
  naming, 23
  Size tags, 23
FontSize property, 15
  editing, 19–21
  points and pixels, 19–21
Foreground attribute, 15, 19
Foreground property, 58
frames, 16
  pages in, 16
FrameworkElement class, 15, 37
FrameworkElement property, 34
FreeDrag gestures, 199–201, 211, 228, 233
  Delta property, 211
  enabling, 224, 235
  handling, 238, 249–53, 271–72
  ignoring, 237
  Position property, 211
  Texture2D positioing, 254
free-fall, 162
FromArgb method, 58

G

game action, 4
Game argument, 294
Game class, 24
  Components collection, 278
  Draw method, 169
  Draw method overrides, 169, 193–94
  GraphicsDevice property, 193
  OnActivated method, 134
  OnDeactivated method, 134
  Update override, 233
game components, 278–82
  adding, 278
  Components collection, adding to, 313
  constructors, 294
  defined, 278
  initializing, 300
  instantiating, 278
  storing as fields, 299
  touch input, accessing, 278
game loops, 26
game time, 145
Game1 class, 24, 144
  back buffer settings, 40–41
  Draw override, 176
  fields in, 24
  instantiating, 24–25
  LineRenderer fields, 208
  splitting, 323
Game1 constructors
  executing, 24–25
  gestures, enabling in, 324
Game1.cs files, 23–24, 323

Game1.Helper.cs files, 323, 326
   Replay method, 331
GameComponent class, 278
GameComponent derivatives, 280
GamePad class, 27
games, 4. *See also* XNA programs
GameTime argument, 145
   ElapsedGameTime property, 145
   TotalGameTime property, 145, 175
GameWindow class
   ClientBounds property, 43
   CurrentOrientation property, 42
   OrientationChanged event, 42
GeoCoordinateWatcher class, 94–95, 98
geographic coordinates, 95
geographic location service, 94–98
geometric lines, thickness, 217
geometry of line drawing, 217–29
GeoPositionAccuracy enumeration, 95
gesture recognition, 53–54
gestures. *See also* touch; also touch input
   Delta property for, 234
   enabling, 199, 233, 324
   Flick gesture, 257–59
   for rotating, 242–46
   for scaling, 237–42
   handling, 200
   ignoring, 242
   in TouchPanel class, 233
   near reference point, 242
   Pinch gesture, 249–57
   Position property for, 234
GestureSample objects, 54, 233
   Delta property, 257
   GestureType property, 200
   Vector2 type properties, 234
GestureType enumeration, 53, 233
GestureType property, 54, 200, 233
GestureType.DragComplete member, 200
GestureType.FreeDrag member, 200
GetAllX method, 220
   if statement in, 221
GetCapabilities method, 49
GetCardTextureSource method, 329, 335
GetCoordinate objects, 95
   distance between, 95
GetData method
   calling on source Texture2D, 229
   overloads to, 214
GetPrimaryTouchPoint(refElement) property, 55
GetRandomPicture method, 82
GetResourceStream method, 75
GetTouchPoints(refElement) property, 55
GetValue method, 182, 184, 191–92
   Boolean argument to, 184
GIF format, 65
Global Positioning Satellite (GPS), 94
GoBack method, 110, 113

GradientBackground project, 215–17
gradients
   background as, 215–17
   interpolating, 215
graphics fields, 24
   initializing, 24
   SupportedOrientations property, 41–42
GraphicsDevice class
   Clear method, 194
   PresentationParameters property, 194
   RenderTarget2D object, setting into, 197
   Viewport property, 26
GraphicsDevice objects, 194
GraphicsDevice property, 193
GraphicsDeviceManager objects SupportedOrientations
   property, 349
graphTexture
   creating, 360
   updating, 362
GRAVITY constant, 367
green color, extra bits in, 194
Grid elements, 15–16
   content organization, 32–33
   content panel/content grid and content area, 16–17
Guide.BeginShowKeyboardInput method, 303–4
   portrait or landscape mode, 304
Guide.EndShowKeyboardInput method, 305

H

hardware buttons, 5
hardware chassis, 5–7
hardware features, 7–8
hardware GPS devices, 8
hardware keyboards, 7
   programs, aligning with, 38
HasTop properties, 378
heap, allocating from, 26
high-level touch handling in Silverlight, 58–61
highlightedSide value, 373
Hold gestures, 233
holds array, 324
horizontal drags, scaling with, 240
horizontal scan lines, filling based on, 219
HorizontalAlignment property, 18, 32–33
   default settings, 33
   Stretch value, 63
HorizontalDrag gestures, 233
HorzBar.png, 171
HTML query strings, 115

I

Id property, 50, 55
identity matrix, 247
image directories, 68
Image element, 68–69, 73–74
   Source property, 68, 73

image transparency, 177
ImageFailed events, 70, 74
ImageOpened events, 70, 74
images. *See also* bitmaps
    camera, capturing with, 76–79
    flicking on and off screen, 259
    flipping, 170
    modifying, 229–32
    via the Web, 69–72
ImageSource class, 73–74
inertia, 257–59
    deceleration values, 257
    handling, 233
    Manipulation events and, 58
    velocity, 257
infinite objects, 288
infinity sign, drawing, 188–89
initialization, tombstoning and, 266
Initialize method, 25–26
    accelerometer startup, 368
    game components, instantiating, 278
Initialize override, 189
    Accelerometer object creation, 349
    components, creating, initializing, and adding
        to collections in, 300
InitializeComponent method, 12, 15, 35
InitializePixelInfo method, 267
insertRow method, 360
instances
    retaining data across, 121–23
    saving as fields, 121
Internet Explorer, 7
interpolation
    calculating, 175
    cubic Hermite spline interpolation, 190
    with Vector2.Lerp, 184
    with Vector2.SmoothStep, 184
InterpolationFactor property, 172, 175
inter-thread communication, 264
inverseMatrix, 324
Invoke method, 87
IProcessTouch interface, 279, 306
    implementing, 279–80, 286
    in Button class, 295
isAnimationGoing field, 174
IsConnected property, 49
isDragging field, 200–1
isGoingUp, 144–45
isolated storage, 130–33
    accessing, 121
    for application settings, 130–33
    for saving data between executions, 123
    saving state in, 121
IsolatedStorageFile objects, 136
IsolatedStorageFile.GetUserStoreForApplication
        method, 136
IsolatedStorageSettings class, 130–33
IsolatedStorageSettings objects, 132

IsSelected property, 298
IsVisible property, 38
Iterate method, 264

J

jitter, eliminating, 354
JPEG format, 65, 306

K

keyboard input, 61
    obtaining, 303
Keyboard method, 303
keyboards, hardware and on-screen, 7
Keys property, 188

L

lambda expressions, 88
landscape orientation, 6–7
    restricting phone to, 42
LandscapeLeft mode, 354–55
LandscapeRight mode, 355
lapSpeed variable, 155
large screen size, 6
lastDateTime field, 46
latitude, 95
launchers, 76
    tombstoning and, 78–79
Launching event, 130
launching programs, 126
layout cycles, notification of, 35
LayoutRoot element, vertical size of, 38
LayoutUpdated event, 35
LCD displays, power consumption, 7
leading, 20
letterboxing, 40
libraries, shared, 4
Line2D objects, 381
    extra, 386
linear interpolation, 152
linear transforms, 245
LineRenderer class, 206–7
LineRenderer objects, creating, 208
lines
    corner points, calculating, 218
    drawing, 206–13, 217–29
    drawing with fingers, 210–13
    geometry of, 217–29
    RenderTarget2D objects,
        drawing on, 210
    RenderTarget2D objects, drawing with, 206
    rounded caps on, 213, 218
    thickness of, 206
lines of latitude, 95
LineSegment structures, 220–21

links, adding as bitmaps, 68
List, 299
LoadContent method, 25–26, 42, 46,
    51, 71, 144, 151, 163
    bitmaps, creating in, 198
    bitmaps, loading in, 326
    borders collection, 384
    canvas, location and size of, 301
    path, determining in, 186
    turnPoints, calculating, 178
    variables, setting, 155
LoadContent overrides
    game components, initializing, 300
    game components, positioning, 285
    in game components, 295
    LineRenderer objects, 208, 211
    RenderTarget2D creation in, 195
    SpriteBatch object creation, 194
    Texture2D, loading, 235
    textures, preparing, 350
    uninitialized fields, setting, 238
Loaded event, 35
Loaded event handlers, 101
LoadFromPhoneService method, 302
LoadSettings method, 132
local bitmaps, loading from code, 74–76
location detection, 8, 94–98
    latitude, 95
    lines of latitude, 95
    map service, 98–105
lock blocks, 350, 353
lock statements, 91–92
loops in Draw override, 195
lossy compression algorithms, 65
low-level touch handling
    in Silverlight, 54–60
    in XNA, 49–53
low-pass filter, 354

M

MainPage class, 13, 107
    partial class definitions, 13–15
    SupportedOrientations
        property, 33
MainPage objects, 13
MainPage.g.cs files, 15
    problems with, 15
MainPage.xaml files, 11, 14–15
    editing, 17
    visual tree, 16
MainPage.xaml.cs files, 11
    structure, 13
Mandelbrot Set, 260–70
    iteration factors, 260
    iteration factors, maximum, 261
    zooming on, 261–62
Mandelbrot, Benot, 260

MandelbrotSet project, 262–66
    iteration maximum, 270
    tombstoning, 266
Manipulation events, 55, 58–61
    origination of, 61
ManipulationCompleted events, 55, 58
ManipulationDelta events, 55, 58
ManipulationStarted event handler, 59–60, 62
ManipulationStarted events, 55, 58
ManipulationStartedEventArgs argument, 61–62
map service, 98–105
Margin property, 33–34, 57
    FrameworkElement property, 34
margin value, 185
Math.Abs method, 202
Math.Atan2 method, 186–87, 192
Math.Min method, 202
matrices, inverting, 276
matrix field, dragging and pinching operations, 250
matrix multiplication, 247–48
Matrix objects, 247
    arithmetical operators support, 248
    creating, 249, 251
    Decompose method, 253
    field initialization, 250
    for affine transform, computing, 284
    in-process translation and scaling handling, 265
    no-transform identity state, 249
    public fields of type float, 248–49
    recalculating, 287
    static methods of, 248
matrix transforms, 246–49
    for {threed}3D coordinate point, 288
    identity matrix, 247
    scaling, rotation, translation components,
        extracting, 253
    third column, 247
Matrix.CreateRotationZ method, 255, 319
Matrix.CreateScale method, 256
    calling, 252
Matrix.CreateTranslation method, 251
Matrix.Identity property, 249–50
Matrix.Invert method, 276
MatrixHelper class, 284, 289
    ComputeMatrix method, 291
MaximumRotation property, 172
MaximumTouchCount property, 49
maxScale, 160
MAXSPEED constant, 163
maze game, 376–88
    cell edges, 378
    intersections, finding, 383
    lines, defining, 381–83
    maze generation, 378
    recursive division for, 376
    walls, defining, 383
MazeCell objects, 378
MazeCell structure, 377–78

MazeChamber objects, 378–79
MazeGrid, 378
MeasureString method, 26, 47
    vertical scaling and, 161
media library, Zune software access to, 306
MediaLibrary class, 79, 82
memory, heap, allocating from, 26
MemoryStream objects, creating, 266
Microosft.Phone.Shell namespace, 302
Microsoft mobile phone market approach, 3
Microsoft Research Maps Service, 98
Microsoft Silverlight. *See* Silverlight
Microsoft Visual Studio 2010 Express for Windows
        Phone. *See* Visual Studio 2010 Express for
        Windows Phone
Microsoft Windows Phone 7. *See* Windows Phone 7
Microsoft.Devices.Sensors assembly, 347
Microsoft.Devices.Sensors library, 85
Microsoft.Devices.Sensors namespace, 85, 90, 347
Microsoft.Phone assembly, 302
Microsoft.Phone.Controls namespaces, 13
Microsoft.Phone.Shell namespace, 38, 122
Microsoft.Phone.Tasks namespace, 76
Microsoft.Xna.Framework DLL, 81
Microsoft.Xna.Framework namespace, 188
Microsoft.Xna.Framework.Media namespace, 79
mouse events, promotion to touch events, 56
mouse input, 61
mouse promotion, suspending, 56
MultiFingerPaint project, 228–29
multitasking in UI, 124–26
multi-touch applications, 7
    scaling in, 245
    testing, 49
multi-touch screens, 5, 49–63

N

NaiveTextMovement project, 143–46
Name property, 35–36
namespace declarations, 12
Navigate method, 109, 113–14
    calling, 110
navigation, 107–14
    around XAML files, 110
    dialog boxes in, 114
    go back a page, 110
    in Silverlight, 107–14
    of the stack, 124–25
    source and destination pages, 113
    stack structure of, 113
NavigationContext property, 116
NavigationEventArgs arguments, 118
NavigationService class
    GoBack method, 110, 114
    Navigate method, 114
NavigationService property, 109
needAnotherSide variable, 375

new expressions, 27
New Project dialog box, 9
new projects, creating, 8
newAcceleration value, 352
NewSize property, 37
nonaffine transforms, 288–91
non-affine transforms, 287
    {twod}2D transform formulas, 290
    in {threed}3D graphics, 287
    in {twod}2D graphics, 288
    mapping points in, 290
    matrix transform for, 288
NonAffineTransform program, 289–91
non-uniform scaling, 249–53
notification services, push notification, 8
nullable properties, 116

O

object class hierarchy in Silverlight, 15
objects
    current thread, accessing from, 87
    defining as fields, 78
    serializable objects, 122
    thread safety, 44
    transforms, applying to, 248
oldAcceleration field, 349, 353–54
OLED, 7
on demand drawing, 44
OnAccelerometerReadingChanged event handler, 86, 91
OnActivated method, 134, 139
OnActivated method override, 301
    loading images in, 314
OnCameraCaptureTaskCompleted method, 78
OnClearButtonClick method, 303
OnDeactivated method, 134, 139, 304
OnDeactivated method override, 302
    saving images in, 314
    storing textures in, 303
OneFingerDrag project, 234–37
OneFingerRotation project, 242–45
OneFingerScale project, 237–40
OneFingerUniformScale project, 240–42
OnGeoWatcherPositionChanged method, 101
OnManipulationStarted method
    events routed to, 63
    handler for, 62
    overriding, 60–62, 108–9
OnNavigatedFrom method, 118–19
    overriding, 127
OnNavigatedTo method, 118
    calling, 116
    overriding, 115, 127
OnOrientationChanged method, 39–40
    overriding, 39
on-screen keyboards, 7
OnTextBlockManipulationStarted method, events
        routed to, 63

OnTimerTick method, 44
OnTouchFrameReported method, 55
OnWebClientOpenReadCompleted method, 71–72
OpenReadCompleted events, 72
OR operations, 363
organic light emitting diode (OLED) technology ,
    power consumption, 7
orientation, 6–7, 31–48
    compensating for, 354–56
    in XNA, 40–43, 349
    LandscapeLeft mode, 354–55
    LandscapeRight mode, 355
    phone response to, 31–32
orientation events, 38–40
Orientation property, 39
OrientationChanged events, 39, 42–43
orientation-independent applications, 38
origin argument, 158, 185, 237
    in RenderTarget2D, 206
origin field, 160
OriginalSource property, 62

P

PackedValue property, 214
Padding property, 34
    for touch targets, 57
page instances, saving as fields, 121
page state, 126–30
page titles, 107, 109
PageOrientation enumeration, 39
pages, 16
    creating, 109
    navigating to, 118–19
    passing data to, 114–16
    sharing data among, 116–21
    state data, saving, 127–30
Paint program, bitmap transparency, 177
Panel class, 16
panels, 16, 32
parametric equations
    for ellipses, 185–86
    text movement with, 153–56
ParametricTextMovement project, 154–57
partial classes, 11
partial keyword, 323
passing data to pages, 114–16
pathDirection field, 151–52
paths, moving sprites along, 176–92
pathVector field, 151–52
performance
    aspect ratio and, 41
    pixel formats, consistent, 203
    pixel manipulation and, 232
    SetData calls and, 232
perspective effects, 287
Petzold.Phone.Xna library, 206
Petzold.Phone.Xna project, 220–23

PhingerPaint program, 293–98
    callback function, 304–5
    canvas for, 299–309
    clear button, 303
    functionality of, 294
    OK and Cancel buttons, 304–5
    save button, 303
    tombstoning, 302
phone tilt
    acceleration vector, relationship of, 364–66
    velocity and, 370
PhoneApplicationFrame class, 107, 110
    OrientationChanged events, 39
    RootVisual property, 13
PhoneApplicationFrame objects, 16
    creation of, 13
PhoneApplicationPage class, 13, 107
    MainPage class, 13
    namespace declaration, 14
    OrientationChanged events, 39
    SupportedPageOrientation enumeration, 31
PhoneApplicationPage objects, 16
PhoneApplicationService class, 122, 302
    Current property, 122
    State property, 122
    XNA use of, 134
PhoneApplicationService objects, 130
phones
    GPS devices, 8
    hardware buttons, 5
    hardware features, 7–8
    keyboards, 7
    photo libraries, 79–82
    unlocking for development, 0–11
photo library, 79–82
    accessing, 79
    saving images to, 316
    saving pictures to, 306
PhotoChooserTask objects, 79
Photos Extra Applications, 7
photos, capturing with camera, 76–79
PhreeCell program, 321–44
    auto move feature, 321
    card moves, legality of, 338–42
    cards, 322
    cards, drawing on surface, 333–35
    cards, overlapping, 335
    cards, positioning, 327
    cards, returning to original spot, 324
    compressed bitmap of playing area, 324
    congratulations component, 321, 343–44
    data structures of, 324
    display matrix, recalculating, 332–33
    Draw method for, 333–35
    opening screen, 322
    play and replay operations, 331–44
    playing field, 322–31
    playing field bitmap, 327

PhreeCell program, *continued*
  playing field, pixel dimensions, 326–27
  playing field, size, 324
  replay button, 344
  rules of game, 323
  shuffling deck and dealing cards, 329, 332
  tombstoning, 329
piles array, 324
  initializing, 325
Pinch gestures, 228, 233, 249–57
  ComputeScaleAndRotateMatrix method
     calls, 255
  Delta property, 234, 249
  Delta2 property, 228, 234, 249
  handling, 249–53, 274
  Position property, 249
  Position2 property, 228, 234, 249
PinchComplete gestures, 233, 265
  handling, 273
  ZoomPixels method, 276
PinwheelText program, 196–98
pixel arrays, indexing, 231
pixel bits, manipulating, 213–17
pixel density, 10
PixelInfo arrays, 264
  looping through, 268
  re-creating, 273
  re-creating after tombstoning, 266
PixelInfo members, shifting, 272
PixelInfo structure, 262–63
  double values in, 264
  static fields in, 270
pixelInfosLock objects, 264
pixels
  as units, 214
  bit configuration, 194
  bits in, 194
  color information for, 272
  color representation, 194
  Color values, setting to, 215
  modifying algorithmically, 229–32
  moved, preserving, 272
  obtaining, 214
  transferring from source to destination, 231
  transferring to bitmaps, 214–15
pixels arrays, 214, 264
  pixel storage in, 299
  updating canvas with, 226
pixels vs. point size, 19–21
PixelSetterThread method, 268
pLap, 160
platforms, choosing, 4
PNG format, 65, 302
  transparencysupport, 177
point size vs. pixels, 19–21
Point structure, 149
points
  four-dimensional, 288
  location, 147

polling, 8
PolylineInterpolator class, 180, 183–85
  GetValue method, 182, 184
  Vertices property, 181
polylines
  scaling factor, increasing, 213
  sprite movement along, 180–85
portrait displays, 6–7
PortraitOrLandscape property, 33
position field, 169
  calculating, 192
Position property, 50, 54–55,
     172, 211, 234
  calculation of, 56
Position2 property, 234
PositionChanged event handlers, 285
PositionChanged events, 95, 286
PositionOffset property, 172
power consumption, 7
PresentationParameters property, 194
  BackBufferFormat property, 194
  BackBufferWidth and BackBufferHeight
     properties, 194
PreserveContents option, 204
PreviousPosition field, 317
  transforms, applying to, 319
ProcessTouch method, 279–80, 295, 317
program content, bitmaps as, 198
program execution, terminating, 10
Program.cs files, 23
programming, 3–5
  development process, 8
programs. *See also* Silverlight programs; also XNA
     programs
  activating, 126–27
  at Windows Phone Marketplace, 5
  closing, 126
  compiling, 15
  deactivating, 126
  launching, 126
  location awareness, 4
  map access, 4
project assets, adding to XAP files, 21
properties, attached, 38
proxies
  calling, 102
  for web service
     communication, 98–99
  using, 100
push notification services, 8
Pythagorean Theorem, 149
  for acceleration vector magnitude
     calculations, 347

Q

Quaternion, 253
QueryString property, 116

R

Random field, 379
Random objects, 203
RandomRectangles program, 203–6
Rank property, 322
raster lines, filling based on, 219
ReadingChanged event handlers, 85, 350
    data smoothing in, 368
    values, saving, 353
Rectangle objects
    nullable, 170
    passing to Draw, 202
RectangleInfo objects, 201
rectangles
    affine transforms on, 282
    drawing with touch, 198–202
    sprite movement around, 176–80
    transforming into quadrilaterals, 288
recursive division, 376
recursive equations, graphic visualization of, 260
reference element, 55
reference points
    for finger movement, 251–52
    for stretching and rotating, 242–43, 245
    rotation relative to, 255
refresh rates, screen, 25
renderTarget fields, setting, 196
RenderTarget2D objects, 193–202
    back buffer, replacing with, 195
    color format, 202–3
    coloring, 199
    constructors for, 204
    contents, preserving, 202–6
    creating, 193
    creating in code, 217
    displaying on screen, 195
    GraphicsDevice, setting into, 197
    lines, drawing on, 210–11
    lines, drawing with, 206
    series of, 195, 198
    size of back buffer, 203–6
    storing as field, 198
RenderTargetUsage.PreserveContentsi member, 204
Replay method, 329, 331
resolution, display, 20
resources
    sharing, 124
    storing, 12
retaining data across instances, 121–23
Rich Internet Applications (RIA), 4
right-hand coordinate system, 84
RippleEffect project, 229–32
rolling ball programs, 364–88
    ball bouncing off edges, 370–71
    ball in corners, 370
    EdgeSlam program, 372–76
    maze game, 376–88

    TiltAndBounce program, 370–72
    TiltAndRoll program, 366–70
rolling ball, creation of, 364
root elements, 12
RootVisual property, 37
rotation, 158
    acceleration and, 162
    affine transforms for, 246
    angle, calculating, 170, 187
    of text, 161–67
    of vectors, 218
    one- and two-finger rotation, 253–56
    relative to point, 159
rotation angles
    calculating, 197, 243
rotation argument, 158, 170, 187
Rotation property, 172
RoundCappedLine class, 307
RoundCappedLine constructor, 225–26
RoundCappedLines structure, 222–23
rounded caps, 213, 218
    filling, 219
routed event handling, 61–63
RoutedEventArgs argument, 62

S

SaveAsJpeg method, 306
Saved Pictures album, 82
    saving textures to, 306
SaveSettings method, 132
SaveToPhoneServiceState extension method, 303
SaveToPhotoLibrary extension method, 305
scale field, 159
ScaleTextToViewport project, 159–61
scaling, 158
    affine transforms for, 246
    based on display size, 191
    bitmaps, 206–7
    center of, 158
    down to zero, 240
    in multi-touch applications, 245
    no scaling, 158
    non-uniform scaling, 249–53
    relative to point, 159
    uniform scaling, 256, 275
    vertical, 161
scaling factors, 237
    checking for infinite or not-a-number values, 241
    composite, 251
    determining, 239
    float values, 240, 242
    limits on, 240–42
scoreText field, setting, 375
scoring
    adjusting, 374
    constants for, 372
screenCenter fields, setting, 196

screens
    multi-touch capabilities, 7
    orientation, 6–7. *See also* orientation
    refresh rates, 25
    resolution, 20
    sizes, 5
    touch points on, 233
Search buttons, 5
secondary pages as dialog boxes, 114, 119–21
SecondPage class, 110
Segoe UI Mono SpriteFont, 196
sender argument, 36, 59
sensors, 7–8
serializable objects, 122, 136
services, 7–8
SetData, 215–16
    calling, 226–27
    calling from Update override, 227
SetPixel method, 363
SetRenderTarget method, 195
SetSource method, 73–74
SetTextBlockText method, 87
Settings class, 134–35
Settings page, 18
shared libraries, 4
sharing data among pages, 116–21
sharing resources, 124
ShiftOut method, 387
Silverlight
    "hello world" project, 8
    bitmap formats, 65
    centering elements, 34
    code-behind files, 11
    Color structure, 58
    dynamic layout, 31
    elements, 15
    elements, organizing, 32
    for applications and utilities, 4
    for games, 4
    frames, 16
    Image element, 68–69
    in cloud services, 4
    navigation, 107–14
    object class hierarchy, 15
    popularity of, 5
    programming Windows Phone 7 with, 4–5
    routed event handling, 61–63
    touch handling, high-level, 58–61
    touch handling, low-level, 54–60
    touch input, 49
    visual composition layer, 45
    visual objects, 15
    visual trees, 16
    WebClient class, 74
    Windows Phone 7 support, 3
Silverlight programs
    dynamic layout, 18
    image directories, 68

    orientation, 6
    XNA classes in, 81
Silverlight standard files, 11–18
SilverlightAccelerometer program, 85–89
SilverlightAccessLibrary program, 81–82
SilverlightBetterTombstoning project, 128–30
SilverlightFlawedTombstoning project, 126–27
SilverlightHelloPhone namespace, 14
SilverlightHelloPhone project, 9–11
SilverlightInsertData project, 119–21
SilverlightIsolatedStorage program, 131–33
SilverlightLocalBitmap project, 68–69
SilverlightLocationMapper project, 99–105
SilverlightOrientationDisplay project, 39–40
SilverlightPassData project, 114–16
SilverlightRetainData project, 122–23
SilverlightShareData project, 116–19
SilverlightSimpleClock project, 43–44
SilverlightSimpleNavigation project, 107–14
SilverlightTapHello1 program, 59
SilverlightTapHello2 project, 60–61
SilverlightTapHello3 program, 62–63
SilverlightTapToDownload1 project, 73–74
SilverlightTapToLoad project, 74–76
SilverlightTapToShoot program, 76–78
SilverlightTouchHello project, 57–58
SilverlightWhatSize project, 35–37
single-finger rotation, 242–45
single-finger scaling, 237–42
SIP, 7
Size property, 55
Size tags, 23
SizeChanged event handlers, 36
SizeChanged events, 35, 37–38, 43
SizeChanged method, 35
skew transforms, 246
small screen size, 6
Soft Input Panel (SIP), 7
source pages, 113
    passing data from, 114–16
Source property, 68
    URL as, 69
SPEED constant, 144–45
speed variable, 163
    increasing, 163
    resetting to 0, 164
SpinPaint project, 309–11
    clear button, 316
    color of paint, determining, 316
    disk rotation angle, 316
    drawing, 316–21
    fingers, tracking, 311
    functionality of, 310–11
    save button, 316
    touch input handling, 311–16
SplashScreenImage.jpg files, 9
sprite movement, 141–43. *See also* text movement
    along curves, 188–92

along paths, 176–92
along polylines, 180–85
around ellipses, 185–88
around rectangles, 176–80
with vector graphics, 151–53
SpriteBatch argument, 176
SpriteBatch class, 67, 157
Begin method calls, 277
Begin method calls for transforms, 247–48
Draw and DrawString method calls, 194
Draw method, 169–71
End method calls, 277
spriteBatch fields, 24
SpriteBatch objects, 28, 171
Begin calls, 335
creation of, 194
drawing on display, 194
GraphicsDevice objects and, 194
SpriteEffects enumeration, 170
FlipHorizontally and FlipVertically members, 158
SpriteFont class, 196
MeasureString method, 26, 47
scores, displaying with, 373
SpriteFont property, 295
SpriteInfo class, 172
Draw method, 176
InterpolationFactor, 176
InterpolationFactor property, 172, 175
MaximumRotation property, 172
Position property, 172
PositionOffset property, 172
Rotation property, 172
SpriteInfo objects
creating and initializing, 173
looping through, 175
sprites, 4, 22
change of direction, 186
displaying, 26
initial positioning, 172
squares, transforming into
quadrilaterals, 288
srcIndex, 231
srcPixels array, 230
srcTexture, 230, 232
stack
emptying, 125
multitasking and, 124
navigating, 113, 124–25
StackPanel elements, 15–16
Start button, 5
navigating with, 124–25
state data
preserving, 127–30
saving in isolated storage, 121
State dictionary
accessing items in, 129
discarding, 130
for transient data, 122–23

preservation of, 127–30
storing items in, 122–23, 129
State property, 50, 122
accessing, 129
State values, 307
static fields, for inter-thread communication, 264
static methods of Matrix structure, 248
status bar
back buffer width and, 352
displaying, 299, 312, 349
status field, updating, 164
Stop Debugging option, 10
storage, isolated. *See* isolated storage
Stream objects, 72
bitmaps, referencing with, 193
Texture2D objects, creating from, 193
Stream type, 71
Stretch enumeration, 33
Stretch property, 63, 69
string types, 46
StringBuilder argument, 46–47
overloads for, 47
status field, updating with, 164
to DrawString, 157
StringBuilder objects, 27
strings. *See also* text strings
dowloading from Web, 70
positioning, 97
storage of, 129
structures, 27
stylus input, 61
Suit property, 322
SupportedOrientations property, 31, 33, 41–42, 349
PortraitOrLandscape, 38
SupportedPageOrientation enumeration, 31
SuppressDraw method, 45–46, 48, 164
surface object, 324
SurfaceFormat enumeration, 194, 213
SurfaceFormat.Bgr565, 194, 203
SurfaceFormat.Color member, 203, 213
SuspendMousePromotionUntilTouchUp
method, 56
SuspendMousePromotionUntilTouchUp() property, 55
system tray, 16
hiding, 41
in landscape orientation, 38
visibility on screen, 38
System.Device.Location namespace, 95, 99
System.IO namespace, 99
System.IO.IsolatedStorage namespace, 121, 130
System.Net library, 71
System.Text namespace, 162
System.Windows assembly, 302
System.Windows namespaces, 13
System.Windows.Media.Imaging namespace, 75, 99
System.Windows.Navigation namespace, 116
System.Windows.Threading namespace, 44, 86
SystemTray class, 38

T

t, calculating, 191, 244
tangents to a curve, 190
    for spline, calculating, 192
Tap gestures, 233
    detecting, 209
    enabling, 208
tapering effects, 287–88
TapForPolygon project, 208–10
task switching, 124–26
tCorner variable, 165
template, Windows Phone Application, 9
termination, program, 126
    on stack, 125
TerraService, 99
testing multi-touch code, 49
text
    centering, 143
    centering horizontally, 144
    flipping, 158
    frequent changes in, 157
    leading, 20
    position, calculating, 165
    positioning on screen, 158–59
    rotating, 158, 161–67
    scaling, 158
    scaling to viewport, 159–61
    vertical scaling, 161
TEXT constant, 144
text movement, 141–43
    acceleration and, 162
    distance of movement, 145
    in one dimension, 143–46
    midpoint, calculating, 152
    nave approach, 143–46
    pacing, 145
    position increases, 152–53
    position of, calculating, 154, 156
    reversing movement, 153–54
    rotation around corners, 164–67
    slowing and speeding, 157
    SPEED constant, 144–45
    speed of, calculating, 154–55
    TEXT constant, 144
    text position, calculating, 152–54
    Update method calculations, 144–45
    velocity, displaying, 163
    with parametric equations, 153–56
    with vectors, 151–53
text strings. *See also* strings
    drawing on display, 194
    measuring, 26
    stacking, 32
TextBlock class, 16
TextBlock elements, 15–16
    centering, 63
    editing, 17

Foreground attribute, 19
    inserting, 17
    manipulation events for, 61
    Margin property, 33–34
    Padding property, 34
    referencing, 36
    Width and Height properties, 34–35
TextCrawl program, 164–67
textPosition variable
    calculating, 158, 166
    defined, 159
    fixed value, 143
    increases in, 152–53
    measuring, 26
    recalculating, 143
    setting, 159
    Y coordinate of, 143
textSize property, saving, 51
texture drawing in XNA, 66–68
Texture2D argument, 169
Texture2D class, 67
    FromStream method, 72, 193, 266
Texture2D data type, 65
Texture2D objects
    center, finding, 237
    color formats for, 215
    creating, 193, 213, 314
    creating in code, 193, 217
    dragging corners, 282–83
    drawing on display, 194
    dynamically manipulating, 293
    Format property, 213
    initializing, 315
    initializing with color, 224
    loading, 173
    position of, 254
    RenderTarget2D instances, 193–202
    saving and loading, 302–3
    saving and restoring after tombstoning, 266
    size of screen, 224
    source and destination objects, 229
    Stream objects, creating from, 193
    updating, restricting, 227
    width and height arguments, 193
Texture2DExtensions class, 266, 302
Texture2DExtensions.CreateBall method, 364, 368
textureCenter fields, setting, 196
TextureExtensions class, 314
texturePosition field, as center of screen, 243
texturePosition vector, adjusting, 235
textureRotation angle, altering, 243
textures, 65–82. *See also* bitmaps
    aspect ratio and, 81
    color information in, 169–70
    dragging around screen, 234–37
    repeating, 363
    saving to Saved Pictures album, 306
textureScale field, 237

themes
 Accent color, 18
 Background color, 18
Thickness structure, 34
this keyword, 25
thread safety, Silverlight events and objects, 44
thread synchronization, 264
three-dimensional games, 4
three-dimensional graphics, non-affine transforms for,
 287. *See also* non-affine transforms
three-dimensional transforms, matrices for, 247
three-dimensional vectors, 345–47
Tick events, 43
tilt, relationship with acceleration vector, 364–66
TiltAndBounce program, 370–72
TiltAndRoll program, 366–70
TiltMaze project, 383–88
TimeStamp property, 55
tinyTexture, 373
 positioning, 376
title panels, positioning, 99
tLap variable, 155, 160
tombstoning, 78–79, 107, 124–26
 in XNA, 134–40
 initialization and, 266
TopCard method, 329
TotalGameTime property, 145, 175, 191
touch. *See also* gestures
 inertia, implementing, 257–59
 over object or outside object, 237
 text movement response, 162–64
touch events
 Margin and Padding properties and, 34
 promotion to mouse events, 56
touch handling
 high-level, in Silverlight, 58–61
 low-level, in Silverlight, 54–60
 low-level, in XNA, 49–53
touch input. *See also* gestures
 Dictionary object for, 50
 game components, accessing in, 278
 handling in Update override, 306
 in Silverlight, 49
 in XNA, 49
 processing, 280, 293
 relative to screen to relative to Texture2D,
  translating, 317
 routing, 61
 TouchPanel.GetState method, 233
 TouchPanel.ReadGesture method, 233
Touch Panel class GetCapabilities method, 49
touch panels, 49
touch points, 7, 233
 converting relative to compressed bitmap, 324
touch positions, storing, 311
touch targets, sizing, 57
Touch.FrameReported event handlers, 55–58
Touch.FrameReported events, 54, 56

TouchCollection collections, 50
TouchDevice objects, 55
 DirectlyOver property, 55
 Id property, 55
TouchDevice property, 55
touchedCardOrigin field, 324
touchedCardOriginIndex field, 324
touchedCardPosition field, 324
TouchFrameEventArgs object, 55
 GetPrimaryTouchPoint(refElement) property, 55
 GetTouchPoints(refElement) property, 55
 SuspendMousePromotionUntilTouchUp()
  property, 55
touchId field, 280
TouchInfo class, 311
 CurrentPosition and PreviousPosition, 317
TouchLocation objects, 50, 228, 279
 TryGetPreviousLocation method, 50–51
TouchLocationState.Moved State values, 307
TouchPanel class, 49, 200
 gesture recognition, 53–54
 gestures supported by, 233
 ReadGesture method, 54
TouchPanel.EnabledGestures property, 233
TouchPanel.GetState method, 164, 233, 279
TouchPanel.IsGestureAvailable method, 200
TouchPanel.ReadGesture method, 200, 233
TouchPanelCapabilities objects, 49–50
TouchPoint class, 55
 Action property, 55
 Position property, 55–56
 Size property, 55
 TouchDevice property, 55
TouchToStopRotation project, 162–64
transfer functions, 156–57
 linear, 157
transforms
 affine transforms, 245, 282–88. *See also* affine
  transforms
 Begin call for, 247–48
 combining, 247
 defined, 245
 for perspective effects, 287–88
 infinite objects, 288
 Matrix fields and, 249
 matrix transforms, 246–49
 nonaffine transforms, 288–91
 skew transforms, 246
transient data, 122
 in XNA, saving, 134
 saving in State dictionary, 122–23
TranslatePixelInfo method, 272
TranslateToTexture method, 317
translation
 affine transforms for, 246
 in two or three dimensions, 247
transparency, 177, 205–6
TryGetPreviousLocation method, 50, 228, 307

TryGetValue method, 129
TryPickUpCard method, 338–40
TryPutDownCard method, 338–39, 341–42
turnPoints array, 178
two-dimensional coordinate system, 147
two-dimensional games, 4
two-dimensional graphics
    non-affine transforms for, 288
    transforms in, 245
two-dimensional transforms. *See also* matrix
        transforms; also transforms
    matrices for, 247
    XNA support for, 247–48
two-finger manipulation, 233

U

UIElement class, 15
uniform scaling, 275
unserializable objects, saving, 140
Update method, 26–27, 51, 144–45
    angle calculations in, 187
    auto move feature implementation, 335
    bouncing ball logic in, 371–72
    default code, 27
    do loop, 374
    drag gesture handling in, 200
    for finger position, 243
    GameTime argument, 145
    multiple gestures in, 235
    parametric equations in, 155
    per-pixel processing in, 229–32
    rotation angle calculations in, 197
    SetData calls in, 229–32
    simplifying, 181
    text location, calculating, 42–43
    touch input, checking for, 49
Update override
    acceleration vector, displaying, 352
    card moving, legality of, 338–42
    color information transfer, 270
    Delta property in, 238–39
    disk rotation, calculating, 319
    drawing based on touch input and image revolution,
        316–21
    FreeDrag gestures, handling, 235, 238
    gesture handling in, 240, 250
    gestures, obtaining in, 233
    landscape orientations, compensating for, 354–56
    RenderTarget2D creation in, 195
    SetData, calling from, 227
    touch input handling, 306
    velocity calculations in, 258, 369
UpdateCoordinateText method, 276
Uri objects for navigation, 110
Uri property, 118
URIs, relative, 109
URLs, as image Source property, 69

user input, 15, 233. *See also* touch input
    in XNA programs, 26
    multi-touch, 7
user interface thread (UI thread), 86
user interface, accelerometer, 345
UserState arguments, 104
using directives, 13
utilities, writing, 4

V

vector graphics
    moving sprites with, 151–53
    points, 147
    review of, 146–50
    vectors. *See* vectors
vector outlines
    filling, 218–20
    parametric equations for, 218
Vector2 objects
    polylines, defining as, 184
    transforms, applying to, 248
    velocity stored as, 369
Vector2 structures, 24, 149
    arithmetic calculations, 149–50
    Distance method, 149
    DistanceSquared method, 149
    properties of, 234
Vector2.Lerp method, 152, 160, 184
Vector2.One property, 150
Vector2.Transform method, 319
Vector2.UnitX property, 150
Vector2.UnitY property, 150
Vector2.Zero property, 150
Vector3 structures, 91
Vector3.Max method, 348
Vector3.Min method, 348
vectors
    adding, subtracting, multiplying, 149–50
    defined, 146
    direction of, 83, 146–47, 150
    length of line, 149
    location, 147
    magnitude, 84, 146–47
    magnitudes, comparing, 149
    radians, converting from, 150
    representation of, 148–49
    rotating, 218
    symbol for, 146
VectorTextMovement program, 151–53
velocity
    Manipulation events and, 58
    of bouncing balls, 370–71
    of flicks, 257
    phone tilt and, 370
    Vector2 object, storing as, 369
velocity vector, 370
VertBar.png, 171

vertexCount, 209
vertical drags, scaling with, 240
vertical scaling, 161
VerticalAlignment property, 18, 32–33
    default settings, 33
    Stretch value, 63
VerticalDrag gestures, 233
Vertices collection, private, 185
Vertices property, 181, 184
vibration, 8
video display
    coloring, 194
    drawing on, 194
video display adapters, 16-bit color, 194
viewport
    retrieving, 42–43
    saving as field, 144
    text, scaling to, 159–61
Viewport property, 26
visibility of system tray, 38
visual objects, 15
Visual Studio
    debugging camera applications, 77
    emulators, connecting to, 9
Visual Studio 2010 Express for Windows Phone, 7
visual trees, 16

W

WALL_WIDTH constant, 383
Web
    downloading items from, 70
    images via, 69–72
web services, accessing with proxies, 98–99
WebClient class, 70–71
    AllowReadStreamBuffering property, 72
    in Silverlight, 74
wide-VGA (WVGA) screen dimensions, 6
Wi-Fi, 7
Windows Azure, 4
Windows Live, 4
Windows Phone 7, 3
    {sixteen}16-bit color resolution, 216
    cloud-readiness, 4
    Device option, 9
    Emulator option, 9
    hardware specification, 5–7
    orientation, response to, 31–32
    Silverlight support, 3
    targeting, 3–5
    XNA support, 3
Windows Phone 7 devices. See also devices; also phones
    {sixteen}16-bit color, 194
    ARM processors, 91
    deploying programs to, 9
    hardware features, 7–8
    multi-touch screens, 49–63
    screen sizes, 5

Windows Phone Application projects
    design view, 9
    project name, 9
    Properties folder, 9
    WMAppManifest.xml file, 9
Windows Phone Application template, 9
Windows Phone Developer Registration program, 0–11
Windows Phone Marketplace, 5
Windows Phone Portrait Pages, 109
WMAppManifest.xml files, 9
WPDTPTConnect tool, 306
WPDTPTConnect32.exe/WPDTPTConnect64.exe
    program, 77
WVGA screen dimensions, 6

X

x
    Class attribute
        in App.xaml file, 12
        in MainPage.xaml file, 14
    Name attribute, 36
x- namespace declarations, 12
XAML, 4
XAML files
    navigation around, 110
    size-dependent, 6
XAP files, 21
Xbox Live, 5
xCollection objects, 299
XML attributes, 16
XML elements, 16
xmlns namespace declarations, 12
XNA
    "hello, phone" program, 21–29
    2D transforms support, 247–48
    drawing, 45
    for applications, 4
    gesture recognition, 53–54
    image transparency, 177
    lines, drawing, 206–13, 217–29
    low-level touch handling, 49–53
    matrices in, 247
    Matrix structure, 247
    orientation, 40–43
    Point structure, 149
    popularity of, 5
    programming Windows Phone 7 with, 4–5
    tombstoning and settings, 134–40
    touch input, 49. See also touch input
    touch panels, 49
    two-dimensional coordinate system, 147
    vector type, 83
    Vector2 structure, 149
    Windows Phone 7 support, 3
XNA game loop, 4
XNA Game Studio font embedding
    process, 22

XNA games
  landscape orientations, restricting to, 42
  orientation changes, responding to, 41–42
  portrait display, 40
XNA programs
  adding references, 207
  Asset Names, 23
  C# files, 23–24
  Content directory, 24
  Content projects, 22
  content, loading, 25
  floating-point values, 24
  fonts, 22–25
  fonts, adding, 22
  fonts, editing, 23
  game loops, 26
  initializing, 25–26
  left- and right-landscape orientations, 349
  orientation, 6
  sprites, displaying, 26
  static displays, 45
  structures, 27
  user input, 26
  WebClient class, 70–71
XNA texture drawing, 66–68
XnaAccelerometer project, 90–94

XnaLocalBitmap program, 66–68
XnaLocation project, 96–98
XnaOrientableHelloPhone project, 41–42
XnaTapHello project, 53–54
XnaTapToBrowse program, 79–81
XnaTombstoning program, 134–40
XnaTouchHello project, 51–53
XnaWebBitmap project, 71
xPixelCoordAtComplexOrigin fields, 264
  new values for, 272
xValues array, 190

Y

yPixelCoordAtComplexOrigin fields, 264
  new values for, 272
yValues array, 190

Z

ZIP files, 21
zooming, 273–74
ZoomPixels method, 276
Zune desktop software, 6, 10–11
  media library access, 306

Charles Petzold

Charles Petzold has been writing about programming for Windows-based operating systems for 24 years. His books include *Programming Windows* (5th edition, Microsoft Press, 1998) and six books about .NET programming, including *3D Programming for Windows: Three-Dimensional Graphics Pro-gramming for the Windows Presentation Foundation* (Microsoft Press, 2007). He is also the author of two unique books that explore the intersection of computing technology, mathematics, and history: *Code: The Hidden Language of Computer Hardware and Software* (Microsoft Press, 1999) and *The Annotated Turing: A Guided Tour though Alan Turing's Historic Paper on Computability and the Turing Machine* (Wiley, 2008). Petzold lives in New York City. His website is *www.charlespetzold.com*.

Collaborative Technologies—
Resources for Developers

For C# Developers

**Microsoft®
Visual C#® 2010
Step by Step**
John Sharp
ISBN 9780735626706

Teach yourself Visual C# 2010—one step at a time. Ideal for developers with fundamental programming skills, this practical tutorial delivers hands-on guidance for creating C# components and Windows–based applications. CD features practice exercises, code samples, and a fully searchable eBook.

**Microsoft
XNA® Game Studio 3.0:
Learn Programming Now!**
Rob Miles
ISBN 9780735626584

Now you can create your own games for Xbox 360® and Windows—as you learn the underlying skills and concepts for computer programming. Dive right into your first project, adding new tools and tricks to your arsenal as you go. Master the fundamentals of XNA Game Studio and Visual C#—no experience required!

**CLR via C#,
Third Edition**
Jeffrey Richter
ISBN 9780735627048

Dig deep and master the intricacies of the common language runtime (CLR) and the .NET Framework. Written by programming expert Jeffrey Richter, this guide is ideal for developers building any kind of application—ASP.NET, Windows Forms, Microsoft SQL Server®, Web services, console apps—and features extensive C# code samples.

**Windows via C/C++,
Fifth Edition**
Jeffrey Richter, Christophe Nasarre
ISBN 9780735624245

Get the classic book for programming Windows at the API level in Microsoft Visual C++®—now in its fifth edition and covering Windows Vista®.

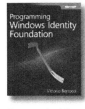

**Programming Windows®
Identity Foundation**
Vittorio Bertocci
ISBN 9780735627185

Get practical, hands-on guidance for using WIF to solve authentication, authorization, and customization issues in Web applications and services.

**Microsoft® ASP.NET 4
Step by Step**
George Shepherd
ISBN 9780735627017

Ideal for developers with fundamental programming skills—but new to ASP.NET—who want hands-on guidance for developing Web applications in the Microsoft Visual Studio® 2010 environment.

microsoft.com/mspress

For Visual Basic Developers

**Microsoft®
Visual Basic® 2010
Step by Step**
Michael Halvorson
ISBN 9780735626690

Teach yourself the essential tools and techniques for Visual Basic 2010—one step at a time. No matter what your skill level, you'll find the practical guidance and examples you need to start building applications for Windows and the Web.

**Microsoft Visual Studio® Tips
251 Ways to Improve Your
Productivity**
Sara Ford
ISBN 9780735626409

This book packs proven tips that any developer, regardless of skill or preferred development language, can use to help shave hours off everyday development activities with Visual Studio.

**Inside the Microsoft Build
Engine: Using MSBuild and
Team Foundation Build,
Second Edition**
Sayed Ibrahim Hashimi,
William Bartholomew
ISBN 9780735645240

Your practical guide to using, customizing, and extending the build engine in Visual Studio 2010.

**Parallel Programming
with Microsoft
Visual Studio 2010**
Donis Marshall
ISBN 9780735640603

The roadmap for developers wanting to maximize their applications for multicore architecture using Visual Studio 2010.

**Programming Windows®
Services with Microsoft
Visual Basic 2008**
Michael Gernaey
ISBN 9780735624337

The essential guide for developing powerful, customized Windows services with Visual Basic 2008. Whether you're looking to perform network monitoring or design a complex enterprise solution, you'll find the expert advice and practical examples to accelerate your productivity.

For Web Developers

**Microsoft® ASP.NET 4
Step by Step**
George Shepherd
ISBN 9780735627017

Ideal for developers with fundamental programming skills—but new to ASP.NET—who want hands-on guidance for developing Web applications in the Microsoft Visual Studio® 2010 environment.

**Programming
Microsoft ASP.NET 3.5**
Dino Esposito
ISBN 9780735625273

The definitive guide to ASP.NET 3.5. ASP.NET expert Dino Esposito guides you through the core topics for creating innovative Web applications, including Dynamic Data; LINQ; state, application, and session management; Web forms and requests; security strategies; AJAX; and Silverlight.

**Programming
Microsoft ASP.NET MVC**
*Covers ASP.NET MVC 2 and
Microsoft Visual Studio 2010*
Dino Esposito
ISBN 9780735627147

Author Dino Esposito leads you through the features, principles, and pillars of the ASP.NET MVC framework, demonstrating how and when to use this model to gain full control of HTML, simplify testing, and design better Web sites and experiences.

**Microsoft ASP.NET and
AJAX: Architecting Web
Applications**
Dino Esposito
ISBN 9780735626218

Rethink the way you plan, design, and build Web applications. Whether updating legacy sites or architecting RIAs from the ground up—you'll learn pragmatic approaches to AJAX development you can employ today.

**Microsoft Silverlight® 4
Step by Step**
Laurence Moroney
ISBN 9780735638877

Teach yourself essential tools and techniques for Silverlight 4—and begin creating interactive UIs for the Web and the latest version of Windows® Phone.

**Microsoft
ASP.NET Internals**
George Shepherd
ISBN 9780735626416

Make Web pages more efficient—and speed development—by understanding how ASP.NET works in depth. This book delves into architecture and provides established patterns.

**Programming
Microsoft LINQ**
Paolo Pialorsi and Marco Russo
ISBN 9780735624009

With LINQ, you can query data—no matter what the source—direct from Microsoft Visual Basic® or C#. Guided by two data-access experts, you'll learn how Microsoft .NET Framework 3.5 implements LINQ and how to exploit it for faster, leaner code.

What do you think of this book?

We want to hear from you!

To participate in a brief online survey, please visit:

microsoft.com/learning/booksurvey

Tell us how well this book meets your needs—what works effectively, and what we can do better. Your feedback will help us continually improve our books and learning resources for you.

Thank you in advance for your input!

Stay in touch!

To subscribe to the *Microsoft Press® Book Connection Newsletter*—for news on upcoming books, events, and special offers—please visit:

microsoft.com/learning/books/newsletter

9 780735 656697